Routledge Revivals

The School in the Bush

The School in the Bush

A Critical Study of the Theory and Practice of Native Education in Africa

A. Victor Murray

First published in 1967 by Frank Cass

This edition first published in 2019 by Routledge
2 Park Square, Milton Park, Abingdon, Oxon, OX14 4RN
and by Routledge
52 Vanderbilt Avenue, New York, NY 10017, USA

Routledge is an imprint of the Taylor & Francis Group, an informa business

© 1967 by Taylor & Francis

All rights reserved. No part of this book may be reprinted or reproduced or utilised in any form or by any electronic, mechanical, or other means, now known or hereafter invented, including photocopying and recording, or in any information storage or retrieval system, without permission in writing from the publishers.

Publisher's Note
The publisher has gone to great lengths to ensure the quality of this reprint but points out that some imperfections in the original copies may be apparent.

Disclaimer
The publisher has made every effort to trace copyright holders and welcomes correspondence from those they have been unable to contact.
A Library of Congress record exists under ISBN:

ISBN 13: 978-0-367-19531-1 (hbk)
ISBN 13: 978-0-367-19532-8 (pbk)
ISBN 13: 978-0-429-20298-8 (ebk)

THE
SCHOOL IN THE BUSH

Alice laughed:
"One *ca'n't* believe impossible things."
"I daresay you haven't had much practice," said the Queen.
—*Through the Looking-Glass.*

THE
SCHOOL IN THE BUSH

*A Critical Study of the Theory and Practice
of
Native Education in Africa*

A. VICTOR MURRAY

New impression of the
SECOND EDITION

FRANK CASS & CO. LTD.
1967

Published by
FRANK CASS AND COMPANY LIMITED
67 Great Russell Street, London W.C.1
by arrangement with Longmans, Green & Co.

First edition	1929
Second edition	1938
New impression	1967

Printed in Holland by
N.V. Grafische Industrie Haarlem

DICK OGAN
IN
MEMORIAM

FOREWORD

IT IS A matter of no small importance that the first edition of THE SCHOOL IN THE BUSH should be exhausted and a second edition called for. It shows that a serious interest in the problems of African education has now spread beyond official and missionary circles, and that a sincere and competent study of them, such as Professor Murray offers in this volume, was widely desired. Of Professor Murray's sincerity I need say nothing : it is a current of disciplined passion which carries the sympathetic reader along from the first page to the last ; but I will explain what I mean by his competence. Although I had for some years the honour of serving upon the Committee which advises H.M. Secretary of State for the Colonies upon Educational questions, I have no first hand knowledge of the African scene. While, then, I can admire the courage with which Professor Murray criticises established persons and institutions, whatever their authority and prestige, I cannot pretend to certify that his strictures are always justifiable. But I can say that I should find it difficult to name a book in which Educational issues of equal range and urgency are treated with so deep and firm a sense of the canons which should rule in educational practice and administration wherever they are carried on.

The strength of my conviction that one of our highest imperial duties is to provide for the African peoples within the Commonwealth an education founded upon humanity and guided by sound principles would, I hope, satisfy even Professor Murray. And it is because his book seems to me to offer invaluable aid to those who are seeking to lead Africa towards such an education that I rejoice in its success and hope that its second and subsequent editions will reach even wider circles of students.

May 1938   T. P. NUNN.

PREFACE TO THE SECOND EDITION.

A GOOD deal of water has flowed over the Victoria Falls since 1929 when the first edition of this book was published. Schools such as Domboshawa and Uzuakoli, which were just beginning their work, have become well-established institutions. Missionary education has become much more coherent and efficient. The various Governments in British territory have accepted the task of the education of future African citizens, although here and there the clock has been put back by politicians who take a short view of their responsibilities. The University of London Institute of Education has established a Colonial Department for the training. not only of Government but also of missionary educationists. An International Committee on Christian Literature for Africa has been established which publishes a very useful quarterly, *Books for Africa*. There has been a number of Commissions of one sort or another dealing wholly or in part with questions of Native education. Of these the Union of South Africa Inter-Departmental Committee and the British Government's Commission on Higher Education in East Africa (which included an African member) were perhaps the most notable. Achimota has had its first official inspection and has also published the record of its first ten years, a really remarkable volume. There have been a number of important Conferences on Native education, particularly the New Education Fellowship Conferences in South Africa in 1934 and the conference on " Jeanes teachers " in Southern Rhodesia in 1935. In 1930 the Royal Institute of International Affairs (Chatham House) collected a very interesting group to study Colonial administration. In 1937 and 1938 summer conferences of Colonial officials have been organised at Oxford. The Press has been pouring out books on Africa and some of them have been notable contributions to the problems discussed in this book. I would mention particularly the report on *Modern Industry and the African*, Julian Huxley's *Africa View*, Schapera's *Western Civilization and the South African Native*, Mumford and Orde-Brown's *Africans learn to be French*, Miss L. P. Mair's *Native Policies in Africa*, Miss M. Hunter's *Reaction to Conquest*, Miss M. Perham's *Native Administration in Nigeria*, W. M. Macmillan's *Africa Emergent*, Arthur Mayhew's *Education in the Colonial Empire*, J. D. Clarke's *Omu* and Mr. H. Jowitt's two books on education in Africa. Above all, Africa is shouted into the world's ears by the strident voices of the Fascist dictators. The ruthless conquest of Abyssinia and the demand for the return of the African colonies to Germany have raised in an acute form the question of the destiny of these "backward" countries. Accordingly there is nowadays an urgency about the subject which was not present ten years ago.

In these circumstances a certain amount of revision of the book has been needed. I have brought up to date the South African story and rewritten the accounts of the schools at Domboshawa and Uzuakoli and of the Southern Rhodesian system, besides making innumerable corrections in other places. I have also given some details about some interesting community work in Nigeria. The main body of the text has, however, been allowed to stand. There are two reasons for this.

First of all it is in the main a discussion of principles, documented here and there by particular instances, and it is the principles that are important. Educational problems are surprisingly similar in different countries and different periods, for they are always concerned with the impact of mature minds upon minds less mature, with human wilfulness and stupidity as well as human ideals, with interested as well as disinterested motives. My experience in Nigeria in 1932 gave me a good example of this. I went out there at the invitation of the Christian Council to discuss a measure of unification of missionary educational policy and the nature of Government supervision. In some doubt as to

PREFACE TO THE SECOND EDITION xi

what I might helpfully read on the way out I finally chose Matthew Arnold's *Reports on Elementary Schools, 1852-1882*. It turned out to be a most useful choice, for although the situations were different the same principles were involved in his problem as in that which I found in Nigeria.

In the second place, I have not had that intimate contact with Africa which is really required if one were to rewrite the whole book. In 1931-2 I visited Nigeria for four months and took particular note of the *local* working of the system of " indirect rule," particularly in the Eastern province of Southern Nigeria. I also had nineteen conferences with Native teachers in different parts of the country, and found their point of view on all Native matters most interesting. In 1934, as a guest of the South African Government, I spent some time in South Africa after the New Education Conferences were over, particularly in Basutoland, in order to get some light on the " Protectorate " system, and in the Transkei—a visit which has led me to modify considerably my views on the success of that " experiment." The Conferences themselves gave ample opportunity for leisurely discussion with eminent teachers, European and African, civil servants, professional men, administrators and statesmen who had gathered in Johannesburg from every part of Africa south of the equator. Apart from these two visits, however, I have not been able to be in very living touch with African problems except through the Reports which the various Governments have so kindly sent me and through conversations with missionary and education officers on furlough.

One question, however, it has been impossible to leave untouched. I had no idea when the first edition of this book was published that my criticism of the system of " indirect rule " would attract so much notice. Mr. Julian Huxley on the one side and Miss Margery Perham on the other have commented on these criticisms and other writers have also discussed them. An article expanding them which I wrote for the *Journal of the Royal African Society* in July, 1935, under the title " Education under Indirect Rule," was so strongly disapproved of by one official that I understand he resigned from the Society, while another not only protested against the publication but also wrote to me two very strong letters. These events gave me food for thought (and also considerable material for a possible volume on " the psychology of prestige " !), but I can honestly say that I did not intend to attack anybody but only to examine the system and to criticize it. These are matters of public policy, and although I do very much sympathize with the annoyance of a man who finds an interfering outsider poking into his affairs I still cannot see that he has any freehold rights in his position. They are not his *private* affairs, and a great Empire can surely not be run on a system of official vested interests. Good friends of mine in Government service may, however, like to know that I was equally abused by some missionaries for other parts of the book!

Nevertheless the subject is of the utmost importance, particularly in these days. " Indirect rule " contains in it a principle of race appreciation which is a standing witness against the racial myths of Hitler and Mussolini. For that reason I am personally quite opposed to the retrocession of the Colonies to Nazi Germany. Under the mandate system and (what is the same thing) that of " indirect rule " I can see some hope for both the persons and the social systems of Africans being respected. I can see no hope whatever if they are *gleichgeschaltet* to the Nazi system, any more than there is hope for the Abyssinian people or for the Ethiopic Church under Mussolini. " *Remota justitia, quid sunt regna nisi magna latrocinia?*" asked St. Augustine, and it is the denial of justice that damns the totalitarian states.

Yet if the colonies are " kept " there will have to be a good deal of modification of the principle of " indirect rule " in order to bring the people to the point when they can " stand on their own feet." The picturesque native custom and the unsophisticated backwoods chief need not and must not be despised and discouraged, but neither ought they to be considered the " norm " of African life. It is a sound principle of progress that the real " nature " of a thing only comes to light in its development, so that the idea of educating a man " along his own lines " contains a contradiction in terms. It cannot be seen what " his own lines" are until after he has been educated. Hence although the educated classes in the African community are at present the minority it is much more likely that among them rather than among the primitives will appear the real *differentia* of African culture.

An illustration of this comes to my mind from my last visit to Nigeria. I met a youth at Uzuakoli called Dick Ogan, one of the most attractive people I have ever known. He was a young teacher, had taken his London matriculation, was keen on games and scouting as well as on academic work, and when I saw him last he was in the middle of reading Jeans' *The Universe Around us*. I was told that some years before this he had been to the Scout Jamboree at Birkenhead, and was afterwards taken round England on a series of visits. When the boy returned home he was asked with other boys to tell the school what it was that had most impressed him in England. The other boys spoke of the ship that had carried them, of telephones, of wireless, of English houses. Ogan said quietly, " The thing that impressed me most was a visit to Westminster Abbey. I found there the grave of Dr. Livingstone, and read the words, " Brought by faithful hands over land and sea—." All at once I realized that those hands were black hands, and that something which the English so much valued that they laid it in Westminster Abbey had been given to them by *my* people."

Three questions seem to me to arise from that story. The first is, how would anyone have known the " nature " of that boy if he had not had those experiences and opportunities? The second is, how many English boys would in similar circumstances have shown a similar sensitiveness to spiritual values? The third is, what place would there be for such as he in the body politic of a country governed by " indirect rule " ?

It has unfortunately not been possible to go very thoroughly into the question of education under indirect rule—that may some day be the subject of a separate study—but I here offer two contributions to its further discussion. Lord Lugard—*nomen praeclarum !*—has sent me a criticism of my chapter XII, and by his permission

PREFACE TO THE SECOND EDITION

it is printed as a "comment" to that chapter. It has added, I think, to the value of the chapter to have this criticism by the founder himself of the system of "indirect rule" in Nigeria, and I am most grateful to him for the kindness shown to an amateur by a master. I have also added an abridgement and revision of the article already mentioned, and express my thanks to the Council of the Royal African Society for allowing it to be reprinted.

In addition to those mentioned in the preface to the first edition I should like to express my thanks to the various Colonial Directors of Native Education and to the Chief Magistrate of the Ciskei, who have kindly and most faithfully kept me supplied with their annual reports, to Mr. T. L. Davis of Domboshawa, Mr. R. S. D. Williams of Uzuakoli, the Rev. A. J. Haile of Tigerkloof (to whom the book owes far more than it reveals), Dr. Wilkie of Lovedale, Mr. Arthur Mayhew of the Colonial Office, Dr. W. B. Mumford of the London Institute of Education, Dr. E. G. Malherbe of Pretoria, Mr. Oswin Bull and Mr. H. Pickett of Basutoland, the Rev. G. E. P. Broderick, Miss Winifred Love of Ituk Mban, Nigeria, and Mr. G. H. Welsh, Mr. H. Storey and Mr. H. Thurlbeck of the Cape Native Education Department. I should also like to thank the officials of the Colonial Office Library, and of the South African Institute of Race Relations, and members of the office of the High Commissioner for Southern Rhodesia and of the office of the Crown Agents for the Colonies for their kindness in helping me to bring my statistics up to date.

My warmest thanks—rather belated—are also due to very many people in Nigeria who made my tour possible in 1932. They included missionary secretaries and school supervisors, African teachers and Government servants. One distinguished name I may perhaps be allowed to mention. Mr. Henry Carr is the *doyen* of the African community in Lagos and I profited very greatly by his ripe wisdom and experience. The University of Durham in 1936 honoured itself as well as him when it gave him an honorary D.C.L. He was the first African to receive such an honorary degree and Durham was the first British University to confer it.

PREFACE TO THE SECOND EDITION xv

I have once again to thank Mr. and Mrs. Edward Cadbury for their kindness. Not only was the original Fellowship their foundation but furthermore they assisted my visit to Nigeria in 1931-2 in various ways and in 1934 enabled my wife to accompany me to South Africa. Her critical observation and judicial mind have been no less helpful in the preparation of the second edition than in writing the book itself.

A. VICTOR MURRAY.

COTTINGHAM, E. YORKS.,
July 17, 1938.

FROM THE PREFACE TO THE FIRST EDITION

This book is the outcome of a tour which I made through Africa from April, 1927, to January, 1928, as the holder of a Travelling Research Fellowship, in order to study the work of Native education, particularly in the training of teachers. The route is given on the map at the end of the book. It was unfortunately not possible to visit Uganda and Madagascar or any of the French territories save the Cameroons, and my only personal contacts with Kenya and Tanganyika were at Mombasa and Dar-es-Salaam.

In the case of the territories that were visited, no attempt was made systematically to see or to report on every school. That service has already been excellently well done in the Reports of the Phelps-Stokes Commissions. My concern was to visit institutions that were typical, and to see from these what general principles were at work in African education as a whole. With this in view I visited schools of seventeen different missionary societies as well as Government schools, and studied at first hand some nine or ten different systems of administration. Industrial and urban areas were visited as well as rural, and schools in the forest and on the veld as well as schools in the bush.

The basis of the book, therefore, is actual observation of the things about which I write.

That, however, is only the basis. Upon it has been built a superstructure of comment and criticism and suggestion which many people will doubtless feel the foundations are unable to bear. Possibly they are right. Yet I think an illustration may make clear what I feel to be my justification.

A good friend in the administrative service in Northern

Nigeria became almost violent because I would not take his word for it that the Moslems do not desire English education and that they would rise in rebellion if mission schools were allowed among them. He pointed out that he had been there for fifteen years and he knew the Moslems, and I had been there just a fortnight and knew nothing at all. There was, of course, truth in this, but in that fortnight I had come across evidence of Moslems who did want English education and who did go to a mission school to get it, and with whom the school was an exceedingly popular place. The missionary, moreover, had been in the country for at least the same length of time as my friend and had quite a different impression of the Moslems. In this case, therefore, I voted for the missionary, as the evidence seemed to be on his side. This method I followed in judging not only as between Government and missions, but also as between one mission and another.

This, then, is my line of defence for having any views at all on questions which many people have studied for more years than I have months. I have tried to write what is really a comparative study, and I believe that every judgement I have made has its justification in the teaching or the organization or the spirit of some actual school.

This comparison has been of a particular kind. It has been a comparison not of one institution with another but of the way in which one school deals with its own situation compared with the method followed by another school in its own situation. It is a comparison of relationships rather than of institutions. Different lines of action may be followed by two schools or by two government departments and yet the relationship to their respective situations may be the same.

In the process of making these comparisons I have been influenced by a conviction which some years of teaching and of the study of education in Britain have impressed upon me. It is this. Education depends upon social structure both for its nature and for its aim. Children are not educated as it were in the air. They are taught by other people and they come from homes that have a certain status in society. The forces governing their education are largely determined by the nature and needs of that society and by the fashion of the moment in thought and in custom. The Industrial Revolution, for example, explains the " monitorial " system, the craft guild throws light on the organization of the ancient universities, the outcome of the Franco-Prussian War and of the American Civil War made Englishmen feel the supreme necessity for technical education in order to keep their hold on the markets of the world.

A study of education is meaningless without this constant reference to the situation in which the education is given.

It is so in Africa. To discover the aim of education and the means to carry it out necessitates a careful study of the status of the African in the modern world and of the forces that are playing upon him. Accordingly, while chiefly visiting schools, I found it no less necessary to consider the nature of industry in Northern Rhodesia, the methods of recruitment for the Rand mines, the effects upon agriculture of the continual soil erosion in the Eastern Provinces of the Cape, the administration of the Transkei. The subject of education is man, and in considering education, nothing that concerns man is alien to our purpose.

While, therefore, the theme of the book is education, it necessarily deals with matters of government, land, labour, politics and theology, in so far as they affect education, and thus it raises many general issues which may be of importance in other places besides Africa.

At the same time the real point of application is the actual teaching in the actual school. My concern has been primarily with the village teacher and with him as a human being. The " educationist " has had a good innings in the consideration of African education, and we may be apt to feel that it is he who is the important person. I do not think so. Men and women in the village schools are the people who count much more. If these are unfaithful or unenterprising the whole system fails, be the Europeans ever so enlightened and able. The knowledge, the faith, the work, and the status of the African villager seem to me to have a far greater relevance in the study of education.

* * * * *

When writing of African schools I have tried—indeed I have felt myself constrained to try—to rescue the subject from some of the meanness with which I feel it is often treated. There is much too much made of it as a " problem," and this breeds the opinion that it lends itself best to statistical treatment and to the " specialist," thereby making a science of what is really an art. African education is being carried on by a truly marvellous body of men and women— people who have stepped out of pre-historic times right into the twentieth century, and now under their little thatched huts are interpreting our age to that ancient past and that past age to ours. The more we think about it the more marvellous it appears, and it is a tribute to the intrinsic energy of the human mind that the work is actually being done. The spirit of man is as clearly the sword of God in these African villages as in our mediæval cathedrals or in our modern inventions. Despite all the ineffectiveness of much of native education I believe this to be nevertheless a fair judgment, and I have taken it as representing the most worthy frame of mind in which to investigate the subject.

We are thus concerned first of all with " the background " against which the African school is set—the geographical conditions, the legacy of history, the tribal system of land tenure and the impact upon it of European industry and agriculture. We then consider " the foreground," with the village school in the centre. In one direction the school is the first of a series which leads to the great institutions like Achimota and Fort Hare. In another direction it is the last of a series, as it is from these higher institutions that the village teacher has come and it is their gifts which he seeks to pass on to his primitive fellow-countrymen. These chapters, therefore, contain the gist of the subject, for " the school in the bush " is in a very real sense the focus of all the forces, European and Native, at work in Africa to-day. They are by no means an adequate treatment of the subject, but I hope that they will be found to raise most of the main issues.

Next there is " the middle distance," and we are occupied with the broader aspects of educational policy. These concern the relationship of schools to the Churches at home, to Governments, and to current theological, political, and educational theories in Europe and in America. In the chapter on " the horizon " there is an attempt to sum up the conclusions of the whole study and to see where they lead.

Finally, there is in the appendix an attempt to burst the bubble of that " uniqueness " which is supposed to be characteristic of the African scene. It is this alleged uniqueness that provides a certain line of argument, not only for the opponent of Native education but also for many of its friends. I have suggested two historical comparisons with the present status of the African, and it will, I think, be found how close are the similarities. " Peasant," " workman," and " native,"—these three terms,—are almost interchangeable in many of the extracts that are given, and it would often be impossible to tell apart from the contexts whether they were written in France in the Middle Ages, in England a century ago, or in Africa to-day. It would almost seem as if the race problem is simply one aspect of the class problem.

CONTENTS.

PART I.

THE BACKGROUND.

CHAPTER I.
                                                                    PAGE
GEOGRAPHY 3
1. The vastness of Africa. 2. Early knowledge of the coast. Mystery of the interior. 3. Importance of communications. Contact of old and new civilizations. 4. Effects of climat on equatorial region and on regions suitable for white settlement. 5. Soil and minerals. 6. Regional survey: East, West Coast, equatorial region, South Africa. Geography and politics. 7. Human geography. Economic influence. African scenery.

CHAPTER II.

HISTORY AND POLITICS 19
1. No indigenous African history. Relation of this fact to "African culture," and to European settlement. 2. The Arabs and Islam. 3. The Portuguese and Spanish. 4. The Dutch. Five factors in the Dutch history of the Cape. Relations with British. The *Voortrekkers*. 5. Livingstone and Stanley. The Belgian Congo. The Chartered Companies. 6. The Union of South Africa. General Hertzog's Native policy.

CHAPTER III.

LAND AND LABOUR 38
1. Land tenure and the tribe. The Scottish Highlands. 2. The European incursion and the land. 3. Village life, and European industry. 4. Native life in the towns. 5. The Industrial and Commercial Workers' Union. 6. Weakening of tribalism. 7. Segregation. Different senses of the term. 8. The Transkei. 9. Agricultural co-operation. Ireland and Africa. 10. Individual responsibility. Influence of the towns. 11. Christianity and tribalism.

CONTENTS

PART II.

THE FOREGROUND.

CHAPTER IV.

	PAGE
THE MISSION	65

Education in the hands of the Missions. 1. The European staff. 2. Nature of corporate life. 3. Characteristics of successful missions. 4. Question of celibacy. 5. Place of intellectual " belief," 6. The cult of perfection. 7. The cult of imperfection.

CHAPTER V.

THE VILLAGE SCHOOL AND THE VILLAGE TEACHER . . . 79

1. A typical village school. 2. Reasons for attendance. 3. Indigenous education. Primitive theory of causation. 4. Initiation. Witchcraft. 5. Some characteristic Native qualities. *Ubuntu.* Imagination and its opposite. Native games. 6. The village teacher, and his education. 7. Teachers' Magazines. *Mthenga. The Natal Native Teachers' Journal.* Exhibitions. Associations. 8. Untrained intelligence. Games. Professional feeling.

CHAPTER VI.

FURTHER EDUCATION AND THE TRAINING OF TEACHERS . . 98

Comparison with rise of European universities. 1. The educational system. 2. Some typical schools. Yakusu (Congo). 3. Uzuakoli (Southern Nigeria). 4. Girls' education. Mbereshi (Northern Rhodesia). Aro Chuku (Nigeria). 5. Domboshawa (Southern Rhodesia). Tsolo (Transkei). 6. Lovedale (Cape Province).

CHAPTER VII.

CHURCH AND STATE IN ADMINISTRATION 118

1. Government control of education. Belgium, France, and Portugal. 2. British territory. Code of Southern Rhodesia. 3. British West Africa and Nyasaland. 4. Missionary Conferences. Advisory Boards. 5. Director of Education. 6. The Natal system. 7. Religion in Government schools.

CHAPTER VIII.

THE MOTHER-TONGUE 134

1. Position of the vernacular. 2. The psychological argument. The vernacular in other than village schools. 3. The scale of utility. 4. The cultural argument. Professor Westermann. The Phelps-Stokes Commission reports. Question

CONTENTS

of a *lingua franca*. 5. The phrase, "the soul of a nation." 6. The nature of culture. 7. The written language. Translations. The Authorized Version of the Bible. 8. Need for indigenous vernacular literature.

CHAPTER IX.

THE CONTENT OF AFRICAN EDUCATION 155

Five essentials of education :—

I. THE TOOLS A MAN USES : THE THREE R'S. 1. The Three R's. 2. Arithmetic. Measurement rather than counting. What is "practical" arithmetic? Nature of "adaptation." 3. Reading and writing. Value of written language. 4. Literature.

II. THE WORLD OF VALUES AND IDEALS : SCRIPTURE AND MORAL INSTRUCTION. 1. A typical Scripture syllabus. 2. Educational value of the Bible. 3. The Land and the Book. Meaning of the term "historical." 4. Moral Instruction. *My Duties.* 5. Nature of morality. How much can "moral instruction" do?

III. THE WORLD OF THINGS : NATURE STUDY. 1. Problem of the curriculum. The Project Method. 2. Agriculture in the village school. 3. Agriculture as a craft. 4. Three aspects of nature study. Appreciation of nature. 5. Hygiene and mothercraft as "liberal" nature studies. 6. Care of animals. Nature study and the town child. The teacher's attitude.

IV. THE WORLD OF PEOPLE : LITERARY STUDIES. 1. Human interests in books.. Literary and practical studies. Training of leaders. 2. Grammar. 3. Biography. History. 4. Geography.

V. CREATIVE ACTIVITIES : ARTS, CRAFTS, AND MANUAL TRAINING.

(a) VOCATIONAL AND LIBERAL. 1. Distinction illustrated by carpentry. 2. Educational reasons for manual training. 3. Fallacy of "character-building." 4. Indigenous art. Achimota. Sceva.

(b) APPRECIATION AND EXECUTION. 5. Drawing in the Transvaal syllabus. 6. Art and leisure. 7. Development of Native industries. Scouts and Guides. 8. An intellectual *ubuntu*. Sanderson of Oundle.

CHAPTER X.

THE FORM OF AFRICAN EDUCATION 226

1. "Literary" nature of African education. Lord Lugard's views. 2. Distinction between studies and social organization. 3. The case for the boarding-school. Character-building. 4. Education "based on religion." 5. Meaning of Christianity in this context. "Atmosphere." 6. School buildings. 7. Craftsmanship. Ritual. Form and content. Discipline. 8. Leisure. Reverence.

CONTENTS

PART III.

The Middle Distance.

CHAPTER XI.

The Missionary Societies 247

1. The Church abroad and the Church at home. 2. The earlier missionary motive. 3. The modern doctrine of development. Chiliasm. 4. Roman Catholic missions. 5. Anglo-Catholic missions. 6. Fundamentalism. 7. Co-operation with Government. 8. Protestantism and the present age. 9. "Edinburgh, 1910." 10. The Peace Conference, 1919. American funds. The Phelps-Stokes Commissions. 11. The Le Zoute Conference, 1926. 12. Current philosophy in religion and politics. 13. Finance. 14. Certain absolute values.

CHAPTER XII.

The Government 270

The theory of trusteeship. The dual mandate. 1. Direct, associated, and indirect rule. British temperament and British policy. 2. Indirect rule in Northern Nigeria. C. L. Temple's *Native Races and their Rulers*. 3. Defects of indirect rule. 4. British quixotism. 5. Christian missions and indirect rule. 6. Economics versus politics. 7. The French point of view. 8. Implications of indirect rule.

CHAPTER XIII.

America in Africa 291

1. Influence of Negro America in Africa. 2. Conflicting cultures in white America. 3. The intimidation of "science" in psychology and education. Measurement. 4. Method of the questionnaire. 5. Formulæ in education. 6. T. Jesse Jones' *The Four Essentials of Education*. 7. Tuskegee and Hampton. 8. Differences between America and Africa. The Phelps-Stokes reports.

CHAPTER XIV.

The Rationale of African Education 311

1. Data for generalization. 2. What is African "culture"? 3. Limitations of anthropology. 4. African history and Islam. Zimbabwe. 5. The sense of continuity. 6. Spiritual ancestry. Fallacy of simplicity. The meaning of "civilization." 7. "Western" civilization. Saint Paul. What is "along the Native's own lines?" 8. Parallel with history of women's education in England. Equality and differentiation. 9. African leadership. 10. The African Native and European culture.

CONTENTS

PART IV.

THE HORIZON.

CHAPTER XV.

THE FUTURE OF AFRICAN EDUCATION 337

1. Comparison of Africa with India. 2. General tendency of the history of education in Britain and in Africa. "Interests" become "forces." 3. Humanization of the State. 4. Future of education with the Government. An "interim Native electorate." Co-operation with missions. 5. Requirements of policy. A constitution for Achimota. 6. Education of African women. Hope Fountain. Ituk Mban. Need for general education for teachers. 7. Training of the European teacher. 8. Christian citizenship. The "two nation" theory. Co-operation between races. Problem of patriotism. E. G. Murphy on "Our race security." 9. Who is sufficient for these things?

APPENDIX I.

TWO COMPARISONS 371

APPENDIX II.

THE PROBLEM OF "INDIRECT RULE"

I. COMMENT BY THE RIGHT HON. LORD LUGARD ON CHAPTER XII 401

II. EDUCATION UNDER INDIRECT RULE 402

1. Indirect Rule a form of devolution. Adaptation. Effect of breakdown of isolation, emergence of educated classes, and better transport facilities. 2. Elementary education. Political education. "Native Administration." 3. Educated classes and their future. 4. Chiefs and chieftainship. Prestige. Education of chiefs. Emirs in Northern Nigeria. "Indirect rule" in S.A. Protectorates. "Natural justice." 5. Women in African society. Women's education. 6. Missions and "indirect rule." Christianity and tribalism. Animism. Denominational missions. Need for religion. Missions and education.

APPENDIX III.

SCHEME OF WORK AT ITUK MBAN 437

INDEX 439

LIST OF ILLUSTRATIONS.

	FACING PAGE
THE "SCHOOL IN THE BUSH"	47
SPRINGS COMPOUND, TRANSVAAL	47
ACHIMOTA: THE ADMINISTRATIVE BLOCK	110
MBERESHI: THE GIRLS' SCHOOL	110
AN ARITHMETIC LESSON, DOMBOSHAWA	167
A PHYSIOLOGY LESSON, KIMPESE	167
ZOMBA: CHURCH OF SCOTLAND MISSION SCHOOL	240

DRAWINGS IN THE TEXT.

	PAGE
A PAGE OF DRAWINGS BY SCEVA, A NYASALAND NATIVE	214
SKETCH-PLAN OF SCHOOL AT ZOMBA	240
SKETCH-PLAN OF DORMITORY AT ADAMS INSTITUTE, AMANZIMTOTI	241

MAP . . . . *At the end of the book*

PART I.

THE BACKGROUND.

WHEN I went out to Africa a kind friend told me that the really valuable book to take with me was Frazer's *The Golden Bough*. The one-volume abridged edition gives you an interesting study of the ways of thought of primitive people, and is a good background for the study of African life at first hand.

I took it, and I had read nearly the whole of it by the time that we got to Kilindini.

There were a great number of passengers who disembarked there, and I went across to the railway station to see off the train for Nairobi. After that I walked along to Mombasa, looked around a little and came back. At the docks our boat was being unloaded by four great electric cranes. Two motor lorries were rattling along by the side of the huge warehouse. Across the waterway the palms raised their heads out of the thick tropical undergrowth. At my feet a small native boy, a Moslem, was saying his prayers.

The question arose in my mind, Which is the background? Is it Frazer's *Golden Bough*, or is it the modern industrial system crashing into a system infinitely more primitive?

The answer is that it is both. Nevertheless, it is more truly the latter, for that includes both. The real *point d'appui* of African education is neither the bush village nor the European factory. It is the point where both meet. And the meeting place is not the compounds of Johannesburg, nor the locations at Cape Town. It is not really a place at all. It is as much to be found among the youths in the Nyasaland bush who order " plus-fours " cash-on-delivery from Oxendale's catalogue, or among the Natives of the

Congo forest who see the shining *SABENA* aeroplanes floating over their heads, as it is present in greater ruthlessness in the streets of Bulawayo or the farms of Natal. It is to be found wherever the mind of a primitive man comes into contact with new ideas, new types of people, new ways of living, new forces. In other words, everything that points a contrast, or creates a conflict, or demands a readjustment of life, is the background of native education.

This, then, is Africa of to-day, and these are the conditions that are to guide Africa of to-morrow. Anthropology alone is not in these days an adequate clue. Still less does it provide a guide to policy. It makes for understanding of one of the factors with which we have to deal. Major Rattray's researches into the meaning of the Golden Stool of Ashanti show how indispensable is that understanding. The stagnation of native education in the hands of well-trained officials in Northern Nigeria shows how sterile is that understanding when it is viewed as an end in itself. It clears a space, but it does not make a road, nor does it indicate a goal. There are also other factors. There are, for instance, the needs of the world market, the nature of the soil, the crops, the minerals, the type of European settler and administrator, the boredom of the native village, the temptations of the towns, the method of land tenure, and a dozen more. These, too, are the concern of the student of native life. He must know the Native. He must also know the world in which the Native lives. And he must know how these act and interact. Education in Africa nowadays cannot be a static thing. It must produce a power as strong as, and indeed stronger than, the forces which have native life in their control. In other words, for the man himself it must create a mind which can stand up and find itself amid the clash of civilizations. This is the beginning, middle, and end of native education. It is a moral problem.

CHAPTER I.

GEOGRAPHY.

1.

THERE is no need to dwell on the vastness of Africa, except to remind ourselves that in area it is one hundred times larger than the British Isles, and in population less than three times as large. It is larger than China, India, Europe, West and South Australia all put together. Yet its population is only one-third that of India. No part of India or Ceylon or the Straits Settlements is below the Equator. At the Equator you are still 2500 miles from Cape Agulhas. The distance down the Congo from Stanleyville to Kinshasa is the distance from London to Constantinople.

It is obvious that in so vast an area there are, and there must be, great differences of climate and of everything else. No sweeping generalizations about the Native are possible, except those which are concerned with the human family as a whole.

2.

Africa has come late into the current of civilization. Egypt, of course, has an ancient history, and the oldest civilization of which we have any familiar knowledge. But although Egypt is geographically part of Africa, it has always marched with Asia. Egyptian influence spread in very early times along the Sudan and across to the highlands of West Africa. But in none of these regions was there ever an Egyptian "civilization." The systems of kingship in Uganda and among the Yorubas on the West Coast may have had Mediterranean origins. We do not know. But no Mediterranean "civilization" was ever set up here. Africa remained shut off from the life of the world practically until the nineteenth century.

For this, geographical conditions were responsible. The African coast-line is very little indented, and there are few harbours. But even where it was possible to land on the coast, it was a formidable task to get into the interior. All round the coast of Africa is a barrier of mountains which is also the long edge of a vast central plateau. It is this configuration of the land that has kept Africa unknown. All that the early travellers ever saw of it was a belt of unhealthy coast-line, the endless creeks of mud and mangrove swamps that were the deltas of great rivers, the mountain barrier, and the unnavigable streams that passed steeply through it from the interior and raced down a series of cataracts to the coast plains. Those who knew the Mediterranean coast found as they went inland only the inhospitable Sahara and the desert region of the Middle Nile.

These facts have had several important consequences. The coast region has had a bad name—

> Beware and take care of the Bight of Benin.
> For one who comes out there were forty went in—

and accordingly the men from Europe who went there were undoubtedly taking great risks. Great risks were only worth taking where there were great profits, and a forty to one chance of survival induced neither scrupulousness nor tenderness. They were wonderful men, these people like our own Sir John Hawkins, but where inclination was lacking—which was seldom—circumstances made them look on Africa as simply a field of exploitation. Their own interest in Africa was to measure themselves against the hazards that she presented, and to get back again to enjoy their spoils in a more pleasant place.

And this feeling has persisted, and still persists. Africa has come late into the world's notice, and nearly all other races are well ahead of those of Africa. Accordingly the African almost inevitably is looked upon as a child, rather a simpleton, to be seen and not heard, and, with unscrupulous or thoughtless men, is there simply to be used by other people. The only observation of Mr. de Waal, the friend of Cecil

Rhodes, on seeing some fine young Matabele, was, " I thought what excellent labourers these men would make for the white man."[1] Just so the Belgians looked upon the Natives of the Congo, the Arabs upon the Masai, the Spaniards on the Natives of Peru, and the British on the negroes of the West Coast. The slave trade was accordingly the easiest form of trafficking, and for generations it was the staple industry.

But in addition to this coastal trade, the mystery of the interior of the Continent provided all kinds of stories. The fable of Prester John and the rumoured magnificence of Timbuktu, drew men of adventure as with a magnet. Africa appeared to be a place of oriental splendour,[2] where a man could get rich quickly. Wealth was to be had if not for the asking, at any rate for the taking.

This again is a feeling which has persisted. It is obvious, of course, in the gold rushes and the diamond rushes that have drawn thousands of white men together in one mad gamble—even as recently as 1927. But it is no less obvious when you hear men in Rhodesia or in Kenya speaking about the land. There is a bewildering extent of it, so it seems, all belonging to nobody; and so, why not take it? The days perhaps of staking out claims everywhere, as did Dr. Jameson's braves, have gone, but the attitude remains.

It is an attitude almost inevitable. With the best will in the world the white man cannot wholly avoid it. Any race with a long history of struggle and achievement is a superior race, and we need not quibble about the fact. Grown men are " superior " in the same sense to children of their own race, but their attitude to them is determined by the belief that the children will grow up to be like them, even, perhaps, to surpass them. Relationships, therefore, are conditioned by the end in view. And it is the same with the African. What we think his future will be determines his present. If it is true that Africa of to-day conditions Africa of to-morrow, it is no less true that our hopes or fears for

---

[1] See de Waal, *With Rhodes in Mashonaland* (1895).
[2] An English newspaper described the visit of Nana, Sir Ofori Atta of the Gold Coast to England in 1928, as " Visit of distinguished Oriental."

Africa of to-morrow condition Africa of to-day. And many people have not very high hopes. Some have no hope at all.

3.

Communications, therefore, are important. If Africa is a land of mystery, an unpenetrated Continent, it can only be opened up as the Romans opened up Britain. Roads and railways can overcome natural barriers. To the Native they are even more important than ports.

The railway has neutralized the barrier of the Sahara in North Africa. It has also supplemented for many hundreds of miles the navigability of the Congo by carrying commerce past the cataracts. It has ruled out the lions and leopards of the highlands of Kenya. It has discounted the silting up of the Shiré river in Nyasaland. It has brought the Moslem areas of Northern Nigeria into touch with European life. It has turned an area of ant-heaps and euphorbia trees in Katanga into the modern gay capital of Elisabethville. The newly-opened Benguela railway provides the shortest route from Europe to Katanga. A railway from Lindi on the Tanganyika coast to Manda on Lake Nyasa would open up a fertile region at present undeveloped.

Roads have supplemented railways. They have opened up the country between Lake Nyasa and Lake Tanganyika. A great road will soon bring the regions of the lower Zambezi into contact with Livingstone and Broken Hill. The Gold Coast has been opened up by a series of fine roads. There is a Great North Road through Northern Rhodesia. Their influence everywhere is enormous.

All this of course involves the European. The African cannot do it for himself; he does not, indeed, ask for it, and in many ways he loses by it. It is he who is taxed in order to pay for it. Yet in the long run it benefits the African, although it is not done for that purpose. He begins to live in a wider world, and if his primitive simplicity is disturbed, the means are also brought to his door to rehabilitate his own life.

The thing which concerns us here is not the economic aspect of all this so much as the human.

GEOGRAPHY

Ponthierville is the place on the Congo where begins that series of rapids known as the Stanley Falls. Consequently you get off the steamer and on to the train. It is a little station set in an area of dense tropical forest. At this station I saw a number of native mothers seeing off their children to Stanleyville. One small boy had on a striped blue blouse and shorts and the peaked cap that schoolboys wear in Belgium. He knew French and was apparently going to school. He was leaning out of the carriage window talking to his mother. She was entirely naked, save for a diminutive loin-cloth. She had come from the forest, where she lived the life that her people had lived for countless generations.

This meeting of the old and the new is obvious all over Africa. It is sometimes referred to as the " shock of contact," but there is not necessarily anything violent about it except to the outsider who does not expect it. It does not always follow that there is any particular shock to the mind of the Native. Railway engines and motor cars are no doubt very odd when they are first seen, just as an earlier generation of Africans were scared at the power of writing, but they make their minds up to these things with astonishing rapidity, and even learn to control them like an expert. The assumption that the mere arrival of European industry of itself changes a man's mind is a mere assumption. It credits external circumstances with a power which is possessed only by the mind which interprets these things. It is not so much the thing that matters as its significance, and the interpretation put upon it.

In the assessment of this situation there are four factors. There is the Native's view of himself and of the European. And there is the white man's view of himself and of the Native. These distinctions seem to me to be all equally important. To the Native, his hut and his customs may, and do, enshrine a system of relationships with his fellows, and to the unseen world, as valuable as anything the white man can offer. But a European may look on the Native's way of life as bestial barbarism. Many people in South Africa even say that. On the other hand, the idealistic missionary of these days has often assumed that the native village or the native language enshrines a culture finer than anything in our machine-made civilization of the West. Yet there are some Natives of Lagos and of the West Coast generally, who look at the white man's way of life and find it good. It means evening dress, spats, walking sticks, motor cars, perhaps also Christianity, perhaps freemasonry, perhaps both. They drive the uneducated Britishers to fury by what they achieve, and the enlightened ones to despair by what they miss. As educated people we feel that these Africans have got the shell of civilization instead of the kernel. What then is the kernel? Do we ourselves know what it is?

4.

Communications are important for opening up a country. If in the first instance they have been used to exploit the Natives, they are later on no less useful to overcome the effects of that exploitation. But there are other geographical considerations which cannot be overcome so easily as the physical barriers of mountain and desert. Of these the chief is climate.

In the Congo basin and along the West Coast we are in the region of constant equatorial rains. There are thick tropical forests, and a climate totally unsuited to continued European settlement. On the other hand, the basin of the Kafue river, west of the railway, is a savannah region of palms and xerophytic plants with here and there a green oasis and a water pan to break the monotony of the sandy soil.

Clearly these two regions have different characteristics, and their needs are different. In the one, if we neglect other factors like disease and modern industry—admittedly a very big " if "—it would be relatively easy to gain a livelihood with little labour; in the other, life is a precarious business. The need in the latter is for skill to get a living; in the former for wisdom in living well.

What I mean by this will perhaps be clearer if I take an example from the Gold Coast. It is within the equatorial rain-belt; it has a Government whose first concern is the stability of native life and customs, and in the region away from the coast it has a tolerably healthy climate, at any rate for the Natives. The land is in native hands, and the main crop is cocoa. It is a particularly easy crop to grow, although in preparing it for export it has to be very carefully fermented and dried. The price fluctuates considerably (the cause of the cocoa strike in 1938), but let us take it at, say, £35 a ton at Accra. The average native farmer who gets that price for his crop is getting more money than he knows what to do with. He is a capitalist with a low standard of living, and little vision. Two grand lines of expenditure are open to him—a funeral and a new house. The road north from Accra is dotted with half-finished cement houses whose building continued until money ran out, and then when next season's crop was gathered they were left derelict, because the owners had capriciously decided on a new site elsewhere! Here, obviously, the emphasis of education should be not so much on how to earn as on how to spend— an even harder proposition. But it is the climate and the soil and the crops which give it this emphasis.

Let us, however, look again at the Congo region, and we shall see another problem which arises out of these same considerations.

The staple foods of the Native in the area around Stanleyville are cassava or manioc, fish, and plantains. Cassava grows easily, but it has to be grown, and it is the woman's weary daily business getting it ready for food. Given this, however, the Native can live contentedly on his own plot of ground.

But cassava is not the crop for which the equatorial region is noted. It provides in abundance rubber, palm oil, copal, and ivory—all of them articles in European demand. There are, therefore, in the equatorial region two sorts of crops—those grown by the Native for himself, and those grown by and for the European. The same Natives have to look after both, for the white man cannot do the work even if he so desired. Here, then, is a problem. It is climate which makes the region for ever a black man's country. But it is climate also which determines the production of crops for which the black man has himself no use.

It is said by many people that the Native must be "educated for industry." The question is, whose industry ? If it is his own, of what value is it if, owing to labour conditions, he does not know whether he will ever see the profits of his own labour ? If it is not his own, how does it benefit the Native to make him simply a superior tool for the white man ?

There is a further consideration. The effects of latitude are modified by altitude. The highlands of Kenya, which are between 4000 and 5000 feet high, although on the Equator, do not possess an "equatorial" climate. They are not purely a black man's country, for they are admirably suited to white settlement. The same is true of Southern Rhodesia, which has an average altitude of 3000 feet. It is true also of South Africa. The presence of native crops and, so to speak, "European" crops side by side is a sufficient complication. But when it is also a matter of native people and European people in the same area for life as well as for livelihood, it becomes very difficult indeed. Land has been alienated from the Natives in both Rhodesia and in East Africa, and European rule has undoubtedly been established on a basis of injustice. Yet there have been sound economic reasons for the white occupation.

This is a peculiarly British problem. For none of the other alien races in Africa have to-day the kind of territory where these conditions prevail. In comparing, as people often do,[1] the way in which the Belgians and the French treat the Native and the way in which he is treated in South Africa, this effect of climate has to be taken into account before the comparison can be used to prove anything.

The effect of latitude is again modified by coastal influences. The warm Mozambique current, for instance, makes the eastern side of Cape Colony much more fertile than the west, and it produces a sub-tropical climate in Natal. One of the leading crops in Natal, therefore, is sugar, and a good deal of black labour is necessary.[2] It was not easy a genera-

---

[1] As, for instance, M. Louis Franck at the Le Zoute Conference, *The Christian Mission in Africa*, p. 138.

[2] The theory, however, of the *necessity* of black labour anywhere in South Africa has been considerably damaged by medical research into the

tion ago to get this labour, and so indentured Indian labourers were imported. By this time it is easier to get native African labour, but of whatever type the labourer is, he is not white. Accordingly there is an overwhelming black population, resented on political grounds, but necessary on economic grounds.[1] What is to be the goal of native education in an area such as this ?

5.

The nature of the soil is thus a vital factor.

The rich soil of the equatorial region produces crops that need little labour and involve few risks. It seemed to early European adventurers a place where money could be got for nothing. Accordingly they demoralized not only the Native but even Nature herself, and wound up by demoralizing themselves. Rubber was over-exploited in the Congo, and the wastage of the country's assets was enormous.

Every region has its own special difficulties. The pastoral areas are on the higher lands, but also on the lower lands where the soil is thin. Cattle are here the source of wealth. They were the mark of sovereignty among the Zulu and kindred tribes, and at a marriage they are the *lobola* that pass from the bridegroom's family to that of the bride as a compensation for the loss of a working member. On the lower lands, where the soil is light, the alternation of dry seasons and heavy rains leads to erosion, and in some parts, particularly in the Karoo in South Africa, the soil is practically useless for any purpose whatever. The cropping is very poor, and the cattle have to travel often great distances for pasture. This gives constant employment to the small boys, and makes school attendance difficult. Where the tsetse fly is found, this rules out cattle altogether, and areas which are not properly arable have to be cultivated as arable land. The soil soon gets exhausted and the village

effects of labour on the health of Europeans. See E. W. Smith, *The Way of the White Fields in Rhodesia* (1928), p. 24, quoting a lecture reported in *The African World*, Nov. 26, 1926.

[1] The estimated population of Natal in 1934 was : European, 188,800 ; Bantu, 1,403,300 ; Asiatic and other, 180,600.

moves *en bloc* to another part of the district and begins cultivating again. This is the condition of things in Central Nyasaland, and obviously here the great need is to teach the Natives to get more from the land by a system of rotation and by growing more profitable crops.

The great arable lands of Rhodesia and East Africa raise an increasing amount of crops for the European market. Mealies are the chief food of the country. But they are also an article of export. Fibres such as sisal are largely grown. Tobacco is becoming a popular crop in Rhodesia, but bad marketing facilities led in 1928 to a glut of Rhodesian tobacco. Part of the difficulty arises from the fact that the chief port for Northern Rhodesia and Nyasaland is Beira which is in the hands of the unprogressive Portuguese. The African Lakes Corporation, which in Britain still passes almost for a philanthropic concern, has in late years shown little progressive policy in the development of Nyasaland, and is far from being philanthropic.

The minerals under the soil are having an increasing influence on life as it is lived above it. The gold mines of the Rand determine the nature of the existence of thousands of Africans who have no connection with the Transvaal. The exploitation of the vast deposits of copper in Katanga have affected life not only in the Upper Congo but also in Rhodesia. The coal for smelting the copper comes from Wankie in Northern Rhodesia, and the cattle to feed the population come from Southern Rhodesia. Many of the labourers come from Rhodesia and Nyasaland. These facts give a unity to that area which is not visible if we regard simply the political boundaries, and English is spoken in Elisabethville more than French. The growth of large mining centres between Sakania and Bukhama in the Congo, on the Rand, at Wankie, between Broken Hill and Bwana M'Kubwa in Rhodesia, between Port Harcourt and Enugu in Nigeria, and elsewhere, is creating a demand for labour. There inevitably follows the movement of large numbers of men from their own ancestral hearths, and the current is set strongly in the direction of detribalization.

This is perhaps the most important element in the background of native education.

6.

The mountain barrier has made it natural that the three coast regions of Africa have each looked not inward to their hinterland, but outward to the opposite coast. North Africa and the Mediterranean lands form one system. West Africa looks to Britain, France, and America. East Africa looks across the Indian Ocean.

The native African is not a trader,[1] and races beyond the sea have come into his midst and traded for him,—Arabs, British Indians, and Goanese in the East, Syrians and Greeks in the centre and North-West, and North Europeans everywhere. East Africa has been dominated by Arabia and India. Indian plants—maize, sugar cane, and baobab trees have all been introduced into Africa from the East. The road south-west from Durban leads through a purely Indian area, with Hindu temples dotted along the side of the road. Indian stores are found everywhere in East Africa. On the road from Blantyre to Zomba the Indian tailor at his sewing machine is the most familiar object in the villages. In a very lonely village—Manda—on the Tanganyika shore of Lake Nyasa, the one tiny corrugated-iron store is kept by an Indian.

The presence of these non-European races has complicated the problems both of the Europeans and of the Africans. It has given the Native two masters instead of one, for common grievances against the white man have not broken down the attitude of superiority of Indian and Arab towards the African. Indians are very frequently moneylenders, and great are the complaints of their extortions. In South Africa, however, one of the signs of the times has been the recent formation of a non-European Conference, including both Africans and Asiatics.

West Africa is very different from the other parts of Africa. The people are negroes. It has had a longer connection with Europe, but it is not a white man's country at all. The coast itself is well within the equatorial belt, it is very fertile, and consequently densely populated. Both

---

[1] This is not altogether true of the West Coast. The Hausa, for instance, are traders throughout Nigeria and the Cameroons, and Efik traders have spread the use of their language on the Cross river.

for its crops and for its potential slaves it has therefore been an attraction to European speculators. After the abolition of the slave trade it became the scene of various political and educational experiments which were designed partly as a compensation to the negro race for the wrongs they had suffered. Liberia was settled by American negroes. Freetown became a centre for liberated slaves. European education, according to the methods then in vogue, was established. The result has been that the West Coast negro has become through education and commerce and his connection with Europe, a much more sophisticated person than any other type of African. And sophistication is the greatest foe to education.

The West Coast and its hinterland are two distinct regions. As we go north, the land rises, and we pass from a region of thick vegetation first to savannah lands and then to desert. The interior plateau is much healthier than the coast, and the extension of railways has brought the two areas together, and made possible a greater variety of marketable crops. The native inhabitants of the West Coast colonies are of three well-marked types—the sophisticated negro of the coast town, who usually writes himself down as a Christian; the primitive tribes of the interior who are animists, even when they are nominal Mohammedans; and the Moslem tribes of the Sudan. Thus Islam is a potent factor on the West Coast, and is particularly strong in the towns away from the seaboard.

The equatorial region is virtually the basin of the Congo, and we have already seen some of the factors in it that affect native education. The country has been rapidly opened up in the last ten years. There are now eighteen wireless stations, an aeroplane service from Elisabethville to Leopoldville, a fleet of large stern-wheelers on the Congo, the Lualaba and the Kasai, and hundreds of miles of good railways. The journey by road and rail from Elisabethville to Matadi takes eighteen days in actual travelling, and twenty-eight in all; by air it takes fifteen flying hours, and three days in all.

The Congo region accordingly presents very violent contrasts. There are extremely modern towns both residential and industrial like Elisabethville and Kinshasa, and the most primitive tribal conditions in Africa, side by side. I have already spoken of the old and the new meeting at Ponthierville. There are to be found rude wattle-and-daub river villages, with substantial European houses rising in their midst inhabited by native administrators. The road from the European town of Stanleyville to the Stanley Falls passes first through an " Arabisé " native village with a fine brick house for the Moslem chief, and then through an animistic village of a quite different type. Disease, particularly sleeping sickness, is rampant in the Congo area, and in addition to this, the Natives suffer extreme dislocation through labour conditions. The concessionnaire companies recruit in the villages, and men are transported great distances from their homes.

South Africa to the European a hundred years ago exhibited the sight of vast untenanted stretches of land. As men trekked north into those great open spaces, there was no need to drive out the people before them; they were simply taken over with the land and settled down to an existence not unlike that of the mediæval European peasant. Wages were paid in kind rather than in money. Gradually, however, the available land became occupied and farms were divided up. The pastoral areas were stricken by a plague of rinderpest in 1896, and " East-coast fever " and other tick-borne diseases were widely spread in the Boer war. A wide farm over which cattle roved at will became expensive; the cattle needed to be kept together and carefully watched, and even in areas chiefly pastoral crops began to be grown. South Africa has, therefore, become more of an arable country within the last thirty years, farms have become smaller, and with the increased demand for arable land, the Native has been driven into the less productive areas. We shall see later that the native problem in South Africa is primarily a land problem.

The mineral wealth of South Africa is a further important factor. The earlier history of South Africa is concerned with the coast, and with the coal areas of Natal, whose trade looked overseas rather than to the interior. These were predominantly British districts, for the tendency of the Dutch was to keep farther and farther away from the sea, which in Holland had been their natural element, and to seek the wide farm lands of the North. Cape Town, Port Elizabeth, and Durban were the most important towns, and they were commercial centres fringing a hinterland primarily of agriculture. Two discoveries, however, disturbed this state of things. The first diamond was found in Griqualand West in 1867, and three years later Kimberley began to attract its thousands. In 1886, there was established on the Rand the gold-mining camp which later became the city of Johannesburg. The discovery of gold shifted the balance of power and interest from the commercial and arable areas of the South to the sparsely cultivated high veld of the Transvaal. Johannesburg became the storm centre of politics, as well as of industry, Dutch versus British, Jew versus Gentile, black versus white, agricultural versus financial, land versus labour. And so it has remained to this day.

This same influence of geography on political conditions was seen in the Industrial Revolution in England, when the agricultural South lost in importance what was gained by the manufacturing North.

A somewhat similar process has been going on in the far North of South Africa. The railway across Southern Rhodesia links a series of mining centres, and on each side of it are vast stretches of farm lands. At Bulawayo the railway goes north through the Wankie coal-field to Livingstone, and thence to the Congo border at Sakania and on to Elisabethville and Bukhama. The railway follows the mines, and of all the mining districts those on the Katanga border are the greatest. It would seem that the supply of copper in those regions is almost inexhaustible. Northern Rhodesia is part of the same region as Katanga, and there are vast copper-fields in British territory as yet unexploited. In the Belgian Congo the *Star of the Congo* mine near Elisabethville used to be the most notable, but of late years it has been surpassed by that at Kambove, while developments at Panda point to this being the chief centre of all.[1] There is thus a cluster of mining

[1] See M. Robert, *Le Katanga Physique* (Brussels, 1927), a very valuable study of this region. My information, however, came from a mine manager in Katanga.

towns right on the edge of British territory which are attracting to themselves labour from all over Rhodesia just as the mines on the Rand attract labour from the South. Meanwhile there is a steady European immigration into the rural parts of both Rhodesias, and a consequent pressure on native land. The cutting down of native reserves at a time when the mines are requiring labour is having precisely the same effect as the coincidence of the enclosure of English land in the eighteenth century with the growth of the factory system.

7.

The " human geography " of Africa is in these days concerned with people in a state of transition. And the transition is being brought about chiefly by economic causes predominating over those purely geographical. The " conditions of life " of African peoples are no longer simply climate, soil, altitude, and vegetation. The man who leaves his hut by the shores of Lake Nyasa for the compounds at Elisabethville or Germiston, has to adapt himself to artificial conditions created by Europeans to whom also they are artificial. The geographical factor is there as a basis, but the relationship that matters is not that between a man and the place where he was brought up, but that between one human group and another human group, each out of its " natural " element. Men move about more than they used to do, and their occupation determines their way of life much more than their way of life determines their occupation. Geography settles the occupations of a locality, but populations are ceasing to be purely local. Labour in Africa is more mobile than might be expected, and this mobility is not always due directly to the European. The growth of industry and the development of transport do not abolish geographical influences on human life, but they make them indirect instead of direct. The work of education is to deal with all the forces at work in an area, and, on behalf of the next generation, to moralize them.

But the economic side of geography is not the only side that concerns the education of the race. Africans no more than other people live by bread alone. Men's minds as well as their bodies need to be adapted to their surroundings. The situation, therefore, needs "moralizing," it needs to be seen in all its meanings if the mind is to find its way about within it.

And there are elements in the geography of Africa which are full of meaning for human life. The fact that the whole world depends on the industries of the tropics is one of them, but it is not the only one. The infinite capacity of African scenery for exciting wonder and reverence is another. The educated Englishman, be he ever so town-bred, finds his joy in the things of the country. The educated African will some day find this joy also, and how much grander are the sights that Africa has to offer! The collieries are established, and copper and gold exercise their influence over the destinies of men. But some day, although that may not be yet, the old fascination of the earth's surface will reassert itself in minds quickened by discipline. And then Africa will really be possessed by the Africans, be our political boundaries ever so European.

CHAPTER II.

HISTORY AND POLITICS.

1.

A FACT of primary importance in African education is that outside Egypt there is nowhere any indigenous history. There is tribal memory of course; there are the elders who stand in the old ways and who " know the law "; there is that deposit of tradition and religion which is handed on to the young in the initiation ceremonies; but there is no history in our sense. There has been no written language, no records. The history of African peoples, therefore, comes to us through the records of other people with whom they have been associated. African history has always been " foreign " history.

This absence of indigenous history in Africa has had two effects. It has prevented the growth of a self-conscious culture, and it has lowered the status of the African in the eyes of the outside world.

The effect on culture I will consider later in connection with the rationale of native education. The people have not taken charge of their own development in the way in which they have done in countries where there has been a written history. Progress has been a slow physical response to environment, just as it was also in prehistoric Europe.

The word " culture " has at least two possible meanings. It may mean those habits of life which are indicated by study of the household and field utensils of a people, by the way they bury their dead, and by the visible tokens of their thoughts. In other words, it may refer to behaviour. On the other hand, it may mean not behaviour only, but also purpose. It may be concerned with the ideals of the people, their intentions, their philosophy and their policy. When we speak of " Neanderthal culture " we use the word in the first sense; when we speak of " French culture " we use it in the second. It is history—meaning by that, written history—which makes possible culture in the second sense.

With one exception there is nothing of this in Africa. Yet the earliest travellers found it impossible to believe in this difference between Africa and other places, and so they invented stories of magnificent and powerful kingdoms in the unknown interior of the Continent. But these stories, unlike those which lured Marco Polo to Cathay, were found to have no reality that corresponded to them. The native Africans when discovered by Europeans were primitive people with no written language, only the simplest arts, and completely objective in their ways of thought. They were physically strong, but docile and easily made cheerful. They could be exploited and oppressed. There was nothing in the past which could rise up again and act as a solace in difficult days and as a rallying-point when opportunity offered. The native African has a short memory for either joy or grievances, and finds forgiveness easy. Through his own disposition, and his lack of a historic past, he has suffered greatly, and the alien has treated him as negligible. Mr. de Waal looked upon the Matabele simply as labourers for the white men, and the history of the Imperial East Africa Company and of the British South Africa Company shows a complete disregard for native races *as a people*. They had to be provided for if they were not to be exterminated, but they were provided for as individuals with no political rights. The " political animal " needs a history in order to be treated as such, or in order to assert himself if he is treated otherwise.

Abyssinia is the solitary exception in Africa which proves the rule. It has a written language and its records go back for centuries. It remained an independent native state until destroyed by Mussolini in 1935.

2.

The first of the alien peoples to enter Africa and to leave a permanent mark on the Continent were the Arabs. Next in order came the Portuguese and the Spaniards, followed by the Dutch and British. The French were the next to establish themselves, and then came the Belgians, the Italians, and the Germans.

With these invasions in detail we are not concerned. We may notice, however, that each one of them had a different incidence, and brought with it both a political attitude and a religious outlook that were characteristic. With the Arabs came Islam. The ships which brought the Portuguese and Spanish *conquistadores* brought also Roman Catholic priests of the Latin type. The Dutch were Calvinistic Protestants almost to a man. The British where they were religious at all represented a more humanitarian form of Protestantism. With the Belgians came a Catholicism in which the Latin element was considerably modified by the Flemish temperament. The Germans brought a Protestantism which was the exact converse of the Dutch type and in which the State governed the Church instead of the Church governing the State. It was Erastian rather than Calvinistic.

Islam presents a comparatively cut and dried situation. To the conquered peoples the Moslems gave the alternative of conversion or slavery, and the negroes of the North showed a decided preference for conversion. " Conversion " was a matter of acceptance of a formula and a few simple observances, and usually also a distinctive dress. It made no inconvenient demands on the animistic converts. Once having joined the Faith the new believer became part of a wide brotherhood with Arabic as its *lingua franca*, and no further progress was expected or required.

Often, however, the native African did not have the option of conversion. Slaves were needed for Mohammedan households, and Arabia, India, Persia, and Turkey kept up a steady demand for native Africans, the supply of whom was apparently unlimited. The Arabs of Zanzibar at a later date conducted vast slave raids into the interior and got as far as the Upper Congo. It was the Arab slave raids round Lake Nyasa that inflamed the pity of Livingstone and roused the British Government to stop the traffic. The Moslem States which had been established at an earlier period in the Sudan were centres of the slave trade, and the traffic was only stopped by European intervention.

Islam, therefore, has no particular "native policy." The Moslems in Northern Nigeria have no concern for the pagans round about, now that they are prevented from harrying them. Were European pressure withdrawn in the North and in the East the slave trade would leap into activity again at once. These Moslem invaders, however, have acted as carriers of products, if not of ideas, from Arabia and India to Africa. Their conquests extended the range of the use of the horse, and of other domestic animals. Civilization in this material sense they developed. They did little else.[1] The unprogressive nature of Islam is seen both in the reaction against it in modern Turkey, and in the attempt to modernize it in Cairo. But while Islam finds it easy to be militant in a physical sense, it is only compatible with intellectual and moral progress by ceasing to be the thing it really is.

Nevertheless, as we shall see later, where it is aggressive it is a serious enemy to Christian Missions and to that education for which Christian Missions stand. Where it is inactive, the attraction of the modern world is too strong for its nominal adherents. In British territory whether active or inactive it is protected.

The European nation that has had most contact with Islam is the French. They have had four main bases on the coast of Africa, the Senegal, Algeria, Gaboon, and Somaliland, and from each they have occupied country in the hinterland. A French empire has been built up in North-West Africa, and the award to France of the mandate over the

---

[1] Islam appears to have stimulated among the Moslem negro peoples poetry of a characteristically Semitic type. The Kanuri, for example, in North-East Nigeria, possess a number of songs which have survived from the old Moslem empire of Bornu. They are extremely interesting, and in places reminiscent of fragments of early Hebrew poetry like the Song of Deborah. But the world of which they sing is a world of despotic and capricious Sultans attended by swarms of slaves and delighting in flattery and slaughter. It is Bagdad transplanted into West Africa, without apparently any of the civilizing Hellenistic elements which it borrowed from Byzantium. Mr. J. R. Patterson, district officer in Bornu Province, has published a translation of some of these songs (privately printed, 1925), and it is interesting to note that although the first of his selection dates from the eleventh century and the last from the nineteenth, the sentiment is not notably different.

HISTORY AND POLITICS

Cameroons is making it possible to link up Gaboon and French Congo with this North-West empire. This has taken the place in French politics of the earlier hope of connecting Somaliland with Senegal. But wherever it has extended, the history of French conquest has been the history of warfare against militant Moslem empires rather than the extension of influence over scattered primitive tribes. Even the British campaigns in Mashonaland or against the Zulus were of a different character from those of the French against fanatical Fula conquerors such as Al Hajji 'Omaru or Samori.

3.

The Portuguese entered Africa from both the east and the west. Their first fort on the west coast was Elmina, established in 1482. Three years later Diego Cam sailed beyond the Ogowe and up the Congo, and in 1491 he went again to the capital of " King " Kongo's country and established the settlement of San Salvador. With him went a number of priests, and the work of proselytizing among the natives went on apace. Almost the same thing happened with them as with the crowds of Saxons and Northumbrians who were baptized in the days of Charlemagne and of Paulinus. There was no preparation for conversion, and the people rapidly became nominal Christians while keeping their old fetish-worship.

A later Portuguese settlement on the west was at San Paulo de Loanda which was occupied in 1574, and from which as a base the Portuguese took possession of what is now Angola and of the islands of San Thome and Principe. The country was worked by slaves for the next three hundred years, and the abolition of the slave trade at the end of the nineteenth century seriously affected its prosperity.

But the mentality produced by slave-owning still exists in Angola and in other Portuguese Colonies. There is compulsory labour on the roads, as there is everywhere in Africa, including British territory, but no wages are given and no *poso* (rations), and the women and children have to work as well as the men.[1] And there is no Portuguese public opinion to force a change of system.

In East Africa the Portuguese established themselves first at the old Arab port of Sofala, then at Mozambique, as a half-way house to Goa. The great Vasco da Gama had called at these places and defeated the Arabs on his return voyage from Calicut in 1498. Quelimane was established in 1544 in consequence of the rumours of fabulous wealth to be found in the gold mines of Manica up the Zambezi valley. There was a great expedition made in 1569, but the dazzling successes of the Spanish in Peru and Mexico were not destined to be repeated by the Portuguese in Africa. They therefore turned to a slave trade as a more certain source of revenue. The Portuguese, however, had not the same religious scruples about the compatibility of slavery and the new religion as had the Moslems. They recognized slavery and the acceptance of Christianity not as alternatives but as concomitants. The ceremony of baptism was a perfunctory act of magic performed by the priest just before the slave merchant took possession. Thus God and Mammon were both excellently well served.

The Portuguese held vast territories on the east and west sides of Africa, and up to the middle of the nineteenth century the land between them was marked on the map "unknown." It was Livingstone's discoveries that drew the attention of the world to the importance of tropical Africa and made the Portuguese desire to join together Angola and Mozambique. There were, however, rivals in the field, the chief of whom were the British, and it was the British South Africa Company which finally ended the Portuguese dream of empire.

Sir Harry Johnston speaks a good word for the old Portuguese *conquistadores*. They

'may have been relentless and cruel in imposing their rule on the African and in enslaving him or in Christianizing him, but they added enormously to his food supply and his comfort.'[2]

---

[1] Of this I was assured in Elisabethville by American missionaries who had spent some years in Angola and had but recently left the country.
[2] Sir H. H. Johnston, *A History of the Colonization of Africa* (1913), pp. 91-92.

They brought to Africa the sugar cane, cocoa, maize, wheat, tobacco, the tomato, manioc, guavas, pawpaws, bananas, and many other vegetable products. It is an extraordinary list, for maize, manioc, and bananas are the three staple foods of the Bantu people from Cape Agulhas to the Congo. This fact alone shows something of the energy of the early Portuguese and also of the adaptability of the Bantu. It is a matter of amazement to the Native at school to hear that the " immemorial " food of his people was introduced by Europeans.

With the Portuguese we may consider the Spanish. The most valuable Spanish possession in Africa is the island of Fernando Po. It became the headquarters of the British when putting down the slave trade in the Gulf of Guinea, and was given back to Spain in 1844. In these days unfortunately it acts as a dumping-ground for lower-grade Spaniards who wish to get rich quickly and easily. Nearly all the clerkships and minor posts which in British, French, and Belgian colonies are held by Natives, are here held by Europeans. Education of the Native is difficult as there is no opening for him in the island itself. Manual labour is all native, but the labourers come from Guinea, Nigeria, and even the Gold Coast on a two years' contract. The Natives leave their tribal environment at home and come into an unaccustomed state of freedom. There are plenty of cafés and idle women on the island, and the chief import from Spain is a crude wine for native consumption only. The Spanish authorities seem quite indifferent to the social results of their policy or lack of policy.

4.

The Dutch, liberated from the stranglehold of Spain, and spurred on by their Protestantism, began to attack the possessions of the most Christian Kings of Spain and Portugal about 1595. On the west coast they supplanted the Portuguese, and after flourishing for over two centuries they began to decline in power with the abolition of the slave trade. Thenceforward their eyes were turned to Java and other

East Indian possessions, and they finally disappeared from West Africa in 1872.

They were destined to leave a more permanent mark on another part of the Continent. Van Riebeeck took possession of the Cape for the Dutch East India Company in 1652, and at first it was no more than a half-way house to the East. Under the van der Stels, father and son, it began to be developed into a colony, and in the forty years from 1679 to 1719 the foundations were laid of an ultimately new nation.

The colony at this time exhibited several marked characteristics each of which was important in its later history.

In the first place there was a dual system, introduced as soon as free burghers began to settle at the Cape side by side with the Company's officials. Devolution was no more understood in the Dutch colonies than it was at the end of the eighteenth century in the British colonies. The seventeen directors of the Company kept strict control not only over their own officials but also over the free burghers. The situation, however, was one in which free institutions were likely to develop, and the burghers had to work out their own political salvation apart from the Company. Accordingly, a " national " party gradually arose, and when during the Napoleonic wars the Stadtholder of Holland allowed the British to protect the Cape against the French, the British found themselves in charge of a people who had learned the lesson of political liberty.

Secondly, the settlement at the Cape was composed of two races. After the revocation of the Edict of Nantes, the directors of the Dutch Company encouraged French refugees to settle in South Africa. They arrived during the time of Simon van der Stel, about 1687. There were not many of them, but they were of a higher social class than the Dutch, they were skilled vine-dressers and artisans, and they had no Fatherland of their own to claim them. The policy of the Company was to fuse them as quickly as possible with the Dutch population. Their children were forced to learn Dutch, while the elders soon ceased to have any organization of their own either social or religious, and to-day many of the most distinguished Dutch families at the Cape have French names.

HISTORY AND POLITICS

A third element in the situation at the Cape was already present in the days of van Riebeeck. The European settlement was very small, and marriageable women were scarce. Van Riebeeck, therefore, allowed mixed marriages with Indians and with Hottentots. The first European to marry a Hottentot " received promotion to the rank of surgeon as a wedding present from the Company." Domestic slaves, detribalized Hottentots and Asiatics formed a large part of the society at the Cape.

'Miscegenation of all these elements began, and soon three-fourths of such slave children as there were, were half-breeds. The Cape Coloured Folk had emerged.'[1]

The fourth factor was slavery. The rigid control of the Company over the Cape Government led to a growing discontent at the Cape itself with the corrupt official bureaucracy, and this discontent in its turn alarmed the directors at Amsterdam. In 1707 therefore they brought to an end the period of assisted immigration, and the colony was thrown back on its own resources for labour. Six years later a plague of smallpox wiped out about a quarter of the total inhabitants, particularly Hottentots and slaves. In these circumstances the authorities decided for slave labour, and thereby prevented the Colony forever from becoming a genuine white man's country. And while this decision was being taken at the Cape the British and the French began to be serious rivals to Holland in all her overseas stations.

There is one more factor, and that not the least important. The Dutch Reformed Church had a hold upon its people only comparable to that which Calvin had over Geneva or John Knox over Scotland. A Calvinistic doctrine of election, and a verbal inspirationist view of the Scriptures which went along with it, characterized Dutch theology, and easily lent itself to a rigid division of classes and races. The Huguenot refugees and the Moravians began to evangelize the Hottentots but were prevented by the Dutch Company.[2] To the Dutch Calvinists the coloured races were of the " perishing progeny of Ham," and the Old Testament religion of those

[1] Eric A. Walker, *A History of South Africa* (1928), pp. 44-45.
[2] Sir H. H. Johnston, *op. cit.*, pp. 241-42.

days sanctioned a complete denial of the human rights of any races outside the pale of divine election. Accordingly a simple personal piety co-existed with a quite un-Christian social attitude, and both were justified by an appeal to the Bible. It is a phenomenon which is not infrequently met with in this type of religion.

The European settlement at the Cape first came into contact with the Bantu about 1778. The attitude of the Dutch towards them was determined both by their Calvinism and by the existence of slavery. They could not look upon the new-comers as equals, because to their eyes the Bantu were simply hordes of thieving savages with no social organization, not even that of the family, which needed to be treated seriously. They were people under the ban of God, predestined to slavery—although, as it happened, the Bantu never actually became slaves to the Dutch. It was impossible that they should be recognized as having any rights of their own to land or property, and they were mixed up with the white inhabitants instead of being given territories to themselves.

All these elements were in the situation at the Cape when the British took over the country. There was a tradition of political liberty, a Calvinistic state, a slave population, another population of half-breeds, and all this in an area of Mediterranean climate suitable both for white settlement and for white labour. The British had a different tradition. Moreover, the French Revolution had produced on the one hand a romantic humanitarianism which blended well with the doctrine of " free grace " of the Evangelical Revival, and on the other, by reaction, a suspicion of popular movements. The Industrial Revolution glorified the work of men's hands, and made industry a means by which a man might wrest the secrets of nature from her. The Napoleonic wars had disorganized the finances of the Cape as well as of countries in Europe. British settlers of the artisan and farmer type arrived in 1820, and their disillusionment helped to swell the chorus of discontent. In 1834 slavery was abolished from London, and the compensation paid to slave-owners at the Cape was so meagre that many of them were ruined. The British authorities, moreover, were inclined to deal with these "heathen savages" as organized peoples, and to make treaties with them. And so from all sides the theological prejudices of the Dutch were seriously disturbed.

The discontent came to a head during Lord Glenelg's Secretaryship of State and Sir Benjamin D'Urban's Governorship of Cape Colony. Glenelg was associated with the "Clapham Sect" which included Wilberforce and most of the anti-slavery leaders. One of his trusted correspondents at the Cape was the famous Dr. John Philip, of the London Missionary Society. The Xosa country round King William's Town had been set up into a new province of Queen Adelaide in 1835, and three distinct views were held concerning it. One was to keep it altogether, a second was to give it back, a third was to keep the province and secure to the natives their land within it. The first was the desire of most South Africans, the second was that of Glenelg and the humanitarians in London, the third was the view of Dr. Philip.[1] The second view carried the day, and the Boers, utterly disgusted with British Rule, began the Great Trek.

With the future of the *Voortrekkers* we are not here concerned. It is however necessary to notice the causes of the Trek, as they persist to this day and are a determinant of South African native policy. The root cause was the abolition of slavery, and it was viewed in two ways. Piet Retief, one of the greatest of the Voortrekkers, declared

'We are resolved wherever we go that we will uphold the just principles of liberty; but whilst we will take care that no one shall be held in a state of slavery, it is our determination to maintain such regulations as may suppress crime and preserve proper relations between master and servant.'[2]

and Mrs. Anna Steenkamp, writing in 1876, gave as one of the causes of the Trek

---

[1] Philip has been about the most vilified man in South African history, but has been vindicated by Professor Macmillan and by D. K. Clinton, *The South African Melting Pot* (1937). Professor Edgar Brookes (*A History of Native Policy in South Africa* (1927), Chapter II.) condemns the treaty system as marking a confusion between the position of an Indian Rajah—with which the Secretary of State had also to deal—and that of a Bantu Chief. Yet, as we shall see, a Bantu Chief was head of a much more coherent social unit than an Indian state.

[2] Quoted in W. M. Macmillan, *The Cape Colour Question* (1927), p. 245.

'the shameful and unjust proceedings with reference to the freedom of our slaves ; and yet it is not so much their freedom that drove us to such lengths as their being placed on an equal footing with Christians, contrary to the laws of God, and the natural distinction of race and religion, so that it was intolerable for any decent Christian to bow down beneath such a yoke ; wherefore we rather withdrew in order thus to preserve our doctrines in purity.'[1]

When at a later date the Trekkers crossed the Vaal river, they determined once and for all to establish it as a principle that there should be " no equality between black and white in Church or State." [2] And on this principle were founded the Republics of the Orange Free State and the Transvaal.

5.

There are many great names connected with the opening up of the interior of Africa, and we need not concern ourselves with all of them. But two cannot be omitted. First of all there is Livingstone, because he is *facile princeps* among all African explorers, and set a standard which has never been excelled. Yet he was first and foremost a missionary. Every other aspect of his life is subordinate to this. Those who speak scornfully of " Exeter Hall " and its influence in politics often lose sight of the fact that it was religious humanitarianism which gave us the greatest name in the European history of Africa. Secondly, there is Stanley, because his work was the direct cause of that " scramble for Africa " which had such an important effect on the lives of European and native peoples.

The explorations of these two men showed that in Africa valuable natural products were to be found in abundance, and that the native inhabitants were simple people who had no use for these products themselves and had indeed no knowledge of their value.

These commercial possibilities, however, did not dawn all at once upon the European Governments. This was the period of the Franco-Prussian War, when a " Continental " policy was forced upon the countries of Central Europe, and

[1] Macmillan, *op. cit.*, p. 81 ; Walker, *op. cit.*, p. 208.
[2] Transvaal Grondwet, 1856.

the eyes of England also were turned in that direction. It was left therefore for the King of the Belgians, whose guaranteed neutrality saved him from undue worry at home, to concentrate on the possibilities of the tropics. He created an International Association for the exploration and civilization of Central Africa, the Belgian branch of which sent out Stanley to explore the Congo and make treaties with the chiefs. Soon the British began to suspect Leopold's alleged disinterestedness, and sought to establish claims in the Lower Congo. This brought in the other Powers of Europe, and the Berlin Conference was called in 1884. The various European countries concerned staked out claims which had hitherto remained very shadowy, and the great equatorial region itself was put under an International Committee and administered as the " Congo Free State." By 1891 its entire administration was Belgian.

Meanwhile British influence was being extended in two directions. In East Africa Sir John Kirk was coming to terms with the Sultan of Zanzibar, and in 1888 the Imperial East Africa Company got its charter and began to govern the country between Mombasa and Victoria Nyanza. Soon afterwards it was compelled to extend its control beyond the Lake, and this forced the British Government itself to come in and accept responsibility for Uganda.

The extension of British territory to the eastern frontier of the Congo state was followed by a similar extension to the southern frontier. Diamonds had been discovered at Kimberley and gold on the Rand, and South Africans began to look to the north. Beyond Johannesburg there lay the rumoured wealth of south Central Africa. The land was occupied by unenterprising native tribes, who, however, had granted " concessions " to various Europeans to dig for gold. The British South Africa Company was founded in 1889 to buy up and work these concessions, and to administer the country as far as Lake Tanganyika and Lake Mweru. It was thus a curious position that Johannesburg, the chief town of a Dutch state, should also be the headquarters of what was virtually a British state. Seeds of trouble were sown in the south.

Leopold was alarmed at the extension of British influence.

Between the equatorial zone and the land of the Chartered Company lay the debatable land of Katanga. In 1892 he sent out an expedition to take possession of it in his name.

As the Congo came more and more into the limelight of European interest, discoveries were made which completely discredited Leopold not only as a philanthropist but even as the ruler of a civilized state. He had declared all the vacant land to be the *domaine privé* of the Government, within which all ivory and rubber were state monopolies. Within this vast area there was carved out in 1896 a *domaine de la couronne* of 112,000 square miles, as Leopolds personal property. The rest of the *domaine privé* was farmed out to concessionnaires who shared their profits with Leopold or the Government. The result to the Natives was the scandal of the Congo atrocities which have left their mark even to-day. In many regions the rubber trees have been ruined, and are having to be re-planted. The native population was reduced in fifteen years from twenty to nine millions—a devastation which, as Sir Harry Johnston puts it, "left the Arab slave-raids far, far behind."[1] Meanwhile the wealth taken from the Congo was used to enrich Belgium, and to this day Belgians are wont to speak proudly of Leopold II. as the founder of their nation. Whatever moral opinion, however, was lacking in Belgium itself to condemn Leopold, indignation was not lacking in the rest of Europe, and the Congo was taken from him and annexed to Belgium in 1908.

In the Belgian Congo to-day the concessionnaire system is still in existence, and the amount of capital represented by the Companies is enormous. Their relations with the administration are very close. In Elisabethville I was given to understand that part of the income of the Governor of the Katanga province is paid to him from the profits of the *Comité Spéciale de Katanga*. In the case of any trouble with the Natives and the Companies, the administration can scarcely be the impartial authority that it ought to be. With the older officials this system works very well, but a more liberal attitude is to be found among the younger men,

[1] *Op. cit.*, p. 352.

HISTORY AND POLITICS

even though in some cases its basis is less a concern for the Native than a nationalist aversion to alien Companies.

The great need in the Belgian Congo is for an independent public opinion. There is a *Société pour la Protection des Indigènes*, but it is under the State and its members are appointed by the State. Except in non-controversial matters it can do little. Public opinion might be created by the missionaries, but the Protestant missionaries are practically all foreigners, ignored by Belgian publicists, although generously appreciated by King Albert himself. The Roman Catholics vary in effectiveness as an independent influence. Most of the priests look upon a good Governor as one who favours the Church and does not favour the Protestants, and there their interest appears to end. But there are some, mainly Jesuits, but also members of other Orders, who have fought hard in Belgium for native rights. The most notable was Father Le Grand, whose speech at the Brussels Colonial Conference in 1925 initiated an official change of attitude. The Belgian Labour Party again is concerned not so much with the Natives as with the capitalists, while it has recently embarked on the production of cotton on capitalistic lines within the Congo itself.

There remains public opinion outside Belgium. It was this which in the first instance, and in spite of defensive casuistry, stopped the Congo scandals, and it is to this alone that Belgium is at all sensitive. On the material side the development of the Congo has been wonderful. The State has done a very great deal in the way of medical service. The gardens of Eala near Coquilhatville are a joy to view, and a great asset to science, and ultimately to industry. The Congo is written up in the Belgian newspapers, there is a marvellous Congo Museum in Brussels, and there is a steady stream of books and magazines about the Congo issuing from the press. What the outsider feels, however, is just this lack of self-criticism, the existence of which in South Africa, in Kenya and in Rhodesia is so healthy a factor in the development of those countries.[1]

---

[1] See footnote on p. 120 below.

6.

Practically every problem that vexes humanity is to be found intensified within the Union of South Africa. Political, economic, religious, educational, moral, and racial questions are clamant for solution, and they are entwined in such a way that it is impossible to touch one without affecting all the others. But the basic problem of all is the native question.

We have seen how it affected the foundation of the Boer republics, and how its emphasis has been distributed in British and in Dutch areas. We have now to notice how it has been complicated by the growing industrialism of the Transvaal.

The *Voortrekkers* claimed from the British a liberty of action which they would not themselves permit to the Natives. In the same way the *Uitlanders* of Johannesburg claimed a liberty of action from the Transvaal Government which they themselves did not recognize when they came to deal with the Matabele and the still more unfortunate Mashonas. The *Voortrekkers* were able to leave the country in which their wishes were flouted and to establish themselves elsewhere. The *Uitlanders* were not able to do that because it would have meant leaving the Rand, which was the only source of their wealth. They therefore stayed, and their claims led to friction, and friction resulted ultimately in the Anglo-Boer War.

The establishment of the Union in 1910 brought a new alignment of parties. The Dutch divided along political lines, between those who, like General Smuts, would unite the races of South Africa under the British flag, and those who, like the Nationalists, would emphasize the racial cleavage and minimize the British connection. The British divided along economic lines in very much the same way as they have done at home, between Capital and Labour. A third section, the Jews, represented political capitalism and have been associated with the British party among the Dutch. Labour associated itself with the Nationalist Party.

In 1924 there came into power a " pact " Government of Dutch Nationalists and the South African Labour Party, and it is due to the courage of General Hertzog that the native question is now the livest issue in politics. His native policy, however, exhibits the two aspects of colour prejudice in South Africa, the social and the industrial.

In 1926 a "colour bar" Act was passed giving the Minister for Mines and Industries power to debar any Native or Asiatic from work in mines and factories. It was petitioned against by leaders of all the Churches—a petition which the Prime Minister strangely described as "unworthy," and the Act was defended by him on the ground that "the white man in South Africa has to fight an unequal fight against the Natives."

In 1926 the Government produced four bills to deal with the "native problem." The "coloured" people were to be incorporated into the community in every way but socially, and a complete cleavage was to be made between Bantu and non-Bantu peoples. These bills did not obtain the necessary majority, and so were remitted to a Select Committee which did not report until 1935.

Meanwhile the "white" position was strengthened. European women got the vote, and in 1931 European men in the Cape and Natal were no longer required to have a property and educational qualification for the franchise. Yet the Native Economic Commission of 1932 and the Poor White Commission of 1933 demonstrated in their reports the essential economic unity of South Africa, black and white.

In 1934 the Smuts and Hertzog parties made up their differences, and the first result of this "fusion" was to put into operation the Statute of Westminster (1931) affirming the sovereign independence of the Union. British and Dutch were now one, and Mr. Lionel Curtis, an old-fashioned Liberal, extolled the patriotism which was "essaying the task of combining the whole people."[1] The "whole people," however, was not held to include the Natives, and "fusion" had clearly made their position worse.

The Select Committee's Report was made the basis of legislation in 1936 on less liberal lines than those proposed in 1926. The Cape Native Franchise, after eighty years of

[1] *The Protectorates of South Africa*, by Perham and Curtis (1935). Pp. 48, 49.

existence, was abolished, just as W. P. Schreiner had foreseen as far back as 1908. In practice it had never been very effective, but as a standing witness against differential treatment it had had an enormous symbolic value. Native voters are now to elect three Europeans to the House of Assembly and two Europeans to the Provincial Councils and to have European representation also on the Senate. The elections of these members are to take place at special times so as further to emphasize the segregation of Native interests. The Government left these matters to a free vote of the House, and the craven fears which underlay this measure were exposed by a member of the Cabinet, Mr. J. H. Hofmeyr, bearer of an illustrious name. He opposed it on first principles and did not hesitate to invoke against it the Christian maxim that " he that seeketh to save his life shall lose it."

There was also set up a Native Representation Council (including some Europeans) to give advice on Native affairs. It has not even the measure of financial responsibility possessed by the Transkei " Bunga," and simply illustrates once more the principle of white domination, while it has yet to be seen how far the Government will pay heed to a purely advisory body. At its first meeting, on December 6th, 1937, it unanimously rejected the recommendation of the Native Affairs Commission of that year that Bantu education should be put under the Native Affairs Department, and it also asked for increasing · " Bantuisation " of the Civil Service concerned with Native matters. On the financial side there are signs that General Hertzog is prepared to deal even generously with proposals for Native development, a possibility violently denounced by the die-hard Nationalist, Dr. Malan, in the election campaign of 1938.

The problem of Native land is most urgent, and the Native Land and Trust Act provides for the increase of the Native reserves from 10 to $17\frac{1}{4}$ million morgen (a morgen is $2\frac{1}{6}$ acres). The area of the Union is 143 million morgen. The white population is roughly two millions and the Bantu six millions, of whom more than half are in European areas. More and more whites are doing what used to be called black men's work and competition in unskilled labour is thus increasing. Hence this Act will assist in driving more Native people into the reserves, and so in spite of the small increase in area these are likely to be still more overcrowded than they are at present.

While political South Africa has thus been becoming more bitterly reactionary and British and Dutch have united at the expense of the Native, there has been, curiously enough, a marked growth of liberalism in the Educational Civil Service. It was very noticeable at the New Education Fellowship Conferences in South Africa in 1934. In 1936 a purely official interdepartmental Committee on Native Education produced a report which was not only humanistic in its ideals but also workable in its details. Its chief recommendation was the transference of Native education from the Provincial Administration to the Union, not, however, to the Native Affairs Department but to the Department of Education, thus in effect equating the importance of European and Bantu education.[1] At the same time it recommended the formation of local committees to support the Native schools and to make them social centres for the community.

There are thus signs of hope even in the seats of despair. Unofficially also, local joint councils of Europeans and Natives have done and are doing good service, for it is astonishing how very few South Africans of European descent have any real knowledge of Native problems or any personal acquaintance with Natives other than houseboys or labourers. And it is not surprising that there is more hope in great centres like Johannesburg, where life is lived at the greatest tension, than there is in the unruffled calm of the country districts.

---

[1] Professor Edgar Brookes had suggested this in 1930 in a small book on *Native Education in South Africa*. (Pretoria, van Schaik.)

CHAPTER III.

LAND AND LABOUR.

1.

IT is a commonplace by this time that the basis of African social life is the land. This, however, if we go back far enough, has been true of every community, and in Africa no more and no less than elsewhere. The situation in Africa is not so utterly strange and alien that we have no guide.

Primitive land tenure has everywhere been communal, and the fact that it is still so considered in the greater part of Africa is not a "native" peculiarity but a characteristic of the human race in general. We need go back no further than the nineteenth century to see it in Ireland, or than the eighteenth to see it in Scotland. It is the case in Russia and in Serbia to this day. The unit of land-holding is not the individual but the group, whether it be a tribe or family, or clan, or sept, or zadruga or village.

In primitive society there can be no such thing as ownership of land outright, any more than there can be ownership of the air or the rain. Land, air, and water are the three essentials of life, and they are the property of everybody, at any rate of everybody in the tribe. The only individual rights recognized are occupation rights, and these are granted by the chief not as landowner but as representative of the tribe. There is no money rent, nothing after the manner of later "contract." A gift to the chief, or a share of the produce from land whose occupier is known to everybody constitutes an occupation title, and it is much stronger than a documentary title, for its sanction is in the common knowledge of the people.

The communal nature of land-holding in Africa is also

indicated by the fact that the land is not only the source of food supply; it is the home of the race and the sepulchre of the dead. In it the race is one—those alive above the earth and those sleeping beneath. The latter are, on occasion, much more effective members of the tribe than the former.

The whole of primitive social life centres round this unity of the tribe, visible and invisible. The obedience due to the chief is absolute because he incarnates in himself the authority of the tribe. He is assisted by a council of old men who remember the past and in whose living memories the dead live again. It is not only therefore in Uganda or in the highly-organized Yoruba communities of Southern Nigeria that the chief has a semi-sacred character. It is implicit in the nature of primitive society.

There is thus a singular toughness about the African tribe, particularly among the Bantu. They have been smitten by disease and famine and reduced by intertribal feuds and war, they have suffered persecution at the hands of slave traders and been upset by European commerce and ideas, and yet they survive and are on the increase. They owe much to their physical constitution, but perhaps more to the closely knit nature of their society. This binding together of the tribe occupying the same land, the sense of a deathless society of which the chief is the living emblem, the feeling of common humanity, *ubuntu*, which recognizes in every man in the community a man and a brother so that food is as common an element as air, are factors that make for survival. Where one member is hurt all are hurt with it, and so it is the duty of the group as a whole to look after any member within it, and there are neither paupers nor are there capitalists. This is a feature of all societies that live close to the land, in the remote parts of Ireland as well as in Tanganyika.

No man will understand Africa who does not grasp the intensity of the tribal Native's attachment to his land. It is not a matter of property-holding. It is something much deeper than that, more emotional, less articulate. In his forcible separation from his land we can see something of the tragedy of Africa. The dumb grief of the Africans who made the " middle passage," or of those Mashonas who saw their land wrenched from them by the foreigner, must have sounded the depths of human misery.

And yet this sentimental attachment is again not a specifically African problem. It is a problem even in modern Scotland. A quotation from a recent Blue Book will show an astonishing parallel with Bantu conditions.

'The problem in the Highlands involves historical, racial, economic, and social considerations entirely different from those in other parts of Great Britain. We are dealing with a community which has never been industrialized, and resists any attempt at industrialization. Land is the basis of its existence and determines the form of its social life. . . . The Highlander not only insists on living in the Highlands, but insists on living in his own strath or on his own island. What seems an obvious fact to an observer accustomed to other modes of life, that there is not sufficient land to provide for the population in an island or a strath, is not accepted as a fact by the Highlander. He insists on being given land in his own district, and would rather have a hopeless patch of his own native heath than a fair holding in a strange glen. . . . The men may go away as seamen sailing from the great ports, or as seasonal workers in different occupations, returning at intervals to their homes. The young people may go out into the world, but as a rule they send home money to keep the family homestead in being, and many of them live in hope of returning home again. But all of them maintain the demand that the land should be opened up to them, so that they may build a home, keep a cow and a few sheep, and grow the food they require.

'To apply the ordinary economic test to land settlement under such conditions would be absurd. It can be shown that a large sheep farm, run by a skilful stockmaster with adequate capital and employing skilled shepherds, will produce better and more stock than the same farm with the best bits of the land laid off in crofts, and the hill ground run as a club sheep farm. . . . But the comparison is between two entirely different things. A sheep farm is a commercial undertaking and has to be judged as such ; a crofting community is a way of living and cannot be judged in terms of a profit and loss account.'[1]

2.

Into African communities organized on this primitive model there came the European and all the instruments of

[1] *Report of the Committee on Land Settlement in Scotland* (1928), Cmd. 3110, p. 25.

modern civilization. We have by this time grown so familiar with this association that we forget the unnaturalness of the process. The distance between the modern European and the untouched native African is as great as that between the Englishman of to-day and his predecessors in one of those quiet lake-villages whose remains can be seen in Somerset. This contact has speeded up progress, and the millenniums that lie between prehistoric man and to-day have been foreshortened almost into a single generation.

The Europeans came in as the stronger race and they have been able to work their will in the Continent. Geographical conditions as well as historical reasons have modified the incidence of the impact in different areas.

The West Coast was for the most part obtained by treaty. It is a " black man's country," and in British territory the Europeans have recognized the *status quo* in native landholding. Where land was communally held it has remained so, and even where it has been allowed to be alienated that alienation has taken the form of occupation rights only, to Europeans and to Natives alike. It was this issue in Nigeria that amused the world some years ago, in the contest between the late Lord Leverhulme who wanted to buy land in Nigeria and Sir Hugh Clifford who refused to let him have it. The British Government here took upon itself the representative character of the native chiefs and held that the land belonged not to it but to the tribe, and as such was inalienable.

In the Belgian Congo, which is also a "black man's country," a different policy has been followed. Land is now no longer recognized as communal. Some of it has been alienated to great firms like the *Huileries du Congo Belge*, and native chiefs are no longer the symbols of their tribe's existence, but are appointed and paid by the State for their services as guardians of law and order. They are, that is to say, magistrates, with no necessary connection with the land. In the Transkei under British rule the native chiefs have a similar status, and the British have adopted the policy in Tanganyika.

In East Africa and in Rhodesia where there are lands as suitable for whites as for blacks, the Natives were dispossessed of their lands. The Imperial East Africa Company acted on the assumption that the land was there for anybody to take who could, and by a judgment in the Supreme Court of Kenya in 1921 native rights in land were held to have "disappeared." The Company looked upon the Natives simply as tenants-at-will. They put a tax on them in the form of "rent," although it appeared in the judgment that they had no right to do anything of the kind. They naturally looked upon any disaffection of the Natives in their areas as discontent among their tenantry, and felt themselves empowered to put it down with any means that was to hand.

The British South Africa Company acted somewhat differently, although the result was the same. They bought up two concessions of land which were held to be grants in freehold from Lobengula, and they proceeded to occupy Matabeleland. The chief had thought, however, that he was simply granting leave to prospect for minerals, an occupation right which might be revoked as easily as it was given. The European idea that land is a marketable commodity was absolutely alien to the native mind, and when it was brought home to him it worked upon Lobengula with the hopelessness of despair.[1] By the judgment of the Privy Council in 1917 both concessions were held to be valueless as conveying a title to land, but by that time the damage had been done, and the only possible landlord henceforth was the Crown.

The Natives, however, are still in the country, and the problem of "segregation" has now arisen. "Native reserves" have been planned out, and they are a subject of controversy in every case. They have necessarily involved a shifting of population, and the transfer of people from land which has an ancestral tie to other land which has no association whatever. This is not only a question of rearrangement of tribes, it is an uprooting for some people of their whole family system. It is difficult to see how it can be avoided, but it necessarily is a weakening of moral sanctions, and of tribal authority.

The South African land question has already been discussed in the first two chapters. With the steady pressure

---

[1] See below, p. 379.

of white settlement, the area belonging to Natives naturally got less and less. Accordingly as the country became more and more congested through white occupation there grew up the practice of " squatting." The landless Native settled on the land of Europeans, and as there were so many Natives in that plight with nowhere else to go every farm had some squatters on it. The Act of 1913 attempted to stop this practice by forbidding squatting, but the dislocation was so serious, because there was no other refuge for the Native except the overcrowded towns, that the Supreme Court in 1917 had to hold up the operation of this part of the Act in Cape Colony.[1]

3.

It is a fact of the utmost significance that the European nations who have had most share in exploiting Africa have been industrial nations. In an industrial country the word " peasant " always has about it a suggestion of inferiority and of poverty, whereas in agricultural communities like the Slavonic lands the peasantry are the most powerful class in society. The rural conditions, therefore, in a country like Serbia are a much closer parallel to those of primitive Africa than are the rural conditions in England.

The average colonist from an industrial country has felt about native agriculture what the small capitalist of England felt about the open-field system.

'In the eighteenth century an advance in agricultural science made the open fields and commons of Europe an offence to economists, and the commons a desirable investment for capital.'[2]

The fact in both cases that the village was self-sufficient, and refused to concern itself with outside affairs, and had a well-knit communal life of its own, made nothing but an unfavourable impression on Englishmen brought up in an urban civilization—even though they may not necessarily have been brought up in a town. Culture is a leisurely thing, and any

---

[1] The fact that it was in the Cape alone where this suspension of the Act took place illustrates the importance to the Native of the Cape franchise. It was suspended on the ground that its operation would adversely affect the Native vote.

[2] H. D. Irvine, *The Making of Rural Europe* (1923), p. 116.

kind of appeal on behalf of the native village seemed to the new-comer an apology for idlers. Miss Gertrude Page's sentimental novels about Rhodesia are full of this spirit. The contact, therefore, has always meant upheaval for the villager.

'It is where there is so-called scientific farming that the tillers of the soil are stinted. Primitive agriculture is almost necessarily for the direct benefit of the cultivators, and is lavish of by-products. And the mediæval peasant lacked an incentive which urges even the unscientific modern small-holder to sell his produce, for he had little need of money. His rent, his tithes, and his alms were nearly always paid in kind.'[1]

It should be remembered, however, that there is a sound case for the economic development of Africa. It is a country of vast potential wealth, and its exploitation will materially ease the problem of food supply to the more densely populated regions of the world. As Lord Lugard has pointed out, the " dual mandate " means not only that the interests of the Natives are to be conserved as well as those of the Europeans, but also that the interests of the world as a whole are to be considered as well as those of the territory in question. While this is undoubtedly true, it is nevertheless unfortunate that the point of view of the large-scale producer has come to dominate Africa as it dominated eighteenth-century England. Not only has it told heavily against the small-holder, but as that small-holder was the Native it has also caused racial discrimination. It may of course be argued that it would have taken a long time for native agriculture to have been so much improved as to provide marketable commodities in the required volume, but even so this would have caused much less dislocation of native life.

This impact of industrialized peoples upon communities that are agricultural has brought with it many inevitable consequences. The incoming Government has imposed taxes in order to help toward the expenses of its occupation. This may have been grossly unjust towards the Native, as in Kenya, where much the lighter burden of taxation falls on the European, but it has everywhere been inevitable. It was

[1] H. D. Irvine, *op. cit.*, pp. 27-28.

impossible to collect taxes in kind, and money has thereby become a necessity. Money is the most mobile form of wealth that exists, except credit, and its introduction has sapped the self-sufficiency of the tribal village. When we find catalogues of British drapery firms arriving in remote African villages, and youths purchasing " plus-fours " cash-on-delivery, it is obvious that rural life is not what it used to be !

Where does this money come from ? It is not to be found in the village itself, and men have to go away to earn it. Here we come to another aspect of the European invasion —the growth of towns and the development of industries. There is an impulse away from the village as there is an attraction on the part of the town. The coincidence of the engrossing of English land in the eighteenth century with the rise of the factory system is not unlike the situation in Africa. Africa, of course, is predominantly rural ; it is indeed one vast rural area. Yet the number of villages every day diminishes in which no inhabitant has been to a town for some part of his life. In South Africa I doubt if there is one at all. In the Congo every village has to provide its toll of men sometime or other for service with the Government or with one of the large Companies. Recruiting agents go through the villages of Portuguese East Africa seeking labourers for the Johannesburg mines, and even though by a recent agreement with the Portuguese Government the number is to be reduced to 80,000 a year, that number represents a great many more, for it is made up only of adult males, and the same people who go one year probably do not go again the next. The towns are a ready resource for the Native who needs money to supplement the produce of his small-holding, or to help to keep his people, or to pay his tax, or simply to see the world. Although, therefore, Africa is and will remain rural for generations to come, it is the towns that set the pace for village life, and even where there is only one man in a village who has been to the outside world his influence is the leaven that cannot but leaven the whole lump. The story of the new way of life goes round and every one becomes interested and inquires about it, and tries to imitate it.

All over Africa there is this slow migration of people, none the less significant because it is in most cases a temporary thing. I have met Calabar boys at Thysville, Nyasaland boys at Kambove, boys from Southern Rhodesia in Cape Town. These migrations are wonderful. Men who have never been outside their own village set out for distant lands knowing little, often nothing, of any language save their own, carrying their own pots and pans with them, perhaps some meal and a chicken, always somehow managing to make themselves understood, never at a loss for somewhere to sleep, always cheerful and purposeful, very good company, simple-hearted and curious. You find them going in all kinds of ways, on the Congo steamers, in trains, on lorries, or on foot. It is the commonest sight in Africa, a Native on the road to or from work. Men who have seen the world like this feel superior to those who have not. The money they have earned has come to them as individuals and by their own efforts. And they do not all come back. Some remain away for ever. They are the "detribalized," and it is the town that has detribalized them.

European influence, therefore, has had a number of results. Peace has been produced among the tribes. Both missionaries and Governments have introduced better methods of cultivation, and have spread a network of schools over the Continent. This has inevitably meant a higher standard of living. A beginning has also been made to check the terrible ravages of disease, although there is a very great deal yet to be done before sleeping sickness, leprosy, syphilis, and other endemic diseases are stamped out. On the other hand, new diseases have come in with the European.

The fundamental change, however, has been the introduction of a more individualistic outlook than is possessed by the tribal Native. This has been shown in the European attitude to land and labour. Both the towns and the rural areas witness to its effects.

4.

Native life in the towns falls into two classes—that of the locations and that of the compounds. The locations are the

THE "SCHOOL IN THE BUSH"
(*A reading lesson in progress*)

SPRINGS COMPOUND, TRANSVAAL

areas set apart for the permanent native town-dweller—house-boys, clerks, shop-boys, labourers, and even professional men—who are not housed in the homes of their European employers. The compounds are the barracks attached to a mine or a works for the men employed there as labourers.

The compounds represent a thoroughly unnatural type of life for the Native. He is cut off for many months from his family and from his tribe, he has to mix with men of other tribes, and tribal faction-fights in the compounds are only too common. Everything is on the wholesale scale, and is at the opposite extreme from the family life of the village. In a typical compound, such as that of Springs, on the Rand, there are 4000 men living in a large quadrangle enclosed by rows of dormitories, each of which holds twenty or thirty men. In the middle of the quadrangle is a large block of buildings which includes a butcher's shop, a kitchen containing several dozen iron cauldrons for mealie meal, a brewery with a tap in the wall from which the men draw their ration of Kaffir beer, a washing place, a place for drying clothes, and a shed for disinfecting them. One of the walls is painted white and serves as a bioscope screen. Everything is communal, but not in the sense in which things in the tribe are communal. There is juxtaposition rather than fellowship, association rather than a common life.

The compound, as I have said, represents a life that is highly artificial and unnatural, but for the great majority of men it is temporary. The man's interest is still in his distant family, his village, and his tribe.

The locations are different. The best of them in South Africa, the Lange location at Cape Town, is set amid the woods near Pinelands. It is a beautiful situation. Down long avenues of mimosa you get a glimpse of the Hottentots Holland mountains. No tree has anywhere been unnecessarily cut down. There are 800 acres of it and it cost £250,000 to lay out. There are single quarters for unmarried men—barracks containing dormitories each holding twenty people, with communal kitchens and dining-rooms. For single men of a rather superior class who can afford it there are single rooms at 17s. 6d. a month, and there are married quarters which are let at 7s. a week. For everybody there are sports grounds and a market, and a powerful wireless apparatus in the central area. There are also gardens for the families.

All locations are not so well arranged as this. Ndabeni location at Cape Town is an area of hideous corrugated-iron sheds. I am told that the Brownlee location at King William's Town is so unspeakably bad that no rent is charged to the occupiers. At Port Harcourt, in Nigeria, the Government has laid down plans of the location, but the Natives have been allowed to put up any kind of shack that they like, and the conditions of the back streets are terrible. Lubumbashi, the native and industrial quarter of Elisabethville, clustered round the copper-smelting works, is one vast unlovely region of ant-heaps and mean dwellings.

And then there are the Africans who serve as house-boys in European houses. The conditions under which these live vary a good deal. In some places it is obligatory to house the men in separate brick houses, in others anything will do. In a town like Durban housemaids are occasionally found. The head of the Inanda girls' school said that it was comparatively easy to get good pay for their girls who leave to go into domestic service, but it was uncommonly difficult to get them well housed. Europeans were quite content to house the girls under a leaky iron shelter at the bottom of the garden. Sometimes even the missions were found wanting in this respect. At a well-known mission which I visited in Southern Rhodesia, abounding in land and building materials, the missionary's house-girl had no place of her own and had to sleep on the floor of the bathroom.

5.

The conditions of labour in Africa have thus become Europeanized. The Industrial Revolution has come and has told heavily against the primitive communal life of the Native. It has by this time gone far enough to produce among the detribalized Natives a new and necessary communal bond. In other words it has led to native trade unionism.

The Industrial and Commercial Workers' Union is an organization which flourishes chiefly in Johannesburg and in Natal, and which counts its members by the tens of thousands. To the farmers and administrative officials it is usually anathema, as for the first time it represents a successful native opposition to what are held to be " white " interests. When, however, men have been found who can speak about it without passion they have witnessed to its utility. It is not opposed to whites as such, but, like the English trade unions, to low wages and bad conditions. All labour is a matter of contract, and while the white employer has power to enforce the Native's side of the contract, the Native is not so well circumstanced against the employer. Unscrupulous people have even been known to withhold the Native's pass from him when his term of service was up, and for him to leave without it, except in Cape Town, means liability to arrest. In nearly every case where employers were summoned for this breach of contract the Union has won its case, and its prestige has become very high with the Natives. The legal position of the I.C.U., however, is determined not by the Acts which affect Trade Unions, but by the Masters and Servants Acts. A strike of Natives is therefore equivalent to desertion from duty and is punishable as such.

The weaknesses of the I.C.U. are obvious. The handling of money is, as always, a difficulty. They have control of large funds, mostly raised from poor Natives, and they are unaccustomed to so much wealth. Their offices are very luxurious and the personal expenditure of the officers lavish. Yet it must be remembered that in organizing work of this kind transport facilities are important, and where Natives, no matter how well educated, are not allowed to ride in trams and have difficulty in getting comfortable accommodation in trains, it is essential that the leaders should have motor cars of their own. Still, there is need for greater rather than less discipline in the matter of display, and the leaders are far from discreet. Moreover, the original secretary, Mr. Clements Kadalie, seems to have been badly served by his subordinates. Many were school teachers who for one reason or another had lost their place in the profession and took up this more lucrative employment. This does not inspire confidence. The talk at conferences is very bombastic and stupid, though no more perhaps than that of our own British Communists. Too much money goes in administrative expenses and in litigation, and not nearly enough in sick and unemployment benefit.

However, when all is said that can be said against the Union and the way in which it goes to work, the amazing fact remains that there are some 100,000 native workers, each paying his 2s. a month, and proving by their unity more than a match for unscrupulous employers. In many ways it is the most hopeful thing in Bantu Africa, not because in its present form it is admirable, but because it bears witness to a capacity for organization and leadership which has not always been believed to be there. The great need in Africa is for leaders, and here is a purely native society which, without aid from the Government and even with opposition from the missions, has of itself produced leaders. In spite of this hopefulness, the German Roman Catholic Mission at Mariannhill in Natal excommunicated all Natives who joined it ! [1]

6.

The necessary effect on the one hand of the engrossing of agriculture and on the other of the development of towns and large-scale industry has been to undermine tribal life. The earning of wages for oneself, and the experience of life on an individual basis, slowly loosen the tribal tie. This is the direction in which events are moving, although it may be generations before the process is complete. The native

[1] The urgent need of the I.C.U. for efficient organization led Mr. W. G. Ballinger, a British trade-union expert, to offer his services as an organiser while Mr. Kadalie was away in Europe in 1928, and the I.C.U. came to be recognized as a legitimate organ of native opinion. One cabinet minister, Mr. Madeley, consented to receive a deputation from it, and was thereby dismissed from his post ! In May, 1929, the Waterberg Farmers' Union agreed to have a joint meeting with the I.C.U. representatives to discuss working conditions on the farms. Internal dissensions, however, have weakened the Union (although it is still useful) and native welfare is to-day being more effectively forwarded by a joint society of Europeans and Africans, the South African Institute of Race Relations, founded in 1929.

reserves in the vast agricultural areas are the last stronghold of tribalism and of tribal religion, just as the Roman *campagna* was the centre of the religion of Numa long after the city had become more sophisticated. But they cannot escape the pressure of the outside world. And it is usually the more independent spirits who go out from them to labour in the towns, and tribalism loses its hold where men become fitted to stand alone.

It is an entire mistake to think that it is the preaching of the missionaries that demoralizes the Native. The driving out of heathen gods and the substitution of Christianity has at any rate a constructive side to it. But contact with the European in industry, where it drives out the evil spirit, leaves the house empty, swept, and garnished.

The town and the country therefore interact. The country is the refuge of primitive life and standards, and will remain so for years to come. It is also, however, a reservoir of labour for the towns, while there are many causes which make it difficult to live even in the country without some dependence on the town.

With the weakening of the tribe as a social unit there is also an undermining of the tribe as a unit of land tenure. The communal tenure of land in the primitive sense is disappearing. It must not be supposed that the change has already been completed or that it is necessarily sudden and violent. In many parts of Africa, as we have seen, the change has been unnaturally violent, but it is the violence that has been unnatural rather than the change itself. Even in circumstances such as those of the Gold Coast and Uganda, in which there has been no violent upheaval in land tenure, the communal method of tenure has been undermined. Occupation rights have tended to become fixed, and there has even arisen that typical phenomenon of European civilization, the individual capitalist landowner.

A further symptom of the new forces at work is the decline of native arts and crafts. In a self-sufficient village community craftsmanship flourishes, for it is the only way of meeting a need of the village.

Here again the same causes are operating in Africa that were seen in eighteenth century England. Holdings have become too small to provide in themselves a livelihood or an income in money. Manufactures have become centralized where there were markets. The capitalist spirit has in some places invaded even rural industries, and gradually the villager becomes a worker, not to supply his own needs and supplement his holding, but to supply a distant market. You see one side of this process in a native market such as that at Oyo in Southern Nigeria, where, in spite of the native skill in spinning and weaving, the spinners and weavers themselves buy cheap cottons exported from Manchester. The other side you see in Kano, where the price of native leather or brass goods depends on the European store which buys to sell in England. The native producer is losing that close association with his work in all its stages which is the mainspring of good craftsmanship.

7.

The word " segregation " is one that crops up continually in the discussion of these questions, but as it is used to cover so many different things it is valueless without definition. The Native may be segregated for the sake of the European or for his own sake, and that segregation may be viewed as a temporary expedient or as the mark of a permanent difference. It may be based on social reasons or its justification may be in the main economic. It may be a distinction of status which may or may not carry with it " segregation " in the territorial sense. But in all its meanings it involves racial discrimination.

Essentially " segregation " is an attempt to give direction to the forces of evolution. In the social sense it puts the Native's life into the control of the European through pass laws, lack of transport facilities, and insecurity of land tenure. The European determines the conditions under which the Native shall live in the locations or the compounds, and the measure of intercourse he may have with the European population. On the economic side it defines the trades in which the Native may not compete with the European worker even where the work in hand may be for purely native purposes, as in a location. In rural areas it marks off the " reserves " in which the Native may live.

This last is the commonest reference of the term " segregation," and yet it is the reference in which there is the greatest amount of fallacy. Theoretically it should mean the complete separation of white from black in different areas. In practice it means the separation of white from black except for those services which the white requires. And the European has it in his power to determine just how far segregation shall be complete. Where they need money for their poll tax, and where the Native land cannot provide a livelihood for the people on it, the Natives are driven out of the reserves to work for wages. The Native areas in the Union of South Africa are now nowhere able to give an adequate subsistence for the inhabitants. In Rhodesia and Kenya and other territories where there is no overcrowding, the policy is often advocated of still further cutting down the native reserve in order to ensure a supply of labour for the white man.

Segregation may thus affect the direction of evolution in several ways. Where, as in South Africa, the Native might be expected to develop into a skilled worker, a discrimination is made against him to keep him in the lower ranks of labour. Where by reason of education and experience his whole thought-world is the same as that of the educated European, he may nevertheless be obliged to consort with people with whom he has nothing in common save the colour of his skin. And where he might, if left alone and given adequate land, develop into an independent agriculturist, he is unable to do so and is perpetually dependent on an alien group of people. In all these, and in other ways, development of the Native is predetermined by the European for his own advantage.

Nevertheless, although there are good arguments for segregation in this sense, where it is applied with discretion and concerns itself not with colour as such but with civilization, it can never be other than a temporary policy. Preferential treatment in economics, in this and in other contexts, is apt to see only one side of the question. It considers the producer and ignores the consumer. The independence of the Native undoubtedly means a shortage of cheap labour for the white man. The opening of skilled trades to the Native of ability means competition with the white worker. On the other hand, the greatest potential market for African produce is the African people. The Native as a consumer is the surest foundation of African economics. As the Native is able to develop a higher standard of living so will his wants increase, and so will the satisfaction of those wants provide labour for a larger number of people, white as well as black. And wants are not created simply by displaying goods on the counter of a store. Wants may be uneconomic as well as economic. Economic wants really depend on mental qualities which are developed where they find opportunity. Skilled work and responsibility in the long run demand a higher standard of living because they involve thinking and comparison and more refined desires. So long as the fact is neglected that the same people who produce also consume, so long there will be artificial interference and dislocation in the mechanism of exchange. Such a neglect causes production to be carried on, so to speak, in the air, for a market that cannot be seen or understood, and it brings about an alternation of booms and slumps and unemployment. And it is the white worker who will suffer most from this dislocation. Racial discrimination is the ultimate cause of the " poor white " problem as it exists in South Africa to-day.

Segregation of another kind is advocated for the sake of the Native. The native reserves are the last resort of tribalism, and of a way of life to which the Native is accustomed. It is felt, therefore, that the more tribalism is strengthened and native independence developed on a tribal basis the better it will be for the Native. Accordingly, the policy of cutting down the reserves is attacked not only on economic grounds, but also because it makes it impossible for the Native to live his own life in his old way. The reserves seem to be the only opportunity left to the Native to develop along non-industrial lines.

It is questionable, however, whether this hope can now be fulfilled. Apart altogether from the increasing demand for labour which must inevitably interfere with any such complete separation, it is at least arguable that the attempt to segregate the Native from the forces at work in the modern world cannot permanently be to the advantage of the Native.

LAND AND LABOUR

Where native life is interfered with already in all kinds of ways, through association with Europeans personally, or in labour, or in education, or through the post, it would seem to be a much better policy to seek to develop in useful ways that evolution whose general trend is already fixed, than to seek to divert the stream of evolution itself into a channel more and more divergent from the main course of history.

8.

We may now look at two attempts to deal with the native problem in the rural areas, each of which involves a measure of native independence without producing this divergence of which I have spoken. The first is the experiment in the Transkei, and the second is agricultural co-operation.

The Transkeian territories are an area of about 16,000 square miles in the eastern part of Cape Province, in which a scheme of segregation has been at work since 1894. 13,000 square miles of the territory are native "locations" and are inhabited by a million natives, while the remainder of the land is taken up by town areas, such as Umtata, the capital, and by the farms of Europeans. The native area is divided into twenty-seven magistracies, each of which is administered by a European magistrate, sometimes assisted by native assessors, and they try cases by native law where that is possible. Eighteen of these magistracies have District Councils, appointed triennially, and consisting of the Resident Magistrate and six members, two of whom are nominated by the Governor-General, and four by the ratepayers. Each District Council meets quarterly and it nominates two members for the General Council of the following year. The Governor-General nominates another, and these three, together with the Magistrate, represent their District on the General Council. The General Council or *Bunga* thus consists of eighteen Magistrates, fifty-four native members, and the Chief Magistrate in the Chair.

These Councils are not executive but advisory to the administration. Since 1926 the revenue of the territories has been made up of the quit-rents in Council Districts which were formerly paid to the Government, and the local tax of 10s. payable by those who do not pay quit-rent. The revenue in 1932-33 amounted to £142,097. This is of course distinct from the native contributions to the national exchequer. The Council employs a Director of Agriculture, engineers for Public Works, and a Superintendent of Plantations. Between 1903 and 1933 it spent, from of course purely native sources, on scholastic education £468,141, on public works £978,686, on agriculture, agricultural colleges, demonstrators, stock-dipping, and industry, £922,013. It owns three agricultural schools which train demonstrators for the districts. They settle down for two years and grow demonstration crops and are available for consultation. Agricultural shows are organized and a quite excellent agricultural journal *Umcebisi Womlimi Nomfuyi* circulates among 3,200 subscribers. The Council contributed £10,000 to the building of the South Africa Native College at Fort Hare. Between 1903 and 1933 it spent in all £2,802,068.[1]

The transactions of the General Council are carried on at a high level of parliamentary procedure. The annual report of the meeting is most interesting reading, and except the names there is nothing to indicate to what race the speaker belongs. As Colonel Muller puts it,

'The material benefit to the Natives is only half the boon. The value of the consultation with the Natives, of the training in the science and practice of local government which the Council affords, the call which it makes for intellectual effort and the value of the interest which the Natives take in the proceedings of the Council, cannot be estimated in pounds, shillings and pence. It can only be appreciated at its full value by those who know how the quality of the members is improving, and can compare the all-round progress of the Council Districts with those that have no council.'[2]

It is interesting to notice that in spite of this prosperity, or perhaps because of it, the country cannot from its own resources support all its people.

---

[1] *Proceedings of the General Council*, 1934, pp. cxix, cxx.
[2] E. H. W. Muller, *Address on the Administration of the Transkeian Territories*, 1924, p. 17.

'It may be taken as a fact that at any given moment nearly half the able-bodied men whose permanent home is in these Territories are earning money for the support of their families in areas outside these Territories.'[1]

Even a trained agriculturist cannot legally hold more than one "lot," about four morgen, while the average holding is under two morgen (4$\frac{2}{9}$ acres). The density of population in the Transkei is sixty to the square mile. It may be said, therefore, that segregation on these lines, with agricultural development and self-discipline, tends to increase the native population. So much is this true that people are to be found who are opposed to it for no other reason than this.

The Transkei experiment has succeeded within deliberately narrow limits. The Council started more recently in the Ciskei has improved on it by giving more initiative to the Native councillors. In comparison with indirect rule in Nigeria and the earlier still more liberal regime on the West Coast generally the Transkei represents the last word in paternalism. In 1934 I asked a (European) magistrate if he anticipated the appointment of an *African* magistrate and he definitely did not. Yet this is surely the next step.

The important point, however, in this experiment is not so much the political as the mental development of the Native which it involves. It develops his general intelligence and initiative. At the Select Committee on General Hertzog's four Native Bills, the evidence of the Native witnesses from the Transkei created a notable impression. It is this type of mind which is the real need of the Native, so that he can stand up in the modern world and not be demoralized by it.

9.

Agricultural co-operation is a further method of making the best of the difficulties of a rural situation. These difficulties, as we have seen, arise from the nature of the soil, the necessity for fertilizers and for machinery, the producer's ignorance of prices both in buying and selling, and the numerous and wasteful stages between the producer and the consumer.

[1] *Ibid.*

The Native in many parts of South Africa labours under all of these disabilities, and the poverty of the people has become almost a menace to the State. Short of more intensive cultivation there is no hope for native agriculture, and such cultivation is expensive.

A situation somewhat similar to this confronted Sir Horace Plunkett in Ireland in the early days of the Irish Agricultural Organization Society. For example, in that bleak district of north-west Donegal known as " the Rosses," the small-holder struggled against granite outcrops, bad supplies of seed, ignorance of marketing, the unscrupulousness of middlemen, and an ever-increasing load of debt. In these days the "Templecrone Co-operative Society " buys for the farmers and sells to them, grades and markets their produce, purchases necessary machinery and hires it out to members, runs a credit bank which will advance any sum from half-a-crown upwards, and a co-operative hall for amusements in the winter months. The Society serves an area of about 70,000 acres, has six branches and 841 members, and the sales for the financial year 1936 came to no less than £82,173. Some time ago it started a small-scale knitting business to employ the young girls of the village who would otherwise have to leave home at an early age to earn money in Ulster or in Scotland. This factory, when I last visited it, had received an order from Manchester for 5000 pairs of knitted woollen gloves. The Co-operative Society has not only made agriculture in this area a paying proposition ; it has re-created the rural community.

Attempts are being made at agricultural co-operation in South Africa. The Roman Catholic Mission at Mariannhill, Natal, has started a Farmers' Association under the ægis of the mission and thereby limited in its scope. There is a Native Farmers' Association, whose secretary is Professor D. D. T. Jabavu of the South African Native College.

But there are certain economic and even political conditions which are necessary to any attempt at co-operation on a large scale. Security of tenure is the first, and after security, motive. It is quite impossible for any group of people to engage jointly in an expensive undertaking unless there is a guarantee that the labour and expense will be of permanent benefit to them. No one can speak with any intelligent native cultivator in South or East Africa without being aware of this sense of apprehension lest the land he works may at any moment be taken away from him. This is not a situation which brings out the best in the Native, and native education is quite beside the point unless it goes hand-in-hand with the betterment of his political and social status. In the equatorial region security of tenure means a guarantee not so much that the land should be left to the Native, but that the Native should not be taken from the land. In the Middle Congo in 1927 the *Huileries du Congo Belge* were actually having to import foodstuffs into villages quite capable of growing their own, because the uncertainty created by labour recruitment had prevented the Natives sowing where they did not expect to reap.

Security having been guaranteed, other factors begin to operate. The holdings if improved may make the village a self-sufficing community. If it is not self-sufficient it may be able to provide for its wants out of the sale of its surplus produce. In this way although the village is still dependent on the towns, it is not necessarily for the native's labour that the towns are a market; they may be markets for his produce. Around Elisabethville, for instance, there are many native cultivators who, instead of being dependent on their labour in the mines, make quite a respectable living from growing garden produce. They sell both to the Europeans and to the Africans. In this case they bring their stuff to market themselves and get the full benefit of the price. But marketing is not and cannot be always so direct as this. In most cases some one else will have to do the marketing, and in Africa the Native has always been at a disadvantage from the fact that the middlemen have been men of other races. Agricultural co-operation,—meaning by that, as in Ireland, co-operation not only in farming but also in craftwork,—involves cutting out the middleman and allowing the society to do its own buying and selling. Without this, the motive for improvement is apt to be weak.

Motive, however, involves intelligence, and intelligence in these matters depends upon education. The real difficulty in the way of agricultural co-operation in Ireland came from the farmer's own ignorance. A campaign of education was first of all required.

In Africa also the success both of agricultural co-operation and of economic self-government as in the Transkei depends on intellectual factors which are the concern of Native education. Agriculture is a valuable subject in school, and it is of primary importance that the Native should learn to get a living as far as possible on his own piece of ground. He needs to be made a better producer. The improvement of agriculture is also necessary to keep alive the spirit of the rural community. Culture has its roots in the soil, but it requires for its existence a tolerable measure of contentment. It withers in circumstances of grinding poverty.

Nevertheless, the villager is not going to be led out of his Egypt into an economic Canaan simply by making him a better producer. He cannot rise in the scale even as a producer without also rising as a consumer. He needs to spend as well as to earn. And his improvement in both directions depends on his education in other things than simply agriculture. As soon as production and consumption are concerned with more than bare subsistence they become determined by mental qualities. Production without any object in view, or consumption for its own sake, are both of them "uneconomic" processes and do not further the ultimate social well-being of the producer or the consumer. With motive, therefore, in this higher sense education cannot but deal.

A long view is necessary in this matter. The kind of thing the Native wants or thinks he wants as soon as he has education enough or has travelled enough to look about him is often something quite ridiculous. It was astonishing to me to find in the purely native village market at Yakusu in the equatorial forest bottles of cheap scent and tins of cigarettes exposed for sale. But that in itself does not matter. It is a symptom of a process which by education can be directed into more useful and sensible channels. The same kind of silly choice was made by our own munition workers in Sheffield during the War. The pity is that when the

Native has developed reasonable wants and a higher standard of living he is so often condemned by the very people who look upon the raw Native as a "savage." He appears to be presumptuous and to be menacing their superiority.

10.

We have seen how native life is developing in the towns and also in the country, and in both cases it is obvious that certain mental qualities are demanded over and above those which are necessary to make the Native a tiller of the soil or a labourer for the white man. Neither in the Johannesburg mines nor on the Rhodesian veld will the Native progress far if his education equips him for no more than the work in hand.

It is obvious that the root factor in native development is the growth of a sense of individual responsibility. The towns detribalize the Native, and in place of the group he can rely only on himself. If he cannot rely on himself he is in a sad case. In the rural areas the native smallholder is hopelessly handicapped, and the tribe in its primitive state is not in these days the kind of group that can hold land in competition with the Europeans. An agricultural society is different. It is an economic group whose success depends on the proper functioning of each individual within it. He comes in of his own choice, his position is not chosen for him. It therefore demands a certain self-reliance and individuality.

Where are these qualities to be gained? I think that negatively they are to be found in the influence of the towns, and positively they are to be discovered in Christianity.

With all its dangers and unpleasantness the town is a place where men learn to look on themselves as individuals. They are treated as such by mine managers, in the compounds and locations, and by the ordinary householder. It cannot be otherwise. And despite the admirable qualities that there are in tribalism, there is no seed of progress in any system which denies to the individual responsibility for his own actions and control of his own life. The life of all communities, including ourselves, was once tribal, and the fact that the tribalism has passed away is an indication that it has not been able to hold its own in the march of history. There are indeed three stages in that progress. First there is the group, in which the individual is nothing. Then there is the revolt of the individual, in which the group is nothing. Then there is the creation of a new group in which the individual finds himself through society and society functions through the corporate action of independent individual wills. The first group is automatic, the later one is ethical. The two may be the same in extent, but they are quite different in spirit.

It is the town which weakens the hold of the tribal group. And as far as Africa is concerned " the town " may be anywhere outside the village. It may even be in England. A Manchester draper's catalogue or the arrival of a motor car may start at once a thousand hopes and fears almost as much as a visit to Johannesburg. It is commonly said that the impact of industrialism has taken away the " sanctions " of the Native's life and that he is suffering from displacement. This is certainly true, and it has its desperate side. The Native with whom the tribal tie is beginning to work loose is a pathetic person, in need of all the sympathy that can be given. But we shall get a false perspective unless we see that this has also its potentially good side. This state is a half-way house which may lead to something worse but may also lead to something better. It will not lead to anything better if it is itself looked upon as a final state around which we must attempt to develop rural industries simply as a barrier of protection.

II.

It is part of the hope of Christianity to provide and strengthen those qualities of character of which the Native stands in need to-day.

The Christian mission in Africa has been viewed in different lights in different generations. Christianity in history has been the force that has created discontent rather than submission. It has opened men's eyes to a new world and made them dissatisfied with the world that now is and given them a will to change it. It was probably this conviction that made an older generation of Europeans oppose native missions and education,—they were "unsettling." In these days the pendulum has swung right over, and Christianity is now advocated by publicists as a co-ordinating and pacifying factor. It is held to be of value in shoring up the tottering structure of the tribe which modern industry undermines.

We have therefore to ask ourselves, " Can Christianity co-exist with tribalism ? "

The minds of missionaries and Government officials are not clear on this point. Some people look upon it as taking the place of tribal control which has vanished for ever, and in that sense it provides a new " sanction." Others feel that it will help to perpetuate tribal control and keep alive that corporate conscience which the individual might otherwise desire to lose.

Obviously there is a difference in this regard between the detribalized Native of Johannesburg and the Native of, say, Northern Rhodesia. Not a great deal is heard of Christianity as affording a " sanction " for the permanent dweller in the town locations. Indeed he is often looked upon more or less as the slum dweller in a European city, and the problem with him is his evangelization rather than the conservation of whatever Bantu culture he may appear to have.

But where the country still keeps a life of its own in spite of the town, the problem becomes vital ; in the Natal countryside, on the Rhodesian veld, in Tanganyika, on the Congo. The Native has a share in both environments, the African and the European. Some would equate Christianity with his African environment, and some (a diminishing number) would make it part of the stock-in-trade of the European.

It is difficult, however, to see how tribalism, as it exists in the untouched native village, can co-exist with Christianity. The root from which sprang that wonderful Old Testament efflorescence of which Christianity was the fruit, was the doctrine of individual responsibility. Ezekiel's "the soul that sinneth it shall die,"[1] was a negation of Hebrew tribalism which had to be emphasized before Christianity could come. This did not dispose in later Christianity of the fellowship. The idea of the spiritual unity and spiritual authority of the Church was inherent in Christianity as preached by Christ, but this was an ethical not a tribal thing. It was based on individual consciousness and acceptance. The results might look the same, for both the Christian Church and the Jewish tribe were communities based on religion, but there was a wide difference not only in the content of their experience, but also in the form of it.

This is not inapplicable to Africa. Smith and Dale in their work on the Ba-Ila show how the nonentity of the individual in his tribe holds back progress:—

'All the personal property held by a Mwila is subject to the rule that his elder relations on both sides have the right to take from him what they want. This is to *nanga* (to seize),—" convey " the wise it call; it is not reckoned as robbery. . . . Young men who go away to work for lengthy periods have very little to show for it after being at home again a few weeks. The chief takes his pickings, and everybody who has any claim to relationship.'[2]

Much of the argument in favour of tribalism and tribal chiefs neglects this point, and makes a confusion between a society that is ethical and one that is involuntary. Tribalism is everywhere giving way before the white man, and if it is to exist at all, it will only do so by changing its form and becoming an association of people rather than a unit of which people are members. In other words, the tribe will have to die to live. It will be born again in the Church or in the self-governing modern community.

[1] *Ezekiel xviii.* 20. " The soul that sinneth it shall die; the son shall not bear the iniquity of the father, neither shall the father bear the iniquity of the son; the righteousness of the righteous shall be upon him, and the wickedness of the wicked shall be upon him." The doctrine comes out still more strongly in the Deuteronomic Code (*Deut. xxiv.* 16, " the fathers shall not be put to death for the children, neither shall the children be put to death for the fathers; every man shall be put to death for his own sin "), where it appears in a context of regulations aiming at greater humanitarianism (S. R. Driver: *International Critical Commentary on Deuteronomy* (1895), p. 277).

[2] E. W. Smith and A. M. Dale, *The Ila-speaking Peoples of Northern Rhodesia* (1920), Vol. I., p. 385.

PART II.

THE FOREGROUND.

CHAPTER IV.

THE MISSION.

By far the greater part of native education in Africa is in the hands of Christian missions. Where Government comes in it is to supplement their work rather than to replace it.

This association of education with organized Christianity has several important consequences. To all intents and purposes the school is the Church. Right away in the bush or in the forest the two are one, and the village teacher is also the village evangelist. An appreciation of this fact is cardinal in all considerations of African education. Accordingly, in view of the fact that the school is an evangelistic agency, and that it is for the Christianizing of the people that the missions are there at all, the moral life and character of the Europeans are of first importance even in the work of running a school.

1.

Let us begin, therefore, by considering the school from the European end. In the village school, of course, the European is an infrequent visitor, but at any rate the teachers have come into contact with him at some time during their training, and the organization of work among the Europeans sets the standard for the educational work as a whole.

The normal organization of a mission is to have a head station with a European staff, and a number of out-stations, each of which is a school as well as a church, and has an evangelist teacher. The Scottish mission at Livingstonia in Nyasaland shows a still further development. Here there is a head station in Livingstonia itself, eight other stations each with a European staff, and around each of these a cluster of out-stations. Whatever the organization, however, be it large or small, the thing that sets the tone of the native education is the life of the European community.

This matter of tone is of the utmost importance. It is of course important everywhere, in England as well as in Africa, but in an old country there is so much that holds up the hands of the teacher. They are upheld by the voluntary agencies of Churches and institutions, literature, public opinion, professional feeling, and in a dozen other ways. The African teacher draws heavily upon the mission for the spiritual strength that he needs, and apart from the mission to what else can he look? It is a tragedy that occasionally happens in Africa that a mission with wonderful apparatus and every appearance of efficiency is weak on this spiritual and human side.

The greatest single problem, therefore, in a mission school is not the question of industrial training, nor that of native custom, nor even the relations of black and white, but the problem of the inner life of the European staff, and it is this problem of which, in many cases, there is least awareness.

2.

The business of living together is itself a difficult thing. People of different temperaments are thrown together in a mission for years at a time with no society but their own. Quite often nothing is done about it. Yet the corporate life of the European staff is an achievement and comes only as the result of stern effort. It cannot be assumed that the fellowship is already there through mere juxtaposition.

Corporate life, if it is to be a really ethical thing, is based on individualism. The individual must be able to live his own life and to develop his own resources in privacy in order that he may give of his best to the group. A group cannot function properly as a group unless each person in it is also functioning properly as an individual. That mutual discipline and forbearance which is the cement of corporate life is only possible as a thing willingly accepted by each for the good of all, rather than imposed on each by the will of all. In this discipline life becomes a deeper thing and a progressive thing. But you cannot discipline a thing which is not there, and where there is not the possibility of private life, not only away from the Europeans but also away from the Natives, there is repression and dissatisfaction.

Three missions will illustrate these difficulties.

In the first it is taken for granted that the unmarried women will want to live together. They have separate bedrooms, but otherwise they can never get out of each other's way. Privacy is impossible and the desire for it is reckoned to be almost disloyalty. Accordingly there is repression and discomfort, and from time to time there is that expensive item in missionary work, a "nervous breakdown."

The second mission is in a hilly district in the South, and every missionary or missionary family occupies a separate little hill. There is a great deal of work which brings them together, but they have the possibility of privacy if they wish.

There was a corporate mind in both missions, but in the first it was the lowest common factor—they came together on the things in which there could be no disagreement ; in the second, there was the friendly clash of considered opinion, and the corporate mind was an achievement, a warm and living thing.

The third mission has features belonging to each of the others. It is right away out of civilization and there is a staff of about a dozen Europeans. They have for the most part not learned to live together because they have not yet learned to be themselves. They have their own private houses and can be as much by themselves as they like. But privacy is only a means to an end. Its value depends on what you do with it. Some of the staff have no real resources within themselves and seem to think about nothing but "shop." This produces an overweening sense of the importance of one's own job, a sensitiveness to criticism, and a certain acerbity in expressing one's own point of view.

In the case of this mission much of the difficulty comes from something which is an effect of the development of native education. It has been obvious that with makeshift teachers you do not get that expert teaching of carpentry or of smithying or of agriculture that you might get from people trained for this particular work. Accordingly the very excellence of the ideal has often been allowed to lower the ideal. Specialists have been appointed who were not missionaries. Of course the two are not incompatible, but it is a question of emphasis. And where a corporate life has to be developed it needs some unifying idea round which to centre, and it is his own experience of that idea which each person has to bring into the group. In community life it is not individual differences that enrich the whole, but individual differences *in the same experience*. The diversity and the unity are both essential.

I have seen missions in which this is being done. There are many of them in Africa, and no society has a monopoly of them. One very good mission in the equatorial region includes on its staff verbal-inspirationists, modernists, medical men, nurses, teachers, and agricultural people,—a very heterogeneous company. There was among them a habit of " in honour preferring one another " of which they seemed to be unaware but which forcibly struck an outsider. They had also a very hearty sense of humour which helped them along. Accordingly the visitor was conscious at one and the same time of their individuality and of their unity. Another mission of the same kind is in Southern Rhodesia, right at the opposite pole theologically, and run by four men who exhibited about the maximum differences of temperament that I have ever met in a group. This could easily have produced hopeless friction and stalemate, yet it was made to produce just the opposite.

These considerations are important, because the agency of the education of native peoples is not simply the teacher as a teacher, but the man himself and the society of which he is a part. The aim is not to give the native information which he does not possess, but to get him to look at life in a new way and to create for himself and his people a new society. This can only be done by people who themselves see life in a new way and are themselves members of that kind of society. In other words, it is not a matter of taking to the Natives of Africa a civilization which we have and they have not, but joining with them in exploring a new way of life in which we are adventurers as well as they.

3.

How do these successful missions achieve their corporate life ? This it is not always easy to discover, but there are certain points which all such places have in common, whatever their theology. They are invariably places which have about them a sense of leisure. The people in them have all taken up Christianity as a serious business, which needs to be cultivated and developed as much as any art or craft. They are all places which do not despise the outward form as an aid to spiritual grace. And everybody in the group has his own job to do and seeks to perfect himself in it. He takes a pride in other men's work and they take a pride in his.

A sense of leisure is an essential part of excellence. It does not imply that people are idle—it rather implies a willingness to learn, and a belief that there is yet more for a man to take in that there is for him to give out. It is strange how busy some missionaries are, and how restless and worried they are, although perhaps not more so than most teachers. After all, to build up a man's life is not a process that you can see—it is something that needs faith and hope, for the wind bloweth where it listeth. But it is very hard for keen people to work for results they cannot see, and to stand back and allow patience to have her perfect work. The constant temptation is to fill up time with things that can be seen and assessed. Accordingly many men's lives are a round of activity. They are for ever giving out, and this leads to weariness of the flesh and an unquiet mind. *Accidia* beset the old monks because they were always taking in and had nothing to do. It besets our modern folk because they are always doing things and have forgotten how to increase their resources.

The sense of leisure is something that needs cultivating. It will not come by just doing nothing. It is much more likely to come by having a hobby which is so far different from ordinary work as to be at once an escape from it and a point from which one can survey the whole of it. Perhaps the most effective mission I saw in Africa was run by a man who took three evenings off every week to pursue his hobby of palæontology. He told me that no matter what cause of worry there was in the mission, he could enter his study and in a quarter of an hour be fifty thousand years away from it. He would go to bed, sleep well, and get up in the morning with a clear head to tackle the problems of the school afresh.

The physical circumstances of life are a further help. The art of emptying one's mind of everything so that God might fill it is something which it is much easier to practice in some places than in others. And in a foreign country, cut off from Christian opinion and the help of civilized society, quite a slight amount of suggestion goes a long way to keep the soul alive. The symbol has a universal appeal, even though there are to be found stern spirits to whom it is only a seduction. A place apart helps to create a mind apart, at leisure from itself and open to God. It is quite a fallacy to imagine that the missionary needs these things less than the man at home because he is busy all the time with "Christian work." He really needs it more. Constant occupation with Christian duties breeds familiarity, and it is among missionaries where this temptation is most subtle. Something, therefore, that is "numinous" and keeps before the mind that the thing with which we deal is far more than can be seen or heard or conceived by the mind of man, helps to create that corporate spiritual life which aids real education.

A certain objectivity is of inestimable value. Where people are brought together constantly they are apt to become interested not so much in the thing which they are all supposed to share as in their own and each other's reaction to it. In other words they tend to become concerned with subjective states rather than with the common purpose. Something, therefore, like a building, or a symbol, or an order of service helps to draw men's minds away from themselves and each other and concentrate them on something outside. Men need to have done for them what the Keeper of the Gate did for Bunyan's pilgrim :—

'He also had them up to the top of the Gate, and showed them by what deed they were saved ; and told them withal that that sight they would have again as they went along in the way, to their comfort.'

And this operates not only as a purge of moods, not only as a point of union, but also as a reminder that outside ourselves there is God, and that this business which we so often look upon as ours alone is really His.

In many missions the sole point of interest is the native pupils. Yet among the junior European staff, and even among the staff that are by no means junior, there are many people who have not found themselves, and who need quite as much sympathetic care and attention as the Natives. It cannot be too emphatically said that it is the European group as a whole that is the chief educating agency, and the group needs to be fitted for its task. Outward observances have their place, but each person has his own individual life to build up as well. The loneliness of Europeans out in Africa is something that needs more consideration than it has received. And where people do not know how to build up their own resources, they are apt to look to the society of other people in order to help them to forget themselves. They therefore come to live in a world upon which they levy a continual tax rather than in a community of free people.

Reading is another necessity to the spiritual as to the intellectual life, and the kind of book that is most help is the kind which demands close attention for a long period so as to give the mind time to get into the atmosphere of creative thought. Solid Bible study with a commentary is of more permanent value than little topical devotional books which require no effort to read and whose effect is sedative rather than recuperative. Good biographies, good novels, a big book on native problems that treats them in a large way, like the works of Lugard or Maurice Evans,—these are things which really build up a man's resources. To keep up reading is a hard but vital task for every teacher.

And there is a man's own special interest to remember. Dr. Arnold of Rugby believed that every man ought to " have his own horse to ride," and nothing creates a greater sense of joy and of dignified self-possession than the mastery of some subject or some craft no matter how small. For a man to have the knowledge that there is a corner of the temple of industry which is for ever his gives him a dignity in his own eyes which will make it unnecessary for him to descend to the meanness of seeking the acknowledgment of his superiority from other men.

4.

The school is often affected by the theories which various missions hold about their work.

The question of celibacy is one of the most difficult. Roman Catholic missions are, of course, missions of celibates, and so, too, are missions of the Cowley Fathers, the Mirfield Community, and the Universities' Mission to Central Africa.

The centre of African life is the home, people marry at an early age, and polygamy is the natural outcome in a primitive society where there is a preponderance of females over males. The missions universally discourage polygamy, and try to set up a system of relationship between husband and wife, and between parents and children, which will be a school of moral virtues. It is therefore a handicap, often voluntarily accepted, if the European community cannot exhibit precisely that kind of society which is so desirable in native life. And the absence of family life is often a sore puzzle to the native mind, especially where European men and European women are together in the same mission.

A great deal of course depends on how the missionary looks at it. If celibacy is looked upon as a limitation, albeit by reason of circumstances unavoidable, its effect on the life of the mission is neither good nor ill, and in individual cases the sacrifice involved may be the means of great spiritual good. It may, however, make it difficult for some people, particularly women, and is one of the considerations that every single woman will face before going abroad.

But celibacy is not regarded in this light in all missions. In some it is looked upon as a higher kind of life than family life, and where this is so, there is obviously a deep gulf fixed between the celibate missionary and the African family. There would thus appear to be a spiritual excellence attainable by the celibate European which is not attainable by the married African. This of course is an arguable point, but where so much morality both social and individual depends on the family, it is indeed a handicap to feel that the people you teach have only a second best as an ideal.

A further practical consequence of this theory is that the life of the European women is separated off from that of the men, and the people of each sex are thrown together a great deal. Each group may easily become a society absorbed in its own states of mind, and where, in the case of women, there are some who have professed vows and some who have not, there are plenty of seeds of friction and often some very lonely people. But even within a closely-knit organization like a Community or Sisterhood, the corporate life of the actual people gathered in one spot has still to be built.

5.

A second theory which affects mission work concerns the relative value attached to intellectual " belief." People cannot be built up in character by words and precept, although such an attempt is often made. Most missionaries, while they might differ widely in creed, would agree that the aim of missionary work is not so much to produce assent as to change life The missionary is usually a man of sense and sympathy, and he loves his people more than to desire simply to add to the number of " professing Christians."

It is, however, the nemesis of certain forms of religion to divorce religion from morality and to aim at the acceptance of formulæ. This is particularly the case with people who are not very intelligent, although they may on occasion be quite well-educated men. A magical view of conversion by words is accepted without any real change of heart. It works out in education in what is called, in the jargon of pedagogy, " the formal training theory,"—the theory, that is to say, which emphasizes the value of subjects *as such* to change mentality and character. Words without the context of life are somehow supposed to have a meaning.

This, however, is not the only corollary of the exaltation of "belief" in this sense. It has an effect upon the Europeans themselves, and particularly upon this corporate life which we are now examining. If moral excellence is a matter of assent the society is not an ethical achievement at all,—it is simply an association of people who believe the same thing. Morality is in the custody of the society in the same sense as the minute-book is in the custody of the society—it is a code of rules which the society interprets. There is no necessary obligation on any member to be his best, because the society is neither helped nor hindered by his exertions or by the lack of them. This attitude is characteristic of types of mind rather than theologies. The Catholic, Fundamentalist and Modernist may each exhibit it, and it arises where men are concerned more about correctness of statement than about that faith which works by love.

6.

There are two other theories which touch on the principles of mission work, and one or the other is to be found in some degree in every mission. One is the cult of perfection and the other is the cult of imperfection.

The cult of perfection is nowadays considered to be just a little old-fashioned. Its favourite text is that new wine cannot be poured into old bottles, and therefore with the change of life which it seeks to produce in the Native, there must be a change of surroundings. A European type of building begins to replace the native type, and European ways of living and of dressing and of thinking are all encouraged. Just as the content of life is intended to be different so will the form be different also. There are missions right out in the wilds whose hospitals are equipped with apparatus that would not disgrace a British Medical School, and whose staff houses are European in every single thing except the soil on which they stand and the sky under which they flourish.

There are good psychological reasons for this position, from the point of view of both the European and the Native.

It is a duty that we owe to our work that we should be at our best when we are doing it, and for that some privacy is needed. And by privacy I mean not only a seclusion from people, but also a seclusion from things. The actual transfer of a man's person from England to Africa is in itself a fairly complete break with his old associations, and to seek to make it utterly complete by allowing the new circumstances to press in upon his life at every point is to do himself violence. Unless a man can preserve for his life a retreat which is his very own, he is not likely to be at his best with other people. Of course a man may be content with keeping his soul "retired unto the Lord," but not everybody can do this easily without the aid—the sacramental aid—of his material surroundings. If physical surroundings help a man to be always on that level at which his soul finds its own refreshment and to which he aspires to lift other people, it is a perverted piety that does not accept that help.

From the point of view of the Native the matter is not quite so simple. When a man becomes a Christian it is a bigger break with his old life than if he started wearing trousers and eating bread. To suggest, therefore, that it is wrong to do the smaller thing while all the time we are seeking to do the bigger thing is just a little odd. But even if the two things were on the same level, there is still much to be said for handing over to the Native everything we have —dress, custom, language, buildings, as well as religion. These things will help to form associations with his new way of life and keep him confirmed within it. Accordingly, in one well-known mission the Natives can learn carpentry in a workshop as well equipped as that of a London cabinet-maker, they are housed in cottages like those in England, they wear European dress and aspire to European habits.

It was obvious, however, on visiting this mission, that a process was going on here not altogether fortunate for the Native. He was being initiated into a new world of ideas and apparatus, and although it was doubtless better for him to find this in the quietness of his own village than in the congested areas of Johannesburg, it was nevertheless breaking up his social life in a way that was to be regretted. There was no scope in their own villages for people who had got accustomed to this kind of thing, and they were leaving the country and seeking work with the Europeans in another territory. This depopulation had indeed become very serious, and it was directly traceable to this cult of perfection.

There is, moreover, such a thing as being too perfect. The educational business of missions is to train people to do things themselves. In the long run this cult of perfection means the triumph of machinery over human nature and a constant effort to keep the Native in tutelage in case he makes mistakes. It must be confessed that a good deal of the educational apparatus of many missions is only so much insurance against failure, and yet where human nature is concerned no such insurance is possible. Education is a matter of faith. The missionary who can stand aside and allow the Native to play with his own material needs to be really well-disciplined. He would do it so much better himself and, yet, in spite of that, he must not do it.

One of the finest buildings in all Africa is the wonderful Scottish cathedral at Blantyre. It was built by an amateur architect, David Clement Scott, and by amateur builders out of the common clay of the neighbourhood. They learned as they went along, for they put their very best work into it. And it was built more to the glory of God than many a mathematically-planned building, coldly sublime and intolerably correct.

7.

Imperfection is also a cult. The aim of its devotees is to do everything as like the native way as possible.

In a certain mission in Central Africa the " hospital " is a hut with an earth floor and a thatched roof, and the patients sleep on the floor. This is not primarily because of lack of funds but because it is held that the Natives are accustomed to it and they would not sleep on beds even if the beds were there.

In a very low-lying district which includes a mile of swamp it did not seem to me that this was a hygienic method of treating any illness, particularly pulmonary diseases. In the same way there is a certain rigidity in many missions in the use of teaching apparatus. Everything must be homemade, irrespective of its relative value for teaching purposes, which after all is the primary reason for the school being there. And in other ways native custom is allowed to set the standard, always excepting doctrine and ritual. The sexes are kept separate in the lower classes not always because of any thought-out view of the best method of education, but again because "the Natives are accustomed to it." There is a great difference in this regard even between missions that agree in theology, and both of which are celibate. The Universities' Mission at Likoma in Lake Nyasa separates the boys and girls in this way. The Mirfield Mission in Southern Rhodesia does not.

Now of course there is again good psychological ground for this point of view. It helps to temper the wind to the shorn lamb, and the Native who becomes a Christian does not make so complete a change in his life as to be utterly bewildered. After all, a change of life is a difficult thing to keep up. The Native does not and cannot become a European all at once, even if it were desirable that he should become one, and it is well to keep all the associations that are not definitely opposed to his new way of life. They will give him a sure standing ground in a new country. There may be a difference of opinion as to what is and what is not a healthy association. Some missions find that they must cut out dancing and the initiation ceremonies; others feel that they can keep both and "sublimate" them. It all depends on circumstances, and it is very necessary to avoid cant at this point. Just because a thing is " native " it is not necessarily along the best line of native development.

Education, like everything else, must be worked out according to its aim, and this touchstone may show some makeshifts, whether native or European, to be good and others to be bad. For instance, in the case of the hospital just mentioned—the real aim of a hospital is to get people well, and where this is hindered by native custom the native custom ought to go, otherwise for the sake of one good a greater good is lost.

The cult of imperfection minimizes the enormous change made by the spiritual and intellectual impact of the mission. A man's whole view of life alters and he himself may need and often asks for surroundings which are more in keeping with that new life. It is not in every case a love of imitation that makes the educated Native seek to have European habits of living: it is sometimes a genuine urge of the spirit to make its surroundings more in harmony with itself. I visited a mission in the Cape Province which strongly objected to its boys wearing shoes because " the Native never wears shoes." At the same time the saintly head of the Mission regretted that it was impossible to use the mealie bread of the country in the Sacrament and he therefore imported European wheaten flour for the purpose.

In a context such as this it seemed to me that the cult of the imperfect was just a little difficult to understand.

When it affects the Europeans themselves it is more doctrinaire still. From time to time there are men who obey a call to "live native." This, however, is surely a special vocation, no better and no worse than other vocations. The men themselves would not be able to have nearly so much influence did they not follow the call that has come to them. But there are others who live in the ordinary European way and who do not lack either respect or love. What a man wears or eats depends on his constitution, his tastes, the climate, the needs of his work. He has a right to be himself and to be at his best, and this the native African respects. If in the cult of perfection there is involved a slight Pharisaism towards the Native, the cult of imperfection brings with it a slight Pharisaism towards other Europeans. And Pharisaism is unlovely wherever it is.

CHAPTER V.

THE VILLAGE SCHOOL AND THE VILLAGE TEACHER.

I.

AFRICA is still predominantly rural, and by far the greater number of Natives who are found in European industry have come from the villages.

The village school, therefore, in the bush, or in the forest, or on the veld, is the heart of the African educational system. It is here that the native African gets his first touch with the world of new ideas which is going to transform his life.

The village schools vary from place to place, but there is a family likeness about them everywhere, not only as between one school and another in Africa but even as between a school in Africa and a school in England. Childhood does not seem to know our racial distinctions, and the beginnings of things are very much alike.

About four hours away from Livingstonia, at the north end of Lake Nyasa, there is a small village school which I will take as the type and symbol of village education.[1] It is a mud building and stands at the corner of a maize field by a tall tree. It is perhaps 30 feet by 16, and has three square holes in the walls for windows. It has an earth floor, and at one end there is an earth platform 9 inches high, on which there is a table. Behind the table stands William, the teacher. He has a blackboard hanging on the wall behind him. In honour of the occasion he is wearing a striped shirt, flannel trousers, a black tie, socks and shoes, and a jacket with a fountain pen sticking out of the pocket. He is a symbol not only of authority, but also of progress.

The seats are branches of trees stuck in the floor. On

[1] See illustration opposite p. 47.

them sit the school—young men and maidens, old men and children, all learning reading, writing, the four rules, and Scripture, and all very serious and intent as becomes the builders of a new Africa. They all crush themselves in, as eager for the new learning as the Florentines of the age of the Medici, or our simple English forefathers who came into St. Paul's to listen to the reading of the Bible. And the parallels are apt. Theirs is new learning, they are mastering the elements of something hid from the wise and prudent of their own people, something that was never in their village life before.

It is important, as we have already noticed, to realize that a village school belonging to a mission is also a church. The distinction between sacred and secular is not so marked as it is at home, and although in some missions the identity results in all the work being secular, while in others everything is bent to the sole end of religious propaganda, there is a large majority of mission schools which keep alive the best in both.

The success or failure of the village school very largely rests with the native teacher. Every mission has scores of village schools out in the bush or in the forest, and the question of supervision is a problem. One mission in Nyasaland has nearly seven hundred village schools to look after, and there is only one European whose specific work it is to supervise them. The Yakusu mission on the Congo is responsible for five hundred village schools. Obviously they cannot be visited very frequently, nor is it always possible to bring the teachers back to the head station for " refresher " courses of training. They are therefore left for most of the time to their own resources. The results are sometimes rather queer !

On the other hand, isolation and responsibility have often the effect of bringing out powers which would never be suspected. One of the Native supervisors in Natal had been the head teacher in a primary school at Umzumbi. He was keen on handicrafts, and he got his school up to a standard as good as that of an intermediate school. In the garden he started experimental plots for growing rice and other crops. His own house was neat and trim, and he was able to show a good mealie plot even in a generally bad season. In the holidays he worked in a store and saved enough money to buy himself a harmonium. At a far-off place called Mbelele, in the Kafue basin in Northern Rhodesia, I visited a tiny village school, and found that the villagers had not only built the school but were also building a three-roomed wattle-and-daub house for the teacher. On a table in one of the unfurnished rooms, along with chalk and pencils, were Bunyan's *Holy War*, and Sir Oliver Lodge's *The War and After*. (I do not know if these were at all connected in the teacher's own mind!)

2.

The matter of attendance is a difficulty. There is, and indeed can be, no such thing as compulsory attendance.[1] A great deal depends on local conditions and on the seasons. In central Nyasaland the gardens have to be watched at night owing to the depredations of game, and accordingly even a five-hour day at school next day is too long. The Lokele people in the Congo are a river people, and this fact affects attendance at school. The men do the fishing and the women do the trading. They are sometimes away for months at a time and take their children with them in a canoe. In the district round Alice in Cape Province the pasturage is very thin, and as stock-raising is the chief occupation the cattle have often to go long distances to pasture. The little boys have to be out all day to watch them, and so there are always twice as many girls in school as boys.

Sometimes the causes for non-attendance are really outside the control of the people themselves. In South Africa there is still in many places effective opposition on the part of Europeans to native education. The labour conditions on the Congo militate against the village school. The recruitment for native labour is said to be voluntary, but as teachers are expressly excluded from the 5 per cent. of its able-bodied men which each village is encouraged to send, this exemption is the measure of their fellows' freedom! If the

[1] The Transkei Native Councillors, however, are very anxious to have compulsion in the Territories, and it is a live issue at meetings of the *Bunga*.

teacher goes (for in spite of his exemption he is not always proof against envy), it means the end of the school.

Apart from general causes of this nature which affect attendance there are more particular and more common ones—some which would indeed be as common in England also were it not for compulsion. At a little Swedish mission school at Imbizana in Natal I found these entered among the reasons for children leaving school,—lack of dress, gone to work, taking care of baby, sickness, kept by her parents to look after the monkeys, too lazy to attend school, afraid to go alone, and, most frequently of all, simply " tired of school."

These are reasons for absence. What of the reasons for attending?

Everywhere there is a widespread desire for education, and all kinds of motives come into it. The sense of power that comes from being able to read and write, the ability to get a place in Government service, are some of them, but these are chiefly the concern of those who are going further than the village school. To the great majority of folk in the rural areas the chief attraction of the school is its own real interest.[1]

This accounts for the easy establishment of schools under all kinds of keen but incompetent teachers, like one " Cabbage " of whom I heard in Northern Rhodesia. This youth had no sooner learned to read and write than he went off into a lonely place in the bush and opened a school of his own! There was perhaps a desire for glory in this missionary enterprise, but this was not the sole motive. The question is often raised whether it is worth while to allow such feeble schools to exist. Have not the children to unlearn later on all that they have ever learned, and are they not only too likely to presume on what little they think they know and to be content with it?

The argument is cogent, and where public funds are to be spent, it is well that the Government should encourage

[1] *Cf.* the position in England in 1816: " There is the most unquestionable evidence that the anxiety of the poor for education continues not only unabated, but daily increasing."—*Third Report of the Select Committee on the Education of the Lower Orders*, p. 56. See below, p. 392.

what is best rather than what is tenth-rate. But when we remember that the percentage of native children of school age who are actually found in schools in British Africa varied in 1935 from under 10 per cent. in Nigeria to no more than 55 per cent. in Basutoland,[1] it is clear that it is a choice not between best and tenth-rate, but between schools and nothing at all.

Of the people's interest and keenness there can be no question. Even a little imagination will bring home to the European how wonderful a thing is education to the African villager. It is to the present generation of adults what a gun was to a previous generation—something which will put them on a level with the European who has come into their midst. For reading and writing are to the "raw" Native not merely a new thing, but a new *kind* of thing. In the same way to our own forefathers the steam engine was not only a new method of locomotion but something which involved altogether a new principle. And it is this thrilling experiment with something, so to speak, fourth dimensional, that provides the absorbing interest in education. It is this, too, which makes reading and writing more popular than agriculture.

3.

It is often mistakenly assumed that apart from the Mission or Government School there would be no Native education at all. But the African peoples like all others have of course their own system of education, for by "education" in the more deliberate sense we mean simply those things which one generation thinks it worth while to pass on to the next. Where life is tribal and the members of the tribe are considered to include equally those who are "dead" and those who are alive, it is obvious that the younger people must be told of those things which bind the tribe together so that they may carry on its tradition. Primitive life is a much more deliberate thing than it often appears to be. Everybody in the tribe counts, and it is therefore a necessity for everybody to be "educated," even the women.

[1] Figures supplied by the Colonial Dept., London University Institute of Education.

There are accordingly among primitive, as amongst all other peoples, two sorts of education. There is the training in the use of tools, the working of handicrafts and the method of getting a living and building a house. This education we may call "vocational." There is also the "liberal" education which is found in the initiation ceremonies and other mysteries which concern the life of the person as a member of a society, mortal and at the same time immortal.

Neither of these types of education goes very far, and their bias is conservative and communal rather than towards encouraging initiative and originality,—not unlike the bias in the education of some English public schools. But there are in them important elements which bear witness to the African's ability to profit by an education which aims at the same thing in better ways. There are to be found discipline and self-restraint, the endurance of hardship, the relation of life to destiny, pride of membership in a group, responsibility for other people, and skill in recognized crafts. These are all familiar traits of caste education everywhere, and they are particularly strongly marked among the Bantu peoples. They have given Bantu society, as has been shown, a toughness which has enabled it to withstand centuries of adverse conditions, and they have only begun to weaken where the closely-knit tribal society has been undermined by forces of individualism introduced by Europe. Tribalism, as we have seen, is bound sooner or later to pass away, and it is one of the tragedies of its passing that the white man who sees the Native in the transition stages so often believes him incapable of those very virtues which the tribal system has fostered, but which seem to disappear with it. It is commonly said by the ignorant that the Native has no restraint, that he is a coarse immoral fellow. It is not the experience of those who know the raw African. Indeed in the matter of continence alone, the restraint that the so-called "savage" can and does put upon his sexual impulses at certain seasons through loyalty to tribal custom is one of the most remarkable things about the make-up of primitive man.

These native qualities are built up, as were similar qualities among the early Hebrews, out of an elaborate system of taboo. But although they are in this sense negative, the materials are all present out of which moral character can be fashioned.

Some of these taboos, however, are concerned not so much with moral character as with a man's relations to the world of nature, and here they are not so helpful or so usable. Agriculture and hygiene are hedged round by prohibitions which give way only to counter-demonstration, if they give way at all. The growing of crops is a process governed from first to last in accordance with strict rules, handed down from dim generations in the past. Iron-working or hut-building is beset by the same system of age-long observances, each of which is as essential for the validity of the process as was every little act and phrase for the validity of an ancient Roman contract. Indeed the two things are not dissimilar. Growing crops, smelting iron, building houses, and all the manifold operations of life can be carried on only through a contract with the spirits. And the form of that contract is the important point.

Effect, therefore, does not follow cause in any automatic way. It is really more true to speak of effort and reward than of cause and effect. The individual act does not really " cause " anything. It simply brings about a set of favourable conditions, which it is then the business of the spirits to acknowledge by suitable action. And so in all primitive societies, for example among the early Hebrews, the idea of " First Cause " is a much more familiar thing than the idea of " cause " in general. Broadly speaking, " secondary causes " do not exist. There is only one real cause for everything.

This is at once a strength and a weakness. It gives to education a usable and a non-usable element. It is a help to morality, but it stands in the way of science. The European whose attitude to the study of primitive life is primarily scientific is apt to fasten on the non-usable element and to neglect the other. It is to the scientific man a rather tiresome thing that in a world which is presumably rational, there should be found human beings who act irrationally. He feels therefore that the great need is to train the Native to think scientifically, and to tidy up his mind. This attitude has various corollaries which we shall discuss when considering the aims of education.

This discussion has been concerned to show that the Native in the village school does not come with a blank mind. He has his own system of education at home. The small children perhaps can be started off on new lines because their previous education has been concerned with things to do with their hands rather than with ideas. But those who have passed the initiation stage have been put in possession of a philosophy of life, crude though it is, against which the education of the village school has to work. Some of it can be used and some of it cannot. But it is a mistake to imagine that it is not there at all.

It is equally a mistake to imagine that everything is there. The European is apt to read into the mind of the African ideas which are in his own mind. The native African attitude to life is not one which can be expressed in words even if he had the words in which to express it. Even his religion is very largely that " religion of the inarticulate " which Donald Hankey found to characterize the average British Tommy during the War. Expression does not come easily if it comes at all, and he is rather apt to be shy of it if he is asked to express what he feels. Therein he is one with the inarticulate everywhere. Consequently he is often accused of lying when all that he is guilty of is a mishandling of unfamiliar material, that is, language.

It is often asked, what do men talk about when they are by themselves ? The old missionaries will tell you that the only way to find that out is to go with them on trek—or *safari* or *ulendo* as it is variously called. And the result is often disappointing. The least little event will keep them going for hours. A teacher was being carried in a bush-car along a difficult bit of road in Nyasaland, and at one place she had to get out and walk. They came to a tiny stream trickling across the road and the men asked her how she proposed to get over it. She said, " On my feet." For hours afterwards they said nothing else among themselves except " The donna said she'd cross over on her feet," and to every person they met they said, " We asked the donna how she was going to get over the water, and she said, ' on her feet ' ! "

4.

"The dark places of the earth are full of the habitations of cruelty," and it would be foolish to attempt to minimize the grim aspect of native life. It does not appear in the village school, with every one so happy and care-free, and quite often the sympathetic white man feels that this idyllic existence only needs a little " informing " in order to make it perfect. Education appears to be so much more the need of the people than " conversion."

From time to time, however, something happens which lays bare a stratum of evil that has been unsuspected, and it is surprising how near it is to the surface. The boys who have just come through the initiation ceremonies have a look of fear about them that contrasts horribly with the happiness of childhood. It is not a matter of surprise that in some missions where the white men have proposed to adopt ceremonies connected with these native rites, it has been the Africans themselves who have begged that they should be entirely cut out.

And then again witchcraft is always rearing its head, even to-day. The cruelty of human nature shows itself nakedly in the recesses of African life. Under the light of the moon, in remote places, men are done to death in strange and fearful ways through the power of the witch-doctor. It is notable that it is not witchcraft itself that is responsible for cruelty, except that the belief in it and the fear of it drive men to take measures against it that are quite as cruel as the supposed influence of witchcraft itself. It is therefore a negative thing. It is not a case of some one going out of his way to do evil, but of people trying to avert or punish the evil that they imagine to have been done. The actual practice of cruelty is accordingly in the hands of a very few people, the witch-doctors. The people as a whole, including often (although by no means always, in these days) the victims themselves, are aiders and abettors through their credulity, rather than in the definite things they do. The witch-doctors play upon their fears and they are willing that they should do so. Death will be remorseless, without pity or pang, but it may come to any of them. They are cruel, but it is to each other and to themselves that their cruelty extends.

5.

There are therefore, in the make-up of every African as he comes to the village school, elemental things which we can parallel elsewhere in a more developed form, and among these are things good and bad.

There are also some more pedestrian qualities, or habits of mind or manners, which the teacher can use in his work.

The rune of hospitality among native peoples is a wonderful thing. True, it often extends only to the tribe, but to-day, with the practical cessation of inter-tribal feuds, it has spread everywhere. I have already spoken of the great distance that men wander from home in search of education or work, yet they have no fear that they will not be helped and looked after. The spirit of comradeship which underlies this quality is what Dudley Kidd mistakenly calls " socialism," and what Father Callaway more rightly calls, without translation, *ubuntu*. It is the link that binds man and man together simply because they are men,—the kind of comradeship that all men feel on rare occasions of common physical danger. But it is also a comradeship which binds together the poor and simple of this earth as it somehow does not bind the rich and the sophisticated. Uneducated British and German Tommies showed it in the War. It is thus that a V.A.D. hut-worker wrote of it :—

' This is the principle of comradeship, that the man next you, not because you like him or he is your chosen friend, but just because he needs it, is to be cared for just as if he was yourself ; his cold, his hunger, his helplessness, his need of a cigarette, are satisfied as if they were an extension of your own personality. There is no difference really between him and you.'[1]

This is also the most characteristic African quality.

Then there are the salutations by the way. It gets in the way of business, sometimes, this stopping and talking—How are you ? Where are you coming from ? Where are you going ?—and the African can appreciate Christ's counsel to

---

[1] *The Army and Religion* (1919), pp. 170-71.

the disciples when they had work to do, "See that ye salute no man by the way." It shows, however, a real interest in people and it is more common among the more common people everywhere. In a Northumbrian mining village every man on the road will greet every other man with, "What cheer?" as he passes along, and even though he never stays for an answer he shows he is not oblivious to the other man's presence.

And then there is the indirect method of dealing with a question. The native African is as wary as the native Irishman of a direct question, but whereas the Irishman will reply to the question "Were you there?" with "I might have been," the African will usually say "No." It is not really a lie nor is it an evasion. It is an answer to what he suspects to be the real question in your mind and to which "Were you there?" is simply preliminary. "No" in this case means, "I didn't do it," although you have not yet asked him whether he did or did not! This method of answering the unspoken question or desire is confusing when you ask—in either Rhodesia or County Clare—how far it is to a place. The "Native" whom you ask ignores the question as you put it, and asks himself another: "What sort of answer will comfort this poor man?" If you look tired, he will say "two miles" and you go on your way rejoicing at the good news,—until you find later on that the real distance is four!

It is not surprising that the anthropologist in search of information is sometimes misled.[1]

This use of imagination comes out as with all primitive people in folk tales, stories, riddles and proverbs, and, in the case of Christian evangelists, in their application of texts. To be familiar with such material, in the native tongue, is an essential for anyone who would rightly understand the people.

On the other hand, this power of imagination when required for unfamiliar uses is singularly ineffective. The native African in matters European is a great literalist. I have heard of a teacher being rebuked by his fellows in a

[1] Lévy Bruhl is continually warning the investigator against possible error of this kind. See, for instance, *L'Ame Primitive*, Chapter 3, Section 1.

"criticism lesson" because he stood on the right of the blackboard, and "the book said" he was to stand on the left! This, however, is evidence neither of his ability nor of his inability to profit by European education. It is simply an example of the way in which the untutored mind everywhere reacts to unfamiliar material. The English schoolboy, no less than the African, feels safer with the book, and we know the tremors into which many people fall at the mere thought of "having the Bible taken away from us." The dislike of being out on an uncharted course, even though it may lead to the discovery of a new world, keeps most people well in sight of land. Partly, too, there is something more fundamental in it than that. There is in it the idea lying behind the old law of contract, that there is a definite form in which a thing should be done in order that its doing shall be effective, and to omit the form is to lose the thing. At any rate this literalism is in evidence in all African schools, and it is to be overcome not by censure but by a growing familiarity with the principles that underlie our European ways of doing things.

And then there are native games to be remembered. One day at a school in Northern Rhodesia I found myself surrounded by about twenty little boys to whom, in the absence of the teacher, I could not speak a word and who could not speak to me. I therefore took a piece of string out of my pocket and began doing a "cat's cradle." Every eye was fixed on it for they knew perfectly well what I was about, although this particular specimen they had not seen before. After that they all started doing them, and they were able to show me very many that were new to me, and to my joy I knew two that were new to them. As "cat's cradles" are about the most widely-spread game that exists, for they are found in Lapland and in the Pacific islands as well as in Central Africa,[1] a knowledge of a few of them would be an effective introduction almost anywhere. On the Congo, among the Lokele people, I found that they knew as many as twenty-eight.

---

[1] See K. Haddon, *Cat's Cradles from Many Lands* (1911), and W. W. Rouse Ball, *String Figures* (3rd edit. 1928).

6.

The village teacher is the hub of the whole educational system. We have already had a good look at William in his school in Nyasaland. He is a child both of his own native village and also of the European school. He has a foot in both worlds. If he is good at his job he interprets the one to the other. His is really a " priestly " function, and both Church and State owe him more than they can well imagine.

We shall only deal rightly by the village teacher when we see what a truly astonishing adventure is his. We forget how much there is in England behind the work that a youth does at school. There is a whole community of thought, organization and action, of which the school is a normal expression. But the village teacher in the Congo forest or in the Rhodesian bush leaves the social life and the ideas of the training school and disappears. He takes with him a Bible, a few small books in the native language, an English or French grammar, and his own notebooks. He has in his head the lessons that he has made his own, and the memory of what is, for all its crudity, an intellectual and religious society. These are his whole stock-in-trade for creating a new world. He is flung largely on his own resources, and yet he is a point of light in an otherwise dark village. To the village he may be the only local element that represents the marvels of the outside world,—the world of white people, of motor cars and railways, of streets and houses, of books, of wisdom concerning the earth, the past of the race, and the destiny of mankind. He is the twentieth century after Christ planted down in the midst of the early days of the world. The thing deserving of comment is not that African education does so little but that it accomplishes so much. It was to me a never-failing source of wonder.

All the territories of Africa are studded at the moment with a large number of teachers who have never been trained at all. They are victims partly of circumstances, and partly of a false educational theory.

The circumstances arose through the desire of missions to spread themselves as far as possible and as quickly as possible. The teachers were like officers promoted from the ranks in the middle of an action to hold a post already occupied. There was little time and indeed inclination to train them, except in so far as the responsibility itself was a training.

The educational theory was to the effect that in order to teach you need be only a little way ahead of your pupils. This is a theory which has proved not only untrue but the very reverse of the truth. It is for the lowest classes that the very best teachers are needed, for theirs is the most important work of all. They give the first approach to a subject, and it is the man who has the whole range of the subject before him who can best see the relative importance of all the parts.

For what, after all, is " training " ? Is it the handing over of certain technical hints as to how the children ought to sit at a desk, or at what point in the lesson the use of the blackboard should come in ? These things of course are valuable, but their value lies in relation to the thing taught and to the people who learn. By themselves they lead simply to that literalism to which the essentially untrained mind clings as to a refuge.

Nowadays the training of teachers is the rule, and it is likely that education in Africa will ultimately go in the same direction as it has gone in England. It has even now to face the question, which is better for the future teacher, a professional training, or a further general education ? Ideally of course you require both, but if both are not possible which is it to be ? As time goes on there will inevitably be a further and further extension of the teacher's own education.

Meanwhile the educational structure as it is has to be underpinned. The men (and women too), who have had little or no training, are brought back to the mission station or training college for "refresher" courses, and in most British territories the Government makes it financially possible to do this. During these periods of training the teachers get into touch with Europeans and with each other, and apart from the technical knowledge which they may gain, they have a time of greatly valued fellowship.

At a "refresher" course at Achimota in January, 1928, there were about sixty men and a few women. There were many different types among them; some were wearing European clothes and were apparently quite familiar with English ideas and habits; others were raw people from distant parts of the bush, and were sitting in a modern lecture-hall with only their blankets round them. They listened to lectures and had discussions, and arranged a concert or two and had European dances, and it was clear that the whole thing inspired as well as edified. And it is this spirit which counts for so much to men in lonely places. A mere brushing-up of knowledge is not enough. One of the most useful courses of lectures was given by the assistant director of Native education on the education code itself. It was invaluable to have the code expounded in this way by one of the officials, and the flood of questions at the end of each lecture showed how much it was appreciated. Another part of the Gold Coast system is the establishment of a circulating library at Achimota, which is freely drawn upon by village teachers.

The mission at Mkhoma in Nyasaland goes one step further. Practically all teachers when they go out into their work get married, and from then onwards it is not only themselves but also their houses that count as an educative agency. The mission therefore brings in to the head station the wives and families as well as the men themselves, and houses them all in a model village of *pisé-de-terre*. Everything in the houses is done as well as it can be in such materials as the Natives themselves have at their own homes. The women are taught housework and mothercraft and also some literary subjects. The houses are inspected and the women are given hints on how to improve their methods of running a house and cooking food. The Training Institute at Kimpese on the Lower Congo is also organized on these lines. The African family functions as a unit much more than the European family, and to keep it together while learning its work is a great gain.

7.

The "refresher" courses are substitutes for, or supplements of, the ordinary business of training teachers. They help to establish knowledge that might otherwise fade away. But there are also other ways of keeping the village teacher in touch with his fellows and with the outside world, and to give him the feeling that he belongs to a great society.

In most places there are magazines. *Mambo Leo* is the well-known Government paper in Tanganyika. The "Jeanes School" at Kabete runs one for Kenya. The mission at Mkhoma has a particularly successful magazine called *Mthenga*. It is published six times a year, at a penny, and has a circulation of about 3000,—a very creditable achievement for a tiny mission press. A copy of it, taken at random, contains five biblical and religious articles, other articles on drink, choosing maize seed, whirlwinds, proverbs, "our lungs," curing tobacco, the Nyasaland census, the journey to Salisbury, the custom of chanting at funerals, and a letter to the editor on tribal names. There are six columns of general news which range as far afield as China, South America, the starting of Achimota, the death of Sir Apolo Kagwa, and the centenary of railways. There is a page for mothers. Other numbers include a serial story. This was the best magazine of the sort that I saw in Africa, thoroughly interesting and varied and cheap. It is a link which keeps together the boys of the mission who go to work as far away as Wankie in one direction and Johannesburg in the other, and is a constant inspiration to teachers in the bush.

Of a more professional nature is the *Natal Native Teachers' Journal*. It is a quarterly magazine of about seventy pages, and is circulated gratis by the Government Education Department to all school "grantees," as the missions in charge of grant-aided schools are called. The value of it is largely due to the nature of the Natal system of native education, about which something will be said in a later chapter. But as a method of creating a common mind on native education among teachers, inspectors, missionaries, and the Department it is excellent. Official notices appear in it, selected reports of schools, articles by inspectors on methods of teaching certain subjects, reviews of books, articles on health, hygiene, and problems of teaching, accounts of schools in other countries, short plays, and an excellent series of practical articles by native teachers. At the beginning of each issue there is a leading article based upon a text in the Bible. The *Journal* is of course very much what the readers themselves like to make it, and it is both popular and well-supported.

The Cape Province Education Department runs an *Education Gazette* which is of a more official nature and circulates among both European and native schools. The Cape Native Education Department is also well known for its *Suggestions for the Consideration of Teachers*, a large and most informative volume based on a similar publication of the British Board of Education. It is distributed free, and within 600 pages it considers questions of school organization, and the teaching of all the eighteen subjects of the Primary School curriculum. I found it sometimes treated as a verbally inspired book!

Occasionally in the South there are exhibitions of the work of native schools, similar to the " Education Week " which is becoming a feature of the activities of the more progressive education authorities in Britain. Some of the missions in Rhodesia and elsewhere have an annual show, which is of value chiefly in exhibiting the results of different methods of agriculture, and also in encouraging native handicrafts.

In South Africa the native teachers have got to the stage where they are members of a professional body, known in the Cape as " The Cape Native Teachers' Association." It was founded at King William's Town in 1921, and the inaugural speech of the Chairman on the need for such an association shed an interesting light on the ideals of native teachers. It was summarized in a pamphlet as follows :—

The salary question—How it has produced misery and poverty.—How Government is moved only by the pressure of a powerful but constitutional agitation, thus unconsciously encouraging agitation. —Need for a reform in the control of Native Education.—The poor, uninformative, and uneducational character of the Cape

Education Gazette for native teachers as compared with the Natal *Native Teachers' Journal*.—Need for a circulating library for general reading of newspapers, like *Health*, the *Express*, the native papers and cheaper good books, e.g. *People's Library, Everyman, and Home University Library*.—Failure of previous attempts at Union, due to indifference, jealousy, puerility, etc.—Value of Union in developing respect for self, for other teachers, for our women, for elders.

On the Gold Coast there is a similar Association.

8.

It is clear that we are here a long way from the simple unsophisticated village teacher of the Congo forest or the Nyasaland bush, and that these are the marks of the urban industrial community rather than of the rural village. But we must not mislead ourselves into thinking that lack of sophistication means lack of intelligence or even of the latent capacity for intellectual effort.

The operations of agriculture and building undoubtedly call for skill and intelligence, although not perhaps for much deep thinking. But occasionally there are signs, even among the most undisturbed native peoples, of powers of thought which need only opportunity of practice and a tradition in order to be quite equal to that of a European. That very complicated form of backgammon which is found all over Africa (and indeed all over the world) is one of them. It is quite as difficult as chess. I have seen it played by native firemen on the Congo steamers on a board of twenty-eight holes, and once in a compound on the Rand on a board of no less than eighty.[1]

One of the most striking things I found in talking to even humble teachers in lonely places was the sense they had of the dignity of their profession. It was always a sure point of contact and the beginning of confidences when they found

---

[1] There is a very good account of it under the name *chisolo*, as played by the Ba-Ila, in Smith and Dale's *The Ila-speaking Peoples of Northern Rhodesia* (1920), Vol. II., pp. 232-37. The Thonga people call it *tshuba*, and it is described by Junod, *The Life of a South African Tribe* (2nd edit., 1927), Vol. I., pp. 345-51.

VILLAGE SCHOOL AND VILLAGE TEACHER

that I also was a teacher. At Yakusu I had a conference with the native pupil teachers and girl monitors. The discussion was vigorous, and I was asked what to do with disobedient boys, how to encourage regular attendance, how much time I felt it was worth while to spend on correcting compositions, and, above all, how to deal with refractory parents!

And if there is brightness and humour among them it is also interesting how much solid learning they can take in if it is interpreted by good teaching. The native teachers at Kimpese study and take away with them into the forest a really advanced vernacular text-book of physiology, compiled by Dr. Catherine Mabie and her native assistant. It is intended to be a scientific basis for hygiene, and has been compiled in discussion classes with the men themselves. It is more advanced than many of the hygiene books which cover all that is required for most of the teachers' training courses in England! And they appear to appreciate it.

CHAPTER VI.

FURTHER EDUCATION AND THE TRAINING OF TEACHERS.

IN African education, for the most part, the greater always includes the less. Every institution, with some few exceptions, no matter how far it takes its pupils, begins at the bottom. Even Lovedale, the largest of all, and Achimota, the wealthiest, have a kindergarten school side by side with engineering laboratories and advanced agriculture.

It is remarkable how similar in some ways is the system of higher education in Africa to the beginnings of the universities in Europe. A place gets a name, and people flock to it—afoot many of them—and they pass by an institution of equal standing in their own territory. A boy in Bechuanaland will wander down to Lovedale, and a boy from the Eastern Province of the Cape will trek past Lovedale and make his way to Tigerkloof in Bechuanaland. Every boarding school is a cosmopolitan place, and there is no guarantee in setting up a school " for a territory " that it will really serve that territory. Thus, too, when the little cathedral schools of the twelfth century branched out into higher studies, men in England travelled to Paris and students from Bohemia found themselves in Oxford. There is something almost sacramental in all this going and coming. It is as if a new world of thought required for its due appreciation a change of circumstances.[1]

Accordingly while missions differ and the efficiency of teachers varies very greatly, there is a certain sameness about African education in every stage. I am proposing therefore in this chapter to look at the system as a whole, and at one

---

[1] This apparently was the mediæval view. " Et quid sit aut prosit, ad vocationem sapientiae, relinquere patriam."—John of Salisbury, *Polycraticus*, Book VII., heading of Chapter 13 (Twelfth century).

or two institutions that are typical of each grade, and then in later chapters to consider details of subject-matter and method, in which there are wide divergences not only of opinion but also of practice.

1.

The majority of African schools are mission schools, but nowadays it is coming to be an accepted axiom, at any rate in British Africa, that higher education, particularly in specialized branches such as agriculture or medical or university courses, is the direct concern of the Government.

In addition to mission and Government schools there are also a few purely native schools. One of the best in the South is the famous school at Ohlange in Natal, founded by the Rev. John Dube, who in 1937 was given an honorary doctorate by the University of South Africa. On the West Coast some are very ambitious and a few are unfortunately rather absurd. The headmaster of one in the Gold Coast claimed in his prospectus to be an M.A., D.D., and F.R.S. !

The grading of schools naturally varies over an area so wide as the Continent of Africa. In Southern Rhodesia, for instance, there are three grades of schools,—boarding schools with a European teacher, day schools with a European teacher, and day schools with a native teacher. In the Livingstonia mission there are village schools, station schools, and head station schools, sometimes called respectively primary, middle, and high schools. In Northern Rhodesia there are four grades,—village, central village, station, and central station schools. On the West Coast schools are graded more after the English fashion. There are, however, all over Africa two main principles observed in the organization of schools : a boarding school is graded higher than a day school, and a school with a European teacher is graded higher than a school with only a Native teacher.

What do these grades represent in terms of the school system in England ? It is roughly the case that the village school corresponds to the English infant school, though not always going beyond Standard I. ; the school of the next grade—where there are three grades—will take children up to about Standard IV. in an English elementary school; while the " high " school, or school of the first class, roughly represents Standards IV., V., and VI. On the West Coast "secondary" school standards begin to appear. The line is nowhere very clearly drawn.

In addition to these grades, there are usually in urban areas night schools for those older people who work in the towns during the day.

A further element in the educational system is the apprentices who are to be found in most mission schools. They have come to learn a trade. The visitor has often a difficulty during the periods of industrial work in discovering who are apprentices and who are schoolboys. The apprentices are paid, and there is usually opportunity for them to continue the literary side of their education. At Livingstonia the apprentices are required to have passed at least Standard II. before they are accepted. In some missions the place of industrial apprentices is taken by medical assistants trained to help in the villages or in the locations.

Accordingly we may plan out the general scheme as follows, remembering that as we get into the higher stages the less people there are in them, the wider the area from which they come, and the greater the part played by the European language :—

As a basis there is the village school, when everybody is, so to speak, in the infant's department. From that a certain number go on to another school usually in the same mission, and begin to climb up the standards. After about three years of this higher education, various alternative routes open before them. They may become pupil-teachers, or medical assistants, or agricultural or industrial apprentices, or, if they are girls, specialize in domestic science, or they may simply continue their general education as far as the top standard of the school.

Beyond this system of education and rather independent of it, there are several large institutions which carry education to a stage which we in this country should call secondary. Lovedale is the best known of these, but in every province of the Union of South Africa there are boarding schools of this advanced type, and there are others in old-established mission areas like Mombasa, and the West Coast. They are naturally more widely scattered as you get into the centre of Africa, and here in British territory the Government has come in to supplement the work of the missions.

At the apex of the whole system in South Africa there is the South African Native College at Fort Hare, a Government institution of university rank for the Bantu people of the Union. There are very few of course who get to this stage. It is established on ground historic in the conflicts between the black and white races, and it was opened in 1916 by General Botha, who in himself symbolized yet another racial conflict. Although Fort Hare is not a constituent college of the University of South Africa, its graduation ceremony in 1927 was honoured by being made a Congregation of the University.

The only other place in Africa which seeks to be a native university (if we except possibly the Jesuit institution at Kisantu in the Lower Congo, Fourah Bay College in Sierra Leone, and the Government College at Makerere in Uganda) is the Prince of Wales College at Achimota on the Gold Coast. It is the biggest thing in native education that there is in Africa and has cost £607,000. It provides a complete scheme of education from the kindergarten stage to the university degree.[1]

2.

In British territory the mission schools of all denominations, and of both British and foreign societies, are, if they so desire, assisted by the Government. In non-British territory grants for schools are given to Roman Catholics alone.

As examples of the organization of education beyond village school work I propose to take one from an area in which there is no Government support, and one from an area where the Government is very generous. The first is Yakusu in the Belgian Congo, and the second Uzuakoli in Southern Nigeria.

[1] *Achimota Review, 1927-37* (printed at the Achimota Press, 1937), gives a concise and inspiring account of its progress.

Yakusu has already been spoken of in various contexts. The infant school at the mission is of course like any other forest school in the country save that it really is for infants. There are no adults.

The children leave the infant school as soon as they can read simple stories, and if they wish to go further they go to the middle school in which the boys and the girls are in separate classes. The boys do more reading, writing, and arithmetic. They begin from their own door to understand something of geography. The study of the weather and the wind, the heat and the rain, gives them their introduction to natural science. A book in the vernacular called *The White Man's Wonders* expounds to them the mysteries of the Congo steamers, the motor cars of Stanleyville, and the aeroplanes that fly over their heads. They begin to learn the history of Africa in the form of biographies of leading Africans, and to study the history of the Bible. There is an hour's community singing once a week. They do gardening, hygiene, carpentry, and French. The French is learned from the English missionaries, and so French as spoken by the Native has been twice diluted and is somewhat below proof! However, while it adds to the gaiety of nations, it also enables him to find his way through Government notices, and to be intelligible to the more patient of the Government officials. As an introduction to the treasures of French literature it is a somewhat clumsy instrument.

The girls' education is much simpler than that of the boys. The morning classes consist of reading and writing only, but by a cunning arrangement of the reading matter they get in some hygiene and nature study and Scripture in parenthesis. In the afternoons the house-girls on the mission station itself have industrial training. They knit, make mats, necklaces, bead bags, and dresses, and they prepare and work raffia. All this of course is an attraction to them, for inducements have to be offered to the girls or they would not come. The mission provides them with some of their food, and they find the rest themselves. The great need at Yakusu is for a boarding school. At present only a few can live in, and for the others there is nowhere to go when their parents go off down the river. All they can do is to go with them.

The next stage occurs as the boys get into the top class in the school. If they wish to carry their education further, they become either pupil-teachers or medical assistants in training.

Those who are going to be teachers do extra French, Scripture, and basket work, and they get more personal attention. On the top of this they have two more years' training, during the first of which they do four hours' class work daily, one hour industrial, and two hours' practical teaching in the infants' school. School management, and that rather depressing but useful subject which an older generation knew as " pedagogy," come in at this stage. In the second year they have more advanced French, carpentry instead of basket work, and they teach in the boys' school instead of the infants. They have preaching classes, or " homiletics " as it is sometimes called, more advanced Scripture, the practical preparation of lessons, and a course in the folk-lore of their own people. This last provides them with a kind of *Gesta Romanorum* from which they can draw popular illustrations for lessons and sermons.

The hospital assistants have a three-year course corresponding to that of the teachers. The first is spent in the top class of the school, and instead of manual work they begin to help in the hospital. In the second year their practical work consists of doing the actual dressings and of medical clerking, and they have their academic work in the evenings. They have an afternoon lecture, and three times they go through a book on hygiene, the third time in French. In their third year they take on actual consultations and attend to the simpler cases. They go journeys with white missionaries who have no medical knowledge. They go out with the doctors taking the census of sleeping sickness. They arrange the operating theatre, give injections, and get into the habit of having instruments medically clean. After this they go for three years to the Government hospital at Stanleyville. This is a scheme worked out in conjunction with the excellent medical system of the Belgian Colonial Government.

There are also at Yakusu a school for older women and an evening school attended by workmen, pupil teachers, and some of the hospital assistants.

Yakusu is provided with a little printing press and many of the text-books are home-made and illustrated by the cyclostyle. The mission buildings are of brick and quite plain—consisting chiefly of two rows of lofty class-rooms with a cement floor, a large and impressive Church decorated all round with pictures of Bible stories, a quadrangle of open class-rooms, carpentry and basket workshops, a girl's dormitory, a fine hospital, houses or dormitories for teachers and students, and the houses of the European staff. It is a compact mission standing on the cliff above the Congo, fifteen miles from Stanleyville. It belongs to the Baptists of Great Britain who support it from their own resources. No fees are charged.

3.

Uzuakoli is about eighty miles north of Port Harcourt, in the Ibo country, and in the forest region of Southern Nigeria. The mission is built on rising ground which has been cleared from the bush, and was started in 1923. The educational institute stands round a sort of campus, and the buildings are delightful.[1]

The school in 1936 had 320 boys. Like Achimota it began in the lower stages of education, which it still continues, but the standard has gradually become higher, and consequently the entrance age has tended to become lower, in order to ensure adequate preparation for the upper classes of the school. This has meant the gradual extension of the boarding department at the expense of the lower classes (nursery to primary) which are composed of day boys. Candidates are recommended by the Mission " supervisors of education," officers appointed by the Mission but paid by the Government. Class I (i.e. Standard VI) is the point at which the secondary school begins and is marked by the introduction of geography, algebra and science, and from there it continues right up to Class VI. Thirty boys chosen

---

[1] It is an interesting sidelight on the services rendered to Governments by Missions that the costs of a neighbouring Government school of the same size and grade should be for the main building £40,000 and the Principal's house £3,000 and salary £1,100, while the corresponding amounts at Uzuakoli, which has better buildings, are respectively £7,000, £400, and £350.

in Class II are future teachers in training, but they do no specific professional work till they get to Class V. Promotions are in the hands of the school authorities until boys get to School Certificate stage or Class VI, when the Government inspectors act as assessors. Tuition fees range from 7s. 6d. a year in nursery classes to 24s. at the top of the school.

The staff is mixed, African and European. All standards up to Standard V are taught by Africans. After this stage specialist teachers may be of either race, although Classes I to III have African form-masters and the upper classes Europeans. Yet masters with special interests, e.g. phonetics, art, physical education, wood-work, agriculture and gardening, may be African or European and are appointed according to professional qualifications. They take their subject throughout the school. The school doctor instructs in hygiene.

The boarding school combines features of the native village and some features of the English public school. It is built on the plan of a compound with a " palaver shed " and it has a chief. He appoints " policemen " or monitors for each of the four " houses." Each house has a captain and under him are the " headmen," each of whom is responsible for four rooms. A " court " is held every fortnight, case books are kept and the sentences are inspected by the Principal, who alone has power of corporal punishment. Usually punishments take the form of cutting grass or doing other useful work.

When the boys arrive they deposit money in the school bank to cover fees, clothes, books, return fare home, and also food (unless sent weekly by their parents). Boys buying their own food get 1s. to 1s. 6d. a week out of the bank for it. A boy can easily get through the year on a total expenditure of £5 to £6. Those who have a full scholarship are allowed £7 10s a year (to include tuition fees) and often have a surplus at the end. No money is paid out except when authorized by the form-master.

The school has a printing press and prints its own magazine, an electricity power house, workshops, labs., a dispensary and sick-room, gardens and extensive playing fields. Text-books in the vernacular are written and printed, and also primers for the kindergarten, illustrated by the senior art class. More advanced books are translated and the school also encourages original work in Ibo. There is thus no domination of the vernacular by English. House matches are arranged in sports, and there is considerable competition in work also. Winning houses are allowed to fly their flag. There are no scouting activities *as such* in the school, although boys may join a village troop and the school runs a full cub pack. There is a library which has been established as a memorial to Dick Ogan, an old boy and teacher of this school and one of the most remarkable Africans of this or any other school. In my opinion his death in 1933 deprived his people of another Aggrey.

The Annual Report on the Nigerian Education Department, 1936, refers to the Uzuakoli institute as one which " approaches nearer the ideal that all West African educationists have in mind than probably any other institution in Nigeria."

The large institutions in the south—Tigerkloof, Nengubo, St. Matthews, Blythswood, and others—are all well-established and well-known examples after the type of Uzuakoli. But I have chosen Uzuakoli partly for its own sake, partly because, like Yakusu, it is in a purely black man's country and the needs of native education can be considered by the Government much more on their merits than is always the case down South, and partly because it seems to me to represent a *tertium quid* in the dealings of Government with missionary education, to which these institutions are more and more like to converge. The problem is how to strike a balance between a maximum of Government assistance and the minimum of Government control.[1] An institution, for example, in the Cape Province, with its long history of Government grants, is very markedly limited in its freedom both as regards staff and as regards curriculum. But this Nigerian institution receives a support from Government almost as generous as that which is given to similar institutions in the Cape and yet it has much greater liberty. From the point of view of administration there is a great

[1] See below, Chapters VII. and XI.

deal to be said for large grants; from the point of view of education there is a great deal to be said for individual freedom. How to balance these two is an educational problem everywhere. They seem very well balanced in the Southern Nigerian system.

4.

Schools of the Uzuakoli and of the Yakusu types are to be found all over Africa, and in British territory through the agency of Government grants the Yakusu type is gradually merging into the other. These two, however, must not be understood as representing rival categories of excellence. There are some large, well-equipped, State-aided schools whose efficiency is that of a soulless machine. They have a great deal to show the visitor, and it is all very impressive, and adventitious. Many of the small schools, with an absence or a minimum of aid from outside, with crude apparatus and cramped equipment, are turning out much better educated men and women.

It does not necessarily follow from this that smallness and crudity are in themselves excellences. They might quite well indicate lack of vision and initiative. But taking the subject all round, it has been my experience in Africa that small, compact, and simple places have the greater educational value. There are fewer cliques, everybody knows everybody else, and the corporate spirit of the whole is easier to realize.

Where girls' education is concerned this corporate quality of an institution is very important. Women in Africa represent—perhaps they represent it everywhere— the conservative element in society. This feature although it does not make for progress at any rate prevents the dispersal of the progress that has already been made. In Africa girls' education, like that suggested for Sophie in Rousseau's *Emile*, has been largely residual. They have taken what the men have left, or they have been trained for the man rather than for themselves. They have accepted that position, and thus one of the greatest difficulties in the way of the emancipation of African women will be the African women themselves.

Conservatism of this kind is a crust that is hard to break but comparatively easy to thaw. And it does not thaw in that type of institution which is merely "institutional." It only gives way in an atmosphere of friendly intimacy and fellowship, in the constant association of the new ideas with the more spiritual side of human nature. It is quite a mistake to imagine that the Native or indeed anybody, is vitally influenced by logical argument. The European often feels that what is so obvious to him ought to be obvious to anybody, and so he is apt to take a short cut and secure conformity when he thinks he is getting consent.

In girls' education even more than in that of boys the silent persuasiveness of a situation is effective where words completely fail. In many villages of the Lower Congo there have grown up more rational practices in midwifery due to the kindly influence and example of the white woman doctor at Kimpese. An unexpected effect of a small, but very well-run, girls' school in Southern Rhodesia has been to revolutionize the girls' attitude to marriage. In a country where the man assumes he has nothing more to do than to demand the girl in order to have her, a young girl teacher flatly rejected no less than five very much surprised young men before she fixed on a sixth. Her reason was not pride, but the fact, which they may have felt to be irrelevant, that she did not love any of the five whereas she did love the sixth. This was a greater proof of the truly educational effectiveness of that mission than if it had simply turned out expert cooks and washerwomen, although it did that also.

There are a number of small boarding schools for girls in different parts of Africa, yet all too few. One of the best known is at Mbereshi, a most remote place in Northern Rhodesia not far from Lake Mweru. From the small plateau on which the mission stands you look down across a vast extent of dense tropical bush, the haunt of lions, to the shining sources of the Congo on the horizon. There are five parts of the mission: the Church, the apprentices' shops, the girls' boarding school, the boys' boarding school, and a small hospital.

The girls' boarding school—with which we are here concerned—is a quadrangular brick building. One side is the missionaries' house; on the left are an open dining-room, four small dormitories and a pottery room; on the right are five dormitories; on the opposite side are an assembly hall, kitchen, and two class-rooms. In the middle of the quadrangle there is a circular grass roof supported on poles, the *nsaka*, such as is seen in every village in that country, and such as you can see in more substantial material in England at Witney, Dunster, and other places. Under it the children play or eat or do anything they like—it is a general meeting ground. This is typical of the school as a whole—it is run by the girls as far as possible like a small village.

Each dormitory consists of a small but high room, with a little raised brick platform down each side on which the girls sleep on rush mats. There are from twelve to twenty girls in each room and they are in the charge of two older girls. These senior girls have a good deal of responsibility, not only for the children under their own charge but also for the community as a whole. They are, so to speak, the elders of the village. They see to the clothes and the health of their own girls, and allot duties to each child, and in this way they are trained in the care of children. The whole of the work of the community, except the heavy manual work, is done by the girls. One noticeable effect of the twenty years' work of this school is that girls stay much longer than they used to do. There is a department for training teachers, and there are three day schools in the neighbourhood, staffed now by girls who have been so trained. School hours, strictly so-called, are in the morning only, and there are the usual subjects which go up to about Standard V. There are seven native teachers.

It is a place of discipline and of joy. There is a good deal of singing in both the vernacular and English, not all of it too serious. There is a band which consists of a shilling drum, ten straps of bells and ten triangles. There are drill and games. The dances are mainly the country dances taught in English elementary schools, but there are some native dances as well. Net-ball is played, and I saw a remarkably good match. In the teaching of everything, including Scripture, much is done by using the dramatic method. At Christmas time the girls stage a play representing the story of our Lord's birth, and it is accepted by the crowds of native people who see it as an act of worship.

There are definite religious exercises—prayers at sunrise and sundown, religious instruction, Sunday school and preparation class. There is a weekly devotional service for the senior girls and for the old pupils in the village. And there is a plain and beautiful school chapel which the girls attend in their neat and simple saffron uniforms.

The mission owes a great deal to its buildings, which have about them the beauty that comes from simple and inspired craftsmanship rather than mere utility or mere ornament. But the atmosphere of the school is quite remarkable—the sort of thing that comes partly from orderliness, partly from the sense of leisure, partly from intense seriousness, and partly from care-free joy. It is a place of true religion and sound learning which at the same time manages to preserve the gaiety of a holiday camp. It combines so well the Catholic and the Protestant elements, the spirit of liberty and the love of order, efficiency and courtliness. And it is in a situation like this that Christian character comes to its full fruition.

In a more advanced area, but also of this happy type, is the Slessor school at Aro Chuku in Nigeria. Here there is no " compound." The school is a real village, set out in huts around a " palaver shed." I remember this school very vividly as one of those few places where people were genuinely " in honour preferring one another."

These two schools are not alone, and one wonders how far their qualities depend on a system or on the personality of the teachers. If it is the latter, the aim of missionary training should be to produce the right kind of person rather than to provide any ordinary person with a few tricks of the trade. This is a trade in which there are really no tricks.

ACHIMOTA: THE ADMINISTRATIVE BLOCK

MBERESHI: THE GIRLS' SCHOOL

5.

It has already been said that in British territory the Government is coming in to supplement the work of the missions, not only with grants but by being responsible for higher education. The example of a Government school which I wish to take is Domboshawa in Southern Rhodesia, because it is primarily an agricultural school, and the main interest throughout the greater part of Africa is agriculture.

The Chartered Company bequeathed to the Government of Southern Rhodesia two schools, one in Mashonaland—Domboshawa, nineteen miles north of Salisbury, and one in Matabeleland, Tjolotjo. Both of these schools have influenced building and agriculture in their neighbourhood.

The school at Domboshawa is situated on a large estate of over 4000 acres, with 100 acres under crop rotation and a plantation of 35 acres of exotic trees. It began in 1920 with 37 pupils, and in 1938 it accommodated 260 and had to turn away three times as many as it enrolled. The annual fee is £4 10s. except for students in Standard IV, the lowest standard, where it is £3. (When the school began the lowest standard was Standard I.) Twelve bursaries are available for students. Nowadays all boys at school in the colony are granted exemption from poll-tax. The success of the school on the side of production can be judged from the fact that the annual yield of maize per acre on the farm has risen from $3\frac{1}{2}$ bags to $21\frac{1}{2}$ bags.

The school has a bias towards industrial work, not only for practical purposes but also to break down the conception that "school" and "work" are two different things. The school authorities have watched very carefully modern movements in rural education in England, such as those in Suffolk and Cambridgeshire, which have many similarities to the policy of Domboshawa. Twenty-one out of the thirty-six hours of the working week are given to agriculture, management of stock, building, carpentry, forestry and gardening, and the aim is to equip the pupils to improve conditions in the reserves when they return. The school has also thirty pupils following a three-year course for the training of agricultural demonstrators, who will qualify for full-time posts under the Government. Their work will be to demonstrate in the reserves new methods of farming, animal husbandry, building and forestry, to combat the ravages of soil erosion, and to foster the spirit of co-operation.

The institution consists of five " houses," each accommodated in a dormitory and each named after an old Mashona chief, just as at Tjolotjo the " houses " are named after Lobengula's indunas. There is a common dining-hall but there are also *madari*, the stone circles usually found outside every Mashona kraal and used as eating-places. The earlier *pisé-de-terre* dormitories are now replaced by burnt brick units, which are fumigable and less expensive in upkeep.

The boys wear uniform on week days. There is a council of sixteen prefects and other features of the English public school. The day begins at 6.30 and lights are out at 9 p.m. There are four standards, IV to VII, although from 1937 to 1939 Standard VII has been suspended until the commencement of secondary classes (i.e. beginning at Standard VI) in 1939. The language problem created by the existence of five different Mashona dialects has been largely overcome by the work of Dr. Doke of Johannesburg, so that by the use of new symbols and some measure of unification the local dialect, Chizezeru, has been retained as the vernacular of the school. The evils of denominationalism which at the beginning affected even the choice of prefects are present only to the extent that the school allows " right of entry " to ministers of all denominations represented.

The staff consists of six Africans on the academic side, all trained in the South but three of them Mashonas, and four on the industrial side, one of them from Tigerkloof, and a European staff including the Principal, four farming and industrial instructors and one schoolmaster. There has been a gradual rise in the qualifications of the African staff. Three of them have the Cape Teachers' Certificate and one of them returned in 1937 to Fort Hare to complete his B.A. degree.

EDUCATION AND TRAINING OF TEACHERS

A course for "Jeanes" teachers [1] was formerly held at Domboshawa and the students worked in the mission schools in the immediate neighbourhood. It was given up in 1934 and this, so to speak, "extra-mural" work was concentrated in one centre, Mungati, at which village live the demonstrators in training and their families. This will develop into a model village with day school, domestic science centre and other activities, many of them already in being. There was also started in 1936 six-months' courses for chiefs. They live in Mungati and have most of their training with the demonstrators. The training therefore is not concerned with any administrative matters (and so differs from such training in West and East Africa) although in the Colony a certain amount of civil jurisdiction is being given to suitable men, but the aim is to get them to understand and co-operate with the work of agricultural development,—an idea which might well be taken up in areas such as Basutoland. Southern Rhodesia is a kind of buffer state between the Union of South Africa with its attempted policy of "segregation" and the territories of tropical Africa, in which the Colonial Office white papers have declared the "paramountcy" of native interests.

We may compare Domboshawa with the Native agricultural college at Tsolo in the Transkei.

Tsolo is of course really a college for men, or at any rate for senior boys. A pupil must have passed Standard VI. before he is accepted. The course for students takes two years, and there are also short courses of four days for native farmers and elderly people of that type. In the short courses, lectures are interpreted into Xosa, but at the school itself, owing to the multiplicity of languages represented, English alone is spoken.

The course consists of twelve subjects—agriculture, veterinary science, stock-breeding, botany, forestry, fruit-culture, entomology, dairying, economics, physical geography, composition (the book studied is Xenophon's *Economist*), and book-keeping. There are examinations in both the

---

[1] See p. 261.

practical and the theoretical work, and diplomas and certificates are awarded. The land available includes two large gardens, an experimental plot, and a farm of 1800 morgen with arable land representing various types of soil. In addition to experimental work in crops there are also irrigation schemes on hand, and experiments to prevent erosion of the soil. There are four hours of lectures and demonstrations every day, and each lecturer also goes through the note-books to see that he has been understood! Reports are issued every week of everything that is going on at the farm, explaining why it is being done, so that the students are kept in touch with the whole of the work. The stud stock is very good—cattle, stallions, and large black pigs. Tasmanian sheep are kept and Australian black Orpington poultry. The cattle are not stalled, except for a short time in order to accustom them to handling. This in itself is an object lesson, for how often does one see native cattle going out to pasture late in the morning! There is excellent ensilage and excellent fencing. There is no elaborate machinery, such as incubators, otherwise the school would make much too big a gap between the raw Native and the one who has been trained. The fees are £10 a year, which almost covers boarding costs. The whole place gives a thorough good training in agriculture and is a credit to the Territories.

6.

Lovedale is part of the town of Alice and is eighty miles inland from East London and 800 miles from Cape Town. It is the largest and best-known missionary institution in Africa, and one of the most famous in the world. It began in days when very little was known of the Bantu people and when the whole of Central Africa was unexplored. The site was chosen in 1836, and two years later a house and a church were erected, and the school was started in 1841. It was typical of the Scottish pioneers that education went hand-in-hand with religion, and Lovedale represented in Africa the system that Alexander Duff began in India. From the earliest days there has never been wanting a due succession of men and

EDUCATION AND TRAINING OF TEACHERS 115

women to carry on that twofold tradition. The chief name in its history is that of " James Stewart, Missionary," whose monument with this inscription looks down upon Lovedale from a neighbouring hill. Stewart was a remarkable personality, an upholder of Natives' rights, and a strong believer in the intellectual side of education. His thirty-five years of rule, 1870 to 1905, left its stamp upon the institution, and it is constantly associated with his name. These things are to be borne in mind if we are to understand Lovedale.

It is a very big place, covers 1400 acres of ground, houses 1255 students, of whom nearly half are girls, and has a staff, European and Native, of 124 people. Its annual report is a book of eighty pages, and its class lists fill another twenty-four. The place itself is somewhat overwhelming for a visitor, especially one who comes into South Africa after visiting the small schools of the territories farther north. There is a central educational block, with lofty class-rooms on two floors, an assembly hall, and a tower, whose stone severity is relieved by a clock and a set of Westminster chimes. There are primary schools, a high-school building, blocks of dormitories, a large dining-hall for the boys and one for the girls, a library, a book department, industrial workshops, printing office, hospital, nurses' houses, staff houses, playing fields, farm, and how much more ? There is an open-air church. The buildings are not arranged in any regular plan, and although this has its inconvenience it adds to the interest and picturesqueness of the institution. It is well planted with trees, and is approached through a long avenue.

There are five schools at Lovedale, all aided by the Cape Education Department. These are the Primary School, which takes children up to Standard VI., the Secondary School (which means Standards VII. and VIII.), the Teachers' Training School, the Industrial School for boys and men, and the Domestic Science School. The hospital provides training for nurses and orderlies. On the roll for 1937 the numbers were as follows : primary 659, secondary 236, training school 214, industrial department 71, girls' domestic science 19, nurses 56, and journeymen. About three-quarters of the pupils come from the Cape Province, in which their conditions of life are very largely urban. This factor is important in determining the type of education that shall be given. In the Cape Province with a settled detribalized Native community, who till lately had the parliamentary franchise, there is naturally more possibility of a system of grading in education. Most of the pupils at Lovedale have come from other schools, and they have come for a special purpose. One of these special purposes is simply to get a higher education that they can get elsewhere, and although a number of those who are in the secondary school go on afterwards to become teachers there are others who come for the education alone. At the same time the system of syllabuses and examinations of the Cape Education Department and of the University of South Africa is a serious limitation on Native education. The examinations are the same as those taken by Europeans, and so the course of studies is assimilated to that in European schools. This, however, raises a question of principle which will be discussed in a later chapter.

There is a curious system of reckoning fees. These are paid in a lump sum for both board and tuition, and are graded not only in accordance with the particular department to which the student belongs, but also according to the food that he eats. There are three " tables," and in the case of the secondary school the charges are £22 a year for the first table, £25 for the second, and £30 for the third. To this division between students according to what they can afford to pay the students are said not to object, although as far as I know it is a unique arrangement.

The institution has a number of " out of school " activities. On Wednesday mornings there is a " Steps " lecture, so-called because it is usually given on the steps of the education building, at which the speaker gives half-an-hour's talk to all who come about anything of general interest, with a monthly talk by the Principal on current events. There are a Student Christian Association, a literary and debating society, a band, and sports. In these things, however, Lovedale does not differ from other institutions of the same kind in the Cape Province and in Natal.

The essential element in Lovedale to-day is its history. It is this which gives a unity to all its manifold activities.

From one point of view it is primarily a large industrial concern. When you realize that this missionary institution takes on building contracts which run into thousands of pounds, such as for a hostel at Fort Hare, or a location at King William's Town, it is obvious that this is no mere school. On the other hand, it is often criticized because it gives a type of education that is too bookish and cut off from the life of the Native community. It creates clerks, it is said, whose aim is to rise in the social scale and leave their fellows where they are. The later career of most Lovedale students gives little evidence to justify such a charge.

But what Lovedale really does, whether it teaches carpentry or Latin, is to put its students into a historical succession and to give them the sense of belonging to a distinguished company. There is a certain meanness about a good deal of African education. The Native is looked upon as a tool to be fashioned rather than as a new partner in the age-long process of bringing the world out of darkness into light. And so everything is so utilitarian, so very much *ad hoc*, so patronizing. It seemed to me that fundamentally Lovedale was different from this. There was a university feeling about the place, even in its buildings. The library is a real library, and not a collection of text-books. There are some thousands of volumes of standard literature, and a good selection also of novels and of newspapers. It is the sort of library that might be found with a different emphasis in an English public school. This in itself carries the business of education beyond the day only, and brings it into touch with the past. The dining hall is reminiscent of an officers' mess in England or a college common room. The walls are filled with hunting trophies, with glass cases containing sports cups, with portraits and photographs of principals, members of staff and old boys. It has a tradition about it which, to an Englishman who believes in this kind of thing, has its value in that elusive process known as " character-building." There are other missions in Africa with a history, and whose small graveyards contain names of famous men who played a great part in the emancipation of the Bantu people, but in Lovedale the sense of that history seemed to me to be woven into the life of the institution.

CHAPTER VII.

CHURCH AND STATE IN ADMINISTRATION.

I.

IN every British territory in Africa the ultimate authority in education is the Government. This is the case also in French, Belgian, Spanish, and Portuguese Africa, although not quite in the same way. In British territory the principle underlying Government control is that it is a proper function of the State to educate its citizens and to train them for citizenship. It is therefore prepared to give grants to missions of all denominations, British and foreign, for their educational work. In non-British territory the connection between the Government and education is much less organic.

In the Belgian Congo, for example, all official schools are run by the Roman Catholic Orders, of which there are 79. No subsidy for education is given to any Protestant Mission, but the Roman Catholics in 1935—during the slump—received over twenty-two million francs, and there is, moreover, a steady alienation of land on a large scale.[1] Apart from this, the Government left the bulk of educational work to the missions, and those of the Roman Catholics alone were subsidized.

'The Government in order to induce a certain number of missions to come to the Congo has agreed to subsidize them. These Missions on their part have undertaken to open schools. The Missions which came on their own account and without subsidies also have schools.'[2]

It will be noticed that this is quite a different system from that pursued in British territory, where the Government is

[1] *Annuaire des missions catholiques au Congo Belge*, 1935; *L'essor économique belge*, I, p. 256.
[2] Louis Franck, *Études de colonisation comparée*, I. (1924), p. 120.

CHURCH AND STATE IN ADMINISTRATION 119

prepared to subsidize the educational work of any missions, Catholic or Protestant, British or foreign, which is in accordance with the Government code for Native schools. When the convention was made between the Belgian Government and the *Huileries du Congo Belge* (Lever Brothers), one of the provisions was that they should be responsible for the schools in each of their five large areas of operation. These schools are all Roman Catholic.[1] I have found it, however, very difficult to convince Belgian Roman Catholic missionaries in the Congo that the British Protestant missionaries in the Congo were not subsidized by the British Government. They seemed to take it for granted but could produce no evidence.

The French regard Native education as a Government responsibility not to be delegated. Consequently Mission schools do not come into the educational scheme. There is no religious teaching in Government schools, but, following the ideals of the Revolution, the triumph of reason and the "moral conquest of civilization" through education are carried forward with an almost religious fervour.[2]

The Portuguese attitude to native education as a function of Government is one of almost complete indifference. The education that is given to their people by the Protestant missions is given for the most part against a great deal of tacit if not of open opposition. It came as a considerable shock to many of the delegates at the Le Zoute missionary conference in 1926 to find that they were reported to have "listened with great pleasure" to a complacent and quite misleading statement by the Portuguese minister in Belgium on the co-operation of his Government with missionaries.[3]

Where a Government has no educational policy as such, its relations with those who carry on schools are arbitrary and spasmodic. A kindly-disposed Governor of a province will make it easy for all efficient schools to do their work, whether Protestant or Catholic. A bigot or a weak man will be the

---

[1] Article in *Progress* (organ of Lever Brothers), July, 1926, by J. T. Irvine, Administrateur-délégué, S.A. des Huileries du Congo Belge, p. 51.
[2] Mumford and Orde-Brown, *Africans learn to be French* (1937), pp. 39, 68, 69.
[3] E. W. Smith, *The Christian Mission in Africa* (1926), p. 160.

cause of hindrances in the way. Where there is no Government direction, everything depends upon the local administration. The strongest protection, however, for any mission is not the chance good-will of this or that official, but rather the fact that its work has its charter in Government policy.

The arbitrary relationships that exist between organized missions on the one hand and individual administrators on the other are very liable to be swayed by moods of the moment. In Latin countries since the war there has grown up a certain nervous sensitiveness about nationality which makes personal relationships between people of different nationalities rather difficult. There is a habit of looking out for slights and for finding them where they do not exist. And the climate of the tropics does not make the situation any easier.[1]

2.

As an illustration of a Government system of education in British territory incorporating Mission schools, we may take the system in Southern Rhodesia as existing in 1938.

It rests on the Act of 1929 (No. 5) supplemented by a Government Notice (676, 1929) and amended by Order in Council on March 1933. It provides for the two Government boarding schools, Domboshawa and Tjolotjo, as well as for grants in aid to Mission schools.

There are six classes of aided Native schools, and the arrangements made for them are as follows:—

I. *Training schools for teachers.*—Candidates are to be between 16 and 25 years of age. The curriculum extends over three

[1] In Belgian books about the Congo there is a notable absence of any self-criticism, even about the evil days of Leopold II. And there are the most meagre references to work done by the other nations for their colony. An excellent anthology recently published called *Le Congo et les Livres*, which contains an extensive bibliography, nowhere mentions Bentley or Grenfell or a single British or Protestant missionary except in one footnote. It is there simply remarked that the campaign against the Congo atrocities was backed up by foreign missionaries (names given), and it is stated, presumably in order to discredit their evidence, that Casement and Morel were both condemned by the British Government during the war (pp. 158-59). An article on " Rural Schools " mentions only the Catholic ones, and an article on " Negro Education " is taken from that notoriously untrustworthy book *Le Sphinx Noir*, by the Comte de Briey.

years of 180 school days each and five hours a day, and it consists of industrial and community work as well as the theory and practice of teaching. Each school has a full-time European teacher and African and European assistants. Capitation grants of £5 10s. in all are made, together with a grant up to three-fourths in the case of Europeans and one-half in the case of Africans of the net amount of salary for approved teachers in the training department (up to a Government contribution of £240 for a man and £120 for a woman), for teachers engaged in industrial work (a varying scale) and for native head teachers of practising schools (up to £100 per annum). Average daily attendance must be not less than ten. No equipment grants are given.

II. *Boarding schools.*—These have the same length of curriculum as training schools, but it is stipulated that two hours daily must be spent in industrial work. The capitation grant is £1 10s. with a further £4 where a specially approved course of industrial instruction is given to classes beyond Standard III, and a further £1 for each girl of 12 below Standard IV who satisfactorily follows a course in domestic training. There are similar salary grants to those in Training Schools, with additional grants for teachers who have passed Standard V of £6; Standard VI, of £10; and for teachers who have the Union of South Africa " Teachers " Certificate, £15. The number in average daily attendance must be not less than 16. No equipment grants have been given since 1932.

III. *Central day schools.*—The length of curriculum is the same as above except that the school day is now four hours, at least one of which must be given to industrial work. There must be an approved head teacher who gives at least ten hours' instruction in the week, together with full-time assistants. Capitation grants are 10s. per annum with a further 10s. where at least *two* hours of industrial training is given to children over twelve, or £1 where two hours of domestic training is given to girls over twelve. Grants for teachers are provided on the same basis as those in higher schools. The average attendance again must be not less than 16 daily, and there are no special grants for equipment.

IV. *Kraal schools.*—These are schools with full-time native teachers, supervised by European superintendents or in special cases by African deputy-superintendents. The school week is 15 hours, to be distributed in any way that is convenient, and 180 days are as usual a school year. Suitable buildings and equipment must be maintained (there are no special equipment grants) and open-air teaching is encouraged. Grants are paid up to a maximum of 5s. per annum per child in average daily attendance, with a further capitation grant not exceeding 1s. for approved industrial work. Grants for teachers are again provided, and no grant-aided school must fall below ten in average daily attendance.

V. *Evening schools.*—These are treated as Kraal schools, except that the minimum schools hours are one hour an evening for four evenings in the week. The staff must consist of approved European or native teachers, and there is no special grant available for industrial work.

VI. *Special schools.*—Under this head come special "refresher" courses for teachers, and various schools for the blind.

Schools open for more than half but less than the full school year are eligible for a *pro rata* grant. Approved missionary superintendents are given grants under special conditions to enable them to visit their schools. The Government may authorize a grant of £250 a year, plus £75 transport allowance, to provide for each denomination one full-time educationist responsible for the oversight of all the schools of that particular Mission. Grants may be given for vacation courses, for publications of approved school-books and for community work.

There are several comments that might be made.

In the first place, the Director is given considerable discretion. Under an earlier system the conditions of grant were presented in greater detail. Such an ear-marking of grants is most useful at the beginning, as Kay-Shuttleworth used it in England, but it ought naturally to become unnecessary as the system becomes established.

Discretion in this particular case is employed also in assessing the merits of teachers.

Secondly, we note the great stress laid on industrial work. It is the only item in the curriculum that earns special grant. There is the possibility of exploitation in this, but in the present circumstances industrial education is a genuine benefit to the villager.

A third point is the relationship between Government and missions, especially in this matter of missionary educationists. The Government is concerned to get educational efficiency and the missions are concerned to have men of a certain religious persuasion. Such a mutual arrangement is quite natural, as it was in England in Kay-Shuttleworth's "concordats". The system operates also in Nigeria and elsewhere.

The fourth and most notable feature of this system

concerns the change in the conception of the school. It is no longer simply a place where reading and writing are taught. It is a community centre, vitally associated with the occupations, homes and social life of the neighbourhood. For this reason the Department of Native *Education* has become the Department of Native *Development*. This naturally raises the question of the segregation of Native affairs. No doubt in Southern Rhodesia to-day it is not yet the burning problem that it has become further south, but it is significant that in the Union the Interdepartmental Committee on Native *Education*, 1936, reported strongly in favour of Native education being equated with *all* education, while the *Native Affairs* Commission, 1937, reported in precisely the opposite sense.[1]

3.

On the West Coast, however, a principle of educational administration is in operation which has never been followed in England, although pressure is often brought to bear on the Board of Education to adopt it. The Education Ordinance for the Gold Coast contains these clauses :—

' 5. No person shall teach in any Government, Assisted or Non-assisted School, unless he is registered on the Register of Teachers, or on the Provisional List as may be prescribed.'

' *Education Rules*, 28.—All Assisted and Non-assisted Schools and other Educational Institutions shall be open at all times to the inspection of the Director of Education or his representative.'

The Code for Southern Nigeria has similar provisions, but also provides that any person who refuses to allow his school to be inspected—whether receiving or not receiving a grant —shall be liable to a fine of £10, and where any school is reported as being improperly conducted it may be closed, a penalty of £100 being laid down for non-compliance with the Government Order for closure.[2] It will be seen that no mission, no individual, can avoid Government control even by refusing to take a grant. The liberty, therefore, which

[1] See pp. 36, 37.
[2] *Ordinance No.* 15 of 1926, §§ 6, 10, 13. Amending Ordinances 14/1928, 25/1929, 7/1931, 42/1933, 9/1934.

is possible in Southern Rhodesia would not be possible in Nigeria or on the Gold Coast.

This is a logical conclusion of the view that the education of the next generation of citizens is the Government's business. Of course, in both of these colonies and elsewhere in British Africa, the Government is prepared to do the work itself if some one else does not do it, but on the West Coast it is considered to be the Government's business even if the Government pays nothing for it. In countries, however, where there is so much bogus education and so much imitation of the superficial effects of European culture, and also where there is a good deal of money in the hands of the Native community and of the missions, it is most important that the Government should protect its citizens against fraud. It has often been argued in England that there should be compulsory registration of teachers as there is of doctors, and that all schools should be open to inspection and closed if they are inefficient. Against this, however, there are in England very cogent reasons. The best guardian of educational reputations is public opinion, and it would be difficult for bogus schools to survive very long. On the Gold Coast, however, Native public opinion is inclined to be easily swayed by pretentiousness, and no Government could stand aside and allow its people to be exploited. And if, as is probable, the universal nature of Government control is mainly of use against incompetent Native schools, it would nevertheless be an unjust application of a colour bar to allow exemption to a mission school merely because it refuses a grant.

On the other hand, a principle which may be justifiable in a situation such as that on the West Coast is not necessarily justifiable in a totally different situation.

In Nyasaland, as we have seen, but also in every territory in Central and East Africa, there are a large number of mission schools run by Native teachers which cannot by reason of their numbers be adequately supervised. They are a continual sorrow to educational administrators, who are apt to dwell on their negative aspect, and to stress the dangers of the ignorant teacher. A good deal of the discussion at a notable Conference between Government and missions in

CHURCH AND STATE IN ADMINISTRATION 125

Tanganyika in 1925 turned on this very point.[1] There are well over 2000 of these " bush schools " in the territory, and there was much nervousness, particularly on the part of the Roman Catholics, about their future.

It is one thing, however, to set a standard below which grants will not be given, and quite another to set a standard below which schools will be closed. The conditions on the West Coast are much more like those in England where church and school are separate, even though they may be separate departments of the same thing. But in the less developed areas in East and Central Africa there is no such distinction. The school is an evangelizing agency, and indeed the evangelization of primitive peoples is not possible without education. They must at any rate be taught to read the Bible. A good deal of hardship would follow from the application of West Coast policy to Nyasaland or Tanganyika. On the other hand, it is not reasonable that the Government should be called upon to subsidize any and every evangelistic centre of any and every denomination. Accordingly, at the Conference between the Government and missions in Nyasaland in 1927, much time was spent in defining " what is a school ? " It was decided that a place in which writing is taught is a school, rather than a purely evangelistic centre, and as such comes under the control of the Education Department ; in order to be free of the control of the Government writing must not be taught.[2] This, as can be seen, is a definition really based on the principle that the Government intends to control the schools whether they receive grants or not.

4.

In every colony or protectorate there has been for some time some machinery which brings together the missions in the area, or at any rate a section of them. In the Union of South Africa there are a number of missionary associations which have an annual meeting to discuss common problems.

---

[1] *Report*, 1925. Speech of the Director of Education, p. 8.
[4] *Report*, 1927, p. 19.

These are organized by provinces, but the Transkei has had a missionary association of its own for the last twenty years. Outside the Union there are regular Missionary Conferences which vary in the nature of their representation and frequency.

The Protestant missions at work in Belgian and French Congo are united in the " Congo General Conference of Protestant Missionaries " and in various joint activities. There is a joint training institute of the British and American Baptist societies at Kimpese on the Lower Congo, a joint mission hostel at Kinshasa, which is of the greatest possible value to all the missions, and a joint magazine, *The Congo Mission News*. The jubilee Conference met at Leopoldville in September, 1928.

In certain territories, by the fortunate existence of goodwill on both sides, or by the statesmanlike leadership of certain missionaries, the Missionary Conference includes all the missions. For instance, the General Missionary Conference of Northern Rhodesia includes every mission, from the Seventh Day Adventists to the White Fathers. It was started in 1914, and meets every three years. The Conferences are marked by cordial relations among the missionaries, and it is obvious that social fellowship is a more solid basis for co-operation than a formal system of " checks and balances."

The functions of these Missionary Conferences depend very much upon their personnel. If there is considerable general agreement on theological questions, the Conference is able to discuss with some freedom the religious side of the work that has brought them all into the same territory. On the other hand, the wider the range of interests represented the more restricted is the ground common to all of them. Yet the Conference of Northern Rhodesia in 1927 was able to deal with native education, welfare work among women and girls and among men at the mines, medical work, leprosy, workmen's compensation, agriculture, language and literature, native customs, and native political representation. The Transkeian Missionary Conference in the same year spent a good deal of its time discussing political agitations among the native community, and the question of native education.

CHURCH AND STATE IN ADMINISTRATION 127

With the growth of Government interest in native education both before, and still more after, the visit of the Phelps-Stokes Commissions in 1921 and 1924, it was inevitable that such important bodies as the Missionary Conferences could not be overlooked. They represented the greater part of the people carrying on the work of native education. They also represented the opinions of a considerable section of the white population in their territory, and in this respect had as much right to be heard on behalf of their special interest as had Settlers' Associations or Chambers of Commerce in defence of their respective constituencies. Accordingly as native education became a more and more prominent subject of policy, the Government naturally turned to those bodies who knew most about it.

The extent of the possibility of co-operation has varied with different Conferences. The Government naturally could co-operate only with a body that was fully representative of all the educational agencies. Where a Conference was fully representative it became to all intents and purposes recognized as part of the Government machinery for native education. In Southern Rhodesia, for instance, the Conference was left to decide the question of the language in which books subsidized by the Government should be written.

In addition to this general recognition there have been set up in every territory under British rule Advisory Boards on native education. These Boards consist of representatives of all the interests concerned in the subject—the Government, the missions, the commercial and industrial community, and (although unfortunately it has not yet become a general rule), the Natives. Where the regular Missionary Conference has not been fully representative, the Government itself has first called a general Conference with all the missionary societies in its territory, and this joint Conference has discussed policy in a way which in other territories has been done at regular intervals in the past by the Missionary Conference alone. Two notable examples of this procedure were the Tanganyika Conference at Dar-es-Salaam in 1925 and the Nyasaland Conference at Zomba in 1927.

5.

The post of Director of Native Education is the key position in the organization of the work. He has to reconcile conflicting interests and to get their representatives to work together. He may enter the schools of all denominations, and no theological prejudice can shut him out. He therefore has the opportunity of knowing the educational situation better than the missions themselves. He has visited schools of all societies, which scarcely any missionary is in a position to do, and he is able to make comparisons and to formulate a general policy for all. If one mission takes the line that a certain thing cannot be done owing to circumstances he is often in a position to say that in similar circumstances only a few miles away it is being done, and what man has done man can do. On the other hand, he is not merely a kind of Government policeman to regiment the missionaries. To the administration he has to stand for the needs of Native education, and there may be occasions when he has almost to be more missionary than the missionaries. The Director of Native Education is going to fail in his work if he is simply a passive instrument of Government.

To be a passive instrument of the missions or of a particular school of missionary opinion would be just as bad. I remember having a long argument with a keen missionary agriculturist in Southern Rhodesia before the place of the Directorship of Native Education was filled. He held that the Director must be an agriculturist, because agriculture is the cry of the hour. This seemed to me to provide an excellent argument the other way. A Director's business is not to be at the mercy of a " cry of the hour," perhaps it is even to withstand it in order to see that the balance of subjects in Native education is not upset. It is a post which calls for independence of judgment and yet at the same time a wide range of sympathy. Many missions are exceedingly backward in the matter of education, and many are very far forward along wrong lines. By persuasion and example, firmness and tact, he has to coax them into better and more progressive ways. If he is dogmatic they will be dogmatic in turn, if he is merely accommodating he will find himself tied up in conflicting arrangements with different people. If he does everything by official routine his work will be merely that of a highly paid clerk. If he does everything through personal relationships and by word of mouth he may find himself committed to promises which he cannot honour. His work is to build up amongst all who are concerned with education that common mind which is the only sound basis of co-operation. He will therefore share his knowledge, and encourage initiative and experiment in other people. He will not let himself be overwhelmed by routine, so that any European or Native who has a difficulty or an inspiration may feel that the head of the whole system is concerned about it and is willing to take time over it. Such men perhaps are born and not made, and it is the great good fortune of the British administration that there are so many of them.

6.

The Natal system of native education seems to me to illustrate thoroughly sound principles. Education is not only looked upon as a co-operative process between black and white, and between the Government and the missions, but is actually organized on that basis.

The word " co-operation " is one that is very much mishandled. It is often assumed that there is co-operation where one part of a job is allotted to a Native and another part to a European, or where it is recognized that the Native is an equal partner in the concern. But there is only co-operation where there is a corporate mind, and co-operation in education means nothing less than building up this corporate mind. The presence of " representatives of various interests " is a mechanical device which often gives the appearance rather than the reality of co-operation.

It seemed to me that in Natal there was this corporate mind, and that the creation of it was due to two things— the *Native Teachers' Journal*, about which I have already spoken, and the co-ordination between the inspectorate and the head office. The inspectors were never away on their districts for more than about three weeks. At the end of that time they came back to Pietermaritzburg and discussed their work at leisure with the Chief Inspector and with the other inspectors. In this way they learned from each other and encouraged each other, the Director was kept informed of things by personal contact, each man knew not only his own work but to some extent the work of the other men also, and the inspiration behind the whole system was a common mind and not an individual will. In addition to the European inspectors there were also the Native supervisors, and the inspector kept in the same personal contact with the supervisors in his district as he himself was kept in contact with the Chief Inspector. The Native supervisors also were known personally to the Chief Inspector, and were often known, at any rate by repute, to inspectors in other districts. The *Journal* was an open forum for everybody, and, as far as an outsider could tell, there were no grievances that were suffered to fester through lack of ventilation. There is an Advisory Board on Native Education, consisting of missionary representatives, together with the Chief Native Commissioner and the Chief Inspector, and of representatives of Native interests who are co-opted by the Board itself. The effectiveness of this Board is largely due to the fact that the members of it meet each other in other capacities also, and their association is not confined to formal meetings.

From an administrative system constituted in this way several advantages follow.

In the first place there is, for there can be, a right use of the power of discretion. Each person in the scheme knows the mind of his colleagues, and when he acts on his own initiative he can feel he is expressing the mind of them all. Accordingly the letter and the spirit have each their proper place. A school which is fully in line with the spirit of the system may be absolved from irksome and often impossible adherence to the letter of it. A school that is out of touch with the spirit is at any rate brought into conformity by the rules.

In the second place, the inspector and the supervisor can exercise their proper functions. They are there primarily not to report defects, but to encourage growth. The Native

CHURCH AND STATE IN ADMINISTRATION 131

supervisors are not a specially trained class, but are men who have made good in their own village schools. Their business is to go round and show the others how it can be done. The European inspectors are themselves teachers. In travelling some hundreds of miles with one of them I saw him take Scripture lessons, geography, arithmetic, and Zulu composition. He obviously knew the ways of Native children, and was very popular both with them and with the teachers. When the lessons were over he had a talk with the teachers about their work, and with the missionaries about the arrangements of the school. It was a consultation among friends, there was candour on the part of all of them, and the whole school was encouraged by the visit. The same inspector had a series of articles in the *Journal* on how to teach geography, useful in themselves, but still more useful because written by some one whom the teachers had seen in the act of teaching geography.

A third advantage is that Scripture can be an examined subject. There is the same problem in Native education in Africa as there is in England with regard to Scripture. Because its subject-matter is "religious," profane hands must not be laid on the Scripture lesson. The result is in Africa as in England that the Scripture lesson is often the one which is worst taught, because there is no supervision, and because there is behind it the old heresy that the content of a book, apart from its interpretation in life and personality, of itself works a change of heart. In Natal, Scripture is as well taught as any other subject in the school, because it is examined like any other subject. But in the present state of Christian disunion and discord this is only possible because there is not only confidence of the missions in the Government, but also a common mind between them.

A fourth and chief advantage is that it makes possible a real understanding of the Native mind and thought. It is sometimes imagined that some easy "adaptation" is all that a subject needs in order to make it suitable for Natives. The doubtful value of this we shall discuss in a later chapter. What is much more to the point is to have Europeans who can speak a native language, who understand native idioms, native politeness, and the habit of indirect speech, together with Natives who in turn understand the European mind. These are not things that can be learned out of a book. They come by frequent and frank association in some co-operative enterprise.

Accordingly, although the political status of the Native in Natal is low and unworthy, and white farmers, white householders, and white juries are often notoriously unjust and bitter, the spirit I found in the Education Department was most encouraging and hopeful.

7.

It is often assumed, at any rate by missionaries, that the co-operation with Government is concerned simply with State interference in mission schools. There is, however, another side of it. It often involves denominational interference in Government schools.

In Africa there is the same belief which used to be held in England that " education must be based on religion." What exactly that means we shall examine later. But as it is held equally by officials and by missionaries it has not been allowed unduly to hang up the progress of Government action in educational matters. Where a British Government has started schools of its own, particularly for the training of teachers, it has often gone out of its way to seek a missionary head for its institution. At Domboshawa in Southern Rhodesia, at Kabete in Kenya, at Mazabuka in Northern Rhodesia, for the projected school for teachers in Nyasaland, and for the Community School for girl teachers at Hope Fountain in Southern Rhodesia, a Principal was in each case appointed from among the missionaries. The missionary Conference of the Gold Coast was asked to suggest names for a Principal of Achimota, and a missionary was appointed. Of these six Principals, two are Presbyterian, two are Anglican, one is a Congregationalist and one a Methodist. The denominational label is of no particular significance, and these schools have what measure of goodwill there is from all the missions alike. Indeed, the " religious difficulty," if there be such, is apt to come not so much from the other denominations as from the other members of the Principal's own denomination. In one of these cases he was looked upon as almost a traitor to his cloth, and the unfriendliness and suspicion with which he met were extraordinary.

The question of a Principal is a relatively simple matter to settle. Given a man of sense and ability he may be trusted not to proselytize, especially as no denominational teaching is allowed in British Government schools. The form of religious exercises that are carried on are very much of the type that exists in English " provided " schools under the Cowper-Temple clause.

Complications arise, however, in the boarding arrangements, and the solution of the problem varies. At Domboshawa, as we have seen, the Roman Catholics live together, and while there are not special dormitories for the other denominations they are at any rate recognized in the appointment of prefects. Futhermore, there is " right of entry " on the part of any denomination. In the South African Native College at Fort Hare there are three denominational hostels, a Presbyterian, a Wesleyan and an Anglican. In no case, however, is the hostel confined to students of that particular Church. The hostels are simply dormitories and studies, for there is one large common dining-hall. The system is a compromise made possible by the smallness of the numbers. The method of denominational hostels was contended for at Achimota, but it was successfully resisted by the Principal, and students were allotted to hostels quite irrespective of denomination.

CHAPTER VIII.

THE MOTHER-TONGUE.

1.

The question that meets us at the outset of any consideration of the work of the Native school is that of the language which is to be the medium of study. We must therefore consider the position of the vernacular.

It cannot be considered by itself. Language is one part of a people's heritage from the past. Other parts are their institutions, their customs, their buildings, their arts and crafts. Accordingly the esteem or lack of esteem with which the vernacular language is treated depends largely, although not wholly, on the estimation we have of the culture of the people who speak it. In these days a much greater regard than formerly is paid to native cultures, and we feel that every culture which is an honest expression of a people's life has a right to respect and to preservation. The case for the vernacular language in the schools is correspondingly strong.

The cultural argument, however, is not the only one. There is also the fact that the vernacular is the child's only language, and the beginnings of education cannot be made except through the mother-tongue. This we may call the psychological argument, and as it applies chiefly to the earlier stages of a child's development we shall consider it first.

2.

In all teaching we have to begin where the pupil is, rather than where the teacher is. To reverse the order is to produce misunderstanding and to prejudice hopelessly the child's approach to the subject. It is not helpful if a class is studying averages, and the teacher is thinking of an arithmetical device, while a boy is thinking of " something that a hen lays its eggs on," because his mother has told him that a hen lays two eggs a week *on an average!*

The language of instruction must be the child's language rather than the teacher's language. An infant in a village school knows only his mother-tongue, and for all practical purposes it will be long before any other is a necessity. Every word for him has a meaning, whereas a word in the European language may only have an equivalent. The distance by which an equivalent may be removed from a meaning is the wide basis of many language jokes against missionaries. And until the foreign language can be a language of contexts and meanings the vernacular cannot but be the medium of instruction.

This difference between meanings and equivalents applies equally to the study of the mother-tongue as to that of another language. Everything outside myself is foreign. The language of Robert Louis Stevenson is a " foreign " language ; it is not the language which I myself use. And if I am a schoolboy I have to do with it what I do with French, I have to " translate " it into my own speech. " Translation," therefore, is the name given to the process by which what I have in my mind reaches the mind of another person. It is not necessarily a matter of words. A shrug of the shoulders may convey my meaning to another person although I know no word of his language and he knows no word of mine.

The psychological argument for the vernacular, therefore, is based on the necessity for putting ourselves in the child's place, and leading him on from what he knows to what he does not know.

This does not involve " verbal inspiration " for any word that the vernacular may employ. In a mission school near Lake Mweru I found the European teacher was laboriously doing arithmetic with the numbers in Bemba, and he justified himself because this was the language with which the children were familiar. This was true, but a number is a different thing from a word. It is a pure equivalent, whereas a word is the centre of an association of ideas. To insist in saying in Zulu, for instance, " amakulu amahlanu anamashumi amahlanu anesihlanu " instead of in English " five hundred and fifty-five," [1] shows not a preference for the " psychological approach " over its opposite, but a doctrinaire preference for a very clumsy tool over a better one. An African number is not more psychological in its use than an English one, any more than the written form " 555 " can be described as English, Zulu, French, Dutch, or Xosa.

In teaching writing, reading, and arithmetic, it is obvious that the early stages must be done in the child's own language. But once we get beyond the early stages, is the same necessity laid upon us ? History, geography, Scripture, science, commerce, industry, represent absolutely new knowledge to the African child, coming to him in an absolutely new context. He might and does easily find a label to attach to these things, or a label may be found for him, but, as we have seen, the essential thing for translation is not the word-equivalent but the meaning. How can he get the meaning ?

This point was discussed at a Conference in Nyasaland :—

'*Mr. Bacon:* In hygiene, how can one express such terms as " germ " or " microbe " ?

'*Dr. Murray:* By the word *chirombo*.' [2]

Now if we look up *chirombo* in Scott's *Cyclopædic Dictionary of the Mang'anja Language* we shall find

'A wild beast, a useless thing, a weed ; an uneatable beast, a noxious insect ; a mote in one's eye, a sharp pain.'

As simply a word-equivalent, therefore, its meaning might be extended to cover the term " microbe." But it cannot do more than this, for " microbe " is connected not so much with a catalogue of animals, but with a theory of disease, and behind the name " microbe " there is a whole thought

---

[1] See C. T. Loram, *The Education of the South African Native* (1917), p. 233.

[2] *Report of the Native Education Conference* (1927), p. 47.

world which it is necessary to grasp before the word has any meaning at all. This may be done in the way of explanation, and just as a lion is different from a leopard, but both are *chirombo*, so the word *chirombo* may be used for " microbe " and the differences of kind may be left to further description.

The point at issue is not, is the vernacular better than English ? but, is this or that word-equivalent the more likely to convey the meaning that we wish to convey ? It may be one, it may be the other. We cannot always tell *a priori* which it is likely to be.

3.

If teaching ought to illustrate the psychological process of conveying a meaning, it is clear that we are concerned not with the African mind as such, but with its relationship to a particular subject. It is this relationship that determines which language should be used, and the relationship varies as between different subjects.

First of all, if the subject is the study of a foreign language, for example English, it is clearly a benefit to do as much as possible of it in English ; that is to say, it is best to use the direct method. We are then handling not two languages but one. There is, however, a weakness in the direct method, for it is apt to produce fluency in the use of word-equivalents without necessarily any understanding of their meaning. We can only appreciate one person's world of ideas by being able to compare it with our own. We need a certain familiarity with the possibilities in our own language in order to understand those possibilities in another language. A mere facility to find word-equivalents does not of itself help us. The failure of the average English schoolboy to get anything like a comprehensive grasp of French is due to his lack of knowledge not of French but of English.

In the second place, if the subject is a technical one, like hygiene, or if it is not a " subject " at all, but a new process, or a new invention, there is, as we have seen, a doubt about the language to be used. In the Mbereshi district the word for a motor-bicycle is *isidukaduk,* a very jolly and expressive word obviously made up on an onomatopæic principle. But it is merely a label for some newly-observed object, and is no more a help to the understanding of the object than the familiar appellation " Ginger " for a red-headed person is a help to understanding that person. And to feel that you have done all that in you lies to translate the idea " motor-bicycle " that is in your brain into the same idea in another person's brain by merely giving him the word *isidukaduk* is to be the victim of a confusion between words and ideas. It is quite different if you are translating *motor-bicycle* into French, for the French word has the same connotation for a Frenchman as the English word has for an Englishman. But where the idea is familiar in one language and unfamiliar in another, the word alone does not necessarily help. If the word is made up by the Natives themselves, like *isidukaduk*, the thing itself needs to be described and explained, and this may need English—indeed how can it *not* need English for many of the technical terms ? If the word is already there like *chirombo*, it needs to be very carefully differentiated from the other uses of *chirombo*, and it is probable that the English word itself would be very much better. The word *chirombo* already has its own connotation. The word *isidukaduk* never existed at all until now, and so its connotation can be built up round " motor-bicycle " and nothing else.

Thirdly, if the subject corresponds to something already there in the Native mind the case for the vernacular in the later stages is much stronger. Where his own history is concerned, meagre though it may be, the geography of his own locality, his own customs, games, handicrafts and occupations, and, above all, the ideas that he has about life and destiny, it is clear that these are matters for the expression of which his own language has already been used and is capable of being used still further.

There is, therefore, a scale of utility for the vernacular, beginning at the things which are wholly new to the African, —where the vernacular plays no part at all except in the very earliest stages,—and working up to things which are more and more familiar. The more familiar they are the more the vernacular can be used. It has been unfortunate that so much of the discussion about the language has been carried on as a debate on the subject, " Which is better, English or the vernacular ? " There is no such complete alternative. When we are seeking to convey meanings to a person's mind, it is this fact alone that conditions the use of one language or the other, and it is this, as I understand it, which is the basis of the " psychological argument." There cannot be a psychological argument " for a language " simply as such ; there can only be a psychological argument in favour of the use of a language for a certain purpose, and it is the purpose that conditions the use. In the beginning of things the medium will of course be the vernacular ; later on, it depends on the nature of the subject.

4.

We now turn to the second, the " cultural," argument for the vernacular.

As texts for our consideration of this subject I will give two paragraphs, one from a private letter from Natal written by a European teacher and administrator of long experience, and the other from the Colonial Office pamphlet on " The Place of the Vernacular in Native Education." [1]

My Natal correspondent gives five reasons for the vernacular. He says—

' We believe in the stressing of the vernacular,

(1) because it is the language of the people and it holds in it all the genius of the race. All that is permanent in their love and culture and aspirations, all their spiritual capacities, find adequate expression only through their mother-tongue ;

(2) because it is at present the speech of every Native in the country, and 75 per cent. do not understand any English ;

(3) because 90 per cent. of their letter-writing and communication is by means of the vernacular ;

(4) because in the case of the Zulu, and I should say all Bantu languages, it readily assimilates new words, and can expand its vocabulary *ad lib.* to meet new situations ;

(5) because 60 per cent. of our children only stay two years at school.'

[1] *African No.* 1110, Colonial Office, May, 1927.

It is clear that three of these reasons are based on practical considerations, and two on more general grounds. It would be hopelessly unsound to seek to replace the vernacular by English where children stay only two years in school, and where Zulu is the most universally used medium of communication. In reasons (1) and (4), however, what we are considering is a hypothesis. It may turn out to be true, and in any case it is a very probable hypothesis, but still, since it is a hypothesis, it is a matter for discussion.

The Colonial Office pamphlet, after a statement of the psychological argument for the use of the mother-tongue in education, goes on to quote from Professor Westermann another line of argument :—

'Mental life has evolved in each people an individual shape and a proper mode of expression; in this sense we speak of the soul of a people, and the most immediate, the most adequate, exponent of the soul of a people is its language. By taking away a people's language we cripple or destroy its soul and kill its mental individuality. . . . If the African is to keep and develop his own soul, and is to become a separate personality, his education must not begin by inoculating him with a foreign civilization, but it must be based on the civilization of each people, it must teach him to love his country and tribe as gifts given by God. One of these gifts is the vernacular. It is the vessel in which the whole national life is contained and through which it finds expression.'

After this argument, however, a somewhat jarring note is struck by the next quotation, from a Phelps-Stokes Commission Report :—

'This emphatic belief in the value of the native languages is not to be interpreted to justify the indiscriminate adoption of all African dialects as claiming encouragement and continuous use. . . . The process of selecting the native languages of greatest value to the native people is often exceedingly difficult. . . . There are also geographical elements that influence the value of a dialect, such as the number of people who speak it, the status and potentiality of the people as compared with others of a different dialect, and territorial proximity.'[1]

It may be said in passing that the juxtaposition of these two quotations in the same page of the same pamphlet indicates to the dispassionate reader our curious English

---

[1] Quoted from the Report of 1924, *Education in East Africa*, p. 20.

facility for both eating our cake and having it. If a Native language enshrines the soul of a people, that soul is surely not measurable in a geographical or any other sense. The language may be to the philological expert a " dialect," but to the people who speak it it is their way of expressing themselves, and presumably has as much right to a place in the sun as any other people's way of expressing themselves. If not more than 20,000 people on the Gold Coast speak Ga, while ten times that number speak Akan, is the soul of the Akan people ten times more worth preserving than the soul of the Ga ? Moreover, even if, as a matter of practical politics, it is not possible to train European teachers and print books in every African " dialect " that exists, whose business is it to decide what shall and what shall not be propagated ? If it is the European philologist's, is he not an outsider who comes to a nation to " destroy its soul and kill its mental individuality," which Professor Westermann tells us we are not to do ? And once it has been decided that a certain tribe's mother-tongue is not to be encouraged, its soul is no more violated if the people learn English than if they learn Ki-Swahili, except that the latter has an African rather than an Indo-European form.

In South Africa it is often said that south of the Zambezi not more than four languages need to be recognized and developed—Zulu, Xosa, Sesuto, and Sechuana. All other languages in that vast area have affinities with one of these four, and to know one of the four is to get the main stem of all its offshoots. So also it may be said that although Danish, Norwegian, and Swedish are different languages and have each its own literature, knowledge of one makes knowledge of the others a very simple matter. In spite of this, however, we recognize that Danish, Norwegian, and Swedish are different, and that there are subtle differences in the way in which they look at life which might be interpreted as indicating a separate national " soul " of which the language is the expression. In the same way, despite all the affinities between, say, Sindebele and Zulu, or between Chinyanja and Zulu, Professor Westermann would hardly allow us to say that the " soul " of the Matabele people, or the " soul " of the Angoni could find just as adequate expression in Zulu.

In East Africa Ki-Swahili is the chief language of the coast, and it is spreading into the interior. In the Belgian Congo it is a recognized language for the postal services,[1] and is commonly used in banks and offices. Its convenience, however, is more obvious to the European and to the Arab or Indian trader than it is to the Native. The European, instead of having to learn a number of languages, or instead of being confined to one small area by reason of knowing only the language of that area, needs to learn only one language, and he has a *lingua franca* which will carry him anywhere. The Colonial Office pamphlet seeks to justify the development of such union languages :—

'The advantages of such dominant and union languages in comparison with English lies in the fact that they are nearer to the mentality of the children, and especially the young children, than a European language can be.'

It is not easy to see, however, what this is supposed to prove. If Ki-Swahili, for instance, is not a child's mother-tongue, then the only sound psychological approach to education is through the mother-tongue rather than through Ki-Swahili. If Ki-Swahili is the child's mother-tongue it needs no further defence as an educational instrument. And if it is not the mother-tongue how can the people, Professor Westermann would ask, express their soul in Ki-Swahili ? It would seem that there are really only two useful courses open. Either the European must learn the Native languages, or the Natives—in British territory—must learn English. For the purpose of communication among tribes other than the Swahili, Ki-Swahili is simply a makeshift. It is a language which is easily " picked up " by different tribes, and people will continue to use it as a convenience. But this does not constitute a reason for the school doing deliberately what individuals do casually.

We may here draw a distinction between a " union " language and a *lingua franca*. In Southern Nigeria the various dialects of Ibo were blended in 1910 into " Union Ibo," which after twenty-eight years' use is a noticeable success. But this union was made primarily in order to create a

[1] *Codes et Lois du Congo Belge*, 3rd edit. (1927), p. 1485.

literature which did not then exist, and a literary language can always act as a focus for widely different dialects. In our own country a Yorkshireman and a Northumbrian speak two quite different dialects and may indeed be mutually unintelligible. But their written language is the same, and in the schools it is the language as written which is the medium of instruction. *A lingua franca* is not adopted for literary purposes but as a conversational convenience. An African case against it has been stated by Mr. Y. S. Bamu'ta, secretary to the Native Parliament of Uganda. Speaking of the strong objection of the Natives to the compulsory teaching of Ki-Swahili, he gives three reasons—Its introduction assimilates Uganda with Kenya and may lead to domination by Nairobi; it is a coast or slave trade language and as such it is " detested by the Baganda people "; and it cuts out English for the poorer classes—the only language which they know will be of any use to them.[1]

5.

The phrase that darkens counsel in a discussion of the vernacular is " the soul of a nation."

The idea in the modern sense comes from Hegel. Fichte's great *Reden an die Deutsche Nation*, delivered in Berlin after the battle of Jena, is the *locus classicus* of the idea in educational literature. After 1871 we begin to hear of the soul of the French nation, and in Alsace that soul was supposed to reside in the French language. In the Italian *Risorgimento* the Italian language was conceived to be the soul of the nation, particularly in unredeemed Italy. And indeed the idea of the " soul of the nation " is the inspiration and battle-cry of irredentism everywhere. In the Southern Tyrol, at the moment groaning under the Italians, the forbidden German language expresses the " soul of the nation." In contemporary Germany there is even a patriotic section which believes that the " Fraktur," or German Gothic type, enshrines the soul of the people !

[1] *Manchester Guardian*, Dec. 3, 1928.

What is this " soul of a people " which Professor Westermann tells us is most adequately expressed by its language ? Presumably it is a differentia, something which marks off one people from another, and exhibits characteristics which are all its own. If we press the question further and ask what kind of characteristics are they—customs of eating and drinking, architecture or art, sense of humour, proportion of idealism to business sense—it is extraordinarily difficult to get a satisfactory answer.

Part of the difficulty arises from the fact that a " nation " means so many different things to different people. If we take up *The Tatler*, " England," means the people who have plenty of money and appear to spend their time going to race-meetings. We learn that a distinguished foreigner has come over to get to know " the English." He meets a few titled people, goes out shooting or yachting with them, and talks political tittle-tattle with a friend at a West End Club, and he goes away to tell his countrymen what " the English " are like. On the other hand, if we subscribe to *The London Mercury* you are with a different set of people altogether. They have more to do that is worth doing, and they do not seek to hide the fact that they have brains. *The British Weekly* circulates among yet a different group of people, *The Daily Herald* among another group, and *The News of the World* among yet another. Which of them represents the real England, and where are we to look for the " soul " of our people ? Is it something inherent in the language itself, so that no matter by whom it is used, or in what context, it is able to express this " soul " ?

It is a constant source of fallacy with the philologist that he necessarily uses the term " language " in a technical sense. " Language " is to the philologist what " botany " is to the botanist and " geology " to the geologist. It is a world of its own containing a co-ordinated body of information with its rules and hypotheses and its place in the scheme of knowledge. It is, so to speak, a static study, and if it exhibits a soul, the relationship between the soul and the language is that of a jewel and a casket. Indeed Professor Westermann uses this very metaphor when he speaks of the vernacular as " the vessel in which the whole national life is contained" although the next words, "through which it finds expression," somewhat complicate the metaphor.

But to the ordinary man who is not a philologist "language" does not mean this at all. He is interested not in what the language is but in what it can do. He is interested not in the thing itself, but in its relationship to other things. The real authorities on a language are not the people who analyse it but the people who use it. J. M. Barrie is a much greater authority on "English" than Mr. Nesfield. It is the man with whom the thing becomes a trumpet on which he can blow "soul-animating strains" who understands the "soul" that is in a language. It is a dynamic rather than a static business.

But a language is not necessarily "the soul of a people," nor is it a necessity in order to "enshrine" such a soul. The United States has no language of its own—although "Say, pop, jump into a boiled shirt" is hardly English—but Americans have a different point of view from Englishmen about most things. Switzerland has no national language, but a Swiss is a very different person from a Frenchman or a German. If we are to hunt for the soul of Switzerland we shall not find it in any "vessel" of this kind. We may find it as some common characteristic that has been preserved through all the changes of its history, or in some point of view that results from a constant life among mountains, or from the peculiar situation of a neutral country, hemmed in by three great nations and able to take a broader outlook than any of them. But whatever it is or wherever we find it, we shall not find it in a Swiss language.

6.

We shall not, therefore, ground our case for the vernacular on any hypothesis that it enshrines the "soul of the people." This does not, however, dispose of the cultural argument. Professor Westermann's Hegelian hypothesis may be defective, but there is a great deal which is cogent in the argument of my Natal correspondent. "All their spiritual capacities," he says, "find adequate expression only through their mother-tongue"; and he continues, "Zulu readily assimilates new words, and can expand its vocabulary to meet new situations."

It is undoubtedly a great surprise to the European to find how flexible is an apparently "barbarous" language. This surprise is due to the preoccupation of all written languages with writing rather than with speech. African languages have been reduced to writing only since the coming of Europeans, and their absence of literature, particularly of indigenous literature, is used to discredit them as a medium of expression. The same attitude has been seen in our own schools in England where "doing English" or "composition" always meant writing. Speech was simply a convenience; when we were going to say something really worth while and over which we were going to take particular pains, we "wrote it down."

The "cultural" case for the vernacular is bound up with this question of writing. It is essentially concerned with the language as written rather than with the language as spoken. The cultural value of a language does not appear until that language has not only been "reduced" (as we say) to writing, but has also begun to produce an indigenous literature. It was with the appearance of Dante and Chaucer and *The Romance of the Rose* and the *Lay of the Nibelungs* that the Italians, English, French and Germans began to feel themselves to be separate nations with characteristics of their own. And the reason for this is that the written language brings with it that element of conservatism without which there can be no progress. It fixes words and syntax, but it does more than that. It fixes experience in such a way that it can be appropriated over and over again by other people.[1]

There are two places, therefore, to which we must go if we would find out the nature of a people's culture—to its literature, and to the ways of thinking of its *common* folk—those who have travelled least either in body or in mind. The one

---

[1] Discussion of the cultural value of a language depends on the interpretation of "culture" in general. See above, p. 19, and below, pp. 313 ff.

is universal, the other pedestrian ; the one looks out towards the world and brings gifts in its hand for all mankind, the other remains by its own fireside and knows nothing about the rest of the world. For any adequate estimate of the " genius of a nation " both of these elements are necessary, and we shall fall into misunderstanding if we omit either of them.[1]

There are two stories of the war which seem to me to illustrate the more domestic side of English culture.

The first is this. During the battle of Jutland one of our destroyers got between our own lines and those of the enemy, and was badly battered from both sides. She put up a heroic struggle which will always be remembered with pride, but she was in danger of sinking. In the height of the action two stokers came up on deck to have a breath of air, talking earnestly as they came up. An officer overheard them. One was saying to the other, " Wot I sez, Bill, is, 'e ought to 'ave married 'er, 'e ought ! "

The other is from *Punch*, but it bears all the marks of being authentic. Some of our Tommies one afternoon captured two Germans and brought them into the base. That night there was a sing-song in the Y.M.C.A. hut, and one of the items announced by the sergeant-major was, " Now, boys, Fritz and 'ans will now oblige by singing the 'im of 'ate."

Both of these stories may ultimately rest upon our insularity, producing in the first place an apparent indifference to thrills in which you yourself have part, and in the second a toleration which makes us extraordinarily bad haters, but I do not think that either of those stories could be told of men of any other nation. They do not depend

---

[1] Art is another illustration, provided that we can distinguish between a local art and those cosmopolitan standards which have no local habitation. The art of a nation, if it is truly " of " that nation, expresses the ways of thinking and of living of the common people, and it rises or falls according as their thought rises or falls. It was a commonplace with Ruskin and with William Morris that the art of a country springs out of its social structure, and there cannot be a noble art where that structure is mechanical or inorganic. The test is what the majority of people are capable of appreciating rather than what a few people are able to do. Thus Landseer more truly represented nineteenth-century English " culture " than Turner.

on language, for they are ways of looking at life. Native Africans also have their own ways of looking on life, and it is in these, as illustrated by their proverbs or in their conversation, rather than in a language considered in itself, that their characteristics most appear.

7.

The presence or absence of a written language makes a great deal of difference to the adequacy of the spoken language as a vehicle for ideas. Thus, from the " cultural " point of view spoken English stands in quite a different position in the English school from that of spoken Zulu in a Natal school. Leaving on one side the use of the language as simply a ready means of communication, it is possible to emphasize spoken English in the English school even more than written English, because there is side by side with this oral language a vast body of literature which is continually growing. But while in England literature came first and schools came afterwards, in Africa the schools have come first. School literature, therefore, is a makeshift produced by Europeans. Literature in the proper sense of the term will be the creation of the people themselves. The day for that is as yet a long way off, but one result of the right sort of education in the vernacular should be to bring that day nearer.

The spoken word passes and the written word remains. The written word captures experience and fixes it. The reader takes it up, and if the form in which it is retained is at all adequate to the content of it, it will become experience in him too. We all of us possess masses of impressions with no very clear thread or pattern connecting them. To read a good book concerned with similar impressions puts as it were a magnet under them, and traces " lines of force " which were not there before. They are still the same, but they have now a form which they had lacked.

It is in this way that reading creates experience,—it focuses impressions. And so long as those impressions are our own, another man's focus of them can become our own

THE MOTHER-TONGUE

too. We can use other people's words in which to express our own ideas if they put that which is familiar better than we have ever had it put before, and in a way which instantly responds to our own experience. Thus good literature creates in the reader the experience of the writer, and builds up a body of knowledge or of experience which becomes the heritage of the race. It is in this way that a language becomes adequate to express " spiritual capacities." This power is not in the language as a collection of words and syntax, but in the language as written, and representing the accumulated experience of a great many people on which all the users of it unconsciously draw. It is unfortunate that in Africa so much of the study of the vernacular is so entirely static—it is the concern of grammarians and anthropologists, who analyse and classify what is already there. It should, of course, be the concern of teachers and preachers, Native and European, using it, writing it, playing about with it, translating into it, and so developing it. We are beginning to get on right lines when we have Mr. A. S. Cripps encouraging one of his boys to translate into Chizezuru a poem from *A Shropshire Lad*.[1]

When we are considering " spiritual capacity," two questions may appropriately be asked. First, can we ever understand the " spiritual capacity " of another people except by understanding their language ? Secondly, can the translation of the record of another people's experience into our language develop our own " spiritual capacity ? "

To the doctrinaire classical scholar, or Irish or Dutch nationalist, or African philologist, the answer in each case is " No." An Englishman, however, can always give the answer " Yes," for the Authorized Version of the English Bible breaks all the rules of the " experts."

'Although men do not go to the stake for the cadences, the phrases of our Authorized Version, it remains true that these cadences, these phrases, have for three hundred years exercised a most powerful effect upon their emotions. They do so by association of ideas, by the accreted memories of our race,

[1] *The Native Affairs Department Annual* of Southern Rhodesia, 1925, p. 12.

enwrapping connotation around a word, a name—say the name Jerusalem or the name Sion :—

And they that wasted us, required of us mirth, saying :—
Sing to us one of the songs of Sion.
How shall we sing the Lord's song, in a strange land ? . . .
And a man shall be as an hiding-place from the wind, and a covert from the tempest ; as rivers of water in a dry place, as the shadow of a great rock in a weary land. . . .

When a nation has achieved this manner of diction, these rhythms for its dearest beliefs, a literature is surely established. . . . The Bible . . . is in everything we see, hear, feel, because it is in us, in our blood, . . . at once a monument, an example, and (best of all) a well of English undefiled, no stagnant water, but quick, running, curative, refreshing, vivifying.'[1]

It is with a start that we realize that this refers to a *translation*. Yet what Quiller-Couch says is surely true, and as an apt illustration for the expression of the " soul of a people " in its language it is worthy of setting side by side with the statement of Professor Westermann. I myself feel that it is worthy to be set above it.

What then is the point ? The most English of all English literature is something that is not English at all, but a translation into English from Hebrew and Greek. But for generations the Authorized Version has represented to the English not Hebrew thought nor Greek thought, but English thought, and, what is more, English thought at its very highest level. Indeed it has so much identified the Bible with our language that we can sympathize with the old preacher who scorned the Revised Version because " the Authorized was good enough for Paul ! "

That translation, moreover, was not in the contemporary idiom, but in the English of the previous generation. The language used was not just the convenient language of intercourse, but a speech which had been well tried in use and had about it a savour of permanence. This is a noticeable point in good literature,—it represents not so much the language of the day, but that part of the language which is well-set and likely to endure. It may arise from the circumstances of the moment, as Burke's *Reflections on*

[1] Sir A. Quiller-Couch, *On the Art of Reading* (1920), pp. 138-39, 155-56.

the Revolution in France arose from the circumstances of the moment, but it is expressed in a medium which is more than a mere fashion. It is doubtful whether in the beginning of things a great literature ever arose full-orbed, so to speak, from the conveniences of conversation. It has an ancestry, be it ever so short. It is tried out in all kinds of little ways that are unimportant save as *juvenilia*. And it is doubtful, too, whether a vernacular literature will ever arise in Africa until a flood of all kinds of books by all kinds of writers has familiarized the people with the written word. It is, I believe, largely through unfamiliarity with writing and through the absence of literature and of the material means of producing it, that so many deep experiences of the spirit among native peoples find expression in weird forms of action and organization, such as the Watch-Tower movement.

Without a vernacular literature it is difficult to see how the vernacular can represent the " genius " of a people. If there is no vernacular literature the spread of education in Africa will more and more put English into the position of the mother-tongue, for in the new world in which the African finds himself the European language is the only one which " fixes " his ideas and makes them transmissible.

The creation of a vernacular literature is therefore one of the essential elements in a " vernacular policy." And as this literature is built up, one of the first tasks of the people who speak the vernacular will be the translation of the Bible into their own tongue. Only in that way will the Bible become an " indigenous " book, for the present translations are and can be only makeshifts. It is as if an English version of the Bible had been written for us not by Wycliffe but by Maimonides. This may sound like a counsel of perfection, but we have to remember that only 200 years separate the age of Chaucer from the age of Shakespeare, and before Chaucer English was to all intents and purposes an unwritten language. In Africa, although we begin in thought centuries behind the age of Chaucer, the rate of advance is far more rapid than in those two hundred years.

Furthermore, the English Authorized Version owes its success to the fact that the translators were translating two things : they were translating from Hebrew and Greek into

English, but they were also translating into English the religious experience of Englishmen. That experience found an echo in the ancient literature which was under their hand, and the one task aided the other. And where this is the case translation is more than transmission,—it is creative, and the English words of the translators are themselves a literary " original." They are, that is to say, the immediate expression of experience as well as a translation of an expression of some one else's experience. In other words the translation fulfils the condition of all good literature—it is an expression of the faith and of the mind of the writer. It is the marriage of knowledge and experience that produces a new creation.

How do we stand in this regard in Africa ? If, as my Natal correspondent maintains, Zulu and other African languages can give adequate expression to the people's spiritual capacities, that expression must be written down in order to be " adequate." And before there can be writing which will be a literature, there must be experience. At present about three hundred African language groups possess either the whole or a part of the Bible in their own tongue. For the most part it has been handed over to them by Europeans who have learned their language, although no translator, of course, works without the help of Native assistants who have a Christian experience. In a few cases translations have been made almost entirely by Africans, but this is very exceptional. A much more general familiarity with the written language by African people who have an experience to record will be needed in order to create a vernacular literature. The work of Europeans is as it were a scaffolding, absolutely necessary in the circumstances, but still a scaffolding, in which the vernacular can be built up into a literature by the people themselves.

Africans are centuries behind European peoples in literary expression. Meanwhile there are lessons in the experience of the world of human nature and of destiny which men as men have been learning in the past, and which they have recorded in their own language for the benefit of the race. We do not expect the African in learning agriculture to start at the next stage to the men of the Stone Age, or in doing science to begin with Aristotle's view of the world. He leaps the intervening centuries and appropriates the lessons that have been learned. In the same way these spiritual lessons also are his to appropriate. It is very odd to find the scientist willing to put at the disposal of the emancipated Bantu all the resources of modern science which he can grasp, and to assume that in matters of the spirit his " genius " is going to be violated by the introduction of Christianity.

But translation involves two or more languages.

The forty-seven who translated the Authorized Version had to know Hebrew and Greek as well as English. The experience they had was something till then best expressed in Hebrew and Greek. We are therefore driven to the paradoxical but I believe the true conclusion that the development of the African vernacular cannot proceed on its own lines alone, but it must be accompanied by, for it is dependent on, development of English. It is the appearance of the European and the African language as alternatives that hinders the proper development of either. It is responsible both for the Baboo English of Lagos and Accra, and for the kitchen-Kaffir of the Cape. The founders of vernacular literature in Europe were all people who not only spoke the vernacular but were also masters of another language with a literature that already existed. Wycliffe has a vast array of Latin works to his credit as well as his English writings. Chaucer knew the language of the court as well as that of the people. A Bengali literature is being created in India at this day by Indians learned in English. And those Africans who are going to create a vernacular literature for the languages of Africa will be people who not only have a familiarity with their own flexible vernacular, but to whom also the treasures of the world's literature are available.

8.

It may be asked, How can all this be carried out in the schools?

We may here draw a distinction between a language as a medium of communication and a language as a means of the expression and creation of spiritual and intellectual capacity. As to the first, the vernacular will be needed in all schools, and indeed without the constant use of the vernacular for this first purpose it can hardly ever be developed for the second. As to the second purpose, the case for the vernacular is also the case for English. The aim is to produce an indigenous vernacular literature, but it cannot be decided in advance who are the people likeliest to produce it. Presumably it will come from those who have an education beyond that of the village school, and it is in these higher schools where the struggle over the place of the vernacular is keenest. But if the vernacular and English have to be developed together, literary studies need a place in the curriculum of boarding schools at least equal to that of manual training, and the farther men go along the educational highway the greater the place that these studies should hold. The creation of a world of thought in the vernacular is at least as important for the race as the creation of skilled carpenters and agriculturists, and unless provision is deliberately made for the encouragement of those who can do this thing it will not be done. For Africa is not like the Southern States of America. In America there is no vernacular, there is the same medium of expression common to white and black, namely English. The "soul" of the black folk, as probably even Dr. Westermann would admit, is as characteristic a thing as the soul of white America, even though they have no language of their own in which to enshrine that soul. The heritage of English literature is the American negro's heritage, as it is written in his native language. In Africa it will have to become the living heritage of some, in order that a vernacular literature may be the living heritage of many.

CHAPTER IX.

THE CONTENT OF AFRICAN EDUCATION.

In considering the content of education let us begin by postulating five essentials.

Let it be granted, as Euclid would say, that a child, that anybody, must know something of the world of things, the world of people, and the world of ideals, that he must have tools to use, and that he must develop his æsthetic and creative sense.

The world of things will include everything in nature outside himself, and himself also as part of nature. It will mean animals and plants, the wind and weather, land, water, and crops, the human body and "the great globe itself." The world of people is concerned with the lives and thoughts of men—what we mean by history, what we mean by literature, and what we mean by industry, commerce, and government. The world of ideals concerns the standards that men have set for themselves in conduct and in thought, the relation of man himself to his own life and destiny, and to the traditions about these things that have arisen in the course of human history. This involves both religion and also *a* religion; it also involves morality and manners. A man needs tools in order to find his way and establish his position in each of these three worlds. They include hoes and knives and reaping machines, they include also speech, reading, writing, calculating, and drawing. And the cultivation of the feelings, or of the æsthetic and creative sense, is concerned on the receptive side, with the appreciation of these three worlds which he is trying to understand —of nature, for example, and of the work of men's hands and brains and voices; and on the creative side, with the use of his own bodily instruments, and the satisfaction that comes from producing something where there was nothing.

Each of these the school should represent. There need only be one " subject " of each type, but there will need to be one. For a large number of people, for the millions of African children, that one will never be more than an " introduction " to each group. But at any given stage the five aspects of life will always be there. I have spoken of them as " worlds," but they are kingdoms without frontiers. They are all part of that universe of the human mind, which respects no divisions since it functions as a whole. And in a sense the more they overlap in teaching the better.

As these five essentials of education are aspects of life, they do not correspond to any hard and fast division of subjects in the curriculum. They are just as much concerned in how we teach as in what we teach. Nevertheless, in this chapter we shall consider the curriculum under five main headings which represent for school purposes these five aspects. The next chapter should make it clear that it is life of which they are aspects rather than a syllabus.

I. THE TOOLS A MAN USES: THE THREE R's.

1.

We will begin with a text.

In an article in the *Journal of the African Society* [1] there is an account of a school in Tanganyika whose curriculum was based on agriculture, animal husbandry, hygiene, and handicrafts. On this basis a very useful and successful school was built up. The headmaster, however, laments that that was not allowed to be enough, and he adds,

> 'Commercial pressure compelled the inclusion of the teaching of English, the three ' R's,' etc.: these were taught in conventional classes. Every effort was made to correlate them with everyday life and thus make them as interesting as possible, and the time allotted was cut down to the morning session only. It was felt, however, that they could be cut down still more.'

This is a really remarkable statement, for the two things put in opposition are not literary and manual work, but

[1] April, 1927, p. 243.

manual work and the three " R's." The case for manual work is clear enough : what is the case, if apart from " commercial pressure " there is a case, for the three " R's ? " It has hitherto been felt that it is impossible to run a school without them, but this experience in Tanganyika would lead us to think otherwise.

The three " R's " are usually put into a school curriculum because it is assumed that they are the tools needed for the acquiring of any other study. Reading, writing, and arithmetic are not so much subjects in themselves as the " form " in which other subjects are cast. Everything which is contained in a book, whether it is Scripture, hygiene, or fiction, requires some one's ability to read. In order to hand on knowledge, whether of past history or of a dog-fight, it normally requires ability on the part of some one to write,— although primitive peoples have managed very well without it. And how can even agriculture be understood without number and measurement ?

The early humorist who grouped reading, writing, and arithmetic under the heading " the three R's " clearly intended them to be taken together. But it is obvious that arithmetic is not the same kind of study as the other two. Arithmetic corresponds more closely to the world outside us. A succession of trees is present along a road and is perceived as such whether or no we can express that succession in symbolic form. One thing may be seen to be not only smaller than another thing, but sometimes by experiment we may find out how many times it may go into the larger thing. It is possible to deal with number and measurement without " doing arithmetic," and there is no need for an abstraction in order to explain them to some one else. But we cannot read or write without employing the symbols of reading or writing, and those symbols have to be learned. It is clear that neither reading nor writing are essential for the ordinary purposes of the communication of knowledge. We can convey our information by word of mouth, whether it is a most advanced subject or a simple story. Reading and writing are crafts, useful to possess, but not essential. Arithmetic, however, in the last analysis is a matter of observation and arrangement.

It is important to draw this distinction between reading and writing on the one hand, and arithmetic on the other, because arithmetic has so often been considered as the same type of learning as the other two. You "do arithmetic" when you play about with marks on a slate or a sheet of paper, but it is something quite different when you go outside and find how many times the end measurement of a field goes into its length. In my schooldays this latter amusement was made theoretical. We never went outside to measure anything, but we drew pictures of things on paper and measured the picture. This was called "mensuration," and was done only by very advanced people!

2.

That phrase, "how many times," gives us a clue to the proper end from which to begin arithmetic.

We begin with the relationships of parts to wholes, rather than with counting a succession of things. It is obvious that the number 8 as expressing a succession is simply an abstraction. We can have 8 of anything, 8 books, 8 pencils, 8 hats. "Eight" is a term brought in from outside whenever we have a certain clump of things together. When not attached to anything it is simply something in the air. It is a *name* of that particular kind of clump of anything.

"One-eighth," however, has a specific meaning; it implies something in which one part goes into the whole eight times. "One-eighth" is a comparison of one thing with another, whereas "8" is merely a symbol or a label. As soon as "8" ceases to be a label and begins to have value it becomes a comparison. I have a certain number of holes into which I wish to put an equivalent number of balls. It is a convenience to know that there are eight of them, as then I can select eight balls to fill them. But what I am really doing in this process is to select as many balls as will go *once* into that particular group of holes.

We can see this comparison in an example which appears

to deal only with a succession. If my son tells me he is "eighth" in his class, it has no meaning whatever until I know the size of the class. If he is eighth out of eight it is rather different from being eighth out of forty-eight. But "eight" in this case indicates not a succession at all but a relationship; it is really a measurement, $\frac{8}{8}$ or $\frac{8}{48}$, and it is the denominator that gives meaning to the numerator. To be eighth out of 48 is a specific instance of eight. We can have eight of anything, strips, marbles, countries, and it does not matter how many more of these there are so long as we have eight. "Eight" finishes the series. But we cannot have an eighth thing out of 48 without having first of all 48, and then arranging them in a fixed order so that the one we have in mind is eighth. If they were boys and were arranged in a row in the playground, we could dispense with the number eight altogether, for what we should then be concerned with is the relative position of my boy to the whole group. We should notice how many times the line from the beginning to where he is, goes into the line as a whole.

The fundamental thing in arithmetic is measurement rather than counting. And measurement involves a unit of measurement, something which has to be measured, and a figure which represents the relationship between them. The psychological order, therefore, is division and multiplication first, and addition and subtraction second. We first arrive at the numbers and we add them up afterwards.

In the process of "learning to count" the assumption that 8 is more advanced than 4 is a pure fallacy. The difficulty in 8 is not an arithmetical difficulty, but a linguistic one. It involves knowing eight words and their meanings instead of four. But whereas counting is a matter of vocabulary and the ability to attach the right name to the right thing, arithmetic is a good deal more than this, and also a good deal less mechanical.

It is important to remember that in our decimal notation, "ten" represents the whole of which 1 to 9 represent a succession of parts. The first ten numbers should all be learned together, not as names, but as parts of a whole thing called "ten." Ten of these whole things called "ten" make another whole thing called a "hundred," and ten of these a thousand, and so on. When we come before a class we have of course objects that they can touch and handle. In one school in Rhodesia they used sticks, ten of which made a bundle, and ten bundles made a heap, and ten heaps were put on a large flat stone. In this way 46 was four bundles and six sticks, and 483 four heaps, eight bundles and three sticks. 1496 means one stone, four heaps, nine bundles and six sticks and is quite comprehensible, whereas the idea of 1496 single things is not. The only numbers that have to be learned are the numbers 1 to 10, and with these it is as easy to go into hundreds as into singles. The "concreteness" of this method consists essentially not in the sticks that are used but in the relationship between them.[1]

Not all native tribes can count up even to ten. Yet it is interesting to notice, in the case of the Thonga, who possess only seven numerals, that these numerals are not the sequence one to seven, but the sequence one to five, ten and a hundred. These, moreover, are all nouns and are therefore names of things. The sequence is based on the use of the hands in counting, a hand being a whole of which the fingers are parts. Following our principles, they count thus ; one, two, three, four, five. Six is five-one ; seven, five-two ; nine, five-four ; and they enter a new series with a new name, "ten"[2] In the Efik language (Nigeria) the word for "nine" is *usuk-kiet*, literally, "it lacks one." In Mende (Sierra Leone) the unit appears to be twenty, as the phrase for "twenty," *rumu yira gboyongo*, literally means "a man finished," i.e. with ten fingers and ten toes.

Clearly, even in the case of primitive tribes, arithmetic, such as it is, is a matter not of the succession of isolated numbers, but of groups and divisions. The psychological method appears, therefore, to be that which is most natural to the African mind as well as to our own.

There is often confusion in the minds of teachers as

[1] The main ideas of the foregoing argument and many more may be found in an excellent little pamphlet by Professor Scrimgeour of the University of Cape Town, called *Arithmetic in the Primary School* (Juta & Co., Cape Town. 1s. 6d. net).
[2] Henri A. Junod, *The Life of a South African Tribe* (2nd edit., 1927), Vol. II., pp. 166-7.

well as in those of "educationists" as to what constitutes "practical" arithmetic. It is assumed that to say "five pianos" is more practical than to say simply "five," and that in the case of African natives "five huts" is more practical than "five pianos." But the number five is an abstraction whichever way you look at it, and "five huts" is no less abstract than "five pianos." Whether you use pianos or huts is no business of arithmetic as such; it is equally relevant in the reading lesson. It would seem that arithmetic, in order to be "practical," should seek to use the common, human way of thought exhibited by the Thonga rather than merely to form a casual alliance with the common objects of the countryside.

On the other hand it has to be remembered that in the case of Native schools a problem arises which makes teaching seem easier, but which makes it really much more difficult; namely, that of the mechanical nature of the untutored mind. Here, for instance, is what M. Junod says about arithmetic among the Thonga:—

'They succeed better when the effort is one of memory, and this explains why they are much more at their ease when learning the English weights and measures, entailing complicated operations of reduction, than when put to the metric system which seems so much more simple and rational. The English system requires a perfect committal to memory of the relation between the various measures . . . and, these being once mastered, all the work becomes purely mechanical. This is what natives like, whilst in the metric system there is one idea pervading the whole, and a certain minimum of reasoning is necessary for its use.'[1]

It is a reliance on this faculty of memory which would justify in a code for Native schools the appearance of an item like this: "Class I., counting 1 to 9; Class II., counting 1 to 20 by ones and twos; Class III., counting 1 to 50 by ones, twos and backwards."[2] Memory work also underlies a text-book of arithmetic that is widely used in the Union of South Africa.[3] It begins with addition and subtraction and

---

[1] Henri A. Junod, *The Life of a South African Tribe* (2nd edit., 1927), Vol. I., p. 170.
[2] Nyasaland Tentative Code for Village Schools, 1927.
[3] *South African Introductory Arithmetic for Native Schools*, by N. D. Achterberg, in four books.

so continues through two books out of four. Lesson I. gives the child the numbers 1, 2, 3, to play with, lesson II., 1, 2, 3, 4, and so on till he gets ten. The second book gives the numbers 11 to 20 in the same way, whereas in a decimal notation the next number after 10 should be 100. The children are also told to "learn by heart" such abstract propositions as these :—

$$1 + 1 = 2, 1 + 9 = 10, 6 - 5 = 1.$$

I have spent perhaps a disproportionate amount of time on this question of arithmetic, but it has been in order to demonstrate one point which is of cardinal importance in all teaching. What is called an "adaptation" of a subject [1] (a rather stupid word, because all teaching everywhere is an "adaptation" and fails of its object if it is not) is often nothing more than a glorified name for "the use of local illustrations." This any teacher can manage as a pure matter of rule-of-thumb, and it can be quite as mechanical and soulless as teaching became in England in the days of "object lessons." On the other hand, underneath every subject there are deep-set principles of human thought and experience which are the only true basis for the development of the human spirit. It is these which constitute the spiritual value of a subject, and without it there may be a certain trick of the trade which can be acquired, and a certain utility in knowing it, but its effect is quite neutral in developing the mind. The teacher has before him the choice between a mechanical process and what is virtually a philosophical one. It may not be in his power to do the latter, and in that case he must do the former as well and as usefully as he can. But he must not blame his pupils if they prefer a purely mechanical means for the accomplishment of a purely mechanical task. That the "philosophical" one is not out of touch with the native mind, the illustration from the Thonga has shown. The teacher there has this choice before him. Is he going to approach arithmetic simply through the occupations and physical necessities of the people, or is he

[1] See the Reports of the Phelps-Stokes Commissions on Education in Africa, *passim*.

also going to base it on what lies behind their habit of counting in fives ? This is one example of the type of choice which occurs in every subject which we shall consider, and so I have begun by elaborating it here. One wonders whether the preference of the Thonga for memory work was not in itself a criticism of teachers of arithmetic who failed to use the valuable psychological material in the Native mind.

3.

The Tanganyika school was also prepared to do without reading and writing. This is quite possible. Far too much has been made of the connection between education and printed matter, and in the more progressive schools in Britain a great deal more of the work is oral than used to be the case. Reading is helpful, and writing is not really essential at all. As we have seen in the case of the Nyasaland *maisons de prière* it has been held that religious instruction can go ahead very well without writing. If that is so in a more or less " literary " subject of this kind, still more is it so where there is a curriculum the chief elements in which are " agriculture, animal husbandry, hygiene and handicrafts."

But is this all that there is to be said ? The life is more than meat and the body than raiment, and, even if we exclude religious instruction, are there not whole tracts of experience to be developed by a greater command of the mother-tongue ? The African, as we have seen, is living in a world that is becoming more and more complicated. New ways of life came in with the white man, and the understanding of them is not a merely mechanical matter but involves a quickened intelligence. It may be argued that reading and writing are matters alien to the native African while agriculture and animal husbandry are familiar. This is true, but it is native traditional agriculture that is familiar, carried on by methods that are wasteful and unproductive. A rotation of crops, or the making of an ensilage, are better ways of agriculture because they are due to better ways of thinking, and they are no less alien to the Native experience than reading. You do not become better at agriculture in the same way in which you become better at playing the piano—by practice. You become better by having new ideas about it, or by grasping the new ideas that are presented to you. The story of the native headman in Natal who cultivated his employer's land in the most approved European style, but his own in the most approved style of the Native, is relevant in this context.[1] Improvement of a manual process should go hand in hand with improvement in a mental one, and there comes a point in all physical development where no further progress is possible apart from a mental change.

To assume that reading brings about this mental change would be to fall into what the pedagogues call the " formal training " fallacy. No subject-matter *in itself* produces mental change, and learning to read may be as imitative and mechanical as learning to decorticate sisal. But the mind is developed not so much by one agency acting alone as by a number of agencies all operating at different angles. The actual business of going into the fields and being shown a new way of tilling the ground awakens the mind. So also does the power to grasp a new method of gathering ideas, which is what reading is. So also does the power to grasp a new method of communicating them, which is writing. All these different kinds of processes going on together are much more likely to awaken a permanent all-round response than only one of them. One by itself may lead only to rule-of-thumb imitation along its own line. And what, presumably, we are after is training a man's intelligence, and not just training his " intelligence-in-agriculture." Indeed the proper grasp of any subject involves the ability to look at it all round and see it in and out of its setting. And if we plead for more than one kind of approach to the African mind it is because this is no less necessary for every mind.

But this is not all. In spite of the Tanganyika school experiment we must hold to it that there is a closer connection between reading and writing and the development of intelligence than is brought about by any manual work.

---

[1] Maurice S. Evans, *Black and White in South East Africa* (2nd edit., 1916), p. 33.

In saying this I am liable to be misunderstood, and I am going to qualify it in a moment.[1] The connection rests, however, on the relation between thought and its expression.

It depends on how we look at language. If language is simply a means of expressing wants or of telling a story or some plain and simple utilitarian process of that kind, we are looking at it primarily in connection with an outside situation. For many of these things indeed no language is needed at all save the language of signs or of acting. The native African finds it much easier to act a story than to tell it. In the case of agricultural work all we should need is a convenient method of telling another person what to do, and the spoken word would be quite enough.

But if we look at language from another point of view, and connect it not so much with the outside situation as with the mind which is trying to deal with that situation, it is obviously more than a mere convenience. It is an outward sign of an inward spirit, and of a particularly intimate relationship between them. Language is an expression of ideas but it also is a means of creating new ideas. Poverty of language is often due to poverty of ideas, but poverty of ideas is no less often due to poverty of language. Every idea within us that cannot find expression (either in language or in some other way) may be alive and vigorous, but it is sterile. It can only produce something else, and be fruitful of more ideas, if it can find expression. For expression is not only an objectifying of an idea; it gives it order and relationship, and so to speak " fixes " it. From this we can go on to further thinking.

We may take a simple analogy from the use of names. I am continually seeing flat things made of wood which have four legs. The first thing I notice when I come into a room is one of these objects, and I can think of nothing else in the room because this strange thing disturbs me. Every time I meet it it disturbs me because I have no name for it. Then I am told it is a " table," and gradually it ceases to be a disturbance. I have now control over it, I take it for

[1] P. 168 below.

granted, and my mind is free to go on to something else,—either the different kinds of tables, whereas formerly I had only noticed undifferentiated flat four-legged objects, or some new objects altogether, such as chairs. This control given by the knowledge of the name is probably the source of the primitive reverence for names. The name is somehow the heart of the thing itself.

In this way language is related to ideas, and a control over and development of language means a control over and development of ideas. We have only to study the difference in our own country between an educated and an uneducated person to see how much this difference coincides with a control, or with an absence of control, over the mother-tongue.

This, of course, may be said still to render reading unnecessary; language can be developed orally. This is true, but only up to a point. One cause of the lack of development of the African peoples would appear to be the absence among them of a written language. Progress so far as it has gone has not been " fixed " in this way for the generations that come after. Progress involves a conservative as well as what is called a " progressive " element, and there can be no great advance without both. That the Bantu races of Africa have within them a strong element of progress is undeniable when you visit the Transkei or Fort Hare or the Bantu Social Centre in Johannesburg. They have not, however, until recently had this conservative element.

It may be objected to this that there is such a thing as memory and oral tradition. This is quite true, and every human society has gone through this stage. But memory is not thought; it is rather a substitute for thought. It is an association, perhaps no more than a " reflex." It leads back to no principle of reasoning, and therefore gives us no data for further reasoning. We only remember what has happened, whether it be an event, a story, or a process of thought, and a national heritage is thereby conceived not as something developed and multiplied through use, but as a talent hid in a napkin. Memory is not the same thing as conservatism, for it acts as a barrier to progress rather than as an assistance to it. Where memory is substituted for

AN ARITHMETIC LESSON, DOMBOSHAWA

A PHYSIOLOGY LESSON, KIMPESE

thought, everything must be done in the "remembered" way, and this easily becomes an authority which is opposed to any advance. The letter has killed, whereas the spirit makes alive.

And of course the reason is that while memory is an association it is a casual and not a *causal* association. We have seen how very weak is the idea of causation among untutored minds everywhere, whether in the African bush or in Shoreditch. The development of education on the intellectual side is concerned with building up in the mind a satisfactory sense of causation. And in order to do this it is obvious that we cannot always be beginning at the beginning. We must be able to establish a position and work from it to the next position. We need what Locke calls "intermediate authorities," from which we can always go back to first principles, but from which we can also go on to further knowledge. It is difficult to see how this can be done on a purely oral basis.

If there is reading there must be writing. If we take in we must also give out, otherwise we become incapable of even taking in. Just as the greater control of language helps us to think, so the attempt to express ourselves in writing gives us a greater control of language. We can think without the necessity of being able to read, but we shall get much further in our thinking if we are able to read. We can learn to read without needing to write, but writing will help our reading and it will also very materially help our thinking.

The compilation of books in a native language assisted by the Natives themselves has been of the greatest help in getting them to classify their minds and evolve new ideas. Such a book is the very considerable treatise on Physiology compiled at Kimpese in the Lower Congo. Of a different, but perhaps an even more valuable, kind was *The Band's Gazette*, an unauthorized publication of the boys of the printing shop in the Government School at Dar-es-Salaam in 1927. They were very proud of the school drum-and-fife band, and they resolved to boom it. They therefore collected the old wooden blocks lying about in the shop and wrote round each picture a story in Swahili about the band. Some of the illustrations mightily taxed their ingenuity. One of them was a cut of a tent, and the story ran like this—" Here is a tent. Why hasn't it been taken down ? Because everybody has gone off to hear the band." A picture of a hospital patient surrounded only by nurses suggested that there were no doctors about because they too had gone off to hear the band ! This, it may be remembered, is exactly the kind of squib that George Morrow and E. V. Lucas once made out of the illustrations from Whiteley's Catalogue.[1] *The Band's Gazette* had, I thought, a real " apologetic " value for the African mentality.

4.

I come now to the qualification which I mentioned earlier.[2]

Agriculture will, for a long time, have this great advantage over reading and writing in the village school; it is always possible to do a lot of it, whereas it is not possible to do a lot of reading. In a great many schools in Natal and elsewhere the children drop off as soon as they have learned to read and write. This is why they come—to acquire a new trick which will help them to puzzle their way through a Government notice or through a letter, or help them to write a line to a relation in Johannesburg. It gives also a sense of importance and power, but as a development of the mind it does very little. All the foregoing argument may be quite true, and the connection between progress and the written language be granted, without it being in the least true that *in a given case* the particular result follows. Clearly it would be quite possible in the time-table of the Tanganyika school to cut down the time for the three R's still more, and yet not deprive the children of that amount of reading and writing which will be of practical utility.

This, however, is not an argument against reading and writing, but an argument of an entirely different kind.

---

[1] *What a Life*, by E. V. Lucas and George Morrow.
[2] P. 165 above.

THE CONTENT OF AFRICAN EDUCATION 169

You cannot read without reading something, and often there is no native literature for the child to read, or what there is has very little variety in it. The constant association of reading with religious instruction, in Africa as a century ago in England, prevents the development of reading·as an educational medium. It needs to be given other associations as well, and until there can be built up for Native peoples a large, or at any rate a varied literature, reading will always suffer by the side of agriculture or handicrafts in the poverty of its " apparatus."

It is astonishing how very little some missions do in this way with their printing presses. One Scottish mission, with printing machines driven by power, had the most meagre output of vernacular literature, although it accepted contracts for printing lengthy reports of missionary conferences. On the other hand the mission press of the Dutch mission at Morgenster, near the Zimbabwe ruins, whose equipment consists of only a small hand press and a guillotine, publishes twenty books in the vernacular. These include devotional books, books on hygiene, action songs, school management, nature study, and an English—Chikaranga dictionary. The price of each was threepence, and the average number of pages fifty. In addition to this they also publish a magazine, *The Mashonaland Quarterly*, in the four chief languages of Mashonaland, each article with an accompanying English translation, which is contributed to by members of different missions in the area. I have already mentioned the magazine of the Mkhoma mission, *Mthenga*, and we have seen the excellent use that the Yakusu mission makes of its small press.

From an educational point of view, however, this is not enough. The value is, of course, very great, but it lies in the information conveyed rather than in the means of conveying it. A Native literature will only be created by Native people who feel they have something to say and that there is a better and a worse way of saying it. This, of course, is a long way removed from the three R's and we shall come back to it in a later context. But reading and writing are the indispensable basis of any such development.

II. THE WORLD OF VALUES AND IDEALS: SCRIPTURE AND MORAL INSTRUCTION.

1.

We must at the outset draw a quite sharp distinction between " religion " and " religious instruction," and between " morality " and " moral instruction." The former in each case is a matter of conduct and attitude; the latter is a matter of words. At the same time the words are important, because they give a certain amount of information about the conduct and the attitude. We shall not, I hope, fall into the fallacy of imagining that in studying Scripture we are studying religion, or that moral instruction is the same thing as training in character. These two highly desirable qualities, religion and morality, belong to the way in which the school work is carried on rather than to any specific subjects themselves. They will be the concern of the next chapter.

The unfortunate identification of Christianity with Scripture has helped, as has been said elsewhere, to make the Scripture lesson that which is often taught worst of all. It is taught worst (not only in Africa but also in England) because no special provision is made for the training of people to teach it better. This hiatus is due partly to sectarian jealousies, partly to the belief that words of Scripture, *however taught*, of themselves work wonders in the human heart without bothering the human intelligence to understand them, and partly it is due to the belief that a good man who is a bad teacher is better able to teach Scripture than a good teacher who is not a particularly good man. Each of these three reasons is ultimately based on the confusion between religion and the words which tell you about religion. Accordingly, native education is often held to be " based on religion " when all that is meant is that the Bible is used in the schools.

Let us see how these things work out in practice, in the village schools and elsewhere.

Here, for instance, were the Scripture requirements of

a certain Diocesan Examination for Native Women Teachers, in 1927 :—

Preliminary: Genesis. St. Luke (narrative and parables). Church Catechism.
Second: Israel in Egypt and the Wilderness. St. Mark. Acts i.-viii. 2.
Third: Joshua and the History as far as the Division of the Kingdoms. St. Matthew. Acts viii.-xxviii.
Fourth: The Kings of Israel and Judah. The Captivity and Return. A selection of minor Prophets. Outlines of their teaching. St. John's Gospel. One Epistle.

With theological or denominational questions I am not here concerned. This syllabus has been chosen at random as typical of most and better than many, for at any rate this particular mission does not labour under the delusion that its " religious training " is adequately met by merely teaching these subjects in school.

But as a teacher I ask myself, which parts of the Bible have the most educational value, and how am I to grade them ? The Bible is in many ways the most highly educational book that exists, and it is so for children of all ages. But it does not yield its fruits anyhow, and the teacher's concern is not with the Bible as such but with the process of relating the Bible to the child so that the child will get the maximum benefit.

It is clear at the first glance that in this syllabus no such relationship has been attempted, at any rate in the Old Testament. Some of the narrative chapters of Genesis are excellent to begin with, the story of Isaac and Rebekah, for example, and the story of Joseph. But the peerless idyll of the Book of Ruth has no place in the scheme, while the battles and sieges of Joshua are apparently studied in their entirety. Those old friends the Kings of Israel and Judah are disappearing from English syllabuses but rule unopposed in Africa. There is no Hebrew poetry in the scheme, the Psalms do not appear, nor the Book of Job, although the problem of the Book of Job arose in a society not dissimilar to that of the Bantu. Many of the dullest parts of the Old Testament are put in, and the sublimity of Isaiah and **Jeremiah** the Native teachers altogether miss.

A scheme of English reading, or of nature study, drawn up in a similar sequence to this Scripture scheme, would at once appear to be wrong. Why does it *not* appear wrong in the case of Scripture ? The reasons are, I think, one or more of those that I have mentioned, while the ultimate reason is a confusion of thought as to what the teaching of Scripture really can do.

2.

Christianity is a historical religion, and it cannot be understood without reference to its historical documents. Accordingly if Christianity is an interest in the minds of the children who come to school and of the people who send them, this intellectual side of the Christian religion is a legitimate subject for school study. But it should be unfolded to them with revelation suited to their growth. The teacher is not absolved from the use of his intelligence in Scripture any more than in arithmetic, and the belief that the words of Scripture will somehow of themselves work a change is a residual belief in magic.

The real argument for any subject to be in a school curriculum must be in the last analysis an educational one. But in England the case for the Bible in the schools has scarcely ever been argued from the educational standpoint. It has usually been argued on lines of doctrine. Both Huxley and Matthew Arnold in their day emphasized the educational value of the Bible. But the schools were not allowed to see it in this light, for the denominations kept these matters in their own hands, and in the undenominational schools the Bible had to be taught " without note or comment." The teachers soon came to lose all interest in the Scripture lessons, and the ignorance of the British soldiers during the War of the simplest truths of Christianity was the fruit of treating Scripture as a denominational issue.[1]

Recently, however, we have come to see that the schools are missing the most valuable educational material that we possess. Accordingly we have the Cambridgeshire and other

---
[1] See the inquiry, *The Army and Religion* (1919).

County Committees drawing up syllabuses of religious teaching, we have the publication of various selected Bibles arranged on educational lines, we have the use in some schools of the little manuals of Dr. Fosdick, and, most significant of all, we have the Authorized Version taking its place in anthologies and general reading books for use in the English lesson. This of course is not the same thing as the building up of "religion," and our boys and girls do not become Christians as a result of the labours of Sir Arthur Quiller-Couch. But it is a recognition of the real place of the Bible in a school curriculum, not claiming more for it than it can do, but not claiming less for it than the best place possible. Under the older system the Bible in the schools was quite negligible, and by pretending that it taught religion it was not allowed even to teach history. But under new auspices, by using it for its literary value, it is having a greater opportunity than ever before of becoming a basis for the growth of the religious spirit.

To this argument the verbal inspirationist, Catholic or Protestant, is unfortunately impervious, for his concern frankly is not with education but with propaganda. The essence of propaganda is unexamined testimony, its aim conformity and its spirit fear. It knows nothing of that glad risk undertaken by every good teacher when he spreads out all his treasures before his pupils and leaves them free to choose, believing that if he has taught them aright they will exercise the right motives in their choice although they may not necessarily choose as he does.[1] Nor does the propagandist care much about relating a subject to the pupils' minds, needs, and circumstances. It is astonishing to recall that in Uganda at this moment there are Native teachers doing seventeen years of Latin as a preparation for the ministry![2]

At a mission in Rhodesia I heard it argued that the "literary" study of the Bible was opposed to its "devotional" use. It is difficult to know what this means except

[1] It has been a great misfortune to the English Catholics that the ideas of Newman did not carry the day with his co-religionists. For Newman had a strong belief in the teacher and no use at all for the seminarist.

[2] For examples of this type of "education," see the Phelps-Stokes Report, *Education in East Africa* (1924), p. 161.

that it involves a lack of appreciation of literature. If the subject of a literary study is a devotional book, that study cannot be literary without being devotional; if it is a historical book, a literary study must include an appreciation of history. How can we assess the aptitude of the means an author uses unless we have some understanding of his end in view? Literature is a study that is concerned with the spirit of man and the way in which it expresses itself in various circumstances. It is not a study of form only, but of the relation of form to content.

Opposed to this is that " devotional " study of the Bible which consists not in letting the Bible speak for itself, but in reading into it things that are not there. I remember the objector referred to above giving an example of the " devotional " use of the Bible at prayers next morning. The lesson was the incomparable twenty-third Psalm, and the reading of it was punctuated throughout with banal remarks. The whole effect of the Psalm was thereby lost, buried under a load of irrelevant comment. Yet it is precisely this kind of thing, although not always in so extreme a form, which so often passes for " religious instruction," and, by a strange perversion, for a " reverent handling of the Scriptures."

3.

Africa is a generation or more behind England in methods of teaching and in school-books, and I am afraid it may be a long time before the African school is able to make the same educational use of the Bible as we are beginning to make of it in this country. But when that day comes there will be at least two great advantages to gain in the teaching of it.

The first will be to bring out the relation between the Land and the Book much more than at present. The Bible —all of it—presupposes Palestine, its geography, history, and customs, and the customs are much nearer to those of the Bantu than they are to ours. The historical method has illuminated the whole background of the Old Testament, and has revealed a society not unlike that of the African village to-day. It was to this society that the prophets spoke, and it was this primitive community that appreciated their message, whether they accepted it or stoned the messengers. And it is around the prophets that the Old Testament history coheres, for they were the agency of its development. Accordingly, if we are to bring our teaching of the Old Testament into contact with native life, it will be done not so much by a mechanical comparison of this custom with that in the Bible, as by emphasizing the prophets rather than the lawyers or the historians. And what is more important still is that we thereby get at Our Lord's own attitude to the Old Testament. He recognized Himself as being in line with the prophets, and He, like them, was struggling against the usurpation of the spirit by the letter. For the African the Old Testament viewed in this way is a living book.

The second advantage is that we get a new emphasis for the term " historical." The value of a thing being historical is not that it happened, but that it happened *then*. It arose, that is to say, out of a certain situation. Events apart from their contexts have no meaning. We read that in 1066 William the Conqueror landed in England. Of what value is that to anybody in England or in Africa ? The value of the knowledge of that fact is bound up with the knowledge of what England was like before and after he came, why he came at all, and what he did when he got here. In the same way the reams of bitterness that have been piled up on the question whether Job ever lived or whether Jonah is an allegory are all so much waste paper. Jonah may have lived or he may not—at any rate from the Book of Kings we know that *somebody* called Jonah once lived—but the value of the story is not bound up with that particular event in time. Its value lies in the existence of a certain situation and how that situation was changed to the benefit of all concerned. The whole point of it is lamentably missed if it is viewed as a " story about a whale ! " It is a belittling of history to look upon it as a number of events in a time sequence, as if their presence in that sequence of itself gave them an ethical value.

To advocate the historical approach to the Bible in African schools is not hoping for the impossible, for I have seen a mission school where it is done. It was a wonderful tonic to meet a group of men who had never known any other way of looking at Scripture than this, who could put all their intelligence into it, and who had at their service the fruit of the best theological scholarship of this generation. To them the Bible was not only full of meaning, but it was inspiring as well, as indeed it cannot fail to be when taught properly.

In the Scripture syllabus of the Natal Education Department (European and Native) a suggested list of books includes the Cambridgeshire syllabus, Sir George Adam Smith's *Isaiah*, Somervell's *Short History of Our Religion*, Driver's *Genesis*, Papini's *Life of Christ*, *The Bible for Youth*, two Student Christian Movement books, and Peake's *Commentary on the Bible*. This list is prefaced by the statement :—

'Whatever happens, we must let the pupils know the truth as far as it is known to reverent and learned men of our own time.'

4.

Scripture is the historical basis of the Christian life and is therefore an essential part of it. But of what is " moral instruction " the basis ? The connection between the Bible and the Christian life is an intimate one, whereas that between, let us say, Samuel Smiles' *Self Help* and the moral life is quite arbitrary.

Let us, however, look at a book of " moral instruction " and see what it contains.

A well-known book of this kind used both in India an Africa is called *My Duties*. It is divided up into five sections, —introduction, my duties to myself, my duties to others, my duty to God, duties in after life. There are seventy-six lessons in all, four of which are poems, and about a quarter of which are biographies. The subjects of some of the biographies are not otherwise known to fame except in books of this kind. There is the story, for instance, of Lafitte, the poor boy whom a banker saw picking up a pin off the ground as the boy left his office. Struck with his economy, the banker called him back and gave him a post, and afterwards Lafitte became a very rich man. There are many examples of self-help, punctuality, industriousness, benevolence, truthfulness, thrift, and obedience. In nearly every case the reward for the acquisition of these qualities is success, and as often as not either wealth or fame. One of the exceptions is Casabianca, the perfect example of an unintelligent interpretation of orders. We have the familiar stories of the choice of Hercules, Regulus, Sir Isaac Newton's dog, Socrates, Leonidas, John Howard, and Florence Nightingale. The whole makes capital reading, and is, as it were, Montaigne in petticoats. Children and Native teachers enjoy books like this, for the stories are a delight while the "moral" can be skipped. The book-shop at Lovedale used to be well stocked with copies of *My Duties*.

The history of the moral story for children is very interesting.[1] Curiously enough it was Rousseau who boomed it most, perhaps as effecting a working compromise between Locke and Charles Perrault. His English imitators laid heavy hands on Robin Goodfellow, Tom Thumb, and even John Bunyan, and made them so "improving" that their original purpose was quite lost. Maria Edgeworth stepped in to repair the damage, and her *Moral Tales* and the *Parent's Assistant* if they provided a pill of morality, were very liberal in dealing out the jam to go with it. They were excellent stories in themselves, and while parents bought them for their morals, children read them for their interest. It is moreover very doubtful whether any one of the thousands of children who have read *The Swiss Family Robinson* or *The Fairchild Family* has ever bothered about the moral. Accordingly, while such stories may not have done the "good" they intended they at any rate provided another kind of good in parenthesis. The child mind has its own way of dealing with well-meaning elders.

The Native mind is probably not dissimilar. So long as such books as *My Duties* are produced, so long will they be read, and so long as they are well written they will provide

---

[1] See *A Century of Children's Books*, by Florence V. Barry (1922).

reading material of an entertaining kind. How far, however, do they or can they realize their serious aims?

5.

To answer this question we need to ask ourselves another: What is the nature of morality? We shall find a great difference, if not in practice at any rate in idea, between the basis of primitive morality and that of " civilized " morality. Primitive morality is primitive custom, and is not consciously concerned with principles, whereas with the advance of civilization morality rests more and more on reason. Moral rules are part and parcel of the social life of the tribe. There is a well-defined sense of the things which are " not done," although no one cares to investigate the reason why they are " not done." With the disappearance of tribalism the sanctions behind these taboos are slackened, and, as we have seen, it is precisely this disintegration which is so great an anxiety to the friends and also the foes of the African to-day.

Customary morality, however, is not a particularly isolated phenomenon. There was a very closely knit tribal morality in England in the nineteenth century, and the disappearance of " Victorianism " has been attended by the same moral dangers. There is also apt to be a variance between idea and practice in these matters. In *idea* the morality of a civilized people is based upon principles; in reality it is often as tribal as that of a primitive people. John Galsworthy's *Loyalties* gives an excellent example of tribal morality, in which the one man who sees right and wrong as something beyond the rules of his caste is at once outcasted.

The alarm which people feel about African disintegration has led to various methods of preserving the tottering structure of Native moral life. One solution is to shore up tribalism by maintaining the authority of the chief. Another is to underpin it with a new set of moral rules borrowed from the white man.

It is apparently the latter which is the purpose of books

of "moral instruction." The illustrations, however, smack of the age of the English Industrial Revolution, and of the qualities which go to make an efficient office-boy or a respected member of a Chamber of Commerce. As examples of "morality" many of them are quite neutral, while the only lessons than can logically be drawn from some are quite *im*moral. There is, for example, no moral virtue whatever in picking up a pin. But the encouragement held out to Young Africa, as in a former generation to Young England, is that by picking up pins you become a millionaire. In another story in *My Duties* civility is commended because a rich old merchant attributes his success to that quality. Yet if morality is worth having at all it is worth having for its own sake. If we are going to exemplify the moral value of perseverance the superb story of Captain Scott's failure is apt, and that of Lord Beaverbrook's *Success*[1] is quite inept. Making money is not a moral achievement, nor is a position in the Cabinet, and whatever may be the literary value of the works of Dr. Samuel Smiles, it is certain that *Self-Help* is not a particularly moral book. And it runs quite counter to the whole Christian way of looking at things. The highest morality that we know is bound up with a Life that was a splendid failure.

Even if we leave out altogether the element of reward—and not all the stories in *My Duties* bring it in—the emphasis is still misplaced. Morality is not a convention of society—it is part of the make-up of the universe. We have consciences simply because the distinction between right and wrong runs through the whole world. But *what* things are right, and *what* things are wrong depend upon society and the way in which we are brought up, until we ourselves challenge these things and make them give reasons for themselves on first principles. One aim of moral instruction is to get people to challenge their conventions, and see if they really do fit, not into another set of conventions, but into the fundamental principles of right and wrong as they can best understand them. The aim, therefore, is that people should

---

[1] The title of a book by Lord Beaverbrook. It has on the jacket a portrait of the author. Free copies were sent to clergy and ministers.

come to have adequate standards of values, and standards cannot be given ready-made. Conscience is something that is infinitely capable of education, and it is educated by experiment, by comparison, by example and by growing intelligence. Its progress is not from one circle of loyalties to a different one, say from the African to the British, but from a narrow circle to a circle more universal. " British " morality is of value only in so far as it has this universal principle in it. Apart from this, its rules are mere conventions, conveniences, or social habits, nor necessarily valueless, but not to be glorified by the name of morality.

My Duties does not make this reference. It is by no means clear for instance why these business-like habits of the British are to be preferred to the unbusiness-like habits of the African. This uncertainty is evident in practice as soon as the Native begins to act on the plane of morality which the book advocates. We say he is pushful, not thinking about his own people but only about himself, despises manual labour and wants to be a clerk. But if a clerk is paid (as he is paid) a higher rate of wages than a carpenter, by our very principles of moral instruction we are bound to say that the man is a fool if he does not aspire to be a clerk. We cannot have it both ways. British morality exalts the climber, and if we condemn him when he climbs it is either because we do not believe in our own morality or because we do not believe in him. British morality like African must be put to the test of some more universal principle. A sectional morality is the product of a society that already exists; it cannot be made the basis of a society that is yet to be.

And if *My Duties* fails to co-ordinate the ideal British shopkeeping qualities with the divine government of the universe, it must likewise fail to seize upon any element of such co-ordination in African morality as it is. If it does not appreciate Britain it will not appreciate Africa. Khama has a chapter to himself in *My Duties*, but what are the qualities for which Khama is commended? None of them are African but all are British. If we are going to draw any lessons from Khama's life they should surely indicate that

THE CONTENT OF AFRICAN EDUCATION 181

he was an African through and through, and represented his people at their best.

It is difficult of course to avoid an individualistic emphasis when we write about morality, because from our point of view morality is individual. But while the individual must bear his own responsibility, morality is concerned with his attitude to the world of things and people and ideas outside him. It is a social relationship. To the African this social relationship is a comparatively easy thing to grasp—we have seen instances of this already. The thing that is not clear to him is that it is intimately bound up with his own self-expression. The phrase " we cannot realize ourselves except in society " has a different emphasis according as you are a European or an African. If you are a European you are, so to speak, here and society is over there, and you must bring yourself to help it. If you are an African you and your society are already linked, and the problem is to render yourself in thought independent of it through the means that society itself supplies.

An illustration should make this clear. Tribal loyalty is a common experience. The educated Native breaks away from it. We either encourage him to be himself and climb up Smiles's ladder of success, or else, with a better instinct, we tell him he must remember to help his own people. But this last is a British way of putting it—it recognizes the very opposition between himself and his people that we want him not to recognize. In the same way we often use the expression that he should " go back to his own people " indicating at once that he is different from them. Why should he go back? Would we ourselves go back? And would we be more inclined to go back if some outside person told us it was our duty to do it? In asking this of the educated Native not otherwise inclined, we are asking for a self-denial which is a fine fruit of the deepest moral reflection. It can only come of itself. If the whole school or the whole mission exemplifies this principle, our scholars will understand it. But we cannot shorten the process by enjoining it as a moral maxim. This whole attitude is a British attitude. From the African point of view it is much easier to begin with the fact that he and his people are one, and that his independence of character is something that arises not because he has left them but because he is a member of a larger society which includes while it transcends them. Tribal loyalty is a very tenacious and a very precious thing, but like all good things it must die to live. It is preserved not by first taking a man away from his people and then adjuring him to go back, but by developing it till it includes an ever-widening circle. The insight of St. Paul into the real nature of the narrower loyalty of Judaism made him the apostle to the larger world of the Gentiles not only without ceasing to be a Jew, but even because he was so very Jewish. He saw the Gentiles not as a group opposed to Jews, but as part of a larger group which comprised the two, and for the service of which were needed the very virtues that made a good Jew. Our loyalty to our country, to the Church, to the company of intelligent minds, are all extensions of the narrower loyalties of the family and the group and are not in opposition to them.[1]

---

[1] A book which seems to me to be excellent for moral instruction is by an American, Dr. Henry Park Schauffler, and called *Adventures in Habit Craft* (The Macmillan Co., 1926, pp. 164. Price $1·25). The title is quite accurate, as a description both of the book and of the nature of moral training. It is a craft, and the attempt after proficiency in it is an adventure. The book takes seventeen qualities and gives a chapter to each. Among them are the habits of "the glowing heart," choosing the best, accepting responsibility, being trustworthy, learning from others, and good workmanship. Each quality is dealt with in five separate ways. First of all one or two problems of conduct are propounded which involve the quality concerned. This at once presents the moral idea in a setting of everyday experience. Having got hold of the idea we then proceed to define it by analysing it and by indicating its opposites. When it is thus defined by this process of elimination it is then illustrated by stories from the Bible and elsewhere. We next collect as many proverbs as we can about it. Finally we build up a cardboard model to symbolize it. These five different ways of learning about the same thing seem to be very practical and psychologically sound. They will not, of course, of themselves make people more moral, but they will help them to think about moral questions in a right way. The book will not simply entertain them, nor will it give them false standards of success. It was written for the mixed population of America and will need to be adapted for African schools. There would need to be African illustrations, and use made (as it is not made in *My Duties*) of the vast storehouse of native proverbs and the native way of illustrating a point.

THE CONTENT OF AFRICAN EDUCATION

III. THE WORLD OF THINGS: NATURE STUDY.

1.

It is fairly clear that the Three R's and Scripture and moral instruction have their place in the curriculum. They emphasize, if they do not adequately supply, two out of the five aspects of life that the work of the school seeks to represent.

When we turn to the world of things demoralization begins to appear. There are so many things which are important to know that we do not see how we can leave out any of them.

Let us take an example. It is held by a good many people that as Africa is chiefly rural the school ought to fit the African for rural life. What then is involved in "rural life"? Clearly agriculture is its basis and so we must have agriculture. Agriculture involves plants and animals, and unless we are simply going to study their external life and no more we must have biology. Biology has two branches—botany and zoology. It may also be a study of structure, which is anatomy, or of function, which is physiology. Physiology leads on to hygiene and hygiene issues in sanitation. Agriculture also involves the soil, and consideration of this leads on to geology and geography. The agriculturist must have a house to live in, and he should know how to build it and how to furnish it. He ought therefore to have a knowledge of trees and timber, and he cannot do without either building or carpentry. He must have tools, and so iron-work is useful. He presumably keeps cattle, and "cattle" is a vast subject by itself. The things that our agriculturist does not have at hand he must buy, and to buy he must have something to sell. If his crops are at all valuable he has to market them, and this process brings in simple economics, methods of transport, and the needs of the people to whom he is selling his produce. How can we do without the study of these things?

I have not mentioned at all the "humane" aspect of his life—his place in the community, his knowledge of its laws, its games and its lore, his reading and writing, the religious side of his life. Yet it is difficult to see how any of these things can come in owing to sheer pressure of time. And it is now in Africa as it used to be in England. Each subject has got its protagonists, and each of them can put up a thoroughly sound case for his own particular fancy.

The attempt has been made to combine them all in the "project method."

The project method may mean one of two things. It may be concerned with the approach to various subjects, and in this it is psychologically sound and admirably fitted for use in the primary school. It is particularly helpful in Africa. Take for example the "project" of building a hut. Clearly this can involve a number of things—knowledge of materials and methods, knowledge of where the things come from, calculations about them, the reading of stories about them, drawing pictures of them, and so on. This is a good deal better than studying all these subjects separately, for here you see them all linked up together. So far so good, and with young children this is far enough.

With older pupils the "project method" may be no more than an artifice on the part of the teacher who is afraid to leave anything out but realizes that he cannot put everything in ! But a method of approach is a different thing from a method of study. The relationship of things in a project is purely fortuitous and arises in a situation which has been artificially created. If the project of building a hut aims simply at building a hut and that is all, the correlation of subjects in that enterprise is admirable. But with older children this cannot take up all the school-time and the subjects still remain to be "studied." Relationships that appear in connection with a certain project are apt to remain only in connection with that project. They have to be pressed back to their original mental source in order to provide "education." An illustration can never take the place of the text, although it may illuminate the text, and there is a difference between seeing a thing clearly and understanding it. A lecture on relativity by Dr. Einstein may be perfectly "clear" and show us what it is all about, but that is a very different thing from "understanding" relativity.

2.

The village school presents little difficulty. It is when we come to the boarding-school and the whole time of the children is taken up, that the difficulty of choosing among subjects begins.

For the village school the most useful nature study is agriculture, and indeed it is the only nature study that is needed. It is not, as has been said, the multitude of school subjects that counts, but the presence of representative sides of life. Agriculture will give "nature study" to us, and so will geography. There is no need in the primary school to have both.

Now what is the educational value of agriculture? As we have seen, it can link up with almost all the other subjects that there are in existence. But this is not its educational value. After all, history can link up with still more, for there is a history of everything—morals, institutions, mathematics, and even of agriculture. But this does not constitute the educational value of history.

The high educational value of agriculture is due to the fact that it *of necessity* has a footing in so many spheres of life. It is concerned with things, for it is chiefly a "nature study"; it is no less concerned with people, for it is the very basis of our existence on this planet; but, more important than these educationally, it has a very vital connection with the world of ideals and values.

It is commonly said by people who have had much experience of teaching agriculture to Africans, that it is a means of overcoming witchcraft and superstition. When new methods come in which involve new principles, they bring with them an idea of causation which was not there before, and they can be used for the destruction of superstition. On this point I have already touched in an earlier chapter. It should, however, be emphasized here as elsewhere, that no study of itself will work the oracle. If it was possible for a skilful headman in Natal to be familiar with all the latest agricultural science and yet to cultivate his own fields in the old way, it is not likely that merely doing the work will produce knowledge of the doctrine. There is no guarantee that the study of nature at school will produce more satisfactory methods of farming at home, or that it will lead to a revolution in the mind of the farmer.

To the mind of the Native agricultural processes and religion are closely intertwined. In changing his agricultural methods we are interfering with part of his religious system. But it will not necessarily affect the other part, unless in the mind of the teacher agriculture is part of another religious system. It is this religious aspect of native agriculture which makes it possible for a man even with modern knowledge to continue to cultivate his fields in the traditional way. There is a religious sanction behind it which more than counterbalances the value of an increase of crops. And as we have seen, the old religious sanction can be used to back up modern methods. The spirits of the corn and wild become re-baptized with the name "Nitrates," but their action is supposed to be the same. This does not make for continued progress, although it does represent a much higher stage than the old one. Educationally, however (and by that I mean something that touches a man's mind) it may have no effect at all. The mind develops through a knowledge not of facts but of meanings, and meanings do not exist in the facts themselves. A meaning is a relationship, and if a man does not see that relationship when he is teaching a subject to another person, he cannot rely on his facts themselves to produce their meanings in the mind of his pupil.

3.

With agriculture as a tool I am not here concerned. Its value is obvious and the results of its improvement are seen in better foodstuffs, better cattle, and a higher standard of comfort.

But from the point of view of the school we have to remember that it is also a craft. The essential value of a craft is the sense of satisfaction that it brings when it is well done. It consists of doing things and of the possi-

THE CONTENT OF AFRICAN EDUCATION

bility of doing them badly, and so requires increased skill and patience to do them well.

This, it may be said, has a value in itself. Accuracy and reasoning are valuable qualities to acquire. This is so, but how is their value assessed ? It is seen in the yield at the end of the season, and in the fact that you have got two crops out of the ground in a year instead of only one. This from the point of view of farming is the main factor, but so it is from the point of view of education also. The relationship here between merit and reward is an organic one : the reward and the merit are concerned in the one process. It is a real connection, whereas to win a football for being top of your class is not a real connection at all. A good yield is organically connected with careful ploughing, whereas a football has nothing to do with learning to do sums. The educational value of any craft comes with doing it well, and the knowledge that it has been done well comes when the result comes. We hear a good deal about disinterested love of excellence, and that a thing is worth doing well even if you get no reward. This is a half truth and a half fallacy. In creative work you are busy all the time making your own reward. The result is bound up with the process and the process with the result.

Craftsmanship is thus self-regulative. It is the perfect example of the discipline of natural consequences. If you do not look after your fields properly, you do not need to be punished by a third person for your delinquency,—you will suffer from your own failure. And if you do your work well, you do not need the praise of an outsider to tell you you have done well,—the day will declare it. It is this elimination of all third-party interference, of merely external talking, or praising, or blaming, or forcing, that marks the stages of educational advance. And of all the various nature studies that exist agriculture more than others has this element in it.

4.

Nature studies, particularly in Africa, lend themselves to the utilitarian. Of course, if they have no practical use they have no educational value. As Herbert Spencer declared, in his own solemn fashion,

'it would be utterly contrary to the beautiful economy of Nature if one kind of culture were needed for the gaining of information and another kind were needed as a mental gymnastic.'[1]

The two go together. It is, for instance, this immediate practicality of biology that gives it a far higher educational value than chemistry. It can at almost every point be tested by every-day experience, whereas chemistry needs the artificial conditions of a laboratory. The word "utility," however, is a word that can mean almost anything, and unfortunately it is mostly associated with the short view rather than with the long view. A thing is considered "useful" if it is immediately useful. But a thing may be useful for many things, and we have always to ask, useful *for what?* It may be useful for the human body, or for the human mind, or for the human feelings. These are all important parts of us and we cannot rule out any one of them. Nature study is "useful" for all three.

The study of nature involves making an adjustment between ourselves and the world of things outside us. But there may be three adjustments, that of the farmer, that of the scientist, and that of the poet, and I doubt whether he can be said to have properly "studied" nature who is entirely lacking in any one of them. A farmer is not necessarily more " in contact " with nature than a scientist, or a poet. One is concerned primarily with results, one with methods and principles, and one with appreciation. Ideally we require all three, and for a "liberal" education we certainly require all three.

One of the things that most strikes the traveller in Africa is the almost complete lack of appreciation in the native mind of the wonderful works of nature that the country exhibits. The great unending stretches of the veld, the marvellous mountain scenery of Natal, the Victoria Falls, the mysterious primæval forest of the Middle and Lower Congo, the cloud effects in the rainy season everywhere, the amazing tornadoes,

[1] *Education: Intellectual, Moral and Physical.* Everyman edition, p. 37.

the thunder and lightning—these things appear to bring no sense of wonder to the minds of those whose natural environment they are. A man in Northern Nyasaland who had built his hut in view of a glorious range of mountains told me that he had not really noticed them till I mentioned them. He had built his hut there because the soil was good and there was plenty of water. He was a Christian elder, and a good scientific farmer, but this other side of life had made no appeal to him at all.

Lest we should feel that this is a defect of the African it is worth remembering, as I have mentioned already, that appreciation of natural scenery is a comparatively new thing among ourselves. Before the time of Wordsworth and the Romantics if there was any awareness of nature at all it was more or less as a vast gallery of sermon illustrations, each of which taught a " lesson." Appreciation was there in germ in the Elizabethans, but it is not really until we come to the Romantics that we get a sense of wonder. And even to-day it is very limited. Among less educated people, in Bermondsey or in Mayfair, there is little of it, for it requires for its growth a retiredness of spirit which neither the slums nor Newmarket tend to foster.

In this respect there is almost completely virgin soil in Africa. Coleridge-Taylor, himself half African, took a mediocre poem like *Hiawatha*, and made of it a magnificent piece of music. The wonder of the forest and of the heart of primitive man come out in it. But it is an interpretation of his own mind rather than that of the primitive. When, however, we think of the amazing wealth of material that there is in Africa to minister to all that is grand and majestic in the spirit of man, what may we not expect when the African spirit has been touched to see it ? But this will come only through people who have seen it first.

5.

Among "nature studies" I have put hygiene. The human body is the most marvellous work of nature, and the study of it involves all those elements which a good educational study should have. It is a natural object, it is also a personal one, and it has relations with other persons; it is a temple of the spirit of man, but it is the instrument by which that spirit expresses itself; the keeping of it healthy and pure brings the same sense of satisfaction that comes from good craftsmanship.

It is from this end that I would look at hygiene. So often hygiene is not a " study " at all—it is a collection of rules of health which the African has to master, and then he is supposed to know hygiene—just as morality is supposed to be a collection of rules of conduct the knowledge of which makes a man moral. Hygiene, although the newest, is sometimes the meanest subject in the whole curriculum, and it is taught with the tacit assumption that the European is a clean person and the Native is not. Yet cleanliness has nothing whatever to do with race. Those ignorant parents in the poorer districts of Glasgow who sew their children up inside their clothes for the winter [1] are much less hygienic than the native sailors on the Congo steamers, who at every anchorage splash into the water and give themselves a good scrubbing with soap. The native hut at night is an unhygienic establishment with its closed door, its central fire, its domestic animals, and its inhabitants sleeping with their heads under the blankets. But so have I seen people sleeping in the wilder parts of County Clare, and so, except for the animals, did our own great-grandparents sleep. There is no need for us to be unduly superior about our views of sanitation, and if we are so, we shall get a bias which may enable us to tidy up the Native's stomach and teeth, but which can never make hygiene a subject of real educational value.

With hygiene is included mothercraft. This again can be simply a matter of rules and information. But at Kimpese, for example, and at Mbereshi, it is much more than that —it is really a "liberal" education. For does not this, above all studies, above even agriculture, focus every side of human life and interest ? The whole question of sex is one of absorbing interest in every native village and is almost an obsession in African life. It is easy to see why it should be so, for there are no other interests of such continuous

[1] For this fact any school-teacher in the Glasgow slum areas can furnish evidence. My information came from two teachers.

THE CONTENT OF AFRICAN EDUCATION 191

importance wherewith to balance it. The creation of other interests is necessary if we would bring this one into its due place. This, however, is not the only need. Sex is part of a religious system just as agriculture is part of a religious system, but while new methods of agriculture may and do co-exist with old sanctions of religion, a new attitude to sex can only come from a new kind of religion. It is, therefore, much more the concern of the mission teachers who deal with the children than even of the doctors who deal with the adults.

A schedule of rules has been prepared by the Director of Medical and Sanitary Services in Tanganyika for the information of African adult women. It begins with this one,

'Expectant mothers should apply for examination at the nearest maternity clinic a month before parturition is expected,'

and continues with nine more.[1] This is intended for older people not specially educated, and therefore presumably the most conservative section of the community, and the least likely to profit by such rules. But the training in mothercraft given to girls is a much more thorough thing. The Church Missionary Society in Uganda is particularly famous for work of this kind.

We have in this study, as in every other study, the vocational side and the liberal side. They are not opposed, of course, but they are different, and I doubt whether any new knowledge of any subject can live and develop unless it is associated with a world of ideals that corresponds to itself. In education a far greater problem than that of getting people to know the right things is to get them to like the right things, and this involves more than mere information.

In this case of mothercraft the "vocational" side, so to speak, is the women's interest. There is nothing that men need to know or to do about it. The whole interest lies in the mother and the child, both before it is born and afterwards. The father, however, is equally concerned. Fortunately in Africa, unlike India, and even unlike Britain,[2] men

[1] *Report of Education Conference*, 1925, p. 123.
[2] See cases cited in *Maternity: Letters from Working Women, Collected by the Women's Co-operative Guild* (1915).

respect their wives during pregnancy and after child-birth, even though that respect may take the form of taboo rather than of anything more positive. But the whole business of child-birth is so intimately known to men, and so freely discussed among them as the most ordinary subject of conversation, that something more is needed than simply specialized advice to the girls. The African home functions as a unit, even though men and women have their own particular spheres of work. Motherhood is the culmination not only of the woman's life but of the life of the home. Ordinarily, however, bearing children is looked upon as the woman's business and the man is not concerned. Unless, therefore, " mothercraft " is more than simply the training of girls in a particularly " female " subject, it is difficult to see how it can ever be a re-orientation of the home. This perhaps is a counsel of perfection, and the desired attitude is by no means common even in England. But the aim of African education should be to give not what is ordinarily done in England, but what is the best possible under the circumstances. And in some ways it is easier to do it in Africa than in England, just because there is no secrecy about it. The fact that there is no secrecy is one that often shocks the European, but on the other hand it makes it more possible to build up a common mind between husband and wife, between men and women generally.

Here is what an experienced missionary says about the training in mothercraft given at her station. After stating that " to the African it is a normal thing to prepare even from childhood for what is to them the one aim and meaning of life, which is marriage," and that merely to ban their customs connected with sex will produce an artificial conscience and do no real good, she continues :—

'I talk to the girls freely and naturally about their bodies, and God's interest in their development, and how large a part our physical natures play in God's purpose for mankind, trying to show how that if our vital energy is all used up in one way there is little left to nourish our mental powers, and God's purpose is that our three-fold nature should be evenly-balanced—body, mind and spirit, keen and alert. If these girls learn to ponder these things in their hearts instead of gossiping with their companions, if they are taught the sacredness of the body as the

THE CONTENT OF AFRICAN EDUCATION 193

vessel of the divine nature, if they are given happy and absorbing occupations and interests, these abuses now so prevalent will in time die out. . . . Repression will do little, a new obsession is the real cure. To me, one woman pure in heart is worth a hundred in body; it is new, sweet, true thoughts of life we need to give them.

'Here, again, it is the teacher who is going to count for more than her teaching, and it is for us who would lead these African girls out into sweet and holy ways to feast our eyes on the beauty of holiness . . . it is the vision that matters.'[1]

This, of course, was said to young girls about the care of their bodies, but it went along with practical teaching about maternity. We must allow for the loss that there is between the word that is spoken and the word that is heard, for not even talking in this way will produce a change of life. But it was not talk so much as a summing-up in words of the general attitude of that girls' school to life, and from this angle " mothercraft " is a liberal education. It has to do with the human body. It has still more to do with the human spirit. And it can awaken a "renascence of wonder."

A question that arises in my own mind is whether this kind of thing could not be done for boys also. The birth of a child is a greater creative act than a well-kept garden or a piece of woodwork, and both sexes are concerned in it. The technicalities of midwifery are no more the concern of the man than the technicalities of carpentry are the concern of the woman. But the real innermost meaning of childbirth is the concern of both, and familiar as men and women are with the purely physical side of it, it should not be an impossible task to interest both in the spiritual reality behind it.

'*Das Ewig-Weibliche*
Zieht uns hinan.'

6.

An important side of nature study is the care of animals, and in this it will be agreed that the African needs educating. Cruelty to animals is due in part to thoughtlessness, and in

[1] *Proceedings of the General Missionary Conference of Northern Rhodesia* (1924), p. 143, paper by Mabel Shaw, London Missionary Society, Mbereshi.

part to his own ability to endure suffering, and hence not to realize it in others. And while kindness to animals is, so to speak, a branch of morals, the problem is how to tackle it. Some schools have linked it up with the care of agricultural animals, and based it on self interest. It is not a subject that can be isolated, for it is part of a person's attitude to life generally.

Two questions remain. The first is, what is the town child to do about nature study? and the second is, what do we expect of the teachers? When you contemplate the long line of corrugated iron school-churches in, say, the Boksburg location, you wonder whether there is anything in the world quite so unnatural as this. The beauty of the forest or the bush has been left a long way behind when you get to Boksburg. And there is likely to be a greater and greater number of people living in such surroundings. It might well be argued that the town child has even more need of nature study than the country child, if only by way of compensation. But in teaching we have to begin with what is there rather than with what we should like to be there, and there are clearly not the same facilities in Boksburg as in a rural area. Agriculture is out of the question, and even a school garden would scarcely be possible. But there are still wind and weather, the clouds and the earth, and the human body. Geography is a more possible subject than agriculture or what is technically called " nature study," but the geography should not be as it so often is in Africa and as it has ceased to be in England, a mere list of names, but something which has in it the capacity for wonder.

It will indeed take a long time to redeem Boksburg and other places like it, but we must not let ourselves suffer from despair. That which appears mean and unlovely to us either may be not seen as such by the children, or may even seem to be a place of the enchantment of the new learning. Even so have night classes appeared to keen pit-lads in grim mining villages in the North of England. Spectacles are not always coloured rose; they are sometimes smoked.

The teacher, as we see all along, is the key of the situation, and therefore European attention concentrates on the African teacher. He has passed beyond the village school and gone on to the boarding school. He is there at his work all the day and the curriculum expands to cover his whole time. Nature study begins to expand also, and from being chiefly a matter of observation and experiment, becomes classified and in fact a "science." Here the difficulties of curriculum of which I spoke earlier are most apparent. A good case can be put up for so much that we do not know what to leave out. But the teacher's need is no different in kind from that of the children. Primarily, however, his need is not to know *more* but to know *better*, so that he can communicate not extra facts but a deeper meaning. And this means a philosophical way of looking at the subject, and a greater capacity for wonder in the marvellous works of God.

IV. THE WORLD OF PEOPLE: LITERARY STUDIES.

1.

Literary studies, if they are really literary, represent that side of human interest which is concerned, not so much with nature as with people, with the things that people have done and thought, and with the development of their minds as they thought and acted, and of other people's minds as they meditated on these things. The word "humanism" is a much misused term, for it is often applied only to literary studies, and only to literary studies of a certain kind. In truth, however, humanism is a way of looking at life. Carpentry can be "humanistic," as we shall see in the next section, while Greek philosophy—"humanism" *par excellence*, so it is said—can be as unhuman as a table of statistics. It depends on how these subjects are handled.

But if they are to be handled in a way which makes for increased respect for the spirit of man, they will need to be associated with the work of that spirit in the past and in diverse other places in the present. They will need to be presented as part of a scheme of things whose beginning no man knows and whose end is not yet. That, to my mind, is of the essence of humanism. Literary studies, therefore, are as it were a background before which the action of to-day takes place.

They involve history—the story of the past, and the attempt to see its relationship to the present. They involve also biography, not only of people in the past, but of contemporary folk as well, in order to make us better acquainted with those who breathe the same air that we breathe. They involve also geography, particularly in its modern aspect of " human " geography—the study of the earth as it affects the human race. This last is not wholly a literary study, of course, but still it is not one to be fully grasped by the mere contemplation of the natural phenomena with which it deals. And while all these studies are going on, it is to be hoped that they will help to broaden the pupil's outlook and give him a sense of proportion about the task in which he himself is engaged.

This last consideration is important. There comes a point in all practical work where a process of " diminishing returns " sets in. It is a point beyond which practical skill cannot be developed further without a corresponding development of intelligence. It is true, of course, that " the job educates the man," but the more he has to bring to the job the more it will educate him. This point was brought out in a slightly different context at the Nyasaland Education Conference in 1927 :—

' It seems to me that what is needed . . . is not the lowering of the literary side but the addition of the technical. . . . To discard or even lessen the literary training would be to block the way for the advancement of native leaders, and means the reduction of the natives to a class of helots, without outlook or aspiration. At the same time it would cripple very seriously advancement in technical work. . . . Without the trained intelligence got in school, the most elementary notion of cost of work is not grasped by the native, and the apparently cheap labour is often very costly in the end.'[1]

The headmaster of a Government Arab school in Mombasa told me that although he was a teacher of commercial subjects he had reduced the time allotted to them in the curriculum because he felt that the boys had not a sufficient general background of English subjects.

The same problem arose a generation ago in England.

[1] *Report*, pp. 23-24. Address by the Very Rev. Dr. Robert Laws.

THE CONTENT OF AFRICAN EDUCATION

After the Devonshire Commission of 1870 there were set up "organized Science Schools" as an alternative to the upper standards of the English elementary school, and science took up more than three-quarters of their time-table. They soon began to fail, however, even as science schools, because the pupils had so little familiarity with the use of English and so little general knowledge.

Apart from the habit of thought, apart from comparison and discussion, manual work becomes merely rule-of-thumb. If it remains at this stage it has ceased to educate and requires a development of the mind in other ways. There are many avenues to the mind, and while it was formerly held that "literary" training was the chief of them, the pendulum has in these days swung in the opposite direction. This has been due partly to a misunderstanding of what it is that makes a study "literary," and partly to a lack of connection between literary and practical work. At Domboshawa, as we have seen, and at Tsolo, agricultural work is preceded and followed by lectures on the subject, and at Tsolo in particular a great deal of care is taken to see that the pupil has been able to write down correctly the substance of the lecture.

But the relation between literary studies and the training of leaders is vital. It is impossible to "train leaders" in advance, to say to this man or that man "you are to be a leader; come and be trained." Leaders are not made in that way, by some third-party choice from outside. The business of the teacher is to give the best that he has to all who are capable of receiving it. He does not know who among his pupils will, by the opportunity of some need or some vision, be called into leadership. The aim of literary studies, as has been said already, is to develop thoughtfulness and a sense of responsibility by placing a man in an environment of thought and history. This is a good thing for all men. For the great majority it may mean no more than to make them able to do well those things which they would have done badly; for some it will give a leisure interest which can grow into a continued source of pleasure; for a few it will mean kindling a flame which will carry warmth and light into places that need them most. These last are a minority, but the good teacher should hope to produce some, and should die happy if he has produced but one.

2.

The ability to use a language for purposes beyond the mere needs of every day is one of the points that distinguish the educated from the uneducated person. It shows itself in an economy of words to express meanings, and in a sense of relative values. An uneducated person who tries to tell you a story becomes hopelessly lost in irrelevant detail. " I said to her, I said, let's go to the pictures, and so we went last Thursday night, or was it Friday, no it was Thursday after all, I'm not sure it wasn't Saturday, yes, it was Saturday, and we saw such a lovely picture all about elephants in Siam, no that was on Thursday, yes well it was on Thursday, and its name was Chang for Chang is an elephant in Siam and the girl played the piano ever so nice . . ." and so on. Do we not know it well? A familiarity with language, and particularly with written language, clarifies thought and arranges ideas in an order of importance. And this power is of value in any subject or in any circumstances where the use of language is needed. To understand a map, or a series of directions, or a message, some more general habit of mind is needed than the beggarly elements of that single situation. It needs control of a language.

Now this does not come from grammar. It used to be said in the elementary school that " grammar teaches us to write and speak correctly," but it is doubtful whether grammar fulfils any such lofty purpose. The case against grammar has been so well argued in England that grammar as a separate subject has now disappeared from the best of our elementary schools. But it is still popular in Africa, partly by tradition, partly by reason of its supposed power of training to think, partly because so much teaching in African schools is necessarily concerned with language, and partly because where you are teaching a foreign language you cannot get on very far without having to understand grammar. But the case against it still remains. Grammar is an analytical study which is dependent upon the possession of something to analyse. In other words, the place of grammar is after rather than before the control of language and vocabulary. I am asked off-hand, " In how many ways do English nouns form the plural ? " I have simply no idea at all, but I jot down as many different kinds of plurals as I can think of, —boys, boxes, oxen, sheep, sheaves, children—and when I can think of no more I say " at any rate six." On reflection, perhaps, I see that these six are reducible to three, and so I say " three." There may be more, but if there are, what does it matter ? It will not help me to speak English correctly to know the exact number, and anyhow the original question is one that would no more arise in real life than would an arithmetical puzzle such as " Reduce to farthings £14,837 16s. 4½d." We get control of a language by discussing and reading, by increasing our vocabulary with more and more new words, and by imitation of other people. Having got it we can then play about with it on the principles of Nesfield or Meiklejohn and see how it is made up.

Grammar is most usefully studied along with composition, related, that is to say, to an actual need for expression rather than done in the air by itself. The rules of a language are studied as they are required, and they are best understood where it is possible to collect a large number of examples. The wider the vocabulary in use the easier it will be to see relations between words and between phrases. Where a single language is concerned we can of course get on for a long time without any study of grammar at all. In the Nyasaland Tentative Code, 1927, no grammar was prescribed at all for the vernacular up to Standard III. The Northern Rhodesia Code introduced grammar only in Standard III. For village children the need is for abundant practice in composition, oral and written, and in reading. Grammar is not a study for the village school.

When, however, we come to study a second language we need some grammar as a beginning. In speaking, distinctions are made between singulars and plurals, between past, present, and future, and in order to express these in another language children have to know just what it is they are doing, and it is difficult to do this without a minimum of grammatical terminology. But the rule that vocabulary comes first and grammar second still holds good, and it is by analysing the language over which we have a control that we are able to understand the language which is new to us. In other words, grammar is best studied comparatively—the structure of Zulu helping us to understand the different structure of English. For grammar is a much more arbitrary subject than, say, botany. Nesfield's *English Grammar* is very different from West's, in a way in which one botany text-book is not different from another.

The grammarian does in a deliberate and ordered way what we all do in a spasmodic way—he analyses the knowledge of the language that he has and classifies it as it seems best to himself. Even his terminology he can make for himself, if he thinks this will give a better clue to his subject. It is therefore sound language teaching to put a child into the same position as the grammarian, to give him plenty of words and phrases and literature upon which to draw, so that "grammar" is for him not so much the application of a rule as the emergence of a rule from a number of examples. It is inductive rather than deductive. We can all of us go to work in this way, because we can all extend our vocabulary. The people, therefore, as I have said before, who are the best "authorities" on English are those who have the most extensive and exact working knowledge of English, rather than the people who simply analyse what some one else has written.

Language study is always more profitable when considered from the point of view of values than from the point of view of mere structure. It is one of the features of Scott's *Cyclopædic Dictionary of the Mang'anja Language* that it deals with language in this way. It is no mere dictionary, but it is a fascinating source of interest even to the English reader who knows nothing at all of the language. Madan's judgment is that it is

'an extraordinarily able and truthful collection of the facts of a single dialect, illumined by the sympathetic insight of a sensitive and philosophic mind, enthusiastically appreciative of the capacity and promise of native thought.' [1]

---

[1] *Living Speech in Central and South Africa*, p. 20.

One of the few books with which we can compare it is Fowler's *Dictionary of Modern English Usage*. They both deal with language as concerned with meanings, and they both are based on a great store of examples of all kinds, not made up for text-book purposes, but drawn from the ordinary use of the language in speech or writing.

To extend the pupil's interests and to acquaint him with an abundance of the best expressions in language of those interests, is a considerable part of "education." For "education" does not mean the "leading out" of what is already in the pupil's mind (that is a popular but false etymology),[1] but the "nourishing" of his spirit in every possible way.

3.

Biography represents an interest that is already there in every African child—and English child too—and is easily capable of development. The little press at Yakusu publishes a small book of biographies of distinguished Africans, ending up with Dr. Aggrey, and this is a scheme pursued by a number of other missions. Its great utility is that it gives the pupil new material for thought and for language, and by enlarging the content of his mind will make it easier in the future for it to take on a definite form. Biography, unfortunately, is so often spoiled by the neglect of the story for the sake of the moral. As we have seen in the section on moral teaching, this nearly always defeats its own end, and besides, "literary" studies should not be subordinated to an ulterior motive. We all have a sense of fraud when we have read a delightful short story which turns out in the end to be an advertisement.

Biography, too, is an excellent approach to history, and is used as such. And here I would repeat what was said earlier in connection with Scripture history—the importance is not that a thing happened but that it happened *then*. It is not the event that is significant, but the event in relation to its circumstances. Accordingly biography is not the same

[1] See *Ignorance*, the Romanes Lecture for 1923, by Professor John Burnet.

as history, but it becomes history when the man's life is studied in connection with his times. It is the interaction of the two that makes history. For history is not dates and facts, it is meanings, expressed not in language but in action. Without those meanings the study of history is not history at all ; it is what our forefathers called " chronology," and was usually classed in school prospectuses with " the use of globes ! "

4.

History is approached in one way through biography. A second approach is through tales and legends. History is primarily concerned with people, and with people who do things rather than think things. The real " form " of history is narrative, and narrative to be successful should be full of colour and incident. Folk stories and traditions have just these exciting qualities about them, and they are an admirable approach to the study of people whose lives have not the same legendary glamour about them, but which can be made exciting if the teacher has the wit and the enthusiasm to do it. Here again the " moral " is apt to get in the way. I read an exciting story at a school in Nyasaland which a pupil had told and which the teacher had written down. It was, I think, about a rabbit and a hyena (one no doubt of a familiar group of folk-tales), but the teacher was just a little worried because she couldn't find any " moral " in it. Probably it had no moral at all, and was told for the sheer fun of telling, but this did not satisfy her.

History for school purposes is the narration of the lives of men, and of the times in which they lived, and what they did in the situations that faced them. But it goes still further. All this can be of interest and entertainment, and it is certainly the most useful psychological approach, but unless it " gets home " to the reader it fails of one of its purposes. And by " getting home " I do not mean the " application " of a lesson, in the way in which lessons are applied as in *My Duties*. " Now, boys, what does the life of George Washington teach us ? It teaches us to be truthful. It teaches us to be brave, etc." This is of no value at all as "history teaching." The only kind of history teaching which gets right home is that which puts the reader himself into the stream of the world's history, and at the same time creates an awareness to the fact that he stands in relation to a certain situation, and according to the way in which he deals with it he " makes history " for himself, for his village, and for his race.

History, therefore, is concerned with the way in which men react to their times. It is this relationship that is their character—apart from this, how do we know their character ? And the point of realizing this is not that we should do as they did—moral values do not exist apart from the situation in which they arise—but that we should recognize that we too stand in a relationship to our times. This connection between the individual and the society in which he lives is to my mind one of the fundamental points that history emphasizes. It is a point that ought to be clear in all history teaching however elementary, and it is the only legitimate way to study " civics." So much of the study of " civics " presupposes that that relationship has not been made clear, and so proceeds to make it clear in a special context.[1] This, if true, is unfortunate, for apart from this, what is history study except at best a thoroughly good entertainment, and at worst a boring catalogue of events ?

From the point of view of " civics," history, while it deals with the past is essentially a study of the present, and its concern is with the person who studies it and not merely with the persons who are studied. It is doubtful whether it is worth while spending a great deal of pains in inculcating a time-sense in the pupils. Africans do not have it any more than our own children, or any more than our forefathers who thought of people in history as dressed in the English costume of the day. By time-charts and the use of spatial equivalents it is possible of course to get the child to see where these things come in history, and for the English child this may be essential. But it does not seem to me to be so essential for the African. A primary aim of history

---

[1] As for instance in *Civics : An Introduction to South African Social Problems*, by R. J. Hall (11th edit., 1926)—not an easy subject to treat adequately in provinces where the Native does not have the vote.

teaching in Africa is to put the African into the stream of history from which he has been absent for so long. The well-known African missionary who, in reporting on his school, said

'Here it is impressed upon the native that his present state of civilisation is about on a par with that of the white man of a couple of thousand years ago,'[1]

is not calculated to understand either the history of "a couple of thousand years ago" or history as it is made to-day. The Native's present position does not matter one whit; the thing that matters is what he is going to do under the circumstances. A right teaching of history would emphasize not the present position of the Native, but the relationship of that position to the position of the world in general. The important thing is not that he is where Queen Boadicea was, but that while it has taken us two thousand years to advance from her type of civilization to our own, he can do the same distance in twenty. It is a consideration of this kind which gives to history that perspective which a mere measurement of distance does not give.

The "situation in which a person finds himself" is a situation not only of people but also of things. In other words, a great deal of history has been made through people's reaction to climate, to mountain barriers, to the sea and to other natural conditions. It is in these days more and more the habit for history and geography to be studied together, and the term "human geography" marks the response of the geography people to the "historical geography" of the historians. In Africa, of course, this relationship is of even more importance than it is in England. The progress of civilization has elsewhere tended more and more to counteract the influences of natural surroundings, but in Africa wind and weather, drought and soil have still a great influence in determining history. Accordingly, if we take history as our centre, we here get a third approach to it—from geography, as well as from biography and from folk-tales. But all these subjects have as their interest people—who they are, what

[1] *The Rotherham Advertiser*, April 28, 1928.

THE CONTENT OF AFRICAN EDUCATION

they did, what they do, where they lived, and when they lived.

5.

Geography, however, has a high educational value because of its link between people and things, so that we can study it from either side we choose. As it is taught to-day in the best English elementary schools, it is one of the most valuable subjects in the whole curriculum. The old political system of classification has been abandoned, and the world is studied as it is before any labels are given to any of its parts. The " regional system " is the only educational one, because it not only represents the actual nature of the earth's surface, but also because it can be dealt with in miniature in the locality of the school. Accordingly modern geography is able to deal both with local conditions and world conditions and use the one to illustrate the other. It follows a more psychological method, and it works well in African schools.

Yet here and there are disappointments. I listened to a geography lesson in Natal given to a class of small children, and the map used was that published in the South African railway time-tables ! And in Kenya I found a class studying the geography of Kenya from a political map on the board. The questions took this form—" Point out Nairobi ? What is the population of Nairobi ? Where is Lake Victoria ? " The text-book that was used was printed in Ki-Swahili by the S.P.C.K., and Lesson I. was on " Geography in general," Lesson II. on " Astronomical geography," and Lesson III. on " Mathematical geography," a method of arrangement long laid aside in our home schools. Perhaps even worse than this is a geography book published by the Christian Literature Society.[1] Although published only in 1925 it goes back to the old political method, and confuses the names of things with the knowledge of them. It is a long catalogue of names of places given under the heading of the country concerned—useful as reference book like *Whitaker's Almanac*, but difficult to justify from an educational point of view. Yet I have no doubt it is exceedingly popular both with Europeans

[1] *A Geography of Africa.*

and Africans, for it saves the Europeans trouble, and the African would only need to use his memory. And for that, a book of this kind, like an arithmetic book, gives plenty of scope.

V. CREATIVE ACTIVITIES: ARTS, CRAFTS, AND MANUAL TRAINING.

It is difficult to find one term which will cover all the interests represented by this fifth aspect of human life which the school curriculum is intended to represent in a typical form. All the other aspects, even agriculture, are " studies," and they require words either spoken or written for their understanding and success. Yet in order to be educational, they must be concerned also with the business of creation and originality. Reading, writing, arithmetic, history, geography, Scripture, need to be worked into the pupil's own life and manner of thought so that he can do something with them for himself.

While, however, this creative element must be in all teaching of whatever kind, and in all learning, there are certain subjects which are primarily concerned with " doing " rather than with " learning." These are arts and crafts, music, dancing and games, and activities such as scouting and guiding.

In these things two sets of distinctions are very prominent, much more than in other aspects of life. We have to distinguish between " vocational " and " liberal," and between " appreciation " and " execution."

(a) *Vocational and Liberal.*

1.

The first distinction is largely a matter of emphasis, but it is nevertheless a distinction which is important. Every study should help to make a man better at his work, and to

THE CONTENT OF AFRICAN EDUCATION

that extent is "vocational," and every study should make him a better man and in that sense is "liberal," but there is a world of difference between a "vocational" aim and a "liberal" aim. An illustration may make this clear.

At a mission in Southern Rhodesia a great deal was said to me about the stress laid on manual training in order "to develop character." I was shown the carpentry shops with a considerable measure of pride. The material chiefly used was petrol boxes, and these were turned into all kinds of things—desks, chairs, cupboards, and tables. Yokes were made for oxen, and with the aid of a small forge and a circular saw a good deal of useful work could be turned out for the farm. But everything was exceedingly crude, and the handiwork of the furniture was all heavily disguised with glittering coats of yellow varnish. No attention was paid to craftsmanship, and the aim was to teach the Native just enough to enable him to make crude furniture and implements for himself. This was vocational training rather than education.

At Mbereshi I saw another carpentry shop of a totally different character. The workshop itself was a very crude place, the only lathe was worked by a large wooden wheel turned by hand, there was no circular saw, and there were few tools apart from chisels, hammers, saws, and planes. The walls, however, were significantly hung with bits of chairs, turned candlesticks, and other samples of carpentry, all, as I thought, quite well done, but nevertheless rejected. They were good enough for the purpose for which they were intended, but they were not as good as they could be made, and so they were thrown out. A thing had to be right, otherwise it was wrong.[1] There was no such judgment allowed as, "it'll do." Beams and other things that would afterwards be hidden by brickwork were nevertheless as well made as possible and were not scamped simply because they would not be seen. It is not surprising after this to learn that the Native boys and men of that mission were busy making a fine circular table for the Board Room of the Missionary

---

[1] This, it may be noted, was an educational principle both with the Hills in their school at Hazelwood (see *The Forum of Education*, Feb., 1923, article by Sir M. E. Sadler, p. 21), and with Edward Bowen at Harrow.

Society in London! This was right on the edge of the equatorial forest, about 250 miles from the railway, but the table was as beautifully made as it could possibly have been by the best cabinet-makers in London.

This is high praise, but here carpentry was a liberal education. The boys and apprentices to whom I talked were proud of their work, and would have been ashamed to turn out crude workmanship even if no person but themselves should ever see it. Both of these missions were turning out carpentry, in both cases serviceable and useful stuff, but in the first it was a business, and in the second it was *ad majorem Dei gloriam*.

2.

Manual training is defined in the Code for Southern Rhodesia as being any or all of the following,—farming, brickmaking, road-making, building, carpentry, iron-work, and, for girls, domestic work. There are good solid material reasons for all of these subjects, and it would do no harm to the average British schoolboy or girl if more of them were made compulsory in the curriculum at home. Where, however, they have such an immediate connection with everyday life as they have in Africa they cannot but come into the purview of any teacher or any missionary who knows his business. The first educational advantage, therefore, of manual subjects is that they are all associated with what is already done in the villages. They are practical and immediately useful. From the point of view of the school they are an easy jumping-off place for the study of other subjects. A second advantage is that they make use of physical means as an approach to the world of mind and spirit. An education in words alone is necessarily an imperfect education. The mind is approached not only through what a man sees but through what he feels and creates with his hands. These of course are only avenues, just as the printed word is an avenue, and they are neither better nor worse than other avenues, but they are too often neglected in education.

THE CONTENT OF AFRICAN EDUCATION

There is here a caution to be observed, for manual training as a mental exercise has limitations. A trick of the hand is learned which enables a process to be done automatically, and as soon as this happens its educational value ceases—it becomes a reflex rather than a thought. A high degree of skill, therefore, while it indicates intelligence, indicates only intelligence of a certain kind. Some people have an extraordinarily high degree of intelligence when playing bridge and yet in every other walk of life they are very stupid. And the workman highly skilled in a specialized occupation may be quite unreliable out of that occupation. To expect it to be otherwise is to fall into the old fallacy of formal training. Specific training gives a specific result. Manual work may be the best avenue of approach to some people's minds, but if the approach continues along that line alone it will produce not general intelligence, but specific skill.

A third and more distinctive educational quality about all physical creative studies like manual training and art and music, is that they have in them an element of satisfaction in the finished product which is a distinct education of the emotions. Education in the past has been very heavily intellectual. It has assumed that the majority of men were concerned with ideas, whereas most people's minds are concerned with things and feelings, and in the realm of thought they are quite inarticulate.

We have already seen how this element of satisfaction comes in in the case of agriculture, but it is of the very essence of every art and every craft. Failure or success in making a chair is finally apparent when the chair is made, but it has grown more and more apparent at each succeeding stage of the process of making it. The educational value of chair-making, therefore, lies in the fact that at every stage you are up against an ideal of craftsmanship by which you can judge your own efforts. Success in the undertaking is found in the fact, not only that you can sit on the thing when it is finished, but that you have fulfilled the ideal of craftsmanship which has been your inspiration all along. All the chairs made at the Southern Rhodesia mission could be sat upon, but it is not the aim of a school or of a mission merely to produce a thing than can be sat upon. The Mbereshi chairs could also be sat upon, and as seats they were probably no better than the others. But they were perfectly made—there was no need for putty or varnish or nails, the wood selected was the best for the purpose, the planing was well done, and every joint was true. There was a satisfaction in the minds of the boys who made them which was quite different from the satisfaction of having made something that could be used. It was an ethical achievement.

In a workshop in Nyasaland I saw chairs which erred in another direction. They failed of their purpose because so much of their good workmanship was unnecessary. It was spent on making fancy backs and elaborate arms. This neutralized the feeling of satisfaction that should have been there, for it transferred the conception of beauty from that which was structural to that which was adventitious. And to emphasize those qualities in a chair which are not *of* the chair is to lower both the educational value of the process and the artistic value of the product. There is about true art a certain reserve, dignity, or severity which avoids all excess as it avoids all defect. It is curious that in many ways artistic values are often better preserved in engineering than they are in craftsmanship. In a large engineering undertaking excess and elaboration mean undue cost, while defect means danger. Accordingly a great work like the bridge over the Victoria Falls avoids both extremes, and can give both to the makers and to the beholders a real artistic satisfaction. In small hand-made work, however, it is so easy both to elaborate and to scamp, and this is probably why manual training as done in schools, however helpful in other ways, is so little educative.

3.

These are all, I think, valid reasons for manual training, but none of them is the reason usually given for the place of manual training in the African curriculum. It is a favourite subject because it is said to produce " character " *in Africans*. Manual training is said to produce character because it trains

THE CONTENT OF AFRICAN EDUCATION

people in habits of handwork, it puts men up against the resistance of physical things, it helps people to become more resourceful, and it introduces into the school the conditions of the outside world. It makes the school more "real." And all this it is supposed to do by some virtue inherent in itself, irrespective of the people who teach it, the atmosphere in which it is taught, the nature of the manual work, or the people for whom the finished products are intended.

It is one of the most cherished fallacies of the human mind that the solution for all its difficulties can somehow be found in the external world. Something that can be touched or seen, or some external piece of organization, or some concrete proposal to do something, is thought to possess a magic power to influence the souls of men. But this quality, as we have seen, resides not in things as such nor in places as such but in the mind that interprets them. While it is no doubt partly true that "there is nothing in the mind that was not first in the senses," this chronological sequence does not determine values. The difficulties that exist in human life are all at bottom spiritual difficulties, because they owe their existence to people.

This general consideration is nowhere more cogent than in the matter of "character building." I have tried to show in the chapter on "The Mission" and elsewhere, that character-building is the effect of all the agencies of education working together, rather than the effect of any one of them. And it is so, because, as has been said before, life can come only from life. A man's character is built up by his association with other people in action and in thought, by facing moral issues in the atmosphere in which they can rightly be solved, and by learning good manners from those who have them. This is not all that there is to it, for the element of instruction comes in also. But character-building is not a property inherent in things or in occupations. It is concerned not only with doing the right things but with liking to do the right things, and the people who "teach" it must themselves like the right things and be able to get their pupils to like rather than merely to do. For the Christian, St. Augustine's phrase sums up the whole matter—*amans ab amante incenditur*—" one lover sets another on fire." For character is a matter of love far more than it is a matter of conduct.

The ability to produce " character " is the first claim of the ineffective as it is the humble hope of the competent. For how can any one tell that he is producing character ? Are the hidden springs of conduct and the shy loyalties of the soul things which any one can see and influence ? It is assumed because Africans are primitive people and have been thoroughly examined by the anthropologist and the psychologist, that the building of African character has become an exact science. Accordingly, Africans are taken in the lump, " the primitive mind works," we are told, " in such and such a way," and when our pupils cease to be " Jacob Makandiwiri " or " Sarah Chulamanda " but " the primitive mind," they become cases in an enquiry rather than individual people. When education gets to this point, character-building is at an end, and instead of " one lover setting another on fire " we have a specialist operating on a patient. Reverence for other people, a great love for them, a desire to be nothing if only they might rise to the best that is in them, a vicarious acceptance of their faults, and a refusal to pry with vulgar curiosity into their innermost hearts are the very fundamentals of " character-building." Set these on one side, and " twelve hours a week carpentry " on the other, and the vulgarity of the claim to train people's characters through manual training as an *opus operatum* is apparent.

Education is at bottom a matter of faith—that is why it is a moral business.

4.

The dogma that manual training is the subject for developing character has put arts and crafts into quite a false position in the African school. They appear as part of moral training rather than as what they are—training in appreciation and in feeling.

In avoiding one extreme we must be careful not to fall into its opposite. At the other end of the scale to the sturdy manual-trainer-of-character, is the curiously negative posi-

THE CONTENT OF AFRICAN EDUCATION

tion of the skilled artist with regard to native arts and crafts. At one extreme is the belief that the teacher has everything to give and nothing to learn; at the other the belief that the teacher has everything to learn and nothing to give.

The art side of a certain African boarding school seemed to me to suffer from this form of dogmatism. I was shown, for instance, a drawing of a chair standing against a door. The chair was drawn about one-tenth the size of the door, and quite out of proportion. It was obviously the crude first attempt of an untutored pupil. But the teacher did not take that view at all. To him it represented something "native," a new idea in the world of art. Although the real height of the chair was one-third that of the door, the fact that the boy saw it as one-tenth indicated a new method of expression which might turn out to be a feature in a new type of art altogether! He felt that for him to presume to instruct the boy in drawing was to cramp his natural genius.

This idea that the more a drawing is out of perspective, or the less real "drawing" there is in it, the more it betokens genius, is one of which we got rather tired after the war in some of the disfigurements of canvas done by Wyndham Lewis and Paul Nash and their school. Art is rooted and grounded in discipline, and freedom in art is the freedom that arises from discipline rather than without it. And the assumption that whatever is produced by the untutored mind of a primitive person is necessarily better art than if that mind had been trained by a European, is part of the philosophical hypothesis of the "noble savage." No sympathetic training will ever destroy individuality; it is rather the very condition of it, and to look upon teaching as interference is as great a heresy as to look upon interference as teaching.

The Nyasaland boy, Sceva, some of whose drawings are here reproduced (p. 214) lived at Mkhoma and went to school there. He never had any lessons in drawing, and these pictures done in an old copy book were quite uninfluenced by any European art teaching.[1] His drawings are as full of vigour as Bushman paintings. It is interesting that

---

[1] A number of his drawings have been published by the Lovedale Press under the title, *Cameos from the Kraal*. The real interest of the book is in the pictures, yet the artist's name does not appear!

A page of drawings by Sceva. (The originals are in colour.)

THE CONTENT OF AFRICAN EDUCATION

once when he was drawing a jackal he drew it in three positions at once in order to show that it was moving. This is precisely the same *kind* of device employed by Rodin in his statue of John the Baptist in order to show that the figure is walking.[1] To argue from this that Sceva would be spoiled by instruction seems to me to argue the precise opposite of the truth.

This negative position appears to be an argument for freedom and it is really an argument for bondage. It is a poor service to the African for the man of goodwill and sympathetic skill to stand aside and allow forces neither benevolent nor thoughtful to do their will. Neither in art nor in anything else can the teacher assume this purely passive attitude, and imagine that he is thereby giving free play to natural ability. Individuality is not developed without education, and if the teacher will not educate, other agencies undoubtedly will. For instance, in Sceva's case it is a pity that instead of his art being trained and fostered it was left as it was, for there was no one to train him, and he joined the ranks of the thousands who go to the Rand mines.

The college at Achimota has done real service to Africa in this respect. The exhibition of native paintings and drawings which was shown in London in 1929 by the art master of Achimota, Mr. G. A. Stevens, illustrated both the artistic possibilities latent in the West African negro and the excellence of their expression under sympathetic direction. The exhibits were original drawings done by students between 16 and 25 years of age, and all that was supplied by the art master was encouragement and suggestion. According to one critic,[2] the distinctive African treatment appeared not so much in the cruder works as in those done by the artist after a period of practice. It would appear to be true that in self-expression through painting and drawing, as in self-expression through the vernacular, an impulse from outside is necessary in order to stimulate later a " native " expression

---

[1] He represents him with both feet flat on the ground, one in advance of the other—an impossible position naturally, but a wonderfully effective convention for the purpose. See *Art* by Auguste Rodin, English Translation (1912), pp. 74-7.

[2] In *The South African Outlook*, May, 1929, p. 85.

from within. In our own British art, as in our own literature, the inspiration of Greece, Italy, and Judæa has helped to stimulate modes of expression which are neither Greek, Italian, nor Semitic, but British.

(b) *Appreciation and Execution.*

5.

It is commonly taken for granted that the aim of arts and crafts is to stimulate execution—to get people to draw, to carve and to fashion. A much more important aspect of the work is to get them to appreciate that which is drawn, carved, and fashioned, particularly in the works of nature.

Let us begin the discussion of this point by considering an actual syllabus for native schools.

In a South African Syllabus for the training of native teachers, 1927, the scheme for drawing was as follows:—

First year: Rectilineal objects—drawing-boards, door, table-top, pile of books, ladder, etc., construction of straight line figures to be used in counter-change patterns.

Second year: Circular objects—circles, cylinders, rings, balls, pail, teapot, plate, etc. Sketch maps and diagrams for use in geography. Continuation of original design work—allowing for simple brushwork in monochrome.

Blackboard drawing: "Simple objects excluding perspective," such as watch, walking stick, vegetables, leaves, spectacles.

Counter-change patterns: The first year course applied to the blackboard.

Third year: The second year course applied to blackboard conditions.

The question that arises as we look at this syllabus is: What is it meant to achieve? It cannot be of any assistance to a youth in appreciating the form and colour of the external world, for perspective is excluded, and the only reference to colour is a permissive use of brushwork in monochrome. Why monochrome? It is provided in the syllabus that in the work of the first and second year drawings are to be shaded—a good provision—but if we are not to use more colours than one, pencil shading is all the colour that we need. Either the thing is to be a drawing or a painting, and monochrome is neither the one nor the other. We may see things as light and shade, or we may see them as colour, or we may see them as both, but we never see them as monochrome.

And then with regard to form ; do straight lines come before curves, in our own minds and in the mind of the African native ? I was told at Likoma in Nyasaland that the schoolboys could draw perfect circles, but they found it difficult to draw a straight line. If this is true in the Transvaal also, this drawing syllabus is psychologically unsound. But even if it is not true (and the geometrical designs on Congo and Transkei huts show that it is not universally true), we still have to enquire whether an object like a drawing-board or a door is an object that any one would ever *want* to draw. The Bushman paintings are all of animals or of people in motion ; Sceva's drawings are of living things ; when an English child starts to draw he nearly always draws men, and it is not long before he colours them also.

The syllabus I have quoted is based on the same fallacy that is apparent in the teaching of grammar. It is assumed that drawings are an association of lines and therefore you begin with lines, just as it is assumed that speech is a collection of words and therefore you begin with words. But surely the impression *as a whole* is the unit in drawing, just as the unit in speaking is the sentence. A work of art, whether a drawing of a chair or of a stretch of scenery, makes its impression upon us as one thing. We begin with this and our appreciation grows as we look into details and see how true they are to the idea of the whole. We do not begin by being impressed with the detail and then working up to the general impression.

In drawing, therefore, we get the child to express a whole in which he is interested, and to express it as he sees it—in form and colour. He is then able to compare what he has done with the original and its shortcomings will be obvious. But out of this discrepancy between what he has attempted to do and what he has done, arises the sense of need of more particular study. The need for studying shades of colour, the necessity for perspective, both make themselves felt, not as academic things, but as related to a particular effect which it is *desired* to produce. Accordingly, behind the drawing there are the interest and the wish which make it a living study.

Furthermore, this approach to drawing puts in its proper place composition, an element which is usually left to the last and hardly ever gets into a school syllabus at all. But the observation of the way in which things are grouped is an essential element in the appreciation of nature. Beginning with colour as well as with form also gives a correct appreciation of light and shade, and it prevents the impression that shade is " black," which it is difficult to avoid if light and shade is first studied in pencil drawing.

It is interesting that in this syllabus the same synthetic approach is made to music. The course begins with scales, instead of beginning with popular songs and analysing them. However, the syllabus is no worse than that followed in scores of English schools even to-day.

There are two facts which should be correlated in all art teaching. Appreciation is necessary to the best execution, and some measure of execution is necessary for the fullest appreciation.

If we are going to do anything properly we must be able to appreciate it as done by other people, and to know what is meant by "properly." In this the good is always the enemy of the best, and if people are willing to do unworthy things well, it is because they have not learned what is worthy and what is unworthy.

At the same time to walk in only a few footsteps of some master craftsman or master artist is to be given an insight into his work which is deeper than that which comes from merely beholding it. To draw even a little will help us to appreciate form, to experiment with colour will give us discrimination in appreciating nature, to write even bad poetry will make us feel a kinship with those who write good poetry, and to sing or play, even if for merciful reasons it be in secret, will quicken our appreciation of music. To create helps us to appreciate creation. " God creates," said Froebel, " and therefore I must create." This, how-

THE CONTENT OF AFRICAN EDUCATION 219

ever, is the case with all good education of whatever kind. It is creative in order to revivify that which has already been created for us; it retraverses a path that has already been traversed *at least once*. Kepler put it into an epigram when he said of his own studies, " an astronomer is a man who thinks God's thoughts after Him."

6.

We seem here to be a long way from the African school, and Jacob Makandiwiri and Sarah Chulamanda are doubtless wondering what it is all about. They have neither of them very much appreciation of nature or of colour. They cannot understand the white man's admiration for their mountains or their waterfalls, and they do not see the shades of colour that he sees. To Jacob, whose other name shows us that he comes from Nyasaland, there are only two colours in the world. Yellow, light green, and pink are all " red," and blue, brown, purple, and dark green are all " black." If, as John Locke says, one purpose of education is to enable us to make distinctions, experimenting with different colours in Jacob's school would probably have had an educative effect upon him. He came one day into the teacher's house and he saw on her wall a poster picture of Lough Derg, which she had got from an Irish railway company. It showed the lake, the blue sky and a large white cloud. Jacob could hazard no opinion whatever as to what it was all meant to represent, and he thought it very queer that she should want to have a thing like that on her wall. Sarah, perhaps, had got beyond this stage, for she had stuck up on the wall of her dormitory at school a picture of a very elegantly dressed young woman which she had cut from a drapery catalogue kindly sent out to the mission from Manchester!

A problem in Africa as in England is what to do with leisure? It is a problem that thrusts itself upon you any Saturday afternoon in a Rand compound, but it is even a problem in the native village. In the absence of other interests men's minds tend to get obsessed with sex, and a good deal of ordinary conversation is about women.

Even in our English and Scottish rural areas this same lack of interests is a frequent cause of immorality. People are not necessarily happier or better because they live in rural surroundings. It all depends on what is in their minds.

Reading is of course a great source of interest, but there is little published in the vernacular, and even where the boy who has passed through a high school can read English easily there is often little sense of discrimination to guide his reading. One day I went into the Bookroom at Lovedale and asked the salesman which books, apart from work books, were most in demand. He mentioned three—*Napoleon's Book of Fate* (constantly asked for, and which they did not stock), *How to be Happy Though Married*, and *Happy Homes and How to Make Them*. This might have justified a criticism of the English teaching at Lovedale that it had not stimulated a better interest in English literature, were it not for the fact that those represent precisely the kind of books that sell by the hundred among certain classes of our own people. Popular science and " occult " publications have probably as large a sale among semi-educated British men and women as they have among educated Natives in Africa. This lack of the ability to discriminate is a symptom of incomplete education.

One problem of native education, therefore, is to enlarge the content of men's minds. The appreciation of nature is one method of doing this. It is not fully or even necessarily produced by " nature study," for it needs the development of the artistic sense also. It is an obvious defect that men should live in the midst of wonderful scenery and that it should mean nothing to them. It is often assumed because of this that it *can* mean nothing to them. Taste is often looked upon as something quite static and unprogressive, just as art is considered to require a " gift "—failing which no one can do anything in the creative way at all satisfactorily. It is here where both the Philistine and the doctrinaire artist stand on common ground. In the case of the Philistine, however, he would say that some people have this gift, and others have it not, and if you haven't it, you haven't it, and there's an end of the matter. The other man assumes that whatever " natural " ability there happens to be is a " gift " and just as relatively valuable as any other man's "gift." But it is one of the most obvious truths that taste can be educated. The art department of the Y.M.C.A. did quite a notable service during the war in educating the taste of the British Tommy until he ceased to think that a picture of a lightly-clad young woman hanging on to a stone cross in the middle of a raging ocean, and entitled "Nearer, my God, to Thee," was the highest achievement of pictorial art. In the same way at Hillcroft College in Surbiton it has been discovered not only that working women can be got to like the music of Beethoven, but also that once their taste has been cultivated they prefer it. Appreciation is not independent of circumstances, and people can only like those things which they have had the opportunity to like, or which have been interpreted to them through the liking of other people. And in African scenery there is a whole world of interest to fill a man's mind and make it rich with understanding.

7.

Many crafts are allowed to perish for lack of appreciation rather than for lack of utility, and the appeal on the score of use is quite irrelevant. Missions in Central Nyasaland have tried for years to get the Natives to spin and weave their own cloth. The same has been attempted in Southern Nigeria. Why should they do it ? It is a laborious business, and when it is done the result is not nearly so attractive to African eyes as the imported cottons from Manchester. We of course can see that these are poorer material and less lasting, and that it is nicer to make your own things, but until we can get that element of appreciation into the Native's mind our advocacy will be mere preaching, words and nothing else. People do not develop their taste in arts and crafts because other people tell them they must. Nor do we "stimulate native industries" by getting Natives to work for the mission. The embroidery school at St. Cuthbert's in the Transkei, for instance, turns out beautifully made altar cloths and chasubles and other things of which the Natives themselves stand in no need. It is no defence of the effectiveness of the training to point out that seven looms have been bought by women to use in their own kraals. The question is, what do they weave on those looms ? If it is Church furniture to be sold to the mission it cannot be called a " native industry." On the other hand, if the aim be to develop people's sense of the beautiful, and to provide that "joy in work " of which William Morris spoke, there must come in somewhere a relation of the product to the producer. It should be something in which he himself has a share, and which he himself can use and test its workmanship in the using. To make elaborate things for other people and for a purpose beyond any purpose of your own is to make a divorce between art and life. It is to associate what is beautiful with what is alien, and one's everyday surroundings are still left unredeemed.

This, of course, is quite a different question from that of developing native resources through industry. The well-known " Kambole industries," for example, in Northern Rhodesia, are an attempt to solve an economic problem, and to provide work and markets for people who would otherwise have difficulty in getting a living. We are here, however, concerned primarily with the educational value of craftsmanship, and that educational value rests in appreciation. When the question of commercial utility arises other considerations come in.

I have mentioned Scouts and Guides. In the non-European communities of South Africa they are called respectively " Pathfinders " and " Wayfarers," and are organized in the same way as in the European movement. In the Transvaal, for instance, a Wayfarers' Council was established in 1925 and joined with other bodies later to form a Wayfarers' Association of South Africa. Detachments are to be found in native boarding schools, in the Rand locations and in remote rural areas. Proficiency badges are earned, the most popular being home nursing, hygiene, first-aid, interpreting, cookery and needlework.

In the first edition of this book I expressed the hope that these special titles would be purely temporary and that the day would come when South African native children would join with European in these movements just as African boys do in West Africa. That day is not yet, but a notable step was taken in February 1936 when the Council of the South African Branch of the Boy Scouts' Association agreed to form parallel, self-governing, non-European Scout organisations which could be admitted into full membership of the world-wide Boy Scout Movement. The Pathfinder Movement is now, therefore, a self-governing unit of the Boy Scout Movement of South Africa. It has taken no more than fourteen years to bring about this change, and it has come not through pressure but through the silent evidence of the efficiency of the Pathfinders, and through the prestige of the Chief Pathfinder and his wife, Senator and Mrs. J. D. Rheinallt Jones of Johannesburg. In 1938 there were 480 troops with 573 officers and 14,786 Pathfinder Scouts. South Africa is a country in which argument goes a very little way to overcome prejudice but it yields in the long run—often a very long run—to demonstration. And these movements are of great importance because they are *activities*, and not only appeal instantly to the African child but also call for disinterested, creative effort on the part of those who run them and of those who are members.

8.

Appreciation is something to be associated not only with nature, and with one's own work, but also with the achievements of the human spirit. European inventions and civilization are often looked upon as something quite alien to the African, and on the whole as rather a bad thing. But there is a relationship among men as men which goes deeper than the distinctions of race. I have spoken of *ubuntu* as the recognition of man's need as man. We require a kind of intellectual *ubuntu* which recognizes man's ability as man. A great bridge, a railway engine, a steamship, or an aeroplane is an achievement not of this race or that race, but of the human mind as such. When we come to add up our indebtedness to the past we shall find that the " barbarians " have brought their gifts as well as the Greeks. For without the primitive inventions of fire, the wheel, iron-smelting, stone carving, and a host of others, the later inventions could never have been made. These have all arisen by wresting her secrets from nature one by one. And the human spirit is the mightiest product of nature. It is the "sword of God." Too much is made of the distinction between a mechanical object and the mind that made it. The object is regarded as something isolated, something, so to speak " artificial." But the *Mauretania* is no more and no less artificial than a coral island, and it is a good deal less mechanical. The little vernacular book published by the Yakusu mission is excellent save only in the title—*The White Man's Wonders*.[1] The wonders are those of the human spirit, resident in the Lokele people as in the British who teach them and the Belgians who administer them. And to look on these wonders in this light has in it a really ethical value. The mind of the humble villager struggling to improve his garden or to master the alphabet differs only in degree and not in essence from that of the designer of the Victoria Falls bridge. It is this which is the lesson of the motor car for the African—that precisely those natural forces which when uncontrolled frighten and afflict us, when tamed and understood are our servants. The native chauffeur in Blantyre or in Kumasi is not driving an object, he is controlling a force, and therein his spirit is more powerful than the forces of nature. This is the " humanistic " aspect of engineering.

Sanderson, the great schoolmaster of Oundle, established in his school what he called a " Temple of Vision." It was to be a demonstration to the boys of the wonders of the spirit that is in man. Representations of the achievements of the ages were to be found there, and in this hall there was to be no work done, no other purpose served than this one. The boys were to be able to go into it at any time to under-

---

[1] See p. 102 above.

stand and think over the mighty works of the men of old, of whose spirit also were they themselves.

A "Temple of Vision" is needed for African boarding-schools too, in order that they may learn to appreciate and take pleasure in the works of men not unlike themselves, and in so doing to take pleasure in the works of their own minds.

CHAPTER X.

THE FORM OF AFRICAN EDUCATION.

I.

THE form of African education has been a matter of perpetual criticism and controversy. The chief defect that has been discovered in it is that it is " too literary."

Let us first of all set before ourselves a number of texts.

The Government Commission that reported on East Africa in 1925 made some strong statements on the way in which teaching was given in the schools.

'... Missionary education has been too literary in character, and not sufficiently devoted to the wider education of the African....'[1]

This charge I have already ventured to call in question, both because it is doubtful whether what is called " literary " education is literary at all, and because a truly literary education could not fail to be of use of the African as a man, although it may not be of immediate use to him as a farmer or as a labourer for the European.

'We do not suggest for one moment that what is termed literary education can be entirely dispensed with ; a knowledge of the three R's is essential. But the danger is lest we import into Africa nineteenth-century English Board-School education with its obsolete emphasis on the earning of marks and the passing of written examinations, and still more with the excessive importance attached to the knowledge and parrot-like repetition of text-books on foreign history and geography.'[2]

This statement loses effect through its very violence. It associates " literary education " with what are called contemptuously " nineteenth-century Board-School " methods.

[1] *Report*, Cd. 2387, p. 50.   [2] P. 52.

The charge is just as true of the classical curriculum of the public schools and of the technical curriculum of the organized science schools that followed the board schools.

Mr. Ormsby-Gore speaks even more strongly in the Report of his visit to West Africa in 1926.

'The next essential weakness of the present educational system in West Africa on the technical side is the excessive " cult of the certificate." . . . The African has a great facility for acquiring information without assimilating it.'

Of this we have already seen a number of examples taken from the West Coast.

'Some of the books which I observed being used in West African schools have long been obsolete in England. Elementary readers with pictures and descriptions of hansom cabs have little value for English children and none at all for West African children. . . . Even in the teaching of geography I found cases where the children had a parrot-like knowledge of the names of places in England, but no knowledge at all of West African geography.'[1]

That amiable bird, the common parrot, seems to be familiar to both East and West Africa, whether the children have actually seen him or not !

A still more valuable, because a more philosophic, witness is Lord Lugard. After discussing in two notable chapters on education the need for the production of a character and ability more suited to native environment, he summarizes his argument :—

'. . . these results may best be achieved by placing the formation of character before the training of the intellect . . . this may be done by boarding-schools ; by an adequate British staff, by . . . the co-operation of the mission societies and . . . the control of Government over all educational agencies ; and finally by the encouragement of moral and religious instruction.' And by this . . . I speak of the controlling force and guiding principle which ministers through creeds and systems of philosophy to spiritual needs—the force which inspires a man to a sense of duty, to unswerving integrity and loyalty, whether in the public or the private relations of life. *It is additional to and greater than the secular and utilitarian education of the class-room.* It is founded generally on religious sanctions, and finds its highest expression

[1] *Report*, Cd. 2744, p. 90.

in the noblest of creeds. It is an essential part of the environment and atmosphere of any institution fit to train and educate a nation.'[1]

2.

I have italicized a sentence in Lord Lugard's statement because I think it unconsciously gives the reason why African education has been "parrot-like," obsessed by examinations, too "literary," and generally useless. A sharp line has been drawn between that which is "secular and utilitarian" on the one hand, and that which is religious and character-forming on the other. Ranged with the secular and utilitarian subjects are the three R's, geography, hygiene, nature study, history, and all those things for which a "school" is more specifically required. On the religious and character-forming side are Scripture, moral instruction, and manual training. Teaching, therefore, is concerned mainly with the giving of information; it is not believed to be capable of doing much more than that. The real business of building up personality is "additional" to the secular and utilitarian education of the class-room. Where school work is looked upon in this material way both by teachers and by administrators, and also by missionaries, it cannot be a source of surprise if in the pupils knowledge puffeth up.

'The output of the schools is described as unreliable, lacking in integrity, self-control, and discipline, and without respect for authority of any kind. The vanity of the young men produced by the schools had . . . become intolerable.'[2]

This is, however, exactly parallel to the similar system in the English public schools, with a difference of emphasis. The African school emphasizes the class-work side; the English school emphasizes the social side. At its worst the African school produces a parody, "a picker-up of learning's crumbs"; the product of the English school at its worst

---

[1] *The Dual Mandate in British Tropical Africa* (3rd edit., 1926), p. 460. (Italics mine.)
[2] *Ibid.*, p. 428.

has been described as " the soul of a prig housed in the body of a barbarian." [1]

It is because this cleavage between the work of the class-room and the organization of the school is accepted by so many people that we require external aids to do the work that the studies ought to do but which we regret they cannot do. As external aids Lord Lugard suggests the residential system, the appointment of monitors, sport, and moral instruction—in other words, Dr. Arnold's programme for Rugby.

All this is to my mind educational heresy. The teacher is a living human being concerned in a co-operative enterprise with another human being, the pupil, and if his work as a teacher is looked upon as secular and utilitarian, it lowers the esteem of that co-operative enterprise. If lawless and undisciplined people are being produced by the schools, this is not due to the subjects taught in the class-room, nor is the remedy to be found in the re-organization of something outside the class-room. It is surely due to *the way in which* subjects are taught.

And by " the way in which " I mean all the associations of the subjects—the sense of wonder and interest with which they are or are not handled, the meanness or the beauty of the place in which they are taught, their association in the pupil's mind with his liking or dislike for the teacher, the atmosphere of helpfulness or of patronage in which the work is carried on. All these things are the " form " of education. They are integral with the work in hand, while monitors and sport, although valuable and necessary to the school community, are not integral with the teaching side of it.

Two examples may show what I mean..

I remember Professor J. Arthur Thomson in a natural-history lecture speaking of the fact that water is at its maximum density at 4° C. This is simply a " fact " which you can observe or get in a text-book. But he went on to show that on this fact had marvellously depended the continuity of life on this planet, for living things were able to exist at the bottom of the pools even in the Ice Ages. The speaker evidently felt that there was more in this than physics. There

---

[1] See T. P. Nunn, *Education : Its Data and First Principles*, p. 1.

was romance and there was even theology! He made us feel it likewise.

The other example is of a different kind. I visited a mission school near Pretoria in which were three European teachers who had been trained in a well-known college in London. One of them took me round. He was thoroughly efficient, knew every trick of the trade, and had "done" pyschology. At each class-room where a Native teacher was engaged he opened the door without knocking. In one room he stood in the middle of the floor and in the hearing of all he said to me, "You know, you mustn't think of these Natives as if they were English. You can't take them very far. They have no initiative."

3.

The question arises whether the boarding-school or the day-school is the better educational instrument. There is a considerable difference between the situation as it arises in Africa and as it exists in England.

It is of course true that if children are segregated and the teacher's whole time is given up to them, he can, as the old phrase went, "mould" them as he wishes, or as the parents wish him to mould them. They will then turn out either according to pattern, or violently of the opposite type: "moulding" is in practice as likely to produce rebels as it is to produce lambs. It of course seems much easier to educate people if you have them with you all the time, but this is an unproved assumption, and often it means a reliance on circumstances to do your work for you. If the home is as keen a place of education as the school, the argument for the boarding-school is weak compared with that for the day-school. It is often the argument of the poor teacher, who needs these external aids to produce his results. But seminarism is always a second-best form of education, for a seminary is a place that seeks to produce a type rather than to encourage people to be their own best selves, whether they conform to type or not.

Africa, however, is not England, and I have touched on

the boarding-school argument only lest it should be taken for granted that a boarding-school is the best form of educational institution. I do not think it is, in England. It certainly is the best in Africa. This is not because it is in itself more "character-building," but because a school of any sort indicates *ipso facto* a quite different society from that of the African village or tribe. It cannot be too emphatically stated that no matter what we teach, even if we cut out all literary subjects, and stick to agriculture and handicrafts and the most familiar occupations of Native life, we are nevertheless doing something the like of which has never been done in that way before. Introduce into agricultural technique a recognition of cause and effect, make knowledge self-conscious and not merely traditional, and you are introducing the Native into a new world.

Education in the formal sense may be defined as the sum of the ideas and knowledge which one generation thinks it worth while to pass on to the next. In Africa this knowledge, even if it be of "native" handicrafts, is knowledge in a European setting, while those to whom it is handed on are Africans. The school is a popular, and by this time a familiar, thing in African life, but in the greater part of Africa away from the coast it is as yet fundamentally an alien thing, even where Natives are the teachers. Accordingly while in England the school corresponds if not to the actual practice, at any rate to the accepted theories, of the world outside, in Africa the world outside does not help at all. The people, of course, help, and parents make sacrifices for their children's education just as they do in this country, but at least in the first generation the home cannot support the work of the school, for each is the centre of its own world.

For the stages beyond the village school the boarding-school is therefore the necessary means of education. And it is so, not because of any intrinsic moral influence, but because it provides a world which more or less represents the world in which the school subjects are matters of familiar knowledge. In other words—to put it with exaggeration—the subjects of the class-room represent new ways of looking at life, the boarding-school represents a new world—an association of people to whom the subjects of "education" are not "subjects" but part of life itself. This, for instance, at Penhalonga and at the Agricultural College at Tsolo, is the reason for the compulsory use of English during the working day. To get hold of the ideas that lie behind the course at Tsolo it is necessary not to study them as "subjects" but to live them, to make them part of your everyday thought, so that when you think of them you will always think of them in a certain way. The boarding-school in Africa is an attempt to provide for the African that general world of ideas in which the English child lives by the mere fact of being in a country where literature, the newspapers, and ordinary conversation assume those ideas. The boarding-school may be an artificial segregation both in England and in Africa, but it is—paradoxically—much less artificial in Africa than in England. In both places it creates a society which is different from the society outside, but in Africa that difference is essential in order to create an appropriate background for new studies, in England the difference is a social difference and has nothing to do with studies at all.

This seems to me to be fundamental, and all other reasons for the boarding-school to be secondary, and to be based on our experience in England rather than on the special conditions in Africa. Dr. Arnold's reasons are largely irrelevant. The possibility of having monitors, of giving the pupils the opportunity for a measure of self-government, of reproducing the tribal disciplinary system within the school, is of course valuable and excellent, and, granted that a boarding-school exists, this is surely the way to carry it on. But the reason for its existence does not lie in these things.

The nature of character-building has already been discussed. It is only when men's effective likes and effective dislikes are touched that the basis for character is laid. *What* things they will like, and *what* things they will dislike depends on the width of opportunity for choice that is offered to them. In the African boarding-school, therefore, those things which normally appear as school subjects are part of the make-up of the place and cannot be found outside. In a literary and debating society, for instance, problems out of a text-book become " causes " to be defended or attacked, and this emotional impulse behind study deepens study and makes it part of one's own thought and life. A library also helps. Subjects which are otherwise confined within a syllabus there break their bonds and are found in all kinds of unlikely places—in illustrated magazines, in historical novels, in popular literature. All this gives men something to think about and to talk over in the dormitories and elsewhere, and so these subjects can become part of them, and, as we say, help to " form their character."

Ideas of responsibility and self-government which are learned only in the artificial segregation of a boarding-school are apt to wither in the open air, particularly if there is a great difference between the society inside and the society outside. Loyalty and discipline, if cultivated by the prefect system, will be effective where the implications of that system are accepted and understood, but there will be a great strain on them where these are not understood nor accepted. The very qualities which have made our old public school boys excellent rulers of subject races have often made them less effective where those races have begun to show symptoms of independence. India in this generation is an acid test of those qualities. The best men come out well in this trying situation, and they triumph over tradition as they triumphed over it at school. But the average man, whose mind has been formed in a " mould," however excellent, finds himself hopelessly at sea when all the foundation truths of his education are despised or questioned.

The African is not likely to be any better. If the arrangements of the boarding-school are emphasized as the agency for the production of character, that character will have no relation to a society with different social arrangements. So far from literary studies being the cause of indiscipline in education in the past, it is more than likely that the social segregation of school life has been the real root of the trouble. It has been intended to produce discipline, and the studies have been intended for information. It is surely mistaken to use the social arrangements of the school for one purpose and the studies for another. If the studies of the school condition the life of the school, and if they are taught in a

" humane " way, morality will be seen to spring out of the nature of life itself rather than out of a particular organization.

4.

There is no educational maxim more widely believed in Africa to-day than that " education must be based on religion." It is recognized in general by anthropologists, administrators, and missionaries that the Bantu—unlike, presumably, his more civilized contemporaries—is a fundamentally religious person, and that any successful education must be founded deep on these nether springs. And in the particular circumstances of present-day Africa, it is also recognized that the old religious sanctions have gone or are going, and new ones are needed if we are to prevent the complete disintegration of native life. While, therefore, the " content " of African education is to be European knowledge, chiefly of practical processes, it is held that the " form " of it is to be religion.

We have first to consider what this phrase is taken to mean in this particular case, and then to consider how far it ought to apply to education in general, in Europe as well as in Africa, and then to study ways and means by which its " religious basis " may be made effective in Africa.

It will help our discussion if we recall the implications of the idea, " based on religion," in our own country. The obstacle that stood in the way of a national system of education and, in earlier days, of adequate inspection of schools, was this very dogma that " education must be based on religion." The modern administrator in Africa means something quite different by this from the meaning given to it by our English forefathers in the nineteenth century, but in practice it often comes to the same thing. An educational system was considered to be " based on religion " when professionally religious people control it. In England the National Society was Anglican, and the British and Foreign Schools Society was Nonconformist, and between them they accounted for elementary education more or less in the same way as the missionary societies in Africa to-day account for Native education. With this they were content. As long as teaching included Scripture, and as long as this and the other subjects were taught by Churchmen and Nonconformists respectively, and as long as these teachers were controlled by the heads of their own denomination, education was " based on religion." The foundation of education in religion was accepted in this mechanical sense because both religion and education were accepted in a mechanical sense. Religion was conformity, and education was instruction.

In Africa this attitude is still present. By " education is based on religion " often nothing more is meant than that it is in the hands of the missions, or that Scripture is a subject of the curriculum.

It is clear, however, from what I have already said in the chapter on " The Mission," that the control of education by the mission by no means guarantees that it is " based on religion." If we turn again to the article already quoted from *The Rotherham Advertiser* we shall see how plain this is. The writer points out that

'Here the discipline is strict, almost military in its strictness, but at the same time eminently just. This can also be said of punishments, including the administration (*sic*) of the cane, which is officially permitted to schoolmasters.

'The result is that a tone of well-being is conveyed, while no fault can be found with the marks of respect afforded not only to the European staff but to *any casual white person*[1] met on the road and elsewhere outside the neighbourhood of the mission. There is no suspicion of pampering of, or pandering to pupils. The native is a child, and must be treated as such, and, though black, he is no whit less quick in his perceptions than a European . . . whom he may take advantage of and flout. Under this heading may be conveniently included the slogan of the " black brother." '

He then gives the sentence I have already quoted on page 204.

It has seemed to some missionaries on reading this that the basis of the education in this particular boarding-school may be religion but it is not the Christian religion. The writer, however, assures us :—

---

[1] Italics mine.

'Six and a half hours weekly, not including Sundays, is devoted to prayers first thing every morning, hymns, Scripture reading and general Biblical instruction. On Sunday there is a short and simple morning service. . . . In the afternoon there is a short service conducted by one of the teachers, while once a quarter Holy Communion is celebrated for converts. There is also every Sunday a class for preparing candidates for conversion and confirmation. . . .

'The newer and fuller life—industrial, mental, social—must have a new religious base. . . . An honest endeavour has been made to produce a better finished article then the raw one, and . . . religion is not the Alpha and Omega of the training given at the mission.'

As far back as 1924 the Phelps-Stokes Commission commended this mission as being run on the right lines, and the head of it as an outstanding missionary educator, whose views may be taken as typical of a certain school of thought about Native education, and about the " religion " which is its basis.

5.

The case for basing African education on religion is the case for basing all education on religion. And by " religion " I mean not simply a man's belief but his *effective* belief; that is to say, something which decides his conduct and his attitude to the world in which he lives. I say conduct and attitude, because both are necessary. If a man looks on the world as very evil, and feels that beauty is a snare and joy a delusion, these are matters of attitude which are concerned with religion, although they involve no particular " conduct." The fundamental thing in religion is loyalty, and in the Christian religion it is loyalty to and union with Christ—looking on the world as He looked on it; loving God and so never despairing of men; finding Him in the glowing heart, the quiet mind, and the spirit wrestling with self; loving men as He loved them; appropriating the witness of Christian folk of all ages to be our witness; allowing history to feed experience, and experience to illuminate history; gladly learning and gladly teaching; rising into " the liberty of the Christian man " and at the same time by discipline and in humility enriching the whole Christian community, which is

THE FORM OF AFRICAN EDUCATION 237

the " body of Christ " ; and above all, holding out hands to receive His gift of life, which is more than we can ask or think or deserve.

I doubt if this conception of the Christian religion is at all visible in the article which I have just quoted. But if it is not this, what is it—a set of words, a code of commands, a number of " services " ? These are surely hopelessly inadequate to convey to other people the mystery of " the life hid with Christ in God." The word " religion " has become terribly cheapened in Africa by its association in this way with education.

If Christianity can be at all adequately described as I have described it, how is education " based " on it ?

We have already seen in earlier chapters something of what is meant by the " religious approach " to various subjects—to nature study, Scripture, manual training, and others. This religious approach will be easier both for Europeans and Natives if the " atmosphere " is a religious atmosphere.

It is unfortunate that the word " atmosphere " has to be used in this context, for there is probably more nonsense both talked and believed about " atmosphere " in this sense than about any other term in either education or religion. A place may be demoralized by inefficiency, and yet we shall be told that it has a religious " atmosphere." " Atmosphere," like " character," is supposed to be a quality that is non-intellectual and even anti-intellectual, something that comes of itself, and yet for which people are willing to take credit unto themselves. It is something unexamined because believed to be unexaminable.

Yet it is a real enough thing. There is an " atmosphere " about one mission which is different from that of another. In Southern Rhodesia a Government Education report referred to the " atmosphere " of Mr. A. S. Cripps' mission and said that it was " all its own " and could not be compared with that of any other mission.[1]

" Atmosphere " is something that yields itself to analysis, although it is not produced by a deliberate synthesis. It is

---

[1] *Report*, 1925, paragraph 424.

like a work of genius, like Shakespeare's "Macbeth" for instance, so brilliantly analysed and criticized by Dr. R. G. Moulton,[1] yet without at all bringing with that criticism the inference that Dr. Moulton could himself have written "Macbeth." The elements that make a successful educational institution may be diagnosed, and yet they may be put together again somewhere else by other people without producing a similar "atmosphere." But given able, good, and unselfish men, the experience of other people and places will always be a help towards excellence.

6.

First of all, then, we observe the religious basis of education, or secure the religious "atmosphere" for it, in a proper regard for the outward form.

By this I do not mean any narrow view of symbolism. The missionary who told me in Nyasaland, "We bank upon symbolism here," really meant, "We bank upon a selected symbolism," and was thinking in ecclesiastical terms. A white vestment may indicate purity, but clearly purity has no necessary connection with vestments, white or otherwise. In the same way a Lamb and a flag may "symbolize" Christ. But symbolism in these cases needs interpretation, and without the interpretation they are simply pictures or clothes. They are a comparison of one thing with another, or, as it were, an acted simile. With primitive people the danger of this is that the symbol may be taken for the thing which is symbolized.

I mean, however, that the form of a thing should correspond to the thing of which it is the form. In the early days of grant-aided education in England it was held that for a school-room a good barn would do.[2] It is clear, however, that if a school exists to make children citizens of a wonderful new world of thought and of action "a barn" will *not* do for a school except as a makeshift. The meanness of a second-hand building is reflected in the production of a second-hand

---

[1] *Shakespeare as a Dramatic Artist* (1885).
[2] H. Holman, *English National Education* (1898), p. 93.

mind, and in the days of that excellent recommendation school children's minds were deliberately second-hand. The content and the form corresponded. And doubtless there are missions in Africa where there is correspondence between form and content at this low level. But if education is to be " based on religion," in the sense in which I have used the word " religion," it will need to seek to make the temple correspond with the spirit that is to dwell therein. I am not here suggesting anything elaborate or costly, but rather that the materials at hand should be put to the best possible use with the best possible craftsmanship. If the school is a mud hut let its building be done with dignity and " formally." At the Mbereshi mission the water-course that had taken six months of painstaking work to construct was first put into operation at a " solemn opening," with thanksgivings and prayer. But this came as the culmination of a process that was carried on in the same spirit rather than as a " dedication " tacked on to a piece of work which in itself excited no interest.

It is here where both the " cult of imperfection " and the " cult of perfection " of which I have already spoken,[1] seem to me to fail—the one because it is content with anything on the spot, the other because it is content with nothing on the spot. A mud hut as an African church is not intrinsically better than a stone building—although some would hold to the one, and some to the other. The standard is neither what the European can afford nor what the Native at present can understand, but what does the situation yield which can best represent the work that we are seeking to do ? The business of a hospital, for example, is to make people well, and everything that can be done under the circumstances to bring about that end should be done, whether it is " native " or not. The business of a school is to fit people to live in a world of higher values than they would otherwise know. Its exterior should therefore somehow correspond to its aim. To associate education with good work, with beauty, with reverence, and with " the best possible under the circumstances," is necessary if we are to base it on religion.

[1] Above, p. 74.

It was an astonishment to me to find in a certain famous mission beautiful houses for the staff and elaborate machinery in the workshops, and a long, mean, unlovely building for a school and a church. There was nothing to suggest that the aim of the work in this building was to turn men from darkness to light, both intellectual and spiritual. It was as grubby as a potting-shed.

On the other hand, there are missions where Government architects, native commissioners and missionaries have come together and evolved buildings worthy of their object. Such a place is the mission school at Zomba, Nyasaland, a rough sketch plan of which I give here,—and which is illustrated opposite.

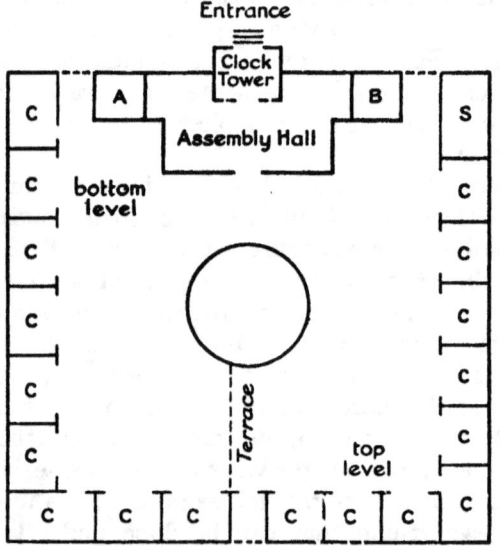

A. Headmaster.   B. Assistant.   C. Class-rooms.   S. Store-room

There are 380 children on the books, from the lowest classes up to Standard IV. There is no wood in the building at all, and so there is nothing for the white ants to eat. Each class-room is entered by a wide arch which is open and serves as both a door and a window. The verandah opening into the quadrangle on the fourth side makes a larger space for the assembly hall, and a little gallery half-way up the wall on the side of the clock tower gives a space for a choir or

CHURCH OF SCOTLAND MISSION SCHOOL, ZOMBA, NYASALAND

THE FORM OF AFRICAN EDUCATION

a few players of instruments. The whole design is thoroughly African, and the school was one of the most pleasing buildings I saw in Africa—suggestive, dignified, and with " roots in the soil."

At the well-known American mission at Amanzimtoti, in Natal, the girls' dormitory was another delightful building. It was built of cement bricks, the window frames were of iron, the windows were wide and the whole place full of light. No plaster was used for the inside walls. In the box rooms where all the coats were kept, instead of pegs there was a rod at a distance of a foot from the wall to give extra space. Everything was made on the mission premises, and it was a highly successful example of what is possible in such a district. Here is the plan.

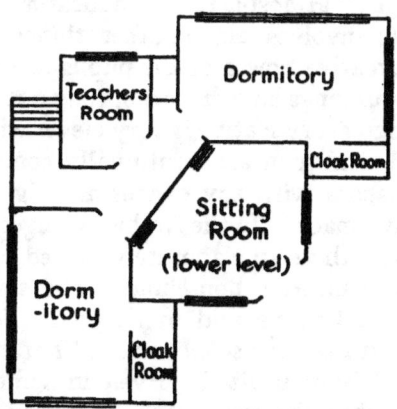

Both of these are brick buildings, but the same principle is found in the model mud houses for the teachers at Mkhoma, and in the *pisé-de-terre* and Kimberley-brick buildings at Domboshawa. " Anything " will not do for a purpose of this kind.

And as with the shell of a building, so also should it be with the internal arrangements of it. One of the most pleasing class-rooms I was ever in was a little rondavel at St. Cuthbert's Mission, Tsolo, in which the upper standards were taught. It was beautifully and yet simply decorated in broad effects of colour, and there were pictures on the wall of a kind which created an emotional interest in the work that was done in the room. It was like a good class-room in a good elementary school at home. Of the same type was the large school-room at Nengubo, Marandellas, Southern Rhodesia. Here the teacher had coloured the walls in two shades of brown, the darker shade at the bottom, and between them a border with stencilled figures of animals that the children were likely to know. It was all very thoughtfully and neatly done, and was a pleasant place to visit.

7.

The element of appreciation is a necessary factor in creating the right " atmosphere " for education. It has many sides to it. It involves among other things the use of as much of the creative power of the pupils as can be used, so that their surroundings have in part sprung out of themselves.

On the Congo every Native is very clever with a knife and a bit of wood, and men are continually coming round the houses at Kinshasa with toy canoes and figures that they themselves have made. In the Arabisé villages on the Congo you find here and there an elaborately carved *porte-Koran* for use in the Mohammedan household. The same skill is exhibited also in Rhodesia and in Nigeria. Yet in none of these regions did I see one school or one Church in which this native gift had been utilized. Even in some of the most beautiful Churches the woodwork had been made in the ordinary way of business in the carpenter's shop. In one mission the head was so afraid that the Natives might " spoil " even the mechanical work done under his direction that he had made carefully measured drawings of everything, and there was no initiative left to the craftsman at all. The building went up, but the Natives had no interest in it, for it was not in any sense theirs. On the other hand, the Blantyre Cathedral is " native " through and through, and the European builder only did the work which the Natives themselves could not do.

Craftsmanship is one form of self-expression. Another is ritual.

THE FORM OF AFRICAN EDUCATION

Ritual is not an ecclesiastical thing; it is a psychological thing. It is one of the commonest characteristics of childhood and is akin to play. The child likes acting a part, and while acting he is showing the emotions of the person or the animal that he is representing. And in children's games the same thing has always to be done in the same way. Even in telling a story to a child you are pulled up sharp if you venture to tell it in a way differently from that in which he first heard it. The " form " of the thing is to a child an essential part of the thing. And in the absence of writing it is this element of " ritual " that has served primitive people as an external memory. Traditions have been preserved because there has been an unalterable form in which to preserve them. And in the same way in all education which aims at " character," at setting a " stamp " on a person's life, there must be form as well as content. The value of form is that it helps to create the liberty which it appears at first sight to check. It is the banks of a river that make it a river rather than a marsh. It is the " sonnet's scanty plot of ground " which by releasing the poet from the " weight of too much liberty " gives him a truer freedom. Children are never so free as when they play and yet they are never so formal.

African life, too, has its formal side—it is formal in work and in play. There are set forms for sowing and reaping, for child-birth, for dancing, for eating and drinking, and for the chase. Part of the disintegration that waits upon African life with the advent of European civilization is due to the fact that European life is a much more shapeless thing, less formal, less symbolic. And accordingly, the aspiring African student assumes that the form of education must lie in the words of the text-book—and these are treasured because they appear to be the outward and visible sign of an inward and spiritual grace. Or the " form " of European life is supposed to be European clothes, or litigation after the European fashion. In Lagos the " form " of religion in Native churches would seem to be found in the truly pontifical language in which they announce their harvest festivals and other services! It is the absence of form in our life that makes the Native at sea in our modern world and makes him do things that appear ridiculous. He would have been much more at home in Europe of the Middle Ages.

It is therefore important that the way in which the new life comes to him should be as carefully studied as the nature of that life itself. The association of new ways of thinking, new knowledge, new morality, with beauty, with dignity and ritual, with creative work, with joy, exhibits forms which he can come to understand and which are so much the expression of an inner spirit that they help him to receive it.[1]

The value of respecting the form of a subject as well as its content lies in the fact that here is the root of discipline. Discipline to be of any value at all needs to spring naturally out of the situation in hand, and respect for the subject creates a discipline which does not require external aid.

The social life of the school is very vitally connected with the " academic " work of the school. The social life will not produce unselfish people if the aim of the studies is to set one person in rivalry against his fellows. The social life helps to create the " atmosphere " in which work is done. It is clear that in the case of the school which had six and a half hours of religious exercises and a discipline " almost military in its strictness," religion was simply a subject, and the social arrangements simply a method of running the school,— neither of them could be integrated into the life of the pupils, for they were both external, alien, third-party. Religion is not a subject, and social life is not created by rule. It is created by people who themselves live in a certain way. To a large extent the thing which " bases " or does not " base " education on religion, is the corporate life of the Europeans on the mission station, or in the school. A mission which is rent by division and jealousy cannot possibly base its education or anything else on religion. Whatever may be thought of the theological implications of the doctrine, it is true at any rate in education that " dominion

---

[1] The " celebrations " of Shakespeare, Darwin, St. Paul, the League of Nations, etc., drawn up by Dr. F. H. Hayward for use in schools, are an admirable method of providing an emotional backing for school studies. See Hayward, *A First Book of School Celebrations*, and Hayward and Freeman, *The Spiritual Foundations of Reconstruction* (1919).

is founded in grace." For the authority of a teacher is not authority in general but authority for a certain purpose, and that purpose is the building up of the lives of men and women. It is a conditioned authority. He may indeed be able to make people obey any orders, and to show " respect to any casual white person met on the road " (thereby saluting race as race, independently of character), but this is a mere exercise of force. It has nothing whatever to do with teaching, it is concerned neither with the teacher as teacher nor with the pupil as pupil. It indicates not authority but the absence of it, not the ability but the lack of ability to keep discipline.

8.

The best mission schools in Africa are those which have about them a certain unmistakable sense of leisure. They are usually busy missions, but they control their busy-ness ; it does not control them. They believe in the value of wasting a certain amount of time.

A very wise head of a school in Southern Rhodesia said to me that the more there was to do, the more time he believed he ought to reserve for himself to be at the service of those who wished to see him. It was an astonishingly difficult thing to do, but he did it. His colleagues, the native teachers, pupils, workmen, apprentices, felt that if they needed help and encouragement he was on hand to help and encourage. This sense of space and of unhurried calm that he kept in his work set the tone for the whole school. Work was done just as well as it was in other places ; it was even done better, because there was time and space in which to see it *sub specie aeternitatis* and not only as a daily grind. And it is a wonderful help to teachers, native and European, to know that interest is being taken in their work, and that what they see only as the trees is seen by some one else as the wood. This is valuable at any time, but in order to base education on religion it is quite essential.

And with the sense of leisure comes reverence, " Be still and know that I am God " is a valuable motto for a school. Reverence is one of the roots of religion. It is akin to fear—

not the base fear lest some one else may hurt you, but the noble fear lest you should hurt the other person—and it cannot be created save by indirect means. It is no more "taught" by making a boy take off his hat than religion is taught by making him repeat a creed. It is an attitude fostered by wide views and deep sympathies and a leisured spirit. The hectic, bustling mind that looks on education as the conveying of so many lumps of knowledge and advice will never understand the religious basis of its work, nor will the manual training expert as such, nor will the proselytizer and the propagandist. The great agency in education is the universe of nature and of people which God made and which manifests Him, and a man can be introduced to it only through those who are freeholders therein and have no need of chaffering. It is this universal element which is present in all great teaching, whether it is in lecturing like that of F. W. Maitland, or in popular literature like that of Sir Owen Edwards, or in ordinary schoolmastering like that of Edward Bowen at Harrow, or of those famous inspired Scottish dominies, or of scores of men and women who teach at the present day in our elementary schools. There is a trick in teaching which can be learned by practice and it is effective for a certain end. The really good teacher has this trick but he has something else beside. You can call it what you will—inspiration, genius, personality—these are simply names for something that defies analysis. But it is not an accidental or casual thing. One element in it is this connection of the work in hand with the universe of which teacher, pupil, and subject are all part. It is the gift which comes to the humble of heart and the noble of soul, for they will take time to cultivate it. And this universal quality is the only real "religious basis of education," against which all mechanical divisions of studies and codes of rules are mere shams.

PART III.
THE MIDDLE DISTANCE.

CHAPTER XI.
THE MISSIONARY SOCIETIES.

I.

THE nature of missionary work abroad is dependent far more than that of the Church's work at home on the current trend of popular theology. Since the seventeenth century the authority of the Church has been loosened from one side of life after another. Art, education, philanthropy, social life, science, and in these days even theology itself, have one by one shaken themselves free and developed on lines of their own. Accordingly there is a great deal of ignorance in many of these spheres of activity now outside the Church as to what Christians really do believe. The doctrine of evolution is a commonplace in nearly all the theological colleges in Britain, and yet Sir Arthur Keith seems to be convinced that the quarrel between religion and science stands where it did.

On the mission field, however, the Church is the agent of an almost complete civilization. Art, education, literature, science, agriculture, social reform, are all aspects of mission work. A well-known missionary near Bulawayo is parson, teacher, builder, carpenter, brickmaker, farmer, botanist, surveyor, archæologist, and licensed slaughterer. And in some missions to this list would be added the further duties of printer and doctor. The missionary is working amid people who need all these services, and who in most cases will get them only through him. Any new current of thought about theology, or politics, or education that flows into his life can find a dozen outlets. In Africa everything is part of the Church's business, and any theory about the missionary's work can at once be translated into action.

2.

The missionary motive which established the great missionary societies during the Napoleonic wars was the evangelical counterblast to the philosophy of the " belle sauvage." The philosophers postulated the happy savage living in an idyllic primitive simplicity. The Evangelicals accepted their view of the environment, but held that where every prospect pleases only man is vile. He was living in ignorance of the blessings of the Gospel and how could he be happy?

The motive has often been stated as if it were purely a theological one, concerned with the desire to snatch perishing souls from Hell like brands plucked from the burning. This of course was present, but there was also a great impulse of pity for the unfortunate. It was this pity which led many of the earlier missionaries to Europeanize their converts. The Gospel had done so much for England, " the Bible," as Queen Victoria was alleged to have said, " is the secret of England's greatness," and therefore where the Bible comes the blessings of civilization ought to come with it. It was a very simple faith, sincerely held and earnestly preached, with no doubts as to its efficacy and its superiority over everything else that the world had to offer. And it was responsible for the exploits in Africa of some of the greatest men of our race, Livingstone being the greatest of all. The missionary motive has never been put into better words than his :—

'In the glow of love which Christianity inspires, I resolved to devote my life to the alleviation of human misery.'[1]

[1] *Missionary Travels and Researches in South Africa* (1857), p. 5.

3.

The missionary motive in those days sprang out of the Evangelical theology and the enthusiasm of Revolutionary ideas. With these impulses men went out to save souls. What is the motive to-day?

It cannot be unconnected with the prevalent ideas of the time. These ideas are very different from those prevalent in the days of the Evangelical Revival and of the first half of the nineteenth century. We have passed over to the other side of the great watershed in thought made in 1859 by the publication of Darwin's *Origin of Species*. We see now that everything, whether institutions, or people, or natural phenomena, has had a history, and it is in the course of that history that we see its real nature. Our estimate of it is formed not by what it is but by what it has come to be. The difference is not so much in the subject-matter as in the method of study.

Theology has not escaped from this doctrine of development. Almost at the same time that the Oxford Movement had drawn attention to origins, the historical method was applied to these origins themselves. Neither the Bible nor the Creeds were taken as having verbal inspiration. They have been examined in the light of the circumstances of their times, and in that light their authority has been assessed. The result of this process has been, in the case of the Bible, not to depreciate but actually to enhance its value.

This evolutionary study of the documents of the faith has been the concern of Protestant Churches. But the principle has been carried farther in a direction in which even Roman Catholics have been willing to follow. This is in the study of religion itself. The comparative study of religion has vindicated its universal quality, and has helped to destroy the very rationalism which it was once thought to prove. In these days it is the rationalists rather than the theologians who are apt to be unscientific sentimentalists. Nevertheless the comparative study of religion has created difficulties for the universal claims of Christianity. All religions have been seen in their own way to lead to communion with God, and the Christian mystics have had no monopoly of the beatific vision.

At the same time the study of psychology—and in recent years, of the " new " psychology—has carried the historical method into religious experience itself. While on the one hand it has authenticated that experience, on the other hand it has often interpreted it in ways that are not religious. By analysing the subjective it has tended to discredit the objective element in human belief. It has traced religious experience back to the instincts, and by explaining its origin has often been held to have explained away its significance.

We are thus living in an entirely different world of thought from that in which the early missionaries lived. That which appeared to them so absolute appears to us as relative. The missionary motive was an absolute command which required absolute obedience. Even where the more human impulse of pity was the prevailing motive, it was pity for people who lacked certain quite well-defined things which the missionary had no doubt that he could supply. In these days there is no such absolute quality about it. The message of the missionary is relative to its historical development, to the psychology of the people, to their previous religious systems, and to the other forces at work in the same field. The missionary comes not as formerly to destroy, but to fulfil.

These tendencies of the present age are commonly summed up in a popular form of "chiliasm." Truth is something which will appear in the future. We do not know it yet, nor will it be known until all the nations and creeds have brought their contribution into the common stock. At that far distant date the Kingdom of God will come, and every good deed that is done, every good cause that triumphs, " hastens " the coming of the Kingdom. It is not unfair to say that whereas in an earlier age the missionary motive was to save souls, in these days it is to hasten the Kingdom. We have thereby grown out of the sense of immediacy which possessed an earlier generation of missionaries. Every single heathen converted somehow represented an absolute act, a turning from darkness to light, a beginning of eternal life. In our generation such an absolute conversion may even be deprecated as standing in the way of that particularly "native" type of Christianity which the world may hope one day to see.

4.

The Roman Church does not of course look at things in this way. Yet while its habit of assurance makes an appeal to many who see in popular theology nothing but a negation, to those on the other hand who feel the positive element in present-day thought the Roman Catholic's assurance carries no weight at all.

In these days it is the nature of authority that is under discussion rather than its validity. But in this the Roman Church as such stands where it did, although individuals in it are more sympathetic to the feeling of the age. The C.O.P.E.C. Conference [1] would have been a welcome opportunity for Cardinal Manning, and he might even have been chairman of it. But the authorities of the Roman Church in England at that time counselled abstinence from it and so lost a chance of leadership.

Rome has its own view of missionary progress, and still holds to its propagandist aims. This, however, does not mean that Roman missions are unworthy. On the contrary, there are few more excellent missions than that of the Jesuit Fathers on the Zambezi—to speak of one of which I have personal knowledge. But it does mean that the primary aim of Roman missions is to produce Roman Catholics, whereas it is fair to say that with the exception of the Fundamentalists, Protestant missions are not in Africa or anywhere else to propagate Protestantism. The trend of present-day thought is too strong within them to allow them to take such a sectarian line. Accordingly in the case of the Roman missions there is to be found an attitude to life as a whole which is apt to come into conflict not only with the Protestant attitude to life, but also with the current ideas of European civilization generally, as represented by the Government official. Particularly is this true where the

[1] The Interdenominational Conference On (Christian) Politics, Economics, and Citizenship, held in Birmingham in 1924.

territory is British and the Roman missions are from Continental countries. This may mean that within a territory which is being developed according to the best ideas of the present time, there is a small group living a life of its own on a fundamentally different kind of basis from that of the society in which it is situated. Sometimes there is actual friction. Roman Catholic missionaries in Nyasaland and in Tanganyika have from time to time caused great trouble to administrators not only because they have been aliens and have had difficulty with the English language, but still more fundamentally because they have been living in a totally different world of values from that which the British officials themselves could understand.

In non-British territory the Roman Church has had more influence in policy than it has in British territory. This is not to say that there is an absence of friction, for instance, in the Belgian Congo between priests and officials. There is often great divergence of opinion and conflict arises, but it is usually a conflict not so much over ideals for the native people, as over personal and property rights of the missions.

5.

The Anglo-Catholic missions are in an anomalous position. As part of the non-Roman system of Christianity they share not only the ethical ideals of Protestantism, but also the belief that those ethical ideals are at the heart of the Gospel. The Anglo-Catholic who is not a mere antiquarian is at bottom an evangelical. In his case, however, the " good news " which turns men from darkness to light is not the words of the preacher but the existence of the Church.

This is a very important emphasis, and it helps to account for the anomalies of the Anglo-Catholic position. For example, it is a source of wonderment, and indeed of offence, in South Africa that Anglo-Catholic bishops who take a strong line on social and racial problems will nevertheless refuse to have communion with their fellow Christians. To the Dutch Reformed minister this attitude appears to show a fellowship with the black man which the Anglican refuses to have with men of his own colour.

This inconsistency indicates how essentially the Anglo-Catholic both shares the modern outlook on the world and at the same time asserts a position which seems to deny it. On the Roman Catholic view the Church conditions the whole system of life which it has to offer to the Native : on the modern political view religion is simply a necessary part of the development of native peoples. It is not in the Anglo-Catholic blood to accept the Roman position. He would, for instance, have far too high a sense of ethical values to excommunicate the I.C.U. even if such excommunication could be effective.[1] On the other hand, the theological heritage of the Oxford Movement forbids him to associate himself with the second position. The Anglo-Catholic needs always to be careful lest his ethical affinities be taken as indicating a theological sympathy. It was almost an acted parable that at the Livingstone Conference in 1927 the Jesuits felt themselves strong enough to be able to turn up in trousers and thus to mingle with their Protestant brethren ; an Anglo-Catholic missionary came in a cassock !

6.

Fundamentalism is Catholicism inverted. It has the same rigidity of doctrine as the Roman Catholic and the Anglo-Catholic, without having the universal system which characterizes the one or the modern social attitude which characterizes the other.

Fundamentalism is particularly strong on the Lower Congo, although there are Fundamentalist societies all over Africa. The history of free-lance Protestant missions on the Lower Congo is a pathetic story of human credulity and failure. There are of course the representatives of well-established societies with a long and honourable record such as the American and European Baptists, the American Presbyterians, the Disciples of Christ, and some others. But there are very many others that have no roots in Europe

[1] See above, p. 50.

or America and fail to show any fruit in Africa. The world of thought in which they live is a world which has long since passed away as a fitting habitation for the human spirit. The motive behind them is often sincere, but also often curiously unreal. I came out on a British India boat with a missionary of this type whose literary stock-in-trade was truly astonishing. He pinned great faith on a little pamphlet which was supposed to be a re-statement of the verbal veracity of Genesis in terms of " modern " thought.

These feats of the human reason are also performed by the Roman Catholics and other Catholic verbal inspirationists, but unlike these, the Fundamentalists have no system to offer along with them. Calvinism, even in the Dutch Reformed Church, has ceased to offer a completely alternative system to Romanism. The Fundamentalist, therefore, is living under a perpetual state of martial law. The conflict between his theological position and present-day thought is a conflict which never ceases and is always held out in the open. He has no territory which he can call his own in which the sound of the battle is not heard, as is the case with the Roman Catholic. Nor can he rest content with an inconsistency like that of the Anglo-Catholics, accepting the world outside and yet affirming a doctrine which is at variance with that acceptance. He recognizes, however, as the Anglo-Catholic does not always recognize, the real significance of present-day thought, and having no system of his own, he is continually at war. This does not create a habit of mind best calculated to benefit the native races.

7.

Doctrinally, therefore, there is a certain rigidity of outlook in all these forms of Christian expression, but the effect of this in Native education differs in different cases. The Roman Catholic, having a world of his own in which to live, is in effect much more ready to admit Government co-operation than any of the others. He knows just where it will fit into the system, and if anywhere it limits his freedom of action more than he would like, his doctrine of submission to the " powers that be " will permit this interference without affecting the validity of the system. It is often the letter alone that is observed and the co-operation offered is quite a static thing, whereas a seemingly intransigent Protestant mission may in spirit agree with an enlightened administration much more than appears.

The Fundamentalist often finds it easy to co-operate with Government, but for reasons different from that of the Roman Catholic. The business of the missionary is held to be preaching the Gospel, and with everything outside this the State can deal; politics is not the concern of the Christian man. There are, however, border-line subjects which create difficulty, and education is one of them. These give rise to frontier actions in the case of the Fundamentalist, and it is a question of interference at this or that point, rather than a conflict between alternative systems.

The Anglo-Catholic finds co-operation difficult, very largely because he does not know what is involved in it. Where the rules are clear as in the Roman Church there is liberty of action within those rules; where there is no visible society assumed, as with the majority of Protestants, it is possible to follow where new light leads. But where a visible society is assumed about whose rules one is not very clear it is safer to stand still than to risk moving.

This uneasiness manifests itself in various ways. Often delegates are sent to meetings with Government who have no power to " commit the mission." A certain Anglo-Catholic missionary who accepted a call from the Government to run a Native boarding-school was visited by ostracism by the authorities of his own communion. This was an indication, however, not of lack of charity so much as of nervousness.

8.

I have spent a little time with the detailed consideration of these three types of missionary society as illustrating three different ways in which societies are affected by current movements of thought. It does not follow, however, that any given mission belonging to any one of these groups is to be characterized in this way. A mission of the Plymouth Brethren in Natal, for instance, professed a rigid and somewhat unlovely theology, but it was held with such a sense of humour and humility that there was no place more popular with Government Inspectors, and no place that did better and happier work. I have already indicated that there are different varieties of Anglo-Catholicism and their attitude to native policy varies greatly. In the same way the French Jesuits on the Zambezi seemed to me to have little in common with the White Fathers in Nyasaland as regards general outlook and ability, although both are Roman Catholic missions.

There now remain to be considered the great majority of Protestant missions.

It is noteworthy that Protestant missions (excluding from the term " Protestant " not only the Roman, but also the Fundamentalist) have most felt the corrosive influence of that relativism to which I have already alluded. There is a good side to this. It is recognized that proselytism, as such, is a violation of another person's personality, and an assumption of conceit in the proselytizer which goes ill with the Christian grace of humility. The idea of imitation has also been given up. The African does not attain excellence by imitating the European, not even in his religion. The goal of missionary work is held to be the creation of an indigenous Church, and if that Church chooses to go its own way it is doing no more than did the Churches of Alexandria or Rome after the sceptre had passed from Jerusalem.

Inevitably this has led to more time being spent than formerly in understanding native races, and also in understanding what precisely it is that the European missionary has to offer. More emphasis is laid on training, and such specialized subjects as anthropology, biology, agriculture, phonetics, and psychology have come to be almost essential to the missionary's equipment. And whereas in the case of the Roman Church this preparation can very well be carried on without interference with the essential aim of the mission, in the case of non-Roman Churches these studies are in effect a re-examination of the missionary aim itself. The Roman Catholic carries with him a social system into which

THE MISSIONARY SOCIETIES 257

the convert passes; the non-Roman system to-day is a system of *thought*, which is largely relative to the thinker. It may be a more satisfactory view of the world and the Gospel than is the Roman view, but it necessarily runs the risks inherent in its own excellence. In the minds of the missionaries themselves it inevitably tends to diminish religious zeal, for zeal is a phenomenon of religious experience, and it is not easy both to have it and to analyse it at the same time. This view does not lack enthusiasts, but the enthusiasm is of a rather different order from what it was a generation ago. It is an enthusiasm for wholeness, and for a tidy, rational system—something, if you will, that is pieced together from outside rather than something which is illuminated in every part from within. Accordingly the scientific temper is the typical temper of Protestantism, and while Protestantism is far more in accord with the spirit of the age than any other aspect of religion, it finds considerable difficulty in raising itself to any height beyond its own reach.

9.

The development of missionary work in the last twenty years throws an interesting light on these tendencies within Protestantism. I will try to deal with it from the angle of education.

The first systematic consideration of African education was made by the Edinburgh Missionary Conference of 1910. This was one of the most notable Councils ever held in the history of the world, and from it dates an altogether new aspect of the world-wide mission of Christianity. Missionary work had been the more or less casual concern of those who had a special interest in that kind of thing. Henceforth it became a more and more united campaign, the concern of Churches as such, and the concern of all Christian princes and governors in so far as they were Christian. It emphasized for individual Protestants that responsibility for the spread of their message which had always been recognized by Roman Catholics and Moslems in the case of their respective religions.

The Edinburgh Conference did not end with itself. It established a "Continuation Committee," and a quarterly paper, the *International Review of Missions*, which instantly became the chief organ of Christian public opinion on missionary and allied matters. The secretary of the one and the editor of the other was Mr. J. H. Oldham. It is clear that the temperament and ability of a man in this position was bound to affect the outlook of missions as a whole, and accordingly the present policy of co-operation with Government is due more than to any other single cause to the statesmanship of Mr. Oldham.

The ecumenical work of the Conference was carried on in England by the Conference of British Missionary Societies, while the Continuation Committee has become the International Missionary Conference. Other sides of its work were represented by the United Council for Missionary Education, and by the Board of Study for the Preparation of Missionaries. All these activities have come to be centralized in headquarters in London known as "Edinburgh House." The name, therefore, "Edinburgh House," has reference to the corporate policy of the non-Roman British missionary societies. The headquarters has come more and more to function independently of the constituent societies, especially in the work of co-operating with the Government.

10.

The wave of idealism that beat against the closed doors of the Peace Conference at Versailles gave the missionary leaders their opportunity. Words were being heard in the mouths of statesmen which had long been current in missionary conferences. The politicians took from the missionaries the idea of the "sacred trust" of backward peoples, while to many missionaries the system of mandates was identified with the simple Christian virtues writ large. The fact that this system was applied only to ex-enemy territories somewhat limited its effectiveness as an inspiration to youth, but once such an idea is set going it is not easy to localize its relevance. The idea of mandates raised the whole ques-

THE MISSIONARY SOCIETIES 259

tion of the purpose of the European nations in Africa and presented a writ of *quo warranto* to all of them. This idealist attitude was in accordance with the new view of the missionary's responsibilities. It meant the recognition by Governments of the right of native peoples to develop in their own best way, which already was more and more recognized in missionary circles.

Nowhere was this new spirit more felt than in the United States. America was not in the League of Nations and received no mandate, but in America the new idealism found an outlet in a generous willingness to advise and subsidize those who had received mandates.

The Americans fastened in particular on this business of African education as something of which they felt they had some experience to tell the world.

' The end of the world war, and the provision of " mandatories " for backward peoples under the League of Nations drew the attention of publicists in Europe and America to the vital importance of adopting wise educational policies in Africa that would tend to prevent inter-racial friction, and to fit the natives to meet the actual needs of life.' [1]

In Europe it was a vague feeling of general goodwill to backward races that inspired political and missionary educationists alike. It needed a touch of that characteristic American genius for nomenclature to give it point and make it recognizable to the well-meaning but puzzled Englishman. And the American drew on his knowledge of negro conditions in the Southern States.

There are in America a number of funds which exist as a kind of charity organization society on a large scale. Philanthropy has become almost as highly syndicated an industry as any commercial concern. It happened then that in 1920 one of these bodies of trustees—the Phelps-Stokes Fund—sent commissioners to West, South, and Equatorial Africa to survey the position of Native education, and to publish their suggestions for the benefit of those whom it may concern. The chairman of this group was an American of British birth, Dr. Thomas Jesse Jones, who had had a thorough

---

[1] *Education in Africa*, Phelps-Stokes Commission, 1921, p. xiii.

training in sociology and had directed the research department of Hampton Institute, the oldest negro institution in the United States. He had also helped with the United States census of 1910, and had written a notable thesis on negro education. The most outstanding member of the, Commission was the distinguished African teacher, Dr. J. E. K. Aggrey, whose lamented death in 1927 was a serious blow to the fortunes of Achimota College of which he was Vice-Principal.

Three years later another Commission came out, on this occasion to East Africa. This Commission again included Dr. Aggrey, and for part of its tour it included Major Hanns Vischer, secretary of the British Colonial Office Advisory Committee on Native Education in Tropical Africa, and Dr. C. T. Loram, one of the Native Affairs Commissioners for the Union of South Africa and a leading authority on Native education in Africa.

Both Commissions were undertakings in which America, Britain, and Africa co-operated, and they both enjoyed very considerable prestige through the interest taken in them by the British Colonial Office. The two reports [1] are a very valuable collection of facts about Native education. The Commissions were most useful in stirring up the authorities and making them aware of what the missions were doing. The Governments of Africa, at any rate in British territory, began to look on Native education as a fundamental part of their work.

The field was, however, already occupied by the missions, and some formula was required to equate the work of both missions and Government. This was found in the phrase that the education of native peoples must be "based on religion." What precisely this phrase meant was a subject on which both precept and practice were apt to vary. It, did, however, involve the closest co-operation between the missions and the Governments. The implications of the phrase in the actual business of teaching we have already considered.

Meanwhile other funds in America were applied on be-

---

[1] *Education in Africa* (1922): *Education in East Africa* (1924).

half of this new enterprise in Africa. Miss Anna C. Jeanes had left a fund to be used in training travelling teachers for Native schools who would demonstrate new methods and instruct the teachers. This was Matthew Arnold's theory of the real function of the school inspector, and had also been the practice of several missions. The " Jeanes' Fund," however, both interested Governments in the work and also enabled such teachers to be produced in larger numbers. They were given a special name and were called " Jeanes' teachers," and the place where they were trained a " Jeanes' School." The first school under that name to be established in Africa was at Kabete in Kenya.

The Carnegie Corporation of New York also began to seek to use a large fund at their disposal—some £2,000,000 —for Native education in British Africa. Their President and Secretary visited Africa in 1927, and a year later had resolved to assist the establishment of a " Jeanes' School " in both Northern and Southern Rhodesia.

II.

Meanwhile things were happening in England. Mr. Oldham seized the great opportunity opened up by the new idealism. His had been the real inspiration behind the idea of the Commonwealth Trust, which carried on the commercial work of enemy missions on the Gold Coast. In 1923 he influenced the establishment by the Colonial Office of the Advisory Committee on Native Education in Tropical Africa. This Committee is an important body more or less representative of the missionary societies, the public schools, and the administration, and its work is to be a sort of liaison between the State and the missions.

The rapid development of co-operation between Government and missions both in idea and in actual machinery was the inspiration behind a special conference in 1926 which was held at Le Zoute, in Belgium, to consider African problems. Here the work of the Christian missionary and that of the Government servant were seen to be for the same end—the coming of the Kingdom of God. The conference was composed of Government officials and "educationists" as well as missionaries, and it surveyed the whole field of African life. Its report,[1] written by one of the most distinguished of African missionaries, the Rev. E. W. Smith, is almost a new *Tractatus Theologico-Politicus*. It laid down that the education of the Native is the proper function of Government, but that as no education of Natives was of any value without religion, it was best to leave it in the hands of the missionaries, aided by Government subsidy and organized under Government direction.

A later development of the new interest taken in native races was the establishment of the International Institute of African Languages and Cultures. It exists to study African life as the data of a science, and to bring together a body of accurate knowledge which will be of benefit to the administrator and to the missionary.

12.

Behind all this apparatus of study and co-operation there are a philosophy of religion and a philosophy of politics that are typical of contemporary thought.

This philosophy of religion affects both the missionary's view of the Native, and the missionary's view of himself.

As regards the Native, the development has been in the direction of "phenomenalism" at the expense of ethics. Witch-doctoring, initiation ceremonies, dances, *ukulobola*, are now so many phenomena which the missionary requires to understand, rather than so many customs which present an ethical challenge to the Christian. So far has this new attitude spread in Africa that at the Northern Rhodesia Conference in 1927 it came out in discussion that while some missionaries wished to keep and "sublimate" many native customs, the native converts themselves wished to make a clean break with them. For the European, however, the scientific anthropologist has come more and more to dominate the situation, and the evangelist has receded more and more

---

[1] *The Christian Mission in Africa* (1926).

into the background. This inevitably has meant an emphasis on external facts rather than on values.

As regards the missionary's view of his own work, it is to be noted that we have now passed away equally from the individualism of Victorian theology, and from its division of life into sacred and secular. It is clear in the first place that a man cannot be a Christian by himself. He is a social being and he has a social responsibility. His environment needs Christianizing as well as himself, and the millennium for him as for the race involves a new earth as well as a new heaven. Secondly, there is the conviction that every good thing is of God—art, music, literature, good craftsmanship, executive skill, thought. Everything which aspires beyond itself to an ideal that is spiritual breathes of God just as do the Bible and the history of the Church.

If we bring these two points of view together we get a third. The Lord of all good life uses engineers and administrators and carpenters to carry out His purposes, just as much as He uses priests and prophets. The task of world evangelism involves a change of sanitation and agriculture quite as much as it involves a change of heart, and hence it is the concern of all Christian administrators as much as of all missionaries.

The political argument is somewhat similar. It is becoming more and more recognized that Government is based on consent, and that neither force, nor even goodwill, can confer a prescriptive title. The desire to apply this idea to politics after the war was part of the reaction to the experience of its opposite. That the desire arose through stress of circumstances rather than through a dispassionate study of the question does not minimise its importance.

The Montagu-Chelmsford reforms in India were the first notable recognition of this need for the consent of the governed and for their association in the work of Government. The mandatory system (with all its many defects) is a still wider recognition of the same principle. The ultimate rulers of a territory are recognized to be the people of that territory, and where they are at present not able to take up this responsibility a more experienced people is appointed as trustee for them. We may be cynical about the effectiveness of any such arrangement, but the principle is there, and sooner or later it will gather opinion around it and will prevail.

Consent is a matter of *morale*. It cannot be gained or kept by mere good works. The boon of railways and the post office in India will not of themselves give us the consent of the governed. It is a more spiritual relationship than that, and requires the building up of an intelligent appreciation of the end in view. What is that end in view is a subject on which opinions may differ, but at any rate in Africa it involves education for the Native. And as the aim of this education is the production of a certain state of mind, it clearly depends on moral and intellectual sanctions well understood and self-administered. A people that has to be kept down by force, or a people who have no discipline, cannot " consent " to anything, and all the high ideals of the Government fail of their purpose.

In Africa the only sanctions of the Native are those of religion. His old ones did very well for his old undisturbed state of life. But new conditions have made them obsolete and a more universal religion is needed to shore up his life. And while the old dogmatic type of Christianity helped to some extent to do this, but was not very attractive to the Government official (perhaps because its demands were as insistent upon the whites as upon the blacks), the new point of view is more acceptable. It integrates dogmatic teaching, Church membership, political loyalty, industrial diligence, educational progress, hygienic habits, into the one comprehensive formula, " Christian education."

It will be seen, therefore, that both the political and the theological positions that lie behind the work of Native education in Africa are aspects of the relativist temper of the age.

13.

There are other causes which tend to bring about this identification of mission work and Government work in education. One is the question of finance. So long as the missionary was concerned only with evangelism in the narrower sense, he was not badly off for funds. His expenses were small, and he could always appeal to an enthusiastic home constituency. But as his work is seen to involve responsibility for almost every phase of human life, his expenses have increased, and at the same time the appeal at home is less to enthusiasm than to intelligence. It is less an appeal to join forces on an issue than an appeal to carry through a programme. And the appeal for a *cause* has a way of getting money out of people's pockets which no appeal to their judgment can effect.

Moreover, the circumstances of the home supporters of foreign missions have greatly changed within the last generation. In a previous generation a large part of missionary money came from wealthy laymen of an evangelical turn of mind. They are in these days a diminishing class, and the missionary societies have increased liabilities and have to meet them with a greater and greater strain every year.

Government co-operation means the subsidizing of missionary effort, particularly in education. But these very subsidies tend in another way to decrease missionary funds. On the field, grants imply a standard of efficiency to be maintained, and may even mean an increased expenditure in order to earn the grant ; at home, it is a not unusual opinion that as the Government subsidizes missions there is not the same need for private subscriptions.

It is not only Government money that embarrasses the missions. American money is also apt to be an embarrassment. It has to be remembered that the funds so generously applied for African education are all earmarked money. The difficulty with ear-marked money is that it tends to increase general working expenses without providing a corresponding increase of general income. It is the very worth-whileness of the work proposed that causes the embarrassment. This of course puts the Government in a relatively stronger position, while it also tends to lead the missions to concentrate on that side of educational work for which subsidies and donations are available, and to pay less attention to the religious work which is their *raison d'être*.

These forces which operate to the embarrassment of the missionary societies operate to the strengthening of

"Edinburgh House." The missionary societies manage their own internal affairs, and they are still left to raise their own funds for general purposes, but it is "Edinburgh House" that speaks with the Government and has the ear of the Americans. Such centralization is a great gain, and it has made the missionary enterprise a more efficient machine than it has been in the past. It is not to be regretted in the least. But in the very nature of the case it also creates difficulties for the societies.

I have spoken of the way in which the missionary appeal has changed, and the difficulty which the societies feel in making it. This is partly due to causes which I have already mentioned, but partly it is due to the denominational basis of the missionary societies. This does not affect those which lay an exclusive emphasis on denominationalism and can appeal to a constituency which does the same. Such are the Roman Catholic, Anglo-Catholic, and Fundamentalist societies. But the denominational basis everywhere operates against an appeal which is general. Denominationalism has ceased to be a "cause" even to the majority of denominations themselves, and this very self-abnegation has operated to the disfavour of the societies. The old type of Evangelical gave freely to those who were to preach the Gospel in which he believed. The new type of interested Christian is quite prepared to help "missions," but is not prepared to help a missionary society. The appeal to men's width of judgment rather than to their enthusiasm is always better made by a body which appears to represent that width of judgment than by one which seems to represent only a small issue. And whereas the romance of missions in an earlier generation was the wistful, domestic kind of romance of poor heathen forsaking their idols and turning to Christ, the romance to-day is that of solving the vast problems of race and industry.

The centralization of "Edinburgh House" is essentially a centralization of business, and this means that the focus of the modern missionary movement is not so much religion as politics, although "politics" in a wide use of the term. Meanwhile the complaint is sometimes raised on the field itself, Why should we ask our people at home to give their money to purposes over which we have no effective control?

This question I frequently found raised in Nyasaland in 1927. The mission funds for general purposes are still contributed from a religious motive. They are more and more diverted by sheer necessity into excellent work which, however, many of the donors would probably feel to be at any rate irrelevant.

The political genius of the modern missionary experts, while it has wrought great good in the conversion to reasonableness of colonial Governments, brings its own problems.

14.

Where the " spirit of the age " is concerned it is not easy to contend against it. The modern missionary society, as I said at the beginning, is dependent on the state of contemporary thought. Everything comes back to that—its appeal for funds and for workers, the response to that appeal, its view of its own task, its attitude to the African races to whom it goes, its relation to Government, and its relation to other societies. It is remarkably sensitive to the world in which it works.

It seems to me, however, that in a world of relative values one or two stand out which are absolute. But there is a danger even in stating them. The acceptance of an absolute value as true may even be a hindrance to making it effective, and the world's progress is assured not by the people who have clear minds and excellent ideas but by the people who live in accordance with those ideas whether they know it or not, and even when they may in theory actually hold the opposite.

I have found in Africa that the really good Christian mission always emphasizes its Christian mission. It may have hospitals and schools, Jeanes' teachers and carpentry, Scripture lessons and moral instruction. But these things are secondary to the aim of the mission. That aim, not only for the Natives but also for the European staff, is a personal, intelligent, sincere loyalty to Christ. This means that the missionary who goes out to a mission school will have this primary qualification. If other qualifications are added, well and good; if they are not to be had except by dispensing with the primary qualification, the mission is better without them. A teacher is not necessarily a missionary, nor is a carpenter, nor is a civil servant, nor is a *preacher*. A " good chap " is not the same as a Christian. The Christian life is the gift of God and the life in grace. No mere *bonhomie* is a substitute. What we are out to do in the world is primarily to rescue it from sin, and secondarily to rescue it from misguidedness, or an untidy mind, or a bad habit. This latter is important, but it is not of the first importance.

The insistence on this first requirement is an ethical duty which cannot be abrogated without loss. It is bound to condition all co-operation with Government. This co-operation will be between two agencies who are doing the same thing only if the representatives of both have a common loyalty. Identity of purpose is determined by the centre rather than by the circumference of a man's work. It is quite true that " education " and " religion " can mean the same thing, but this is not because the area of the one coincides with the area of the other, but because the highest ideal for both is the same, a view of the universe and of human duty springing out of a change of heart through Christ. This is a perpetual challenge both to the missionary and to the administrator. It cannot mean that the missionary should cease to regard himself as a buffer between the Native and the Government. There may be occasions when his very presence as a Christian missionary demands it. But whatever he does, the standard for him is not that of Government approval (or *dis*approval !) but that of his conscience as a Christian. Conversely, the administrator is not of service to the Christian education of the Native unless he has the Christian standard himself.

A doctrine of grace is in this context more important than a doctrine of nature.[1] The business of the Christian teacher is to see that the beginning is right and that the direction is right. What the end may be he cannot know. There is surely something fundamentally non-Christian in a great deal

---

[1] That well-known book, *The Christ of the Indian Road*, by Dr. Stanley Jones, takes this same line with regard to Indian missions.

of this elaborate planning and detailed programmes that are the concern of missionary experts. It leads them into a sense of identity of purpose with anthropologists and publicists whose interests may be the same, but whose point of approach to those interests is quite different. In much of this search after the specialist and the yielding to the intimidation of science, men may quite easily lose all effective belief in the fructifying influence of the spirit of God.

CHAPTER XII.

THE GOVERNMENT.

THE change in missionary theory concerning the Native corresponds to a similar change in the theory of government. Just as it was formerly held that the missionary's business was to impose upon men a wholly new way of life, so it was held that the business of a dominant people was to impose upon a subject territory new and alien methods of organization. As change has brought about the growing conviction in missionary circles that the Gospel should fulfil rather than destroy, so there is also a political doctrine that the government of backward races is to be carried on along Native lines as far as possible, rather than in a way more suitable to those who govern them.

This is a point of view which, as we have seen, has become of greater prominence since the Peace of Versailles established the system of Mandates. But it was arising before the war, and is indeed a very typical product of the best side of the British character. The war, however, brought into prominence two things: first, that the peoples of Europe had become more and more dependent on the products of tropical Africa, and that the earth's resources in that region needed to be developed; secondly, that as the people of these regions were not able to do this themselves, nor were they able to protect themselves in the conditions of the modern world, the government of them was a fiduciary trust; it was to fit these people for self-government, and gradually to hand over government to them. The one point was economic, the second was political, but both affected the work of administration. The trusteeship had two aspects—one, to see that the economic needs of the world outside Africa were being met in so far as Africa could meet them, and the other, that the Natives of Africa were being protected and developed.

Both white and black were therefore concerned, and Lord Lugard has called this the " dual mandate." His great book on the subject is the most comprehensive and authoritative statement we possess.[1]

I.

There are at least three methods of governing a subject people. There is the method of direct rule, in which they are governed from above with no share in the government themselves; there is the method of assimilation, in which they are associated as far as they can be with the system of their governors; and there is the method of indirect rule, in which they are associated with the work of government as much as possible through their own institutions. The first is the method of the conqueror, open or implied, and was followed by the Germans in Africa, and in an earlier generation by the British in India. The second is very typical of the Latin countries, and is perhaps a heritage from the days of the old Roman Empire. It is exemplified by France. Every inhabitant of Senegal or of Algiers can call himself a Frenchman just as a native of Tarsus in the first century could call himself a Roman citizen. The third is the later colonial theory of Britain, and is best exemplified by Lord Lugard's administration of Nigeria. He found there in existence a system of Moslem Emirates, and he shaped his policy so as to govern through them rather than to supersede them. It is obvious that of all these methods the third is the more difficult, because its essential business is .to expand and develop the native faculty for government instead of doing without it. It therefore demands a type of officer who can educate people in this way, neither a mere mechanical servant of a State Department, nor a person wedded to his own methods and his own position.

The scramble for Africa, as we have seen, began after the Berlin Act. It was characteristic of Britain that while other nations of Europe were out to achieve greatness, the

[1] *The Dual Mandate in British Tropical Africa* (Blackwood, 3rd edit., 1926).

British had greatness thrust upon them. The hesitancy of successive British Governments to accept any responsibility in Africa at the same time that the French and Belgians, Portuguese and Germans were almost feverishly staking out claims, is only remarkable if we ignore the British habit of mind. Obviously these newly-discovered territories could not either morally or legally be held to " belong " to the Powers whose nationals had explored or settled in them, and the scruples of the British on this question led them to overlook the fact that it was a question not of British occupation versus non-interference with the Natives, but of British occupation versus Belgian, or whatever the other nation might be. The astonishing French claim to the northern territory of what is now Nigeria as the " hinterland " of Algeria, at last made the British Government take steps to delimit its frontiers. Again, with the typically British attitude to have your cake and also eat it, the first " occupation " of three large areas in Africa was not official at all, but was carried out by three chartered companies—the Royal Niger Company, the Imperial East Africa Company, and the British South Africa Company. It was only when this policy was seen to be impossible that the British Government itself took over direct occupation. Meanwhile, however, the habit of hesitancy had lost us Katanga. It had also lost us any interest in the equatorial region of the Congo, although Stanley did not turn to King Leopold until he had finally given up all hope of the British Government.[1] It also very nearly allowed Gladstone to withdraw from Uganda.

The British preference for the method of the indirect rule of backward races is consequently very much in accord with the British hesitancy to act with decision when there is no very clear legal or moral title. It is quite against the British habit of mind in the twentieth century to domineer over a less advanced race, or at any rate to do so with a good conscience. The absence of any monument to British arms in Palestine, and the existence of the mendacious monument

---

[1] A. B. Keith, *The Belgian Congo and the Berlin Act*, p. 37. (A valuable work, but biassed by the year of its publication, 1919, when the British estimate of the Belgians was clouded by sentiment); Sir H. H. Johnston, *The Colonization of Africa*, p. 343.

THE GOVERNMENT 273

to the French in Beyrout is a parable illustrating two distinct attitudes. It has, however, to be remembered that if the British position has one root in political ethics, it has another root in national temperament. It may be a moral thing, and it may be a non-moral thing. Policies which appear to be the same outwardly may result from two very different motives.

2.

The present state of education in Northern Nigeria is a good illustration of this contention. Lord Lugard laid down the principle of indirect rule twenty years ago.[1] The Moslem Emirates were not abolished, but were retained and moralized. Moslem authority under the guidance of Britain shed its capricious character and began to be more and more responsible. In deference to the Moslems no Christian missions were permitted among them, save only one, the famous C.M.S. mission at Zaria, which was already established. Education was in accordance with Moslem ideas—the Koran was taught, there was no English, no modern subjects, no provision for girls' education, and to all intents and purposes the British suzerainty limited itself to enabling the Moslems to do better what they had previously done badly. Schools of arts and crafts were established at Kano and elsewhere in order to foster native industries which, however, had shown no very obvious signs of dying out.

In the disturbed state of the north in those days, and the barbarism that exhibited itself among the Moslem peoples, this was a wise and courageous policy which justified itself during the Great War.

That which, however, was with Lord Lugard a policy, appears gradually to have become with his successors a formula. The C.M.S. School at Zaria is a somewhat acid test. So far from being an offence to the people, it is the most popular institution in the place. Both boys and girls attend, and Dr. Miller when head of it taught hygiene and English, two of the subjects which are said to be in conflict

[1] On the general subject of this chapter see Appendix II for Lord Lugard's comment.

with the views of the Moslem rulers. The chief Mallam is friendly, and even enthusiastic, and pupils come from all over the Moslem areas of Northern Nigeria in order to study at Zaria those subjects which the Government formula forbids to be taught elsewhere. The evidence is abundant that the Moslem people desire a wider opportunity for education than that which is open to them in their own Koran schools and in the Government institutions.

A discussion of these matters, however, with the authorities in Kano was held in the atmosphere of a detective story. I was assured by men who otherwise showed a keen sense of humour that the Moslem Emirs were sullen and suspicious, and that to attempt to allow the missions to introduce modern schools on Christian lines, like that at Zaria, might cause a *jehad* to blow up at once. The loyalty of the people during the war was not taken into account. There was no attempt to assess the value of the Zaria school, and indeed there was evidence of a wish to have it closed. The known desire of the Moslem Natives for modern knowledge was discounted, and there seemed to me to be almost a perverse enjoyment of a thrilling sensation of plots and diplomacies which in reality began, continued, and ended in the minds of those who enjoyed the thrill. This was the more evident because I was informed that the Rev. A. G. Fraser, of Achimota, had recently made an inspection of the educational system of the Northern Territory and had apparently treated with rude common sense the romance of imaginary dangers which had been allowed to justify administrative inaction. The British authorities at Kano resented this ruthless examination, and took refuge in Lord Lugard's theory of indirect rule. The fact that there are Christian mission schools in the Moslem areas in India, Syria, East Africa, and Iraq, and the fact of Mr. Fraser's own distinguished record in Ceylon, were held to be irrelevant, because the circumstances of Northern Nigeria are " so peculiar." There was, however, some difficulty in describing this peculiarity, and no argument that was put up for special treatment was logically able to stand against the evidence of the desire of the people.

The theory of " indirect rule " was never meant to be a formula. It was meant to be, and in Lord Lugard's hands

THE GOVERNMENT

doubtless it was, a progressive policy, modifiable in detail and direction as its results were seen to work a modification in the minds of the people who were governed. To ignore the results, and to discount evidence of change in order to avoid a development of policy, is to exalt the value of a formula over the value of the people for whose benefit it is presumably intended. And this is the plain lesson of Northern Nigeria. In education the authorities have done practically nothing to develop the Moslem people, although there are many Government schools among them, and by being true to the letter of " indirect rule," they have missed the spirit of it.

A book which well illustrates the theory of verbal inspiration which fastens on the work and words of a great statesman, is *Native Races and Their Rulers*, an otherwise admirable book, by Mr. C. L. Temple, late Lieut.-Governor of the Northern Provinces of Nigeria. He makes excellent use of the comparative method, and illustrates his points by references to mediæval European customs and English history. This is all to the good, but the value of a comparative study is surely to point out not how this situation in mediæval Europe is like this situation in Africa, but how the transformation of mediæval into modern Europe may suggest a clue for the transformation of modern Africa into Africa of to-morrow. The question is not, what is this now ? but, what is this likely to become ?

Mr. Temple, however, approaches the problem as static rather than dynamic, and this involves the use of formulæ. For example, here are some extracts from his summary table of contents :—

' The natives are in the feudal condition, with the bump of veneration developed to a great degree. . . . This is their sheet anchor, and if we remove it, we produce chaos, as we have nothing to replace it. The absence of economic stress renders retention of feudal system necessary. . . .

' Deterioration can be avoided if native institutions supported.' [1]

In the body of the book he states with great cogency the case for indirect rule, but that in his mind it is becoming

[1] Pp. vi, vii.

a formula is evident from a passage such as the following, where he is stating an objection to his case for segregation :—

'But, I can imagine one such saying . . . there is no reason at all why European society should be to the native in the manner which you indicate. You have said that he is a man just as ourselves, why therefore should we not enter into social relations with him on lines of absolute equality ? . . . To this I would reply, "Are you prepared to advocate free inter-marriage of the races ? "' [1]

There we have a formula, " Leave the Native to his own institutions," met by an imaginary formula, " Social relations on lines of absolute equality," and answered by another formula, " What about inter-marriage ? " and this *non-sequitur* is supposed to prove the first formula. There are certain places in South Africa where the expression of the deepest thought on the Native question is this same formula put in these words : " Call no man your brother unless you are prepared to call him your brother-in-law ! "

Mr. Temple has a good chapter on " Missionaries, Education, and Slavery," which, however, further illustrates this use of formulæ. He states with insight and experience the Moslem attitude towards Christian missions, and points out that it would not be at all hostile. Their presence would not be resented by the Moslems as adherents of another Faith, but by the Government as representatives of an influence which might upset the formula.

'The missionary . . . may very probably be thoroughly imbued with the value of the " individualistic " system as opposed to the feudal system : many native customs . . . and many other observances may well strike him as ridiculous and puerile and even degrading to the natives. This feeling he will impart consciously or sub-consciously to the natives with whom he comes into immediate contact.' [2]

This is surely an example of the logical fallacy known as the " undistributed middle." " The missionary *may* be imbued . . . and this feeling he *will* impart." Clearly the author knows nothing of the Edinburgh Missionary Conference, and with what ideas the missionaries are as a matter

[1] P. 55.   [2] P. 233.

THE GOVERNMENT

of fact imbued. Accordingly he again puts up an imaginary formula in order to demolish it. And as to education :—

> 'The policy which I have outlined certainly does not admit of the institution of schools where young natives are to be taught to read and write English, and as a natural corollary, European habits and customs. Nothing could be more subservient (sic) of the policy than this.' [1]

The formula is evidently in danger again.

Clearly the foundations laid by Lord Lugard have not been built upon, and by this time it would almost appear to be treasonable to disturb them in any way.

Before going on to discuss the corollaries of this attitude in general, it might be well to consider the position of the " expert " in these matters.

It is not infrequently found in this as in other walks of life that a position which cannot be justified on first principles is taken to be justified by " special knowledge " which the critic is not likely to possess. If a man has a weak case he often defends it by saying, " I have lived here for ten years, and you have just come." This is more or less the attitude of the Northern Nigerian authorities, and it has the advantage of being true, even though it is a truth which is irrelevant. There is a certain subtle temptation to human nature to assume authority from the possession of recondite knowledge. This authority is not considered to have anything to do with intelligence, or prejudice, or self-interest. Merely having one's person for a number of years at the same place on the earth's surface is supposed to give a man an authoritative opinion on policy. I do not think so. It may even disqualify him from any such recognition. Policy cannot disregard environment, and in order to have an authoritative opinion on policy, the claimant must know quite as much about the world into which his special subject fits as about that special subject itself. To be ignorant of the world outside is to disqualify him from any claim to deference because of his knowledge of the world inside. The " expert," therefore, is the person whom the statesman uses ; his " expertness " is not in itself statesmanship.

[1] P. 219.

3.

The principle of " indirect rule " has an important corollary wherever it is applied—in Tanganyika and Northern Rhodesia as well as in Nigeria—but the situation in Northern Nigeria again illustrates it. The corollary is this. The aim of the European administration is to reinforce native authority, whether of the tribal chief or of the emir. But the emir is thereby held to be responsible to no one but the suzerain. It is therefore extremely difficult for native opinion to express itself in favour of any change. In other words, the European Power comes in and finds a certain system of government in existence. With its past or its future it is not concerned. It recognizes what is, and by so doing it can check the development of what might be. A native system of government is looked upon as a matter of static organization rather than as a living thing growing and changing because it must.

In Northern Nigeria the Emirs[1] are Fulas and Moslems. But this has not always been so. It was so, however, at the time when the British Government took over the country, and the policy of " indirect rule " has confirmed the Fulas in their power. But the Hausa have never admitted this alien domination except under protest. The British recognition of an authority which to the Hausa is an accident, has deprived the Hausa of any possibility of a government by men of their own people. In other words, the indirect rule of the British has established the direct rule of the Fula Emirs.

This is a special grievance in Northern Nigeria, but it is consequent upon indirect rule everywhere. The European suzerain retains the tribal chief, irrespective of whether the people under that chief wish also to retain him. In the Gold Coast the authority of the tribal chiefs on the seaboard is scarcely recognized at all by the native inhabitants of that region. In South and Central and East Africa inevitable economic causes have undermined tribalism, and indirect rule—applied as a formula—would impose upon the people a system which can less and less command popular respect. And if no opportunity is given for the native system of

[1] See Appendix II.

government to develop and even to transform itself in accordance with the new situation in the world in which it exists, indirect rule by the European suzerain will result not in justice but in injustice. Even for societies without representative institutions, Burke's axiom remains true that " a state without the means of some change is without the means of its conservation."

This is not an argument against " indirect rule," but it is rather an argument in favour of a developing system of government which will conform more and more to the development of the people. A rule which simply perpetuates an accidental situation is indirect only in form.

It is this which accounts for the official attitude towards education in the Moslem areas of Northern Nigeria, and we can see the germ of it even in Lord Lugard's book. I have already discussed his views on character-training in native schools, and the way in which he contrasts with this vital task the " secular " tasks of the class-room. If we look again at his list of the agencies for the training of character, we shall find them to be these : residential schools, a more adequate British staff, the delegation of responsibility for discipline to monitors, field sports, grants to be given for tone and discipline, religious and moral instruction.

Now where does this list come from ? It is an adaptation of the ideas of the British public school to African education, and one essential element in the theory of the public school system is that it produces capacity for government. Under the system of indirect rule in Northern Nigeria the only form of education which the Government will tolerate is that which is supposed to fit the sons of the ruling class to be rulers, and the sons of the people to be ruled. Yet Lord Lugard himself has to confess that

' Contrary to expectation, it has been found that in some of the schools—notably in Sokoto and Bornu, the religious headquarters in East and West—English is becoming more popular than Arabic, but the latter will always serve a useful purpose for the sons of Emirs, and for the training of native judges.'[1]

This reference shows that English has been introduced into these Nigerian schools—" very cautiously," so I was

[1] Lugard, op. cit., p. 454, note.

told at Kano. But the caution does not appear to have been necessary, and the fact that the popularity of English even in these Moslem headquarters, was " contrary to expectation " makes the observer wonder how many more changes would have a popularity " contrary to expectation." The experience of the school at Zaria seems to point to a good many.

This bias, however, that is given to the Government schools in the Moslem areas, makes them less places of education than seminaries. The evidence produced by the Phelps-Stokes Commissioners of the high order of intelligence of the students in the Survey schools at Kano,[1] makes it very unlikely that the Natives can be entirely satisfied with the system as a whole. The school for training Moslem teachers at Katsina is very well ordered, but it is simply a seminary, although a seminary of a good kind. But even the best kind of seminary, as Cardinal Newman pointed out long ago in his correspondence with Archbishop Cullen, falls short of an education that is free. And if, as seems likely, only a seminarist education was possible in Mohammedan Nigeria in the early days, there is not a great deal of evidence to show that the people have been guided to appreciate a different sort. Indeed in this matter the people are probably in advance of the Government. And little has been done for the women.

4.

I have spoken of the British temperament, and the hesitancy which is its characteristic in undertaking responsibilities which have a moral aspect. Allied with that is a certain perverse quixotism which over-emphasizes the importance of the point of view to which it is opposed. In dealing with the opposition, actual or possible, of any group which has accepted the main principle of British authority, the administration is apt to go to an almost unreasonable length in order to ensure conciliation. The rule of the Moslems in India or in Nigeria is a case in point. The less the authorities themselves believe in Mohammedanism, the more likely they are to favour it ! The community in India whose rights are

[1] *Education in Africa*, p. 172.

least attended to is the Christian community. This is the case in all British Moslem areas. It was interesting to walk round Mombasa and come upon a Government school under the ægis of the "Fidei Defensor" in which nothing was taught for the first few years but the Koran. The same is true in Northern Nigeria, and cases have there been alleged of Moslem boys in Government service having been dismissed because they became Christians. This, of course, if true, would have been done in order to show to the Moslems how broad-minded a "Christian" Government could be, but it is an act of injustice all the same. Justice cannot flourish in a morbid atmosphere of nervous conciliation. But this kind of attitude is not only unjust, it is also stupid. Many Government servants truly believe that somehow Islam is a better religion for the black man than Christianity. Yet even if this is due, as it often is, to an ignorance of Christianity, it is none the less a tacit admission of the inferiority of the black man.

This quixotism shows itself again in the treatment of Roman Catholic Missions. The ardent Protestant usually looks upon the Roman Catholic as a deep intriguer who does not scruple to pester private individuals in the Government in order to gain his ends. But as likely as not, any most-favoured-nation treatment of Roman Catholics is due not to the Governor's Catholic bias, but to his anti-Catholic bias. Governments are so anxious to be scrupulously fair to those with whom they disagree, that this "impartiality" in fact works injustice to those who are of their own way of thinking !

The educational situation in Nyasaland in the middle of 1927 is a case in point. Here the Government was faced with Roman Catholic Missions which had made a habit of setting up in Protestant areas "prayer houses," for which they wished the status of schools without, however, the obligation of inspection. Against them were two types of opposition, one on theological grounds, and one on educational, but both in the circumstances necessarily anti-Roman. The Administration quite failed to distinguish between these two different kinds of anti-Romanism. The theological kind, the Government, as a neutral in religious matters, was bound to ignore. The other, based on a genuine concern for the standard of education in the country, the Government, as the chief promotor of educational progress, was bound to consider. But as it happened, the characteristic British attitude to the side it likes least resulted in the Government respecting the Roman Catholics as a theological group, and thereby favouring an educational policy which was reactionary. The difficulty straightened itself out later, but it is a constant complaint in British territory that the Roman Catholics are much more likely to find favour with the Government than are the Protestants.

5.

The principle of indirect rule is a political principle, and as I have shown, it may easily result in the direct rule of an alien Native authority. At the same time, where, in a second generation of administrators, it has become a formula rather than a policy, it is apt to ignore all factors save the political.

The story of the Golden Stool of Ashanti is by this time familiar through the use made of it by E. W. Smith in his excellent study of the relations between European Governments and Native civilizations.[1] Here were an adventure and a policy based on purely political considerations, and ignoring social factors which the later anthropological research of Major Rattray revealed. But the policy which in this case led to war, is just as likely in other cases to lead to mistakes.

In Bantu Africa the chief is a sacred person. He is, as we have seen, the representative of the spiritual unity of the tribe, alive and " dead."

' The Bantu believes intensely in the divinity of chiefs. . . . Ceremonies connected with the worship of the spirits of the dynasty would be invalid unless he [the chief] presided. The clash of the power of kindred with that of the state, which did so much to shape our Anglo-Saxon polity, is, therefore, constantly at work in Bantu tribes.'[2]

The authority of the chief therefore is a religious authority, and anything which undermines that sanction undermines

---

[1] E. W. Smith, *The Golden Stool* (1926).
[2] W. C. Willoughby, *Race Problems in the New Africa* (1923), pp. 97-98.

chieftainship: The European Power coming in sees this system of organization at work, and equates it with that of an English magistrate or Lord-Lieutenant. The chief becomes invested with magisterial powers which make him an official. In the Congo the Belgian Government chooses suitable people to be " medal chiefs." They are given this badge of office from the authorities. There are " medal chiefs " also in Uganda and in Tanganyika and elsewhere. The standard by which the " indirect " ruler judges has therefore no reference to this religious character of the chieftainship, and in the very nature of the case the attempt to foster " tribalism " as the European understands it does not necessarily establish tribalism as the Native understands it. Native institutions are rooted in religion, and the mere decision to keep this institution and reject that does not of itself bind or loose. It all depends on how far the religious basis remains.

Mr. C. L. Temple recognizes this, and observes that Christian missions are a disintegrating force. They undermine tribalism and are thereby a danger to the stability of Native life. Accordingly the Government (in Northern Nigeria) is justified in restricting their activities in order to preserve the *status quo*. The only condition under which the missions could be tolerated would be to require the missionary to inculcate in the Natives

' that ready and willing compliance with all the lawful orders of his Emir or chief, and observance of all sanctioned tribal customs and manners is their first duty, and to place such secular instruction in the forefront of his teaching.' [1]

It is not explained on what grounds certain tribal customs are " sanctioned " and others are not. And if political considerations alone are to be the guide it is quite possible that the Government by refusing to sanction a certain custom may itself be cutting at the root of tribal discipline.

Mr. Temple's book, however, indicates very clearly the confused attitude of the " indirect " ruler to Christianity. In untouched pagan areas there is apparently no harm in allowing the missionary full scope, as the primitive pagan is a " very robust fellow " ; he will cling to his hereditary custom, and the missionary will not be able to shake him.[2] Where,

[1] *Op. cit.*, p. 217. [2] *Ibid.*

however, such a community emerges from this untouched stage and disintegration begins, the Government will be forced to send away the missionaries in order to preserve the native institutions.[1] The Moslem areas are presumably different. Their institutions exist intact, but the Government will not allow the missionaries to come because they would be a " danger to the native administration," except on the conditions mentioned above. In other words, where a community has strong institutions, the Christian missionary may come in if he will agree to back up those institutions. If decadence has already set in (from some cause unexplained but *ex hypothesi* not Christianity) the Christian missionary may come in if he will help to rebuild those institutions. This is really a rationalizing of a position based on other grounds, namely that Islam is a much more useful religion for Government purposes than Christianity. The Christians are here felt to be as much a nuisance in Africa as were the Jews in the Græco-Roman Empire. The political officer alone is to have the power of the keys to bind and to loose, and political considerations alone are relevant.

6.

The fundamental fallacy in this position is that it altogether ignores the inexorable pressure of economic change. To Mr. Temple it is a matter of political versus religious authorities, and he objects to the religious authorities. But Christianity is not the enemy. The enemy, if it can be called such, is European economic influence, and Mr Temple could only preserve his little enclave intact if he kept out the trader, the railway, the motor car, and the post office. These are the disintegrating forces, and against them the political officer is powerless. Mr. Temple declares that " deterioration can be avoided if native institutions are supported," and he looks upon the problem simply as one of government. This was precisely the attitude of the ruling classes in England in the days before the Reform Act of 1832, and it is just as fallacious. The Industrial Revolution had changed the

[1] P. 218.

whole balance of power in England, the squirearchy was losing influence, the manufacturing classes were gaining, and new aspirations were taking possession of the working class. England was in the throes of change, and the sanctions of centuries were being shaken. Of all this the ruling classes were profoundly ignorant. Yet the power-loom, the spinning machine, the steam engine, were to remodel England in the space of a generation.

An absorption in political government tends to make a man strangely unaware of forces which are not under his control. He is naturally conservative, and considerations of law and order are apt to become the sole concern of policy. To declare, as Mr. Temple declares, of the primitive pagan, that " it requires nothing short of the full weight of the government machinery to create a decadent condition in the case of such robust constitutions as these," is to say something that is contrary to experience right throughout Africa. It shows a quite disproportionate estimate of the actual power of a political officer, and assumes that positive law is of far greater consequence than any moral or economic force. It is a common form of self-deception. In Africa the political authorities and the missionaries are simply two factors contained within the *continuum* of African social life. The influences which affect that social life, some of which we have considered in earlier chapters, make necessary a continual re-adjustment of relationships. No political principle can operate in a vacuum, not even an excellent principle like "indirect rule." Principles, like everything else, are conditioned by circumstances, and an incorrect knowledge of the circumstances renders faulty the working of the principle. Every " factory " that is opened in Kano, every motor car that squeezes through the Nassarawa gate, every Hausa who leaves his native city to seek his fortune in other countries or to learn the white man's language and ways in Southern Nigeria, is an influence that is modifying every day the situation which the political officers of the North have to meet. Whether they themselves change or not, the circumstances change. And to keep the native rulers of that great country away from influences which are playing all the time upon their people, to keep them as far **as** possible ignorant of English, and wedded to Arabic and Moslem law, is to widen the gap between rulers and ruled. This is not to educate people " along their own lines " ; it is to seek to perpetuate a stage of development which they desire to leave, but whose continuance has become a prejudice of administration.

7.

I have discussed the political theory of " indirect rule " in connection with education in Northern Nigeria, because the situation there brings into clear perspective the implications of that policy. It is the policy, too, in Basutoland and in the Bechuanaland Protectorate, and indeed it is recognized as the official policy everywhere, and it accords with the principle of mandates.

The French point of view in colonization is interesting, especially as found in the study by M. Albert Sarraut to which reference has already been made.[1] It was written after the war, and after the setting up of the mandatory system, of which—in compliment to his Belgian editor, M. Louis Franck—M. Sarraut professes to see the germ in the system of Congo rule inaugurated by Leopold II. M. Sarraut will not have it that the French believe in " assimilation," understanding by " assimilation " the fusion of colonial government with that of the mother country. He would reject, for instance, the British system of Crown Colony government, under which the colonies are governed from London. It is noticeable, however, that he speaks of the effect of

' le libéralisme de notre politique, de l'assimilation progressive des races indigènes à notre action, de l'ensemble en un mot des gestes de civilisation que nous accomplirons ' (p. 25),

and he considers whether all this progressive assimilation will lead to the possibility of the colonies some day desiring to " cut the painter." This is an interesting point to raise, because it has been raised in Britain only in connection with

[1] *Études de Colonisation comparée*, t. 1. (Brussels, 1924), pp. 4-29. *L'oeuvre coloniale de la France*, par M. Albert Sarraut. See p. 119 above.

the "self-governing dominions," and in later years with India. French policy, however, has developed considerably since 1924, and M. Sarraut was raising a purely hypothetical question. The aim of France in Africa is quite different from that of Britain. Strictly speaking, France has no colonies at all. All the lands over which the tricolour waves are regarded as the very soil of France. They send their Native deputies to the French Chamber,—a matter, no doubt, of some embarrassment to Colonial Governors. French citizenship is open to their inhabitants, the highest grade of which—that of *citoyen français*—is granted to Natives who can speak and write French, who have been in military or public services for ten years, who have been legally married to a French woman, who have served for one year in the army overseas or have received certain military decorations. Even the organisation of the French Colonial Office bears witness to the theory. It is organized not " vertically " according to territories but " horizontally " according to interests,—agriculture, education, etc. Thus the territory is not the unit, " Home Rule " cannot be considered an ideal, and there can be no differential development on territorial lines as there is in the British colonies. The French colonies contribute to the " metropolitan " budget and are, moreover, looked upon as reserves for the army. In the one year 1928, for example, the *recruitment* of native troops in Madagascar exceeded in number that of all the Native troops in training in the whole of British Tropical Africa, a population ten times that of the island!

The aims of education are consonant with this policy. They have been defined very well by M. Brévié, Governor General of French West Africa.[1] The primary object is to secure the evolution of a more and more highly qualified corps of *elites*, " of whose zeal for a thorough and exclusively French culture signs are already visible." Consequently, while the British officials get on best in Africa as in India with the uneducated villager and not so well with the educated classes, the French tend to have little patience with the primitives but mix on terms of equality with the others.

[1] Mumford and Orde-Brown. *Africans Learn to be French* (1937) Chap. V. See also Chap. III.

8.

The principle of mandates does not of itself involve any particular policy. As we have seen, M. Sarraut equates it with the organization of the Congo Free State ; he also equates it with French colonial policy to-day. To these two interpretations we may add others from the British side. Indeed the vogue of the mandatory principle has affected—by what M. Sarraut excellently calls " une exosmose inévitable " —the government of all territories whether mandated or not.[1] This may work in one of two ways. In the case of Tanganyika and Kenya, for example, the accident of juxtaposition may drive the Kenya Government to equate itself with that of Tanganyika, and introduce what is virtually the mandatory principle into its own territory ; or it may do precisely the opposite, and by an interpretation of the mandatory principle to cover the present direction of policy in Kenya, may equate Tanganyika with Kenya. This is the issue raised by the Hilton-Young Commission, and it exhibits the dangers that lie in the use of terms which can bear quite a different connotation according to the goodwill or intelligence or self-interest of the people who use them.

The necessary implications of "indirect rule" are the education of the people to meet the new conditions in the world in which they live, and a flexibility of mind in the governors to meet these same changes. And, if I may here adapt an argument which I have used in respect of " African culture," a people's " own institutions " are what they make them. When we speak here of an institution, we do not speak of it in the sense in which a building is called an " institution "—something fixed and static and dead, unchanging and unchangeable. Yet this is the sense in which it is all too often used in questions of this kind. An institution has to fit a certain situation. If tribalism obviously does not fit that situation, the remedy is not to bolster up tribalism in spite of the changed circumstances, but to enable the minds of men to develop from tribalism a new institution which will fit the situation. And if this is impossible in the case of tribalism, then the minds of men should be pre-

---

[1] See p. 258 above.

pared in order that they might invent, if need be, a totally new thing. It is no honour to the African's intelligence to assume that he is incapable of this development. The Transkeian General Council is a new thing of this kind. It was invented by Europeans and "imposed" upon the Natives. But it has developed beyond its original, and is being developed further. It is an admirable expression of the people's will, and has their confidence.[1] A visit to the *Kgotla* at Serowe, where Khama used to preside, and where his young son reigns in his stead, gives one the same impression. Here is a purely native institution, presided over by a young man educated at Lovedale and Fort Hare. There is about it a very keen awareness to the world forces which condition the lives of the Bamangwato people. It is no less "native" but it is more intelligent than it would have been had Khama been confined to animism and to the Sechuana language. Accordingly, the visit of the Colonial Secretary to Serowe in 1927 marked a meeting of two responsible people, both political officers, and both acquainted with the world in which they live. A visit of the Prince of Wales to the Emir of Kano was a durbar staged by the Resident— a very different kind of proceeding altogether. All parts of Africa are not so advanced as Bechuanaland or Uganda, but the principle remains the same. It is a principle of progress and flexibility. When it becomes a mere formula, the life has gone out of it.

The principle actuating the government of backward races is very closely akin to that actuating missions, and they are both part of a more general point of view. In education the corresponding principle is that of letting the child discover things for himself and find his own feet. In social life it means the end alike of patronage and of irresponsibility. In business it means the recognition of the workers' right to control his own life.

This moralizing of human relationships is the most vital element in contemporary thought. It makes for wholeness in thinking and is opposed to the departmental mind. For this very reason missionaries, teachers, business men, government officials are not fully equipped if they have only a technical

[1] See, however, p. 57 above and Appendix II, p. 402.

training. To understand a job and yet not to understand it in all its bearings, may work as much mischief as not to understand it at all. The last word in the government of native races at this point in history does not rest with the professional administrator as such. The development of cotton in Uganda or of cocoa on the Gold Coast, the concession areas of the *Huileries du Congo belge*, the vast estates of European settlers in Kenya, the going and coming of labour on the Rand, all represent forces whose effect is ultimately political but which cannot be controlled or even understood by reference to political considerations alone. The government of a people cannot be divorced from the nature of their social life. This is true of an African territory as it is of England. It has been recognized, particularly since the war, that the education of the native people is a proper function of Government. It is not a matter of private arrangement between a mission school and a native community, nor is it a matter depending on the enthusiasm or prejudice of a native chief. It is a national concern. That being so, it is not a violation of the principle of indirect rule to seek to interest people in education and to offer them the best education which is possible : it is rather a corollary from it. The " direct ruler " has no particular interest in his subjects except in their docility and their capacity to pay. But indirect rule carries with it the responsibility for an enlightened and progressive system of training to fit the pupils for life in the world as they will find it. That world is a world not only of things and of people, but also of developing ideas. No man has the right to say to any people " thus far shalt thou come and no further."

CHAPTER XIII.

AMERICA IN AFRICA.

I.

ONE of the most important factors in African education to-day is the influence of America, both black and white. The educated Native is beginning to be conscious of his kinship with the Negro people across the Atlantic and they in turn are showing an increased awareness of him. At the same time the white Americans have come to feel that their experience of the black and white " problem " in the Southern States is something which may help to the solution of a similar problem in Africa. They have also experimented a good deal in education, and the trustees of the various educational funds which are in existence have shown a generous willingness to finance schemes for Native education. In British territory the authorities have facilitated American research, and have also been willing to co-operate in plans put forward by the educationists. America, therefore, cannot be neglected if we would have a true view of the position of African education.

My concern here is with white Americans rather than with the Negroes. Yet Negro America is a very important factor. Even apart from the actual contact with Africa of Negro leaders like Marcus Garvey, the status of the American Negro is a constant stimulus to " Ethiopianism." In the Transkei, for instance, in 1927, the mission schools were feeling very keenly the competition of schools set up by " the Negro Self-Improvement Society," whose founder called himself " Dr. Wellington." On the very day on which I was first in Umtata [1] a large number of " red Kaffirs " collected together in the town in the earnest hope that Wellington was going

---

[1] Friday, August 26, 1927.

to appear in an aeroplane with General Hertzog and some American Negroes, and that the government of the Natives was going to be handed over to the Americans ! In Southern and Northern Rhodesia the " Watch-Tower Movement " has had a numerous membership, particularly in the coal-fields. This movement, whose constant expectation is the " millennial dawn," is called in America, where it was founded in 1884, the " Watch-Tower Bible and Tract Society," and in England the " International Bible Students' Association." It has a great attraction for a certain simple type of mind, and its prophetic view of history has raised apocalyptic hopes among large numbers of Africans.[1]

What the Watch-Tower Movement stands for in idea, Marcus Garvey tries to realize in practice. He is an African born in the West Indies and is seeking to build up among Africans everywhere a common consciousness of race. It is obvious that in any case this is likely to be one result of Native education, and it is among the educated, or at any rate among the sophisticated, Natives of the West Coast that Garvey has his greatest following.

2.

The Southern States of America exhibit the problem of black and white on a large scale. It was claimed at the time of the Civil War that this was a domestic problem for the South alone, while to the Northerner the status of the Negro in the South was a constant challenge to his political theories. To the South, therefore, in spite of all the machinery of repressionism which exists, the situation has nevertheless appeared in the light of a human problem. Where the Southerner has begun to think seriously and dispassionately about it he has thought of it in this way. It is this which lies behind so solid and stimulating a book as Murphy's *The Basis of Ascendancy*, written by a Southerner. It also gives point to the remark of an American Negro woman leader to the effect that where the Southerner is with you (i.e. with the

---

[1] See Appendix, p. 383.

Negro) he is with you through thick and thin.[1] To the North, on the other hand, the problem has been looked upon as one of political ethics requiring clearness of head rather than warmth of heart for its solution. Mrs. Millin, in a comparison with the situation in South Africa, speaks of this difference as a thing of the past, as that

'which once existed between the Northern and Southern United States. The Northerners fought for the rights and privileges of the Negroes, but the Southerners had an affectionate intimacy with their darkies which was not customary among their more highly principled countrymen.
 'Such aimiability, however, springs from the same source as its complementary harshness : the connection between owner and chattel.'[2]

In the years succeeding the Civil War the South was left to struggle with the terrible problem of " Reconstruction," in which the feeling between black and white assumed a bitterness not known before. The North meanwhile was pushing ahead with railroads to the Pacific and with the expansion of industry in East and West. Accordingly the Northern ideas of business efficiency have come more and more to dominate America, and it needs an effort on the part of the Englishman to realize that there exists another America beside that of the hustling tourist and the millionaire merchant. In some degree the American Rhodes Scholars represent this more cultured element in England, but the publication of the letters of Walter Page, perhaps beyond any other influence, have helped this generation of thoughtful Englishmen to have a more balanced view of the United States.

Page was a Southerner, but the difference of types is no longer wholly a territorial one. It is a contrast of cultures which can be met everywhere.

Nowhere is this contrast more visible than in education. Education has become in some places and in some aspects a large-scale industry, with all the defects that spring from such a conception. This is the side of it most familiar to England, and it is the noisier side. But it is still only one side. The

[1] Miss Davies of Nashville, Tennessee, in a speech at Birmingham in 1928. She is an organizer of schools in Liberia, West Africa.
[2] S. G. Millin, *The South Africans* (1926), p. 169.

difference between the two is well illustrated by the history of the " Robert Brookings Graduate School for Economics and Government Research " at Washington.

'In the five years of its existence it has built up for itself a reputation not only all over America but also . . . in Europe as well. In addition to being a highly successful co-educational residential college, it made a positive attempt to break away from the standardisation and narrowness of the average American graduate school. Instead of the large numbers of heterogeneous students, coming into little or no contact with the members of the staff, the authorities of the School concentrated upon a small number, less than forty, of selected students, who enjoyed a common life with the resident staff.

'It is becoming more and more generally recognized that what America needs is not more high-class researchers, but individuals of wide culture and intellectual independence, trained to develop ideas rather than to complete treatises.'[1]

Unfortunately the founder of the Brookings School appears to think otherwise, for in 1928 these distinctive characteristics were given up and it became merely a training place in research methods.

In Professor Flexner's Inglis lecture at Harvard, 1927, called " Do Americans really value education ? "—a lecture important enough for Africa to call forth a leading article in the Johannesburg *Star*,—another point was emphasized. Mr. Flexner points out that while the administrative officers of colleges—the presidents—are ranked in public esteem with bankers and railroad magnates, the teachers have no such recognition.

'The executive is valued because the American loves administration and organisation and esteems highly those charged with responsibility for it, whereas he gives less recognition to superior intellectual achievement.'[2]

These characteristics of big business dominate one side of American education, and it is this side which is the more prominent in American contact with Africa.

---

[1] Article on " Higher Education in America," *Manchester Guardian*, August 7, 1928.
[2] Flexner, *op. cit.*, p. 15.

3.

The regard that is paid to the organizer, and the desire for results that are measurable, when applied to intellectual studies result in a method of treatment which is commonly but incorrectly called " scientific." To be " scientific " is the intellectual equivalent of business efficiency.

Yet the word is hopelessly overworked both in England and in America. It is applied to everything from salesmanship to religion, and it commonly means the logical grouping of facts about the work in hand, and a disposition to act according to rule. It means the elimination of everything spontaneous and incalculable, and the reduction of everything else to quantity and number. It is the use in other spheres of a method which strictly applies only to the physical sciences.

In the physical sciences, of course, measurement is essential, and a merely qualitative study of chemistry, for example, is not " science " at all. But with the greatest scientists while measurement has been essential as a routine method, it has not of itself made a study " scientific." It is the hack worker, the man who has gone only half-way, who takes this to be the whole. There is, in fact, a certain *moral* quality which is necessary in science. No one exhibited this moral quality more than Huxley. To him science needs accuracy of measurement and of statement because it is the highest expression of the spirit of man. There are in it faith and humility and meaning. The truly scientific is the truly humane and the truly religious. for it helps a man to find his place in the universe.

Even in the physical sciences the mere routine measurer falls short of the highest scientific standard. But when we come to sciences which involve mental qualities, the use of rule and plummet alone is still less scientific. We have witnessed in England the failure of any mechanistic theory of the universe to maintain itself among scientists of repute,[1] simply because it ignores mental factors that are no doubt

[1] Of whom two of the chief are the Professor of Astronomy at Cambridge (Sir A S Eddington), and the late Professor Sir J. Arthur Thomson of Aberdeen. They have both been Gifford lecturers.

inconvenient to the logician but are strictly relevant to a scientific consideration of the subject. It is curious, therefore, to find that methods which are found to be inadequate in the physical and biological sciences are in these days being applied to still more human studies such as psychology and education. If, however, the scientific authorities on these subjects succeed in reducing human life to an exact science, we shall not be surprised if it is done only by ignoring everything that is human and everything that is living.

Whatever inclinations Professor McDougall may have had while in England to develop the study of psychology along these lines, the logical conclusion of it as he saw it in America appears to have acted as a strong corrective :—

'This mechanical psychology is decidedly preponderant at the present time : and my book therefore is largely a polemic against all psychology of this type and on behalf of purposive psychology. . . . Its latest exponent, Mr. Bertrand Russell, has performed the service of reducing it to the lowest level of banality (in his *Analysis of Mind*). Recently it has begotten upon physiology a most misshapen and beggarly dwarf, namely, " behaviourism," which just now is rampant in this country.'[1]

This is one way in which the " scientific " method has been seen to act upon the study of psychology. It has eliminated precisely that element of purpose which is most characteristic of the human mind.

This limitation of scope has been dependent on a limitation of method, for that method alone has come to be considered " scientific " which is based on measurement. In the desire to be " scientific," therefore, there has been a wonderful outburst of " experimental psychology," and intelligence, attention, and even character have been assessed and charted as if the reactions of human beings were as invariable and as certain as the action of sulphuric acid on zinc. Mathematics, the *organon* of the physical sciences, has been made the *organon* of humane studies also. It is certainly more possible to measure the mind in action if we ignore purpose. But it is purpose which makes it a mind at all.

It is from this angle, therefore, that we may ask what

[1] W. McDougall, *An Outline of Psychology* (1923), preface, pp. viii, ix.

precisely is the relevance of an otherwise admirable book like Thorndike's *Educational Psychology* or like Rusk's *Experimental Education?* They are both a mass of figures and tables and charts, and it is all very well done. But it is difficult to see their bearing on the craft of teaching except to help the teacher to look on the children as cases instead of as human beings. As Ruskin said of the science of political economy in his day, " The reasoning might be admirable, the conclusions true, and the science deficient only in applicability." [1] If we compare either of these books with the late James Ward's *Psychology Applied to Education*, we find ourselves in a different world. Ward is primarily concerned with purpose and with " educational values," and the whole treatment has an ethical bearing which is absent in the other two. This, doubtless, to the scientific psychologist is a defect, but again how can any scientific study of mind ignore purpose ?

4.

The use of measurement is one factor in the " scientific " study of humane subjects. Another is the method of the questionnaire.

Questionnaires are of several kinds. One of the most common is that sent out to elicit opinions on subjects of interest or of controversy. It is a kind of scholastic equivalent of democracy, the belief being that a large number of answers to a question will get you nearer the truth than that same question passed through a massive individual mind. It may of course be the case that what a thousand casual citizens think about, say, the value of tradition, represents a worthier opinion than that of Burke, but I cannot myself believe it. For opinions need to be weighed as well as counted, and if they are collected at all, they might as well be collected from the minds of men in the past as from the minds of men to-day, with the additional value that the opinions of the past have already been subjected to careful scrutiny. *Die Weltgeschichte*

---

[1] *Unto this Last* (1862), Essay 1.

ist das Weltgericht, and if we are seeking to have a judgment on matters of value it is as well to seek judgment in a court qualified to try the case.

Of course all questionnaires are not of this kind. They often seek facts rather than opinions, and here they have their value. But in matters of education, what kind of facts are they that have relevance? Somewhere we must come up against principles though we be ever so logical and scientific, and if we ignore them in our list of questions they surely appear in the way in which those lists are drawn up. And a collection of facts brings us no nearer to reality than a collection of nebulous opinions. The value lies in their interpretation rather than in their collection and classification.

The questionnaire habit of mind persists even in regions which would appear to be incapable of this kind of treatment. What the collection of evidence is to the physical scientist, so is a " source book " to a historian. But this has been pushed further, and we get, for example, Professor Kilpatrick's *Sourcebook in the Philosophy of Education!* This consists of a series of headings under each of which are grouped a number of quotations from books about education. It is difficult to see the utility of all this. The implication is that the value, for instance, of Kant's writings on education lies in one or two epigrams or purple passages which have appealed to the compiler. They are taken from their context, and Kant's whole argument is missed. The " philosophy of education " is assumed to be a patchwork of little pieces stuck together from a variety of authors. The idea of a solid coherent study by a single mind is discountenanced as being " unscientific."

This popular " scientific " method has given education a psychological basis which ignores purpose and uses mathematical measurement, and a philosophy based on the questionnaire. It has resulted in a multiplication of published theses, and the Universities have become factories for research. There is yet one more characteristic feature. It has evolved formulæ.

5.

The temptation of all logical thinkers is to strive after some comprehensive term in which the results of their thinking can be exhibited. It was in this spirit that Herbert Spencer invented a formula for evolution—the "survival of the fittest," an indefinite phrase which conceals more than it reveals. A formula has a certain utility, and like the slogan of the advertiser, it draws attention to itself if only to deceive. Unlike the advertiser's slogan, however, it is apt to include the inventor himself among the victims of the deception.

Formulæ are nowhere more rampant than in education. "Education is adaptation" is one formula, "education must be based on religion" is another. "Manual training for character"; "education by doing"; "educate the negro along his own lines," are three more. Of a more specialized kind are "the Dalton plan," "the Jeanes' Teacher," "the Project Method," where these are used not as descriptions of something but as slogans.

Now there is no harm whatever in formulæ, provided they are not used to economize thinking. So long as we know what we mean by these things, and so long as we have thought out the implications of them in the actual business of teaching actual children, it is quite helpful to adopt this kind of shorthand way of speaking about it. But as every one of these formulæ is vague, different people understand different things by them, and they become a mere nuisance. The mischief comes in their application. Not always having been thought out, they are applied by people according to their own ideas, and although the application itself may be all wrong, some magical quality is supposed to be inherent in the formulæ themselves which will make it all right. I have alluded several times in these pages to the fallacy of the *opus operatum*. It is the Nemesis that waits upon the use of formulæ.

The formula, therefore, is the logical conclusion of the scientific method applied to human life. No ultimate analysis is possible of something that is alive and purposive, and so the formula is a substitute for it. In the ordinary affairs of life a formula is a favourite way of dealing with people of another nation and it is particularly vigorous in war-time. It saves reasoning, and it prevents that erosion of patriotism which might ensue if once we recognized that there is a variety of groups and opinions inside another nation just as there is inside our own. It is the method, of which Burke said he was ignorant, of " drawing up an indictment against a whole people." And in educational writings about Africa this indictment is only too frequently made. All Africans, for example, are lumped together and considered to be eminently suitable for education by manual training.

6.

The three factors already discussed stand out very clearly in a small book by Dr. T. Jesse Jones called *The Four Essentials of Education*.[1] It has gained a considerable reputation, more because of the name of the author than through any intrinsic merits of its own, and it is typical of the present " scientific " attitude to education.

The author begins by asking " What is the school for ? " and he finds the clue to the answer in the formula " Consciousness of the community." This involves four essential elements which are " to guide the educator in the study of society, and to enable him to become conscious of community conditions and needs." The perfect educator, therefore, is the person who is aware of what is going on in his community, and who makes his pupils aware in their turn. He is clearly intended to be a researcher.

This view is confirmed in the chapters that follow. The first essential of education is " health and sanitation." We have a startling array of statistics which tell us how many people in the United States suffer from divers diseases, and altogether give an impression of physical unfitness which is appalling. What, then, has the educator to do about it ? Apparently he has to ask questions. This will make him conversant with the conditions of living, or rather of dying, in his own area, and he is recommended to have " patience,

---

[1] New York, Scribner, 1926, pp. 188. Price 6s. net.

persistence, and tact in the questioning of physicians, ministers, and undertakers." [1] We are not told whether all the teachers in a school or in a district are to go round asking these questions, or what they are to do after they have gone round, but we are shown how the information may be used in a class in order to make an "adaptation." Here for instance are the possibilities of the "adaptation" of arithmetic to hygiene :—

'Even the younger children may count the number of people in a village or town area, such as a portion of a street ; the proportion of children to the number of men and women ; the number of sick people ; the number living in a house . . . the amount of money spent on useful or harmful sweets or drink ; the sleep requirements. Vital statistics with their vital meanings, now practically unknown even by College and University graduates, could be discussed arithmetically in the upper elementary grades.' [2]

The second essential is "appreciation and use of environment," and again we are to ask questions. In a rural area we inquire among other things about the acreage of arable land, value of live stock, marketing facilities and historical associations, and in town areas about the census of trades and professions, hours of work, insurance and municipal services. And as to the value of this :—

'Among the results of such a consciousness of environment will be the recognition of the educational importance of agriculture both to city and to rural youth. Urban schools will help to counteract the indifference to rural life. Rural youth will learn to appreciate the essential value of their agricultural surroundings to all society. . . . Another result . . . will be a better understanding of the educational value of industrial training and the processes of physical science.' [3]

The assumption here seems to be that knowledge of facts somehow brings with it not only knowledge of the significance of those facts, but also *ex opere operato* a disposition to change one's own attitude of mind because of that knowledge. In the same way we are told :—

'Statistical comparison of the egg production of the country with the value of wheat, will add greatly to the appreciation of fowls.' [4]

[1] P. 47.   [2] P. 61.   [3] Pp. 83-4.   [4] P. 88.

It is difficult to see how statistics can do anything of the kind, unless " appreciation " has some unusual meaning. Wordsworth " added greatly to the appreciation " of the celandine by writing a poem about it. This was probably a more effective method than an investigation of the number of celandines on the hillside above Grasmere.

The method of achieving the second essential is again to make the school staff aware of these facts.

So also is it with the third essential, " home and household," and the means of doing this is by the " scientific interpretation of social forces, the marshalling of statistics for general use." [1] The list of questions to be asked by individual researchers into this third essential as they go from house to house, begins as follows :—

' *Homes and Households.* How many? Number of persons in them? Average membership of each household? How many fathers in all households? mothers? children of school age? children below school age? above school age? How many widowed parents? Divorced? How many relations other than parents and children? How many males in all households? How many females?' [2]

The fourth essential of education is " Recreation—physical, intellectual, and spiritual," and under this omnibus heading come seven " agencies of recreations," as follows : the homes ; the schools ; the churches (" numbering about 238,000, with a membership of almost 50,000,000 persons, and an annual contribution of $548,000,000 ") ; public recreation centres such as playgrounds ; libraries and museums ; philanthropic organizations like the Y.M.C.A. and Boy Scouts, fraternal societies and Clubs ; and commercial amusements. " Recreation " apparently means the adjustment of yourself to one or more of these " agencies."

Dr. Jones walks with a slightly faltering step when he here forsakes statistics and finds himself on the less solid ground of " appreciation of art." We read :—

The people should have an opportunity to be thrilled by symphonies, oratorios, and operas : to be awed into grateful appreciation by the great Madonnas and motherhoods of the ages ; to be inspired by the sculptured presentations of humanity.' [3]

[1] P. 103. [2] P. 110. [3] P. 148.

"Appreciation of art" is apparently to be provided for by setting up "agencies." And in the case of religion, which comes under this fourth heading, we are told that the best instances of the educational use of religion are Hampton and Tuskegee institutes. As evidence of this we are told about the second Principal of Hampton, Mr. Frissell, who

'deepened and extended the correlation of body, mind, and spirit in education by his emphasis on the mental and spiritual value of work and study, and by his constant reference in prayer and sermon to the realities of the unseen world.'[1]

If this means anything very definite it means that an essential of education is duly present by telling people about it, and making them "conscious" of it.

This, then, is the gist of a book which represents in more detail the point of view of the Phelps-Stokes trustees, and which is therefore widely recommended by missionary experts as a guide to educational policy in Africa. There is the complete ignoring of function; there are the use of statistics, the method of the questionnaire, and the application of formulæ. It is rather melancholy to discover that the "essentials" of education are simply four groups of facts of which the educator has to be "aware," but this is the kind of Herbartianism into which people are apt to fall when they write of education "scientifically." It is as rampant in the works of Dr. J. C. Maxwell Garnett in England as in this book under review. To "know the doctrine" is assumed to be equivalent to "doing the will." Moreover, if we have here Herbart's fallacy that "the will originates in the circle of thought," we have also Herbert Spencer's fallacy of the nature of a scientific education. In his book on education, published in 1861, Spencer takes the line that the school ought to make people aware of their environment, and that everything that there is in the environment should be in the school. He therefore advocated a curriculum containing all the sciences on which human life depends. This,

[1] P. 152. In the Phelps-Stokes Commission Report, 1924, p. 15, we are again told that Dr. Frissell "regularly referred in his prayers to the realities of the unseen world." This is mentioned as apparently a very unusual occurrence.

however, cannot be done in the time, and so Dr. Jones would substitute for these subjects statistical information about the environment.

The fundamental objection, however, to the book is that there is no grasp of principles in it. Do we realize our " consciousness of the community " more by getting up statistics about it, as Dr. Jones does, or by realizing our spiritual one-ness with it as Aristotle does ? Awareness of our membership of a community may mean much, or it may mean nothing at all. What does mean something is the attitude of life we adopt when we have become aware of it. And if it is this quality that counts, we have to ask ourselves what is the most likely way to produce this quality. I see no hope of doing it through sociological investigation. It is much more likely to happen through an appeal to the educated emotions, and that is what the philosophical approach really is. True, it also means creating a sense of " awareness." But to what is it " awareness " ? Not simply to the dry bones of a statistical survey, but to a world of thought and feeling that has functioned in the past and functions now. In other words, it means awareness to the existence of a " realm of ends " and purposes.

The difference between the quantitative and the qualitative view of life is the theme of an old parable. Two men were each given a shilling with which they were asked to buy something to fill up an empty room. The one bought straw and filled it as far as he could in that way. The other bought a lamp and the light flooded the whole room.

7.

Dr. Jesse Jones is the Educational Director of the Phelps-Stokes Fund, and he prepared the Reports of the two Commissions. Both reports naturally show those traces of the scientific educationalist which we have already discussed. They also, however, have as a background the Southern States of America.

Two assumptions are common in this context. The first is that the educational ideals of Hampton and Tuskegee are the best for the Negro community in America, and the second is that what is best for the American Negro is also best for the African. We must remember that these are assumptions not axioms. They require proof and such proof is not always attempted.

Now the Southern States of America exhibit a society widely different from that of New York. Among the Negroes there is a really rural community which bears almost the same relationship to the Negro life of Harlem as the Native conditions of Rhodesia bear to the Native locations in Johannesburg. (I say " almost " the same, because tribalism in Africa makes a difference.) To people, however, who are familiar with New York, the Negro communities of the South seem by contrast to have in them the possibilities of idyllic excellence.

It is in much the same way that the town-dweller in England sees the beauty of rural life when he escapes to it for a week-end. This nostalgia for the country and for simple habits and crafts is one of the products of our town-bred civilization. The countryman does not always see it in the same light.

'It may be as well to remind anyone who intends to go back to the land by working on a farm, that his new neighbours will not think " how sensible is this man to leave a stuffy office, and do a man's work in the open air." They are much more likely to say, " a bit cracked, 'e must be, poor lad, or p'raps got pinching money and putting it on the 'osses, naught else'll make a man chuck a decent job to come and lead muck." '[1]

The excellence of the country life is a thought rather than an observation, and it is often a wish which is father to the thought.

The two great Negro institutions, Tuskegee and Hampton, have behind them not only this rural community of the South, but also this philosophy of the countryside which exists in the minds of their white—and black—supporters.

We have to allow for this fact when assessing the value of Mr. Booker Washington's evidence in favour of the type of education given in Tuskegee. He was not himself produced

[1] G. T. Garratt, *Hundred Acre Farm* (1928). The author was a farmer in Cambridgeshire.

by the institution which he founded, and the sphere in which he was most distinguished was not carpentry or farming, but in thinking and getting other people to think with him. There is a curious self-deception often present in men's minds with regard to education. The thoughtful man comes either to exaggerate the importance of the elements which were lacking in his own upbringing, or, conversely, to attribute his present position to elements which were there but which may have had nothing whatever to do with it. The man who has had a classical or literary education becomes an ardent advocate of geography or agriculture—two of the things which he himself missed. The working-man becomes excessively addicted to books. On the other hand, the man whose real education has been through his hobbies, often gives the credit to his more formal studies. It is not unlike the way in which a centenarian passes judgment on the cause of his own longevity. It is due to total abstinence, or to a glass of beer a day, or to early rising, as the case may be. In other words, he observes an association, and he gives it the status of a cause.

I am not, therefore, inclined to base very much upon even Booker Washington's verdict of the causes of Negro advancement. His own humility biases his judgment. In the case, moreover, of the white men who support manual training as the way of educating the Negro " along his own lines," this judgment is much too easily combined with the will to keep the Negro " in his place." I do not say that this desire is in the least present in the mind of Dr. Jesse Jones, but the fact that it can be so combined with such an educational ideal should make men more and not less critical of the educational ideal itself. Instead of that, the Phelps-Stokes Reports appear to regard as axiomatic what is really an unproved assumption.

This is the more important because we cannot dissociate education from social structure. It is part of it and is conditioned by it. The education of women and the emancipation of women went together. The development of working-class education in England coincided with the extension of the franchise and the growth of trade unionism. In the same way the education of the American Negro and the raising of his status go together. The one is of little use if there is no intention of doing anything about the other. At a Methodist Ecumenical Conference in London in 1921, Bishops of the American Methodist Episcopal Church South would not sit down at table with the Bishops of the American African Methodist Church. So long as this feeling exists and is condoned, an agricultural and technical education for Negroes keeps the Negro in his inferior state. It will not of itself produce leaders.

8.

When the ideals of education for the Negroes of the Southern States are transplanted to Africa, there is a certain dislocation. It is held, therefore, that they have to be " adapted " in order to make them fit. True, but of what nature is that adaptation ? Is it the kind of adaptation that a living thing makes in response to a change in outside conditions, or is it the cutting up of a long piece of cloth to make it fit a square table ? Dr. Jones' " adaptations " are, as we have seen, a purely mechanical process.

In America the Negro population has a unity about it which is not present in Africa. There is only the one language, and owing to the passage of generations, the Negro is the inheritor of the same culture as the white man.[1] But in Africa we can divide up the native population not only into tribes and languages, but also into two quite distinct classes, the tribal and the detribalized. However different the Negro rural communities in America may appear to be from the Native locations in Africa, I believe that in reality they are much more akin to these groups of detribalized Natives than to the African rural community. The African tribal community is a religious group including the living and the dead, and with a special relationship to the land. It has its own immemorial customs and its own primitive language. The American community is a social group living in the country, who might without spiritual change quite well be living in the town. English is its language, and its life is part of

[1] See E. G. Murphy, *The Basis of Ascendancy* (New York, 1909), Chapter 1, " The Indivisible Inheritance."

modern civilization. To emphasize the economic simplicity of the rural community and to apply that conception to Africa is to miss the whole significance of the tribe.

There is the same source of error in emphasizing the racial difference between black and white. Americans have never quite recovered from the object lesson of Negro incompetence during the " Reconstruction " period. The belief persists that the Negro as a Negro is no use as an administrator, or in any clerical post, and that he would be far happier and " realize " himself better in the simple manual trades required in the rural community. When an American with this point of view comes to Africa, he thinks the same about the African. And yet in the Union of South Africa, and in a less degree in every other territory of Africa, there are thousands of Natives who have ceased to have any roots in the soil. Of the numbers on the class lists of Lovedale in 1927, including boarders alone, 223 out of 614 came from urban areas and had no touch at all with the country or with any tribal organization.[1]

The rural society that is visualized in the Phelps-Stokes Reports is a static society. It sets before the educator and would set before the Native, the old way of life, amended and rationalized, as something in itself desirable for those who were born to it. It would avoid the conflict between the new and the old by avoiding as far as possible contact with the new. This is an educational policy possible only in theory, for it ignores that very community which Dr. Jones would have us remember. The " community " of which the Native is part includes in these days the white man, and the destiny of black as well as white is bound up with this fact.

In the library of the Native college at Achimota there is a copy of Norman Leys' *Kenya*. I should imagine that this might quite well distress both the Government servant and the Phelps-Stokes educationalist. It is a disturbing book, and it makes neither for contentment with general conditions nor for respect for the white man. But if education is a part of social structure, it is useless to educate people to till the

---

[1] Ten years later the proportion was much greater. See p. 115 above.

soil if the conditions of land tenure make it impossible for such labour to end anywhere else than with itself. It is part of the non-moral attitude to education induced by the modern " scientific " method to ignore a challenge such as this. Under the old system of literary education it was forgotten that men had bodies to feed and clothe ; under the new it may be forgotten that they have minds to develop and spirits to kindle. And through ignoring this intimate connection between social life and education the Phelps-Stokes Reports emphasize differentiation before there has been attained equality. Differentiation without equality means the permanent inferiority of the black man.[1] This is why with the best will in the world on the part of the Government the missions cannot resign their independence of judgment. Their education is vain unless they seek also to bring about a social adjustment through which the educated Native may be acknowledged as a citizen of his own country.

These considerations discount somewhat the verdicts of the Phelps-Stokes Commissioners on certain of the educational centres which they visited. They were very much wedded to their formulæ. If during the rapid visit of the Commission the school was seen to conform to the formula, it was a good school ; but the " goodness " of a school which did not appear to conform to the formula was often precisely of that kind which could not be assessed in this external and mathematical way. For instance of Lovedale they report :—

> . . . there are a number of important differences that rather seriously disappoint any visitor who believes in the adaptation of education. The most important of these differences are the very limited instruction in gardening, hygiene, and handwork related to simple needs, and the slight relationship of the school to the community. Most important of all is the fact that the graduates go out without an adequate sense of their responsibilities to the communities in which they are to work.'[2]

We may well ask of what use would be an extended training in manual work to the detribalized Native, and further, how it was possible to tell that the " graduates " left without an

---
[1] See the discussion of this point, pp. 330 ff. below.
[2] *Education in Africa* (1922), p. 201. See above, pp. 114 ff.

adequate sense of their responsibilities? This is an obvious case of the application of formulæ.

A school in Rhodesia impressed me so much with its quiet, unhurried efficiency and its sense of wonder and peace that I felt it to be one of the best schools in Africa. I therefore visited it on four different occasions and in widely different circumstances in order to be sure I had made no mistake. It earned this report from the Commissioners:—

'The school plant is exceedingly simple and greatly in need of development. . . . Though the buildings are simple and in some respects even primitive, they are kept in sanitary and even attractive condition by the well-directed activities of the girls. The success of the Principal in administering this institution so effectively with such a primitive plant and such a small income is to be highly commended.'

Nevertheless, although disagreeing with the methods and many of the judgments of the Phelps-Stokes Reports, we must recognize their value. The minds of the administrators in Africa were open, and the authorities themselves were willing as perhaps never before to try to grapple with this great work of Native education. The Commissions were happy in their opportunity, and they made good use of it. They conducted a most detailed investigation, and presented those whom it may concern with a body of information unobtainable in any other way. They gave both administrators and missionaries concrete proposals to study and concrete criticisms to meet. That in doing so they took a line which we may hold to be unfortunate, is, after all, no great loss, but rather a service. It compelled people to think of better ways for themselves. Their work was productive of many local conferences in Africa between Government and missionaries and in the strengthening of such conferences as already existed. The Commissioners themselves had sufficient weight with Government to get a new attitude thoroughly set. The working out of policy will follow, and in this co-operative task the teacher will take more and more his place, and the " educationist " will be less necessary than formerly.

CHAPTER XIV.

THE RATIONALE OF AFRICAN EDUCATION.

I.

The " content " of African education is the three R's, the study of nature, of people, and of ideas, and the development of creative skill. The " form " of it is religion. What is the underlying idea which links the form with the content?

The two first considerations are concerned with education in general, with the African as a human being. The third is concerned with the African situation alone. Its implications take in all those questions which we have already seen arising out of the " background " of the school in the bush—questions of climate, of geography, of history, of land, labour, and politics. They concern Governments and Churches, and the relations between them.

It is here where the teacher of African children leaves his class-room and looks at his children in their setting of contemporary life. I have purposely not done this until now, for the work of the " educationist " is a small thing compared with that of the teacher, and it is now of the educationist's point of view that I would speak. The educationist is essentially a generalizer. He has to look at the work of the class-room as it is related to the outside world and to the world of nature and history. But the data for his generalizations are supplied in the class-room. In education we begin at the wrong end altogether if we begin with policy and try to frame the people into the policy we have thought out for them. Accordingly, before considering African education in its wider aspects, as the " educationist " looks at it, I have thought it not merely worth while but quite essential to consider the actual work of teaching, and to allow that to be regulative of educational policy.

We have looked at the elements in the background, we have studied the content and the form of teaching. We are now, I hope, in possession of enough data to enable us to consider the *rationale* of African education.

2.

I have already referred in an earlier chapter to the modern attitude to African customs and culture. It has a sympathetic regard for the African and recognizes the value of his own civilization. An older view looked on everything African as wrong and useless, and everything British or European as valuable and right. We have passed away from this form of self-conceit and are willing to recognize that the African may have something to give as well as to gain by coming into the world's life even at this late stage.

The rationale of African education from this point of view is to seek to preserve a characteristically African culture, and to train the Africans themselves to develop it and purify it and bring it into the common stock of the world's good. The African, therefore, should be educated along his own lines, and individual Africans who are able to profit by a high degree of education should be encouraged to go back to their own people and help to educate them.

This is a view which, although creditable to the white men who hold it, is nevertheless not held by a good many educated Africans. They feel it can co-exist far too easily with an unjust segregation policy, and relegate the African to a back seat. They do not want to prolong African civilization as it now is, but to have the best that the world to-day can offer. This affects their attitude to the English language, to European clothes, to standards of comfort and to political rights. It is not a particularly South African question, although I heard it discussed with most earnestness at the Bantu Social Centre in Johannesburg and at Lovedale. The teachers from the Congo forest at Yakusu were just as much interested in it, and so were the Gold Coast native teachers at Achimota. It must be admitted, of course, that these were all either young clerks or students in the training

THE RATIONALE OF AFRICAN EDUCATION 313

schools—a very small proportion of the whole number of native teachers. But they are picked people, and unless we are to discount the native African's opinion except where it agrees with our own we cannot ignore their testimony. And to them this favourable attitude to " African culture " appeared to be much more a European attitude than an African one.

How far is it in accordance with what we have seen in the class-room ? We have already touched on this question in connection with the vernacular. It is, however, wider than that of the vernacular, although the conclusions to which we came in that discussion very largely determine the answer to the wider question.

It is with this as a text that we shall consider the rationale of African education. What is African culture ?

3.

The word " culture " is exceedingly hard to define, and the definition of it has been left either to the anthropologists or to the nationalists, and it changes its emphasis as it passes over from the one to the other.[1] Thus Tylor speaks of " Primitive Culture," and analyses for us the content of a system of which he himself is an outside observer. Mussolini speaks of " Italian culture," of which he is an apostle. To the anthropologist, it is essentially something static ; to the nationalist, it is something which has a mission. The anthropologist is content to preserve it and allow it to be itself, the nationalist is much more concerned with other people's attitude to it. And this is natural, for the nationalist shares the thing which he describes, and his business is with its future rather than with its present. There is thus a marked difference of emphasis between the plea for " African culture " in the mouth of the most sympathetic European, and the same plea in the mouth of the educated African. It is this difference of emphasis which I wish at the outset to emphasize.

It may be considered hazardous in a context of this sort

[1] Cf. above, pp. 19, 146.

to enter into disputation with the anthropologists, but it is up to a point unavoidable. With the results of their research I have no quarrel. They have entered the jungle of African studies and reduced it, if not to the semblance of a garden, at any rate to the decency and order of a forest reservation. This is all to the good, and even if the amateur student of Africa understands that "trespassers will be prosecuted" he will at any rate rejoice that the palings are put up to protect that for which he cares. My only question is whether such a warning notice is good in law. In other words, while the work of the anthropologists is invaluable in the study of African culture, I query its relevance in the matter of education. Anthropology gives the scientific method by which we understand primitive people, but it affords no basis to indicate the future of that people in the modern world. The later history of the British race was not deducible from the remains of the lake villages of Glastonbury, and the future of the African people is not to be inferred from an examination of the social customs of the Bantu. And it is with the future that education is concerned.

It is somewhat of a paradox that anthropology, in spite of its frequent occupation with a particular field, is essentially a comparative and generalized study. Its results shed light on the nature of the human mind in general rather than on the development of the particular people who provide the data. Thus an anthropological study of the Melanesians describes what the Melanesians do and say, but it can only arrive at the significance of what they do and say by comparing them with perhaps the Malays or the Thonga. Apart from the possibility of such comparison with other primitive peoples or with other people who are not primitive, the anthropologist has no criterion of judgment. In other words, the data that lie outside a certain specialized field are as necessary as the data discovered within that field in order to assess the significance of the latter. If that be so, that significance, which involves at least two factors, must concern something common to both.

When the anthropologist fails to make this comparison, or makes a comparison only over a small range and seeks to establish uniqueness for his particular field of study, he is apt to err. It is in this way, I believe, that M. Lévy-Bruhl has gone astray in characterizing the thinking processes of the primitive mind as " prélogique " as against the civilized mind which is " logique."[1] If instead of taking as the " civilized mind " the modern European intellectual he had brought into his comparison other strata of modern society, or an earlier stage, say the mediæval, of the European mind, the uniqueness of the African or Melanesian mind in this particular would have disappeared. But when this distinction is accepted as true, and a system of education is built on it, mischief can be done which far outweighs mere error in analysis. Where it deals with mental characteristics (and the place of a people in the world depends on this consideration), anthropology is more likely to be authoritative where it detects similarities than where it emphasises difference. For the meaning of a difference depends on the history of the process of differentiation (for which anthropology can provide no evidence), whereas similarities are more likely to be discovered since the raw material of all anthropological studies includes the common element of the human spirit.

It is a further paradox that the data of anthropology are in the present rather than in the past. The study of the past is the concern of history and depends on data which testify to development. Where there is no evidence of this kind, everything is present, and can only be assessed for what it is to-day. It is evidence of development that gives a thing a history. In history, therefore, the two points of comparison needed are points in time, England in the age of Alfred with England in the age of Elizabeth; in anthropology the two points of comparison are points in distance, the Masai in Kenya with the Matabele in Rhodesia, or the caves of the Matapos with the caves of Altamira. History looks at the same thing at different times; anthropology at different things at the same time. Until we

[1] L. Lévy-Bruhl, *Les Fonctions Mentales dans les sociétés inférieures* (7th edit., 1922), Chaps. 2 and 3. See the criticism of this in Allier, *La Psychologie de la Conversion chez les peuples non-civilisés* (1925), Vol. I., p. 86, and in C. C. J Webb, *Group Theories of Religion and the Individual* (1916), Chaps I and II

reach history, there is nothing discoverable in the consideration of any one " stage " to prove that it has at some time been some other " stage," and to show what it has preserved in the process and what it has developed away. Without the possibility of finding out what things were like before they are what they are now, our study cannot be said to deal with the past at all.

Accordingly there are severe limitations in the study of anthropology. Within those limitations it is authoritative —outside of them it is irrelevant. The anthropologist examines Bantu handicrafts, the custom of *ukulobola*, methods of agriculture, ways of thought, the quality of *ubuntu*, and all the other characteristics of a primitive people of the present day, and he describes these things to us as " African culture." So far, so good, but when he goes further and declares that these things represent the " law of the African's own being," and that these are necessary if he is to be educated " along his own lines," he has forsaken the province of the anthropologist. He has ceased to deal with the present, and has laid down a rule about the future. He has become a prophet, and in so doing he has had to lay aside the authority which clothed him as an anthropologist.

This may seem a little hard on the anthropologist, but the nature of his subject makes it inevitable. For while it is true that all these Bantu characteristics are present, there is nothing to show how they came to be there, or what was there at an earlier stage. And if a common element linking various stages cannot be found, any theory of the future based upon African " culture " is as much an assumption as the theory that the Africans are the " perishing progeny of Ham." What is the " law of his own being," or what are " his own lines " along which he is to be educated, depends not on anthropology at all, but on the historical method, and how can there be a historical method apart from history ? If no comparison of the same people at different stages is possible, the inner core of development which has persisted through all the stages cannot be discovered. It is this permanent element which gives us the clue to " culture," rather than the evidence provided by a people at a given point in time. We have to see a people not static but

THE RATIONALE OF AFRICAN EDUCATION 317

in transition in order to discover the law of their own being. Apart from the evidence at different stages we have no means of knowing what are the constant and what are the contingent elements in their character and social structure.

Culture, in the dynamic sense, is a deposit of history.

4.

When we come to look at the culture of Africa, we are at once made aware of the difficulties. A clear line can be drawn between those African stocks which have a history and those which have not. The first will include the races living north of the equator from the Atlantic to the Red Sea. The second is conterminous with Bantu-Africa.

The predominant factor in the northern area is Islam, but it is not the only factor. There are Mediterranean influences noticeable among pagan households in the Yoruba country, and of course Egyptian influences right up the Nile Valley into the plateau of the Great Lakes, and signs of pre-Islamic Arab culture in the Sudan. It is the Moslem invasions, however, which are the great historical event in the development of these tribes. Yet nowhere is the real spiritual deadness of Islam more obvious than in its contact with the Negro peoples. It has brought with it to Nigeria and elsewhere on the edge of the Sahara a system of walled cities, an oriental nomenclature and dress, an Egyptian style of architecture, and it has made the Negro a trader. East and North of the Congo Valley it has produced the so-called " Arabisé " villages with more substantially built houses, and Arab designs in wood and ivory carving. It has done all this, but it has opened no one's mind to a new world of progress, although since its first appearance its converts have amounted to millions.[1] With all the objections that can be brought against the " Europeanization " of African habits and crafts and buildings, it can at least be said that behind the European importations there is a world of thought which is not only developing but which is capable of stimulating

[1] See note on p. 22 above.

development in others. There is nothing of this in Islam. The European importation is the beginning of a process; the influence of the Islamic importation ends with itself. In a Moslem city like Kano in Northern Nigeria it becomes clear at once that the wonderful Islamic civilization of Bagdad and of Cordova was but a late flowering of Byzantine Hellenism. In Kano there is Islam without Hellenism—naked, unprogressive, dead. Through it all the animistic African remains himself, as he has remained for centuries.

This introduces us to the first of our difficulties in the search for " African culture." If culture is a deposit of history, here are Africans with a history, but who can tell what their " culture " is ? Everything about Moslem Africa is borrowed, and those things which are not Islamic are at the same stage to-day as they are in other parts of Africa. Races, like individuals, exhibit a strange anæsthesia which enables them to pass through the most terrifying and novel experiences and to come out unchanged. Development does not necessarily come about through the mere flight of time, or through the impression of some experience. It is not *ex opere operato*. It arises only where the new experience presents a challenge which cannot be avoided, and awakens in the minds of men a conflict which must be solved. Events alone do not produce the change. Movements of the human spirit come about in conflict—conflict, that is to say, not of physical mass and might, but of ideas. Ideas may and do depend on physical events, but they must be events which confront the observer with a new fact which is inexplicable on any of his previous theories, and of which he himself demands an explanation. Nothing is more remarkable about Islam than the ease with which it can accommodate itself to new minds. But in its relations with North Africa the essential element in progress—conflict of ideas—seems to have been absent and so the Negro tribes kept the even tenor of their way, with little clue to the powers latent within them.[1]

---

[1] It is possible that the lack of a written African language may have had something to do with this immobility. Although Arabic records give us a very early date for the invasions of what is now Northern Nigeria they are a mere chronology and in an alien tongue. See the

THE RATIONALE OF AFRICAN EDUCATION 319

We may compare this situation with that of the Norman invasion of England, with its stimulating effect on national life, or with the Industrial Revolution at the end of the eighteenth century. This latter upheaval, despite its attendant evils, forced simple villagers into situations which stimulated their minds, and in this disturbance there were crystallized out the characteristics which differentiated Englishmen from other people, and exhibited the nature of "English culture." For the characteristic thing is always the common thing, the trait exhibited by the great mass of the people. " Culture " as the word is used in that nuance of meaning given to it by Matthew Arnold, is a cosmopolitan thing, and often refers simply to "widely read" people, as we should expect the intellectual classes of any country to be widely read. But there is a great deal of truth in the contention of James Conolly, the Irish leader, that the real inheritors of the culture of a people are its working class rather than its intellectuals.[1]

When we look at Bantu Africa, south of the Congo, as distinct from the Negro and Moslem north, the most significant fact is that although the Bantu has a past he has no history.

Amid the kopjes of Mashonaland there rises the chief ancient monument of his country—the ruins of Great Zimbabwe—yet the only thing that is at all certain about it is that he did not put it there. By whom it was erected—Phœnician, Arab, Portuguese—and when and why it was erected, are mysteries hitherto insoluble. And Zimbabwe is a symbol of Bantu civilization. How that civilization began, what steps have marked its growth, what are its essential features, are questions that have exercised the minds of the ethnologists as Zimbabwe has puzzled the antiquarians. But the conditions of solution are not present, for it depends on the historical method. Without the possibility of observation at various stages, the essential element in that civilization cannot be discovered. And if the highest rule for education is that it should be " along the line of one's own being," how

article by H. R. Palmer, on " The History of Katsina " in the *Journal of the African Society*, April, 1927, p. 216.

[1] An argument advanced in his *Labour in Ireland*. Cf. above, p. 147.

can there be any adequate education where the "line of one's own being" is unknown?

5.

This deposit of history which is "culture" is a mental and not a physical thing, and there are in it individual as well as corporate elements. It implies continuity and it implies change. The sense of continuity is that of a greater society than that which now appears, a society, be it understood, whose ideals one accepts and of whose existence one is conscious. It implies that kind of solidarity through which an Englishman can say "We beat the Spanish Armada," and elderly gentlemen in vicarages declare "We have won the boat-race." And if there is no beginning of days neither is there end of life. Both past and present look to the future and believe that then as now in the midst of a changing world the society will continue, and that those features which made it a society in the past will remain. It is this which is the spiritual principle of aristocracy—the memory of a society in which I was represented in earlier days by a person whose name I know, and which I represent to-day, and in which I shall again be represented in the future. I am not therefore just myself, I am a representative person, and while this fact brings with it a dignity it also brings with it a restraint. I must not do anything to "let down" the family. Accordingly it is not only in the past that is gone but also in the *past* that is yet to be that the present finds its stimulus and its security. Posterity must not be ashamed of *us*.

The features of this society are again mental and not physical. It is not the possession of things that marks it, but a quality of mind. The outward aspect of it is something that can be seized by any impostor, by any *nouveau riche*, but the imposture declares itself because it has no roots in the past. "Dignities" may be bought and sold, but you cannot create "dignity" by a single transaction. Any betting man can take the Oxford or the Cambridge side in the boat-race but he cannot say "We won it."

As these features are mental they cannot be static. The restraint on the individual means simply that conservatism which makes for progress. It avoids side issues and fads and fancies and keeps the stream of development within channels and prevents it from becoming a marsh. We can see this in the society of scholars. The fact that a man has to have respect to the work that has gone before him, while it limits his freedom, prevents him wandering away into a wilderness of vain hypotheses and profitless disputation. And so, if he is a historian, he will try to produce a well-documented but original and trustworthy work instead of rubbish like *The Divine Plan of the Ages* or speculation on the Great Pyramid. The influence of a great heritage is chastening but also exhilarating; if it curbs eccentricity it creates individuality. And this individuality is developed by the shocks of conflict which it finds as it goes along, and by its method of dealing with them. Accordingly, in spite of all the contrary arguments of the lawyers, the United Free Church of Scotland in 1904 was the true continuator of the old Free Church of 1841, and those who stood in 1904 for precisely the same things as the men of 1841 were no true successors at all. Continuity means continuity of life, so that as conflicts arise they are dealt with not by the same formulæ but in the same spirit. The identity of a society is not identity of form, but identity in relationship between form and content, so that a change in the one involves a change in the other. Otherwise culture is merely traditional and dead. The talent is given to be used, not to be hid in a napkin.

6.

If, however, culture is a mental thing, it is obvious that the continuity in it is not something predestined or determined, in the way in which a duke's son automatically becomes a duke. It is the spiritual principle that counts and not the automatic descent. It is therefore open to all who will to choose their spiritual ancestry. If a man is concerned for the things of the spirit he at once ceases to be a mere individual. He steps into membership of a republic of thought which goes back thousands of years, and whose ancestry becomes his own. For him artists and poets, thinkers and men of action, have seen visions, dreamed dreams, subdued kingdoms and wrought righteousness. There is an excellent story told of Huxley and a dock labourer with a taste for science. This man had bought a shilling microscope at a fair and he corresponded with Huxley about his observations with it. Huxley was enthusiastic, and writing about the man to Sir J. Donnelly he said, " in that first letter he has got—on his own hook—about as far as Buffon and Needham 150 years ago." [1] The casual labourer had become a member of a distinguished and ancient society. And this possibility is before any man.

The purpose of education—or at any rate one of its purposes—is to give people this possibility of entering into such a spiritual line of descent as I have described. It is to enable them to put themselves into a stream of continuity which will give them something to be proud of, something which brings both dignity and humility, something conservative but also the condition of progress. The past has laid up for us a heritage of deeds and thoughts open to us if we will but accept it. Acceptance has its conditions. It means discipline and we are not always ready to be disciplined. It means examination of what we already hold and believe and are, and the possibility of conflict with what we might have and might become. The more we have lived our life in solitude the more difficult will be the struggle to understand and accept what is offered to us. But nothing is here for tears. The real tragedy is to be out of reach of this offer, even though the offer itself should work revolution in our ways of thought.

' The singers have sung and the builders have builded,
　　The painters have fashioned their tales of delight ;
For what and for whom has the world's book been gilded
　　When all is for these but the blackness of night ? '

Thus William Morris sang of the British working men of his day.[2] The African is in a position not dissimilar. For

[1] *Life and Letters of Thomas Henry Huxley.* Eversley Edition, Vol. III., p. 311.
　[2] *The Message of the March Wind.*

them as for us the treasures of the world's past have been heaped up. We received the treasures of Greece and Rome and Judæa, and have added to them. And if for us, barbarians and Gentiles, Plato thought and Virgil sang and Jeremiah agonized—and Christ died, these things happened for the African too. For him also in later days Beethoven played, Leonardo painted, Shakespeare wrote, Pascal disputed, and James Watt invented. There is no " African culture,"—as yet. There is this universal heritage waiting to be taken up by them. What will they do with it ? How will they come out of the conflict that it brings to their familiar life and ideas ? We cannot say in advance. At any rate not until this conflict has been overpast will it be possible to tell what is the " law of their own being " and what is African culture.

For while the African has no history in the sense which I have held to be necessary for culture, no recorded stages of development through which we can see some mental quality persisting, he has at any rate before him history in the making.

European trade, medicine, politics, and Christianity are coming into Africa with an even greater momentum than any movement which has affected Europeans themselves. The white man has come and he has stayed. His habits, his tools and inventions, have remained as a perpetual whetstone to curiosity and imitation. The unchallenged assumptions of a thousand years have been challenged, while to the new-comer the ancient oracles are dumb, meaningless, and stupid. Change does not come about all at once, and, as we have seen, there is often an unthinking acceptance of the new as but an allotropic form of the old. Men are willing to put by their old gods, and yet to hail Paul as Mercury. But the political and industrial development of Africa is forcing men to think. European Governments have come in, and by regulations of land and labour have sapped the basis of tribalism and have left people in a state of bewilderment. Men have been transported to vast distances from their homes to work for ends they did not see and did not understand. They have been taxed on an individual basis, and money has taken the place of primitive exchange in kind. People have become more mobile, and Bantu Africa is once again on the move. Christianity has come in to challenge the ways of life of those with whom it comes into contact, and to force men either to choose it or to know why they do not. Either response has helped to awaken their minds. And if they have chosen it, they have for the most part not been able to choose easily, but have had to undergo long probation.

The fact that there is to-day no armed resistance, and that the sword is not in evidence even in the hand of the intruder, disguises from us the real mightiness of the revolution. But there are many white men who do see it for what it is, and have become alarmed about it. We have, therefore, in this generation an ideal of education which aims to some extent at tempering the shock of contact, and at educating the Bantu " along his own lines." But these lines are thought to lie in the pleasant places of the undisturbed native villages of a generation ago, rather than with the African as he is to-day.

This assumption is based on a comparison between African ways of living and the political and commercial mechanism which is crushing out his primitive simplicity. But this is a comparison which, like Matthew Arnold's comparison of the scholar gipsy with the modern man, proves nothing. The one has obviously the rural outlook which the other has not, but it tells us nothing of the mental quality behind the appearance. Simplicity is after all an achievement, and the highest achievement of mankind. To become as a little child is to enter into the Kingdom of Heaven. But the untutored mind is very far from being simple—it lives in a world of strange happenings in which cause is related to effect in a most complicated and arbitrary manner. And this is true whether we meet it in the African bush, or in the remote English village. Mr. Lascelles Abercrombie has well portrayed the complicated nature of English rural " simplicity " in his play *The End of the World*. The assessment of rural life as a more simple and desirable thing than town life is the typical fallacy of the town-dweller. The desirability lies in the mind of the observer and not in what he observes. To use moral categories in such cases is to credit things with an ethical nature which things do not possess. And to assume that the unspoilt native community in, say, the Kafue valley, represents the Bantu as God intended him to be, while the educated young men and women from Fort Hare and Tigerkloof are exotic products, exhibits a personal preference rather than a dispassionate judgment. The theory, which I shall consider in a moment, that European civilization is in danger from the increase of the Bantu is no more and no less a fallacy than the belief that Bantu " culture " is in danger from the increase of the Europeans. It is based on the belief that we know what Bantu culture is, and that it is the unspoilt native village.

The only historical comparison which to my mind is valid and which will give us any data for the law of the African's own being, is a comparison between the African in the setting in which we have hitherto usually found him and the African after he has absorbed European civilization and made it his own. For this we need long views. The first contact produces mere imitation on the one hand or opposition on the other. But European civilization in Africa is quite unavoidable. The African cannot but make up his mind to it. Unfortunately, what European " civilization " really is is often hid from his eyes. He sees it in the person of the trader, the labour recruiter, the Government demand for taxes, missionaries of every sort of view, and administrators of every sort of policy. This multiplicity of aspects is bewildering, and the poor African makes all kinds of shots in the dark at the real nature of this thing which has come upon him. To some it is essentially a matter of clothes, to some a bicycle, to some a cigarette, to some simply the English language itself. I have seen men in the Rand compounds holding English books upside down and deriving great satisfaction from the very feel of them ! [1]

It is here where we come to the real function of the school, to the rationale of African education The school (above the village vernacular school) should present this alien civilization *as it really is*. And what it really is is a mental and spiritual thing, not motor cars and money and armies and possessions, but mind. An aeroplane is not just a thing which

[1] Cf. pp. 243-4 above.

flies through the air, but an expression of the mind of man triumphing over the force of gravitation. The electricity which as lightning will strike a man dead, will when tamed in a motor car, obey his control and carry him from place to place. These things which testify to the wonder of the human spirit, and to the majesty of the God who made it, are not mean, sordid, commercial things, but symbols of the glorious heritage of all men. For the spirit of man is everywhere one, and the spirit of man is the sword of God.[1] It is a form of cant to write off European civilization as artificial and unlovely simply because its most characteristic expressions are in the hands of people who are uncouth and selfish. It is the makers of these things that determine their nature rather than the people who use them and buy them. Otherwise we might hold that one of Leonardo's pictures is poor stuff because it hangs in the mansion of a vulgar millionaire.

Moreover, this civilization is seen not only in the mind behind scientific invention, but in the ways in which that same mind has dealt with the problems of God, man, nature, and destiny. In other words, it is to be found in literature. If the material side of European civilization forces itself upon the African's attention, the school can at least present a more balanced picture by giving the other side. It seems unreasonable to introduce rotation of crops and to withhold Shakespeare. A wise old missionary in the Congo assured me that she had found it just as easy with some boys to make a contact through Shakespeare as through a mortise-and-tenon joint ! This was her verdict after a quarter of a century. And a boy at Uzuakoli at the age of 15 was thrilled by *Julius Cæsar* and asked, " Are people writing plays like that to-day ? " The missionary thereupon followed up Shakespeare with John Drinkwater's *Abraham Lincoln* and Bernard Shaw's *Saint Joan*.

7.

What we call " Western " or " European " or " modern " civilization is a blend of various elements not all of them

---

[1] Cf. pp. 223-4 above.

Western or European or modern. It has come to us from Greece and Rome and Palestine, and doubtless the cultured Roman of the Augustan Age would have been shocked to think that the barbarian British could ever have " carried on " his culture.

Forgetfulness of this fact is a fruitful source of panic, and in South Africa it allows men to alarm themselves about the future of what is called " white " civilization. The rapid increase of the Bantu is held to put this " white " civilization in danger. The assumption seems to be that civilization is, as it were, a commodity, and that any white man, by sole virtue of his whiteness, is somehow a custodian of " white " civilization. When stated in this way it is clearly seen to be nonsense, for it is obvious that the civilization of Greece and Rome, of Florence and Weimar, is much more likely to be in safe keeping with the educated Native students of Fort Hare than with the " poor whites " of the Orange Free State.

This is not to say that there is no problem. There is a problem, an intricate and difficult one, but it cannot be solved until it is stated, and stated correctly. We cannot say whether European civilization is safe or is not safe until Bantu have come into it. Like all moral questions it cannot be solved *in vacuo*. Of one thing we may be certain. The Bantu cannot be kept out. Their numbers are too great and their desire is to come in.

There is good historical precedent for this problem. There was a time in the early days of Jewish Christianity when the minds of men were occupied by the problem of safeguarding " Jewish civilization." Christianity had its roots in Judaism, and it seemed unthinkable that the off-scourings of the slums of Corinth and Rome could possibly be trusted to carry it on and develop it without control. The problem was characteristically tackled by Paul of Tarsus. The argument of the *Epistle to the Romans* is to the effect that from now onwards the " Israel " of God is in point of fact the Christian Church, and it inherits all the promises made to ancient Israel. These foreigners, of course, were not by physical ancestry part of the Israelitish strain at all. They had come late into the field, and were indeed drawn from a lower stratum of civilization altogether. But in culture it is not the physical descent that counts, even for those who have it,—" a Jew is not he that is one outwardly." The thing that counts is the spiritual ancestry that a man can choose for himself. By " adoption," therefore, the Gentiles became Israelites, and " Jewish civilization " was in their keeping as well as in that of the Jews who had seen the larger vision.

This has been the normal way in which Christianity has advanced. That ancient Hebrew-Christian tradition has passed from Jerusalem across the Levant into Greece and thence to the Latins and so into Teutonic countries. And at each stage the same thing has happened. Another group has taken it over, together with all the enrichment that has come in the intervening centuries. It has now come to the Africans, and no missionary save the mere proselytizer has ever taken up the line that the Bantu folk are incapable of entering into the Christian heritage and must therefore be content to be for ever dependent on European direction.

At this point the anthropologists begin to be divided. The missionary anthropologist holds that the Native can accept Christianity but that " secular " civilization is not " along his own lines." The scientific anthropologist is only too apt to think that a scientific attitude is possible to the Native, but that accepting Christianity is not." along his own lines." If, however, European culture simply means the material side of it and is to be presented by people who see that side alone, then the missionary anthropologists have a measure of justification for their preference for the native village. And if Christianity means nothing more than dead formulæ, the scientific anthropologist can easily see more warm and living elements in animism.

For good or ill the African is now in the stream of the world's life. It is quite impossible for him to develop apart from the white man, even if he would. New desires have been awakened, which only the white man can satisfy. This is the prelude to conflict of ideas, and conflict is the prelude to development. And just as among the white races it is given to some to be producers of things, some producers of ideas, some to be traffickers in other men's goods, so it can hardly be that a huge section of the human race should for ever find their self-expression in agriculture and rural industries for no other reason than that these were their occupations when the white man came. In the process of development the African peoples will become as highly differentiated in occupation as are the whites : there will also come to be as many mental differences among them as among the whites, although this is bound to be a slower process than the other. And all the while it will become more and more possible to compare one stage with that which has gone before it, and so historically to discover some idea of the common element of distinctive African culture that persists through all the stages.

The work of the boarding-school, therefore, is to give young Africa the best that it is capable of giving and that he is capable of receiving. We foreigners cannot give him *African* culture, because it is not ours to give. We can only give him European culture, because that is what we have.

But it will be *culture ;* it will not necessarily be clothes or bicycles or any particular external; these things he cannot avoid getting from the trading world around him. It will be the real thing, *sub specie aeternitatis,*—the principles by which men live and die ; the scientific temper ; the philosophic mind ; the eyes wide open to beauty of colour and form and function—all illustrated in detail in the life of the teacher and in the presentation of what he has to teach. It will challenge his thinking at every turn, but through the conflict he will enter into the company of all good men of all ages and peoples who have made the great adventure, and the school will give him the sense of the historic continuity of this great society. The history of the race will become his history. This has already been done (often in parenthesis) when men have become Christians. They have been set at once in a stream of progress which leads back to Christ, and Christ has become as much part of Bantu history as He became part of the history of the nameless converts of St. Paul. But the African heritage includes all that has ever taken place since the world began, if only it can be put at his disposal.

What will he do with it?

He may reject it—but that is hardly likely. He may uncritically accept it—this is only too probable. Much of the Native opposition to the college at Achimota arises from this very attitude. It appears to offer a " native " thing, whereas the Native wants the European thing. It is no use railing at this point of view, it can only be accepted, and in the case of many people it may be the best possible under the circumstances. The educational system which sets out to insure itself against failure of this kind is a crude logical machine rather than an association of free spirits. Given time, however, the African who has accepted this alien culture at first without question, will begin to modify it and to work out for himself a new creation. That this in the long run—probably generations hence—is likely to happen is a conclusion fully warranted from the analogy of history.

8.

It will be noticed that there are two stages in the development of culture, and African culture is hardly likely to develop otherwise. There is the stage of acceptance of the new thing, and there is the stage of its metamorphosis into something else. In other words, there is first equality and then differentiation. In the first stage the new-comer wishes to have everything on precisely the same terms as those who have them already; in the second he begins to develop along a line of his own according as his own mental ability asserts itself in its new environment. And the first stage must come first. It is useless to emphasize the difference between the Black and the White until we have first of all vindicated the equality of the Black and the White. Otherwise difference means not so much difference as the inferiority of the Black. This is why the educated Native is so suspicious of the attempt to educate the African " along his own lines." It is also why the South African Native clings to the Cape franchise and will not even consider the specious alternatives that General Hertzog offers.

These two stages can be paralleled by those in the history

THE RATIONALE OF AFRICAN EDUCATION 331

of women's education in England. Up to the middle of last century women were supposed to be not so much different from men as inferior to them. They were held to be more emotional, less persistent, less practical, less intellectual. Suppose these things to be granted, at most they amount only to difference. But in the context they were held to denote inferiority. "Women," said the cynical Lord Chesterfield, "are but children of a larger growth." Accordingly women's education was residual to that of men. It was framed to encourage habits of self-repression and docility in order that the women might be made more attractive to men, who were supposed to like this sort of thing. And it was a standard which women accepted.[1]

This was the disheartening situation when the pioneers of women's education began their work. The first necessity was to vindicate the essential equality of men and women, and until this was done no thought of difference could possibly be entertained. To have started with differentiation would have been to acknowledge the inferiority which went with it and thus to play into the hands of the enemy. Equality came first, and men had to be met on their own ground and beaten on their own ground. The contests in those early days were all "away" matches! Accordingly at Girton, Bedford, and Somerville, and in the London hospitals, women took the same examinations as men and occasionally beat them. After two generations or so of this salutary process the battle has been won and the vindication has been made. No one but a die-hard would ever dream of thinking that a woman is "inferior" to a man.

Yet she is different. And to-day the attention of teachers is being given to the differentiation of curriculum between the sexes in order to allow for that difference, and to educate girls "along their own lines."[2] But in these days "difference" really does mean difference and not inferiority.

In the same way, I imagine, it will be with the African people. It is excellent apologetic that one of the best motor mechanics in Blantyre is a black man, that one of the most

[1] See Appendix, pp. 395 f.
[2] See the Board of Education Report on *Differentiation of Curricula between the Sexes in Secondary Schools* (H.M. Stationery Office, 1923).

able medical men in the Cape Province is a Native, and that black administrators and skilled workmen in the Belgian Congo give the lie to the easy assumptions farther south that the Native can never be anything else than a hewer of wood and a drawer of water. It is also excellent apologetic that the Native students of Fort Hare take the same examinations in the University of South Africa as the white students of Pretoria and Grahamstown, and hold their own with marked success. There will have to be much more of this kind of thing before we can think of differentiation along lines of " African culture." The nature of education depends to a much greater extent than is often realized on political and social conditions. So long as politically and socially the status of the African is inferior, so long will education " along his own lines " serve to emphasize that inferiority.

In England, moreover, the first stage in the progress of women's education—the vindication of equality—required the support of sympathetic men like Sidgwick, T. H. Green, and Maurice, while the second stage—the search for a *differentia*—is the work of women themselves, meeting on an equality with men, but themselves giving the lead.

It may be presumed that the same principle will be true of African education also. The first stage will need the support of men of goodwill among the Whites. This may involve a sacrifice and perhaps a persecution such as Sidgwick and Maurice suffered, and such as is not the lot of the white men who advocate an " African " education for the Native. It it most unfortunate in these days of conflict, when vindication of the case for equality is urgently needed, that so many men of goodwill are to be found playing into the hands of white reactionaries because they draw false conclusions in education from what are sound premises in anthropology.

The second stage—laying down the lines of differentiation—will not necessarily be the work of the white man at all.

A distinction of course has to be drawn between the village school and other schools. For the great mass of the people education will be on quite different lines from that of the European. It will be more concerned with manual work and more immediately practical. As long as the few who are able to profit by it have the opportunity and encouragement to vindicate their equality with the white man, the many who do not have that ability are not penalized by the chance of development along such lines as are possible. But the *rationale* of education is concerned not with what is for the moment possible for the majority, but with the general direction in which policy is moving. It depends on permanent elements and not on the fortuitous disadvantages in a given situation.

A further distinction has perhaps to be made between the West Coast and the rest of Africa. Given the West Coast system of land tenure, the development of agricultural education is going to enable the Native to help his own country. But this again is a matter of deciding what is best in the circumstances. The same rationale of Native education may quite well issue in two different systems for two different areas.

9.

What then are we to say to the appeal to the African to " go back " to his own people and help them out of their darkness ? This is one of the commonest aims held before the educated African by the European missionary or teacher. We may doubt, however, whether it is the business of one race or class to determine arbitrarily the vocation of individuals in another.

It has occasionally been the complaint in societies such as the Co-operative Movement or the Trade Union Congress, that young men of the working-class who were sent to Oxford to be trained as leaders have taken a line of their own, and have not " gone back " to their own people. This of course is a misfortune to the people who send them, but it was a risk which could not be avoided. Nor were the men necessarily to be condemned who thus disappointed their patrons. There is a sense in which it was even a good thing that some men should not " go back " to their own people. Men are so apt to associate values with origins that every example of the same value associated with a different origin is a good thing, and helps to break down prejudice.

The African who does not go back to his own people may have a vocation to help them as much as the man who does go back. It depends on his motive and on his right or wrong assessment of his own gifts. A man's sense of vocation is the expression of all that he is, it is his view of himself in his relation to the world, and the possibility he has of serving his fellows. It cannot be bought by two years at Oxford or Tigerkloof or Fort Hare. And a sense of vocation can only be produced in pupils where it is already present in the teacher. It means a very real sacrifice for a man to come into the light and then to leave it again for the dark, to be rich and yet for the sake of other people to become poor that they through his poverty might be made rich. This is no irreverent use of St. Paul's words, for the quality of spirit required in men who " go back " to their own people is in a very real sense that mind which was also in Christ.

But this finest flower of Christian morality does not flourish on any soil, nor does it spring up at the bidding of any Simon Magus who tries the experiment. If the atmosphere of the school has in it those elements of reverence and wonder, of industry and peace, of which I have already spoken, some men with this vocation are likely to be produced. It is not so much the school's business as the school's privilege to produce them; and there is no guarantee that even a good school will produce them at all. But to make the thing a mechanical process, and for Whites to set out to train certain Natives as leaders of their own people quite irrespective of their standing with their own people, is to run the risk of training not leaders for the Natives but servants for the Whites.[1]

The theory of " going back to one's own people " nevertheless involves a true conception of progress. Men belong to groups which are not of their own choosing. These are pure accidents, like a racial or colour group, or are due to historical and geographical causes, like a proletarian group, or a national group. One side of progress consists in the transfer of a man's loyalty from these adventitious societies

---

[1] This indeed is precisely what happens in French and Belgian territory, and has to be set in the scale against that absence of colour prejudice for which many people uncritically commend the Latin races.

to voluntary groups based on intellectual and moral associations. Yet there is a permanent moral value even in the involuntary group, for its existence devolves upon its members the responsibility to take their fellows with them into any new Canaan to which they are called. For one working-man who is able to profit by a wider education, or for one African who can get the benefit of European culture, there are thousands of others equally qualified who do not have the opportunity. A man's ability to choose a more natural grouping for himself than can be provided by the local area in which he lives often blinds him to the existence of others who would if only they could. And so there is laid upon him an obligation to consider his involuntary society, and to value it not for what it is but for what it might become, through the fuller expression of many who share its life with him. He is thus saved from pure individualism, and he does not lose the element of discipline which is necessary in all character. At the same time the ideal society which eager hearts expect is saved from being a group of people all of the same temperament and outlook, an association of self-determining atoms, a kind of universalized Chelsea or Hampstead.

10.

Education, therefore, needs faith and courage, and, what is more, it needs a belief in other people's faith and courage —a much more difficult achievement. What "African culture" is going to be depends on the African developing on his own lines, and what these lines are depends on the African also. From the anthropological view of what are "their own lines" this development is no longer possible. They have come into the general scheme of the world's life through the mere presence of the European. No segregated education or religion can now abolish that influence. The Dutch missionary in Northern Rhodesia who told me that we "must educate and Christianize the Africans, but cannot have anything to do with them socially" was attempting a quite impossible dualism. It was only thinkable through the previous acceptance of a mechanical view of education and of religion. The whole thing moves on together,—trade, politics, religion, social life.

The African has also begun to enter into the heritage of the centuries which is his through loyalty to Christ. Men whom I have met in lonely places by Lake Mweru and elsewhere have absorbed more of that Christian culture in one generation than many Europeans whose forefathers had lived in it for centuries. On them it sat as " naturally " as on any missionary, and much more naturally than the animistic life of their old kraal.

And as it is with religion so it is or will be with the rest of European civilization. The " belle sauvage " was a theoretical person invented by the philosophers of the Enlightenment. There is invention, too, in the idea of the Bantu living a simple life in contact with nature, with his own art and culture and joy. These things are present in the minds of the thoughtful European, and they will not be present in the mind of the African until he, too, in this sense becomes thoughtful.

> At dusk that look'st on Senegal, at noon America,
> That sport'st amid the lightning flash and thunder cloud,
> In them, in thy experiences, *hadst thou my soul,*
> What joys! what joys were thine![1]

Culture is a matter not of things, but of meanings. The African will give his own meaning to these things when he has the opportunity of assessing them in the light of new knowledge. That is his own business.

The business of the European is to give him of his very best and to believe that he will use it aright. The work of education consists in helping a man to set up standards of judgment, and those not always intellectual. These are not so much given to a person as—to use Pauline language —" formed in " him, and thus education is the effect of one whole life, individual and corporate, upon another whole life, individual and corporate. Life comes only from life.

---

[1] Walt Whitman, *To the Man-of-War-Bird* (italics mine).

PART IV.

THE HORIZON.

CHAPTER XV.

THE FUTURE OF AFRICAN EDUCATION.

1.

In matters of human interest there are so many indeterminate factors that prophecy is apt to be an amusement rather than a serious task. The spirit of man breaks out in unlikely places and in unforeseen ways and falsifies the expectations of the prophet. Who, for instance, could have foreseen the immense changes that would come over the whole world through the advent of an inspired cattle-driver among an unenterprising desert people? And did it seem possible that a quiet rural civilization such as that of England in the early eighteenth century should ever give place to the life of the modern nation, based on steam, electricity, and petrol? There was nothing in previous history to cause men to anticipate the arrival either of a Mohammed or of the Industrial Revolution. The wind bloweth where it listeth.

What unknown forces are pent up in Africa we cannot estimate. They may be no less powerful than those which in the middle of the nineteenth century turned a picturesque Oriental people into the modern Japanese nation. The great leader may arrive, or the great discovery be made, which shall antiquate all our plans for the future. We see in Africa to-day only a few thousand village schools, a few boarding-schools and colleges, and their pupils living in a subordinate position in a country which might still have been their own had they stepped into the path of progress sooner. They have no dead weight of historical superstition about their necks like the people of India. Animism is lower in the scale of religions than Hinduism or Islam, but it has a greater possibility of becoming something higher. It is not bound by its past, and its characteristics are, in the main, distortions of elements in the normal make-up of mankind. Animism is a description of a certain outlook on life, it is not a system, it is not independent of the individual. Hinduism is a faith rooted in written history, real or imagined. The African villager, therefore, does not move about in a world of traditional antipathies, and with relative ease he is free to attach himself to something better. He has no intellectual defence to offer of the same kind as that of the Hindu or the Mohammedan. In the race of human development the African is a late starter, but I am not sure that he is not far less handicapped than the Indian or the Arab who looks down upon him in the narrow streets of Zanzibar or in the towns of Natal. And the education of such a people may make for them a future quite unlike anything that their past has led us to expect.

2.

It is not, however, with such high speculations that I am here concerned. The goal of African education is something hid from our eyes, because we do not know what new factors may appear as we move towards it. But although we may be uncertain of the goal we may at any rate know something of the direction. That direction we may find by applying the historical method to the progress we have already made.

Education is usually considered to be the concern of a number of interests besides that of the pupils themselves—the parents, the teachers, the employers, the State, and the Church. As "interests" they are quantitative. Each has a territory called its own, and an accommodation among them necessarily means compromise, giving up as little as possible in order to retain as much as possible. No one of

THE FUTURE OF AFRICAN EDUCATION 339

them can be satisfied except with the knowledge that none of the others are satisfied! It is an uneasy relationship, and cannot in the nature of things be a happy one.

This point of view cannot be final, and along the line of progress we find that the metaphor ceases to apply. These rival "interests," each jealously watchful over its own possessions, become "forces." It is not what they have but where they are going that is the important thing. They have momentum and they have direction, and an accommodation among them leaves them unchanged in momentum while their resultant direction is determined by the forces themselves each acting with its maximum of effect. It is a dynamic association.

This change has been gradually coming over education in England. The competing representatives of Church and State, class and creed, employers and teachers, parents and administrators, who went to battle with shouting and confused noise in the days of the School Boards, have had their ardour cooled in the last half-century and have taken fresh stock of their position. The present generation is somewhat amazed at the language used by its forefathers over issues which nowadays seem to be unreal. The schools were " garrisons against Popery " or, alternatively, " outposts of the Catholic Church," they were " nurseries of patriotism," or, at a slightly later date, " the guarantees of our industrial supremacy," and all who would these truths deny were infidels, or sedition-mongers, or " idealists " (used as a term of abuse). Well, those were hearty days, and there are still folk who lash themselves with whips in order to bring them back again. But the future is not along that line.

To-day education is becoming more of a co-operative enterprise. Its nature is determined by an aim which all of the competing factors can share. Although each may be travelling along its own lines there is a general direction common to all, and on which all converge. And this has come about through a more disinterested concentration on the child whom they all seek to educate. The pupil's own personality, its development for his own sake, and a respect for it at every stage of development, provide an aim which transcends the demands of this or that " interest," and by so doing changes those interests into forces whose goal is something beyond themselves.

This metamorphosis is still more striking in Africa. The four interests in Africa were and are the missionaries, the Government, the Natives, and the other Europeans.

In an earlier generation the chief educational task of the missionary was, so to speak, the compilation of a " grammar of assent." Belief was relatively the most important thing, and along with belief went European civilization. The schools were in the hands of the missions, and they were primarily schools of catechumens. This still continues. But in these days the emphasis has somewhat shifted. The aim of missions is more and more expressed in terms of the " Kingdom of God," and even where this is identified, as by the Roman Church, with a single denomination,[1] the content of the idea involves much more than merely church membership. It is concerned with the development of the Native on every side, as a social and economic as well as an ecclesiastical unit. And with the Protestant missions it means some day an independent indigenous Church.

A similar change has come over the Government. Instead of leaving Native education to the missions as a matter of private concern, the Government has now come in to strengthen and to generalize this side of mission work. At an earlier stage the administration may have been indifferent or even hostile, for it, too, looked upon itself as an " interest," often as nothing more than the interest which keeps the ring in which rival sects conflict. It recognized the missions in so far as they appeared to be a Europeanising agency, and helped to mould the Natives after the desirable Government pattern.[2] Gradually, however, the

[1] See an amusing and, within its limits, a capable book, by Father T. Gavan Duffy, *Let's Go!* (1928), an account of a journey across Africa by a Roman Catholic missionary from India. It is unfortunately marred by an incredible wildness of statement and bitterness, and only becomes judicial when as an Irish Catholic the author seeks to find excuses for the attacks on his fellow-Catholics, the Belgians of the Congo, by his fellow-Irishman, Sir Roger Casement!

[2] W. P. Livingstone, *Laws of Livingstonia* (1923, Popular Edition), p. 266. " On his part the Doctor told of the Livingstonia Mission and its

Government also has come to look upon its position as conditioned by the end in view. The development of the Native as a citizen more and more capable of self-government is a dynamic way of looking at the Government's task. Administration is less concerned than formerly to be a mere end in itself. It seeks co-operation rather than acquiescence, not only from other Europeans but from the Natives as well. The disastrously stupid policy connected with the story of the Golden Stool of Ashanti is not likely to be repeated.

The position of the Native has also changed. Europeans used to be interested in him not for what he is in himself but for what he might be made. His customs seemed barbaric and out of date, while his religion held his land in "error's chain." On the whole there was nothing to be expected of him unless he received Christianity and the civilization of Europe. The attitude to-day is different. The Native is seen to be the centre of an intensely interesting human system not dissimilar to an earlier stage of our own. He is in possession of characteristics which appear to have been lost in the evolution of the European, a loss which we may have cause to regret. He, too, is no longer an "interest"; he is coming to be reckoned as a "force." He is seeking to develop a way of life of his own—free, intelligent, and responsible.

The domiciled Europeans are also feeling the pull of this new orientation of life in Africa. To people a generation ago the Natives represented an unlimited supply of cheap labour, and the only thing which stood in the way of European industry on this basis was the opposition of other "interests," notably the missionary, and to a less degree the Government. But times have changed, although there are still backwoods where men cannot read the signs of the times. A debate on Native education in the Legislative Assembly of Southern Rhodesia in 1927 was remarkable for the measure of agreement there was among all speakers on the need for the Native

success : how it was civilizing the tribes and providing industrial education for them ; how the native boys were being eagerly sought after by the Administration and the planters ; and how his dream was to establish a great central institution which would be a kind of educational and technical University for Central Africa. The bigness and boldness of the venture appealed to the imagination of Rhodes, who asked for details" (in 1894).

to be trained as a potential citizen.[1] The Report of the Hilton-Young Commission to East Africa equates Kenya with Tanganyika and emphasizes the conception of the " sacred trust " as the governing idea in the British rule of native races.

' The creation and preservation of a field for the full development of native life is a first charge on any territory, and . . . the Government having created this field has the duty to devote all available resources to assisting the Natives to develop within it. But if, after having settled what is necessary for the above purpose there appears to be room for immigrant settlers—still more if these are likely to assist the advancement of the Natives— then immigration can be permitted and even encouraged. Once this has been done the immigrants also deserve consideration, and it is equally a duty for the Government to protect their interests, provided that their needs do not involve any interference with the development of the Natives in the field that has been created for them.' [2]

This is a complete reversal of the policy of the Chartered Companies.

3.

We have seen in the course of this book the way in which these different factors in Africa have developed. If we wish for a word to sum up the whole process in all its aspects we might call it " humanization." The concern of these agencies is gradually being turned away from the narrower interests of their own particular group and toward the services which that group can render to humanity.

It is in Africa as it has been in Britain. Nothing has been more remarkable in Britain in the last generation than the growth of legislation on " social " questions. We have come to see that the wealth of the State is in its people more than in its property. There were of course at an earlier period Acts of Parliament dealing with the factories and mines, trade unions, and the welfare of the working classes. But the idea behind such legislation was different from that behind, say,

---

[1] Hansard (Southern Rhodesia), Vol. VI., Nos. 2, 4, 5, 6, 9, particularly the speech of Mr. Gilchrist, M.L.A. (Cols. 154-5).
[2] *Report* (1929), Cmd. 3234, pp. 40-1.

the Insurance Act. The one was concerned with an unprivileged class whom the upper classes desire to help, the other was primarily concerned not with a class at all but with the well-being of the State of which all classes form part. In other words, we have come to hold a much more organic view of national life than formerly. It is only among extremists at both ends of the social scale that "class consciousness" is believed in and desired.

As this class consciousness is weakened the class idea of education is also weakened. Education ceases to aim at perpetuating existing groups and at standardizing types. As the term "people" comes to mean not only the governed, but in a more and more real sense the governors as well, so "education" comes to mean the preparation of the young for public life. This has no narrow reference but includes all honest service of which the country stands in need. It is the ideal of the modern State that everybody should in this sense be a "public servant," whether or not he draws his salary from the State funds. Education, therefore, is concerned not with any sectional aim but with a national aim. The progressives of all three political parties are closer together now than they have ever been before.

The emergence of the humanized State has been made easier by the growing humanism in religion, in industry, and in education itself. In Britain at any rate, we have begun to feel impatience with the sectarian, whether in religion or in anything else, and although this attitude makes life much less exciting than it used to be, it also increases our regard for men as men, irrespective of the party to which they belong. The business of the Church, for instance, has been emphasized in a new way, not to exalt itself but to serve God through serving humanity. With this emphasis, the term "Christian" has a greater significance, while the terms "Catholic" and "Protestant" are more and more simply party badges, symbols of

> . . . old, unhappy, far-off things,
> And battles long ago.

It is clear that with this convergence in political, religious, industrial, and educational progress, the humanized State has an importance of a kind which it never had before. It is the great society which includes all the others, the *communitas communitatum*, not, as formerly, simply because it could impose its will on all the others, but because it represents human nature in all its aspects in a way in which the others do not. This is not a defence of Nationalism nor an exaltation of Government, but an acceptance of the obvious fact that if humanity is our standard the most human organization necessarily approximates nearest to it. Nietsche's glorification of bureaucracy is in effect a lowering of the humanity of the State to serve a sectional end in the worship of power. The State is not an aim in itself. It serves, because it represents, human nature, and it is conditioned by this fact.

In other words, the State no longer means simply the Administration. It is gradually coming in practice to mean the same as society.

4.

The future of Native education in Africa rests with the Government. If there is any lesson to be learned from the history of education in other countries this conclusion is inevitable. It is even to be welcomed, in so far as human interests come to condition government, and the building up in Africa of the humanized State accompanies the work of education. Apart from these considerations, education by the Government will mean, as the missions have often feared, simply an additional element of official routine.

The growing spirit of humanism naturally first shows itself in the personnel of the Education Department, and in their attitude to their task.

Of this the Natal system of Native education, which I have already described,[1] is a good illustration.

Native education in Natal is under the same Superintendent as the education of Europeans. Something of the spirit of the Department may be seen in the preface to its Scripture syllabus :—

[1] See above, pp. 129-32.

THE FUTURE OF AFRICAN EDUCATION

'Believing that all teachers in their hearts most earnestly desire the spiritual welfare of their charges; believing, too, that our supreme task is the training of the children of this Province to love and reverence God as revealed to us in the Old and New Testaments and to translate Him unto our daily life; recognizing that the insistent and crying need of the world to-day is the simple admission of the love of God; desiring that we should tear the veil of cynicism from our eyes and the gag of silence from our life; realizing that never more urgently rang the call of example and precept to youth, the Department asks that this syllabus be treated by all who handle it in the reverent and responsible spirit in which it has been cast.'

It is not surprising, therefore, to find that Scripture is an examined subject in Natal, and that the missions co-operate closely with the Department. One of the American missions has already handed over seventy of its schools to the Government and would be willing to hand over more if it were able to receive them.

In other territories the same spirit works out in other ways. The existence of six important Government schools in different parts of Africa which have missionaries as principals is a good omen. In a certain Central African territory the Director of Education is not only a member of the Missionary Conference but has even been appointed to various sub-committees. And this kind of thing is becoming general. A new type of administrative officer is finding his way into the educational services, and whereas a few years ago the educational branch was looked upon as being very much inferior to the political, it is now becoming the case that men are found who desire to go into the educational service because of the opportunity it gives to help the native people. It is a hopeful line of advance to strengthen the Government service with men of educational experience and enlightened outlook.

Personal factors play a large part in all the instances that I have given, and in these cases they have worked out beneficially. But there may also be disadvantages. In the case of the Director of Education whom I have just mentioned, his sympathy and goodwill may even create an impossible situation if his successor did not have the same attitude. The present Director is honoured in this way because of his personal qualities, but on an education committee even of a Missionary Conference it is difficult to dissociate his official and his personal positions. There is also a further difficulty. He happens to be an Anglican, and as such it is quite open to him to have his own point of view and to act on it, irrespective of the opinions or "authority" of the clergy of his own communion. But if his successor were a convinced Roman Catholic, would the same conditions hold? On controversial matters such as segregation, the education of half-caste children, and the question of religion in Government schools, the Roman Church has quite definite opinions which a Roman Catholic Director of Education would necessarily share. In these matters his is not an independent opinion. Here is a case in which an accident of personnel may divert the administration of Native education into a channel which it might not otherwise have followed.

Something more is needed than the sympathy of individual administrators. Here and there even under bad systems kindly officials have flourished, and have humanized their administration. But the system itself needs to be made independent of personal favour or disfavour.[1] It requires a certain status in the governed as well as a certain sympathy in the governors.

The control of education by Government agencies raises no insuperable difficulties where it is really the nation that controls. But in Africa there is no "nation" in the European sense, not even in South Africa. There is government by a foreign power representing the views of a minority who belong to the white race. The majority are not yet enfranchised. It is not of course a unique situation; it is a stage through which every nation in the world has had to pass.

The acceptance by a Government of the task of Native education necessarily involves some day the end of this dissociation, and the development of an educated Native electorate who will take charge of the guidance of their own destinies. The situation in Africa is in this respect different from that in Britain. In this country the view of

---

[1] Cf. above, pp. 119-20.

education as a right derived from society itself has only recently been accepted, and it has come with the extension of the franchise and the more organic ordering of society. In Africa education has come first, and those who are being educated are not yet citizens, nor is it possible for many years for them fully to be citizens governing their own country. While in Britain the nature of education has depended on the nature of citizenship, in Africa the nature of citizenship is bound to be dependent on the nature of education. An education which does not develop independence of thought will not issue in a citizenship that is worthy of the name.

Accordingly, since in Africa " Government " means in effect the local agency of the foreign power, it becomes a matter of some importance to see that education has this direction given to it. In the absence of a native electorate some body, some group of people, must act in a capacity corresponding to that of the British electorate. In default of an effective Native public opinion this group itself must act as the organ of such an opinion. An unchecked bureaucracy is a bad thing even for the bureaucrats. Nothing but good can come from the presence of a well-informed, independent, critical body of opinion. The wise administrator has nothing to fear from it, and indeed welcomes it. The foolish person confuses it with obstruction and dislikes it. The British constitutional practice of referring not only to " His Majesty's Government " but also to " His Majesty's Opposition " indicates a healthy element in all government.

The missions are the obvious interim equivalent of a Native electorate. They are run by Europeans, but they include Native members, and in the best missions the Natives are having more and more influence. The Christian Church to-day, as often in the past, is a school of politics, and it is there where the Native ought to have his first opportunity of self-direction. Moreover, the weakening of the sectarian emphasis in missionary work makes it more possible to co-operate with a Government whose bureaucratic attitude is also changing. The existence of an ideal of citizenship towards which both agencies are able to work defines the relative positions of the two. Government and missions will still remain opposed, but in the matter of education only in the sense in which the electorate is opposed to the legislature, or, perhaps more aptly, as the legislature is opposed to the executive. It is as two separate parts of the same system rather than as two completely separate systems that the missions and the Government are likely henceforth to function in Native affairs.

5.

These considerations do not affect very much the practical work of the village school. The effective direction of these schools for some time to come will remain in the hands of the missions. There are so many of them and their standard is so elementary that apart from the spending of money it is doubtful if the Governments could run them any better than they are run by the missions. In actual practice, therefore, a sympathetic administrative staff, and the joint advisory councils on education, meet all requirements in the lower grades.

In the case of the higher institutions, however, the contention which I have advanced is urgent. This is partly because in these places, subsidized directly by Government, a considerable part of the work is the training of teachers for village and other schools. It is still more because Government has now come in to run institutions of its own. The non-existence of a Native electorate means that the formulation of Native educational policy rests with people of another race, and with an administrative body which has to consider other questions besides education. This may give a bias to Government policy which may not be to the best interest of the pupils, or the exigencies of office routine may considerably limit that opportunity of experiment and that elasticity which are of the essence of true education.[1]

Considerations of this kind have led to an interesting and far-reaching proposal in the case of Achimota. It has been proposed (and the proposal has already the approval of

---

[1] That this, however, is not necessarily the case is witnessed by the excellent Government school at Dar-es-salaam.

THE FUTURE OF AFRICAN EDUCATION

most of the parties concerned, including the Colonial Office), that this great institution should be taken away from the control of the Government and put under a Council. The Council, it is suggested, would consist of four European members appointed by the Governor, six African members similarly appointed, four members of the college staff, and the Principal. It is provided that each of the three groups of members should include a woman. This Council would be free to develop the college in any way that seemed suitable, conditioned only by the provisions of the document which establishes it. The Government would continue to be responsible for the salaries of the senior staff and for upkeep, and would act as the interpreter of the instrument of foundation. The position, in other words, would be similar to that of a grant-aided public school in England, such as King Edward's School, Birmingham. The King Edward's foundation has its own governing body which administers the school in accordance with the terms of the statute, and so long as that is done it is free from interference from outside. The Board of Education and the local Education Authority between them contribute about £40,000 a year to the foundation, and their relations with it are confined to inspection and report and to representation on the governing body. Something of the same kind of system is aimed at on the Gold Coast. The difference, however, lies here, that whereas the Birmingham school started independently of Government and is now State-aided, the Government itself founded the Gold Coast school and is now devolving its authority to an independent body. This, too, is the difference between Achimota and an institution such as Lovedale.

This freedom from official administration is of the utmost importance in education. For a college is not a factory or an office; it is a living and growing community. It cannot be decided in advance how it will grow or what traditions it will make. A school that is to produce character needs liberty to be itself, a throbbing vital society of intelligent people who are learning in common the lesson of self-direction. Bureaucratic control of a society with this intention is as the savour of death unto death. When, for example (to quote an actual case), it has become a matter of serious controversy to decide what uniform the staff of a Government College should wear, the emphasis has clearly shifted from the word " college " where it ought to be, to the word " Government " where it ought not.

There is no reason why higher education in Africa should not be as dignified and generous a thing as that of the best type of English school. The existence of this quality at Lovedale, as I have already mentioned, gives a value to that institution which far outweighs the limitations of the Cape syllabus. And Achimota, young though it is, gave me the same impression. There is everything there which can make a living tradition.

An illustration of this in the case of Achimota is the annual Conference of the staff with representatives of Government, the trading interests, Native chiefs and people, schoolmasters and missionaries. It is usually a time of great freedom of speech and criticism. At the Conference in 1927 a significant feature was the choice of a speaker on the subject of the " Relation between Achimota and the schools." With the whole of the Gold Coast to choose from, including the Government Education Department and Africans with English university degrees, the Principal nevertheless chose a humble village schoolmaster out of the bush. This man had been there for thirty years and had always refused promotion as he believed the village school represented his real vocation. It was a choice which was not lost upon the African people present, and it did a great deal to win them to a belief in the college as an independent and living community, very far removed from their ideas of a Government institution.

The possibility of higher education in Africa on such lines as these is one of the happiest elements in the present situation. For it indicates a type of education, neither missionary nor Government, but a new thing. It would be a mistake to contrast it merely with an unenlightened Government Department; it is just as marked a contrast to many unenlightened missionary institutions. Indeed there are few missions in Africa whose educational work is as truly educational and as truly religious as that of Achimota. It is, of course, a wealthy institution, and while money does not of itself produce excellence it is difficult to see how the best kind of school can flourish without money. And it is the Government that is best able to provide the money.

6.

From the Native point of view the future of African education means the emphasis of three features which were very much neglected in a previous generation. It means the development of his economic life, the education of the Native women, and the more general education of the Native teacher.

The first of these has already been dealt with in some detail. The second is of equal importance.

It was my experience that the education of girls in African boarding-schools was on the whole better than that of boys. The reason is not far to seek, and it is a reason that operated also in England a generation ago. The education of boys is affected by the requirements of vocational training, and often there is little more in it than the preparation for a job. These requirements are less obvious in the case of girls, and even where domestic subjects are the chief part of a girl's education they are a more " humane " study than those of the boys. They concern people as people rather than as potential labourers of one kind or another. Moreover, most boys come to these higher schools in order to learn a trade ; this motive is much weaker with girls. Accordingly the education of girls is done much more for their own sakes than for any other motive, and the average of girls' schools give a more " humanistic " education than the average of boys' schools. At least so it seemed to me.

This is a factor that is worth emphasizing, and for two reasons.

In the first place, the women are the more conservative element in the community and there are few matters in which people stand so much in the old ways as in the rearing of children. The elaborate system of taboos relating to it is even stronger than that relating to agriculture. Even among ourselves new ideas of every kind get a footing much sooner than new methods of bringing up children. " They say," is a common justification for this or that practice, and it is difficult to discover who "they" are; at any rate "they" are not usually the most advanced authorities on the subject! Experience, too, is often of the most curious kind. There is the story of the washerwoman's contempt for the health visitor: "Fancy 'er talkin' to me about bringin' up children, and I've buried seven!"

This kind of taboo is not easily dissolved. It takes some time before the results of new practices can be seen, and meanwhile it has to be taken on trust that the new will be better than the old. Moreover, there is naturally a fearfulness in the minds of most parents that their children may grow up to be quite different from themselves, and this fear makes for conservatism. The dissipation of it depends on more human factors than the exploration of new and better ways of doing things. It is a psychological process needing a stimulation of intelligence and imagination and an emotional attachment to an ideal. It will be best started by women of the same class who understand their own people. This is as true of Africa as of England.

In the second place, the family is a community and the training of one element alone is going to create dislocation unless all the others are trained with it. This perhaps does not matter so much if the boys simply learn a trade, but in Africa to-day learning a trade involves other factors. The boys leave home, and that in itself is a great experience. Travelling brings them into contact with other people and with a wider world of ideas. Community life in a boarding-school brings its own lessons that are not learned in the village itself. Close contact with European teachers leads men to imitate even where they do not understand. And if when such boys come home they can marry only girls who have never left the village and who are complete strangers to the new experiences that have come to their husbands, there is a necessary dissociation in the home life.

This has been a problem in England also, at any rate until recently. In the middle of last century the boys of the upper classes went to a public school while their sisters stayed at home and were not supposed to be interested in serious studies. A generation ago the education given by the

THE FUTURE OF AFRICAN EDUCATION 353

Mechanics' Institutes, Trade Unions, Adult Schools, the Co-operative movement, and the Workers' Educational Association, was almost entirely an education for men. The women were neglected, and this meant a serious cleavage of interests between men and women. The balance is being righted in this generation through political action like the enfranchisement of women, through the education of women on equal terms with men in colleges and schools, and through agencies such as the Women's Co-operative Guild and the Women's Institutes.

A scheme which is being put into operation by the Government of Southern Rhodesia indicates a very hopeful line of advance in the education of African women. It is an adaptation of the method employed in the Transkei and elsewhere for training agricultural demonstrators. The girls' school of the London Missionary Society at Hope Fountain has been chosen as a centre for the training of women in community work. In a memorandum to the missions in Rhodesia, the Principal writes:—

'The general idea of the scheme is to bring together a small number (in the first instance) of native women, and to give them a two years' course of training in such subjects as shall enable them to improve the life of the communities in which they live. . . . The high rate of infant mortality, the ignorance of the simplest elements of first aid, the deplorable lack of personal and community cleanliness, are a direct challenge to us who believe that the preaching of the Christian Gospel should go hand in hand with an upward civilizing influence among the people. We have, therefore, decided in consultation with the Director of Native Education, that the course shall consist of home nursing and first aid, maternity work, personal and community hygiene, simple physiology, child welfare and mothercraft, simple cookery with special reference to infant and invalid diet, dressmaking and housecraft, simple civics, vegetable gardening relating to the cookery, simple household arithmetic, letter writing and reading, and Scripture. . . . It is the intention of the Government that when the students have completed their course they shall be appointed to work in their own areas on a definite salary basis, which the Government will provide. The actual cost of the training will also fall upon the Government. All that it is hoped the Missions will do is to provide suitable students. . . . Standard IV. is aimed at as a minimum qualification.

'A word in reference to the kind of student we hope to attract may be useful. While there is no objection to the admission of unmarried girls of mature age who are likely to be married before long, it is rather hoped that we shall receive married women, particularly those who, having passed through our training schools, have married teachers and others in positions of influence. . . . The ideal student would, I think, be one who took her two years' training here while her husband was undergoing a similar course for a similar period at Domboshawa, or was taking the teachers' course at one or other of our institutions.

This community work at Hope Fountain is neither specifically missionary nor specifically Government, but shows a wise co-operation between the two. Community work under other auspices is very well developed in Uganda, the lower Congo, Liberia, and elsewhere.

As an illustration of what is possible on simple lines in a very primitive bush community, the centre at Ituk Mban, a little place in the Efik country of Nigeria, is most inspiring.[1] There are in the year four sessions of nine weeks each. In the intervening weeks the head of the school goes on trek around the villages to keep in touch with former and present members of the centre in their own homes. Most of them are girls about to be married. They come usually for two, three or four sessions, some longer, very few for only one. The effect has been to stimulate attendance of girls in bush schools, dwelling-houses have been greatly improved and " home life " appreciated, the general health of the people has been better, the revolting custom of fattening girls for marriage has come under criticism by Africans themselves, and the Churches have grown stronger.

The training of Native teachers is already engaging the attention of the Governments of Africa, and the Jeanes fund of America is making it possible to create a body of supervisory teachers who will train others in the right way. It is likely that the training of teachers will go through the same stages in Africa that it has gone through in other countries, and indeed it already shows signs of doing so. There is first of all a period during which the aim is more or less exclusively technical, and is concerned with learning the tricks of the trade. In England for two generations it was generally believed that the teacher need be only very little ahead of those whom he has to teach, as long as he knows

[1] See Appendix III.

THE FUTURE OF AFRICAN EDUCATION 355

how to impart what he knows, and for teaching beginners very little skill is needed. The old Home and Colonial Training College for infant school teachers believed that with an effort the necessary training might be given in six weeks. These ideas were not only fallacies but the very reverse of the truth. As the results in practice of these ideas were seen to produce mechanically-minded people with little real education it gradually became clear that a good general education was a necessity for every teacher. After the Bryce Commission of 1896, therefore, instead of tinkering any longer with " pupil teachers " and " monitors," the country organized a wider system of secondary schools, and made a good general education a necessary preliminary to training for elementary school teaching.

The day for this has not yet quite come in Africa. The lack of money is the chief drawback. In some places, moreover, there is still a belief that the teacher's work is to hand over knowledge rather than to communicate a spirit, and even in places where mere knowledge is discounted and " character-building " is emphasized, it is often felt that this is largely a matter of sleight-of-hand. But there is a slow progress towards better views. And it is here where the new spirit in Government is likely to be effective. Such general education as is required is relatively costly, and the missions are finding difficulty in giving it. But the training of teachers is a very suitable subject for combined effort.

7.

I have spoken of the position of the missions as an " interim Native electorate." If this is so, it involves a special training for the missionary. He needs to be a person who has a real " political sense," not that he need be keen on what is narrowly called " politics " or that he should acquire the fatal habit of lobbying or of running after men of influence. This latter kind of man has forgotten the essential dignity of his calling. But by a " political sense " I mean the ability to grasp what is really essential in a situation, the ability to estimate beforehand the probable effect of this or that line of action on this or that group or individual, and generally to know when to take a stand on principle and when without loss of principle to give way. Not everyone has such habits of mind, and they are primarily developed by experience. But they are much less inborn than they are often assumed to be, and they are largely the product of reflection and quietness of spirit.

Quis custodiet ipsos custodes ? is a question which continually rises to the lips as one looks at the schools of Africa, both Government and missionary. The European's responsibility is, and is necessarily, so great, as he prepares young Africa for the coming day, that one wonders who is to prepare *him*. In many places it is pathetic to see very commonplace and uninspired people tackling this task of creating a civilization that shall be inspired and the reverse of commonplace. They pass on to others the lessons they themselves have never learned. Yet again in many other places the work is often so wonderful. " That we may be used beyond our own proper efficacy " is a prayer of Jeremy Taylor, and the answer to that prayer is self-evident in the mission-field. While complacent and stupid men, ignorant of their own stupidity and blindness, attempt tasks too big for them and do not know that they have failed, humble and modest men, conscious only of their own limitations, are often unaware of how very far they have succeeded. The grace of God is wonderfully operative in mission work of this latter type. Is there anything that man can do to allow this factor a greater and greater field of opportunity ?

" Training " has in these days become a fetish. There is no task so elusive or so inspired but that some one will arrange a " course " which a man may take to fit him for it. It is felt that one set of men can be fitted to do the work of the world by hearing another set of men speak about it. It is a curious recrudescence of the fallacy of " formal training " among people who would see through the fallacy at once in the case of teaching children. And in its least imaginative form it is part of the intimidation of " science."

A man must, of course, find the tools for his job. If he is a missionary he will need to know something of anthropology, something of phonetics, something of psychology, in addition to the primary qualifications of being a Christian and a gentleman. But what precisely is it that he should know about these subjects ? I have heard a man commended because he knew by heart all the various complicated tables of affinity of the Melanesian Natives ! It is not really the content of these subjects that is of most use. They are more valuable for the question they raise than for the answers they give. A subject, for example, like "principles of education," which is part of every course for a teacher's diploma, has a practical value that is very nearly nil (*experto crede!*) What Raymont, Bolton, Dewey, Findlay, Thorndike, Bagley, and all the others have said about these matters is in itself of little practical importance. I doubt if there is one teacher in a thousand to whom it makes any difference at all. What is, however, of real worth is the way in which these men approach the subject, the questions which they think are relevant, the ground which they feel the subject ought to cover. And that being so, their work is suggestive rather than informative, they stimulate us to give our own answers to questions which their books suggest, and it is our own answers and not theirs which are of value to us. In other words they present us with as it were so many magnets, each of which attracts to itself a number of scattered ideas which come out of our own experience and reading.

Subjects of course vary in their content value, and in the case of some, such as the ethnology of a primitive people, the real aim in studying them is to acquire information which we did not previously possess. In cases of this kind solid reading is to be commended rather than lectures, and a " course " of training would consist of guided reading rather than the substitute of taking notes. Attending lectures is for the pupil one of the most frequent sources of self-deception, and giving them is not infrequently the same for the lecturer ! In subjects which combine both values of information and suggestiveness there is most of all opportunity for self-deception. Such a subject is psychology. It can be exceedingly helpful, but about it also there can be talked a great deal of nonsense. The psychologist's business is to tell us something about our minds and bodies which we did not previously know, and to stimulate us to ask ourselves the right questions about ourselves and about other people, and about the relationship between these two. The practical teacher is concerned not with the psychologist's researches but with his results and their applicability. Yet psychologists are apt to have a morbid interest in their own experiments, and to feel that experimentation is the important thing in " doing " psychology. Yet if, for instance, it is proved by experiment that it is easier to learn poems in wholes than in bits, that is all we need to know. It raises a question which the practical teacher will have in mind when he teaches poetry to his class, and it is this stimulation that is the important thing. A knowledge of the experiments themselves is of no particular value, and a " course " in psychology which laboriously presents these before the wondering eyes of youth may give both the lecturer and the student the feeling that they are being scientific whereas they are merely being irrelevant.

The " training," therefore, that the missionary—and Government—educator needs is less one of " courses " than one of reflective study with the opportunity for discussion. It needs to make a man a good human being, with a power of mastery over his own thinking and of seeing the wood as well as the trees. Quietness of mind and thoughtfulness, flexibility, imagination, thoroughness, self-criticism, an understanding not only of the subject but also of the philosophy of the subject, even if it is only arithmetic, are all very desirable qualities in those who are going to train African teachers. They will need to know how to teach elementary subjects and to enable elementary people in their turn to teach them also, the knowledge of a handicraft, or skill in some direction not merely literary, an acceptance of all that is implied, politically and socially, in their position as teachers, an understanding of themselves not less than of Africans, and experience of school organization and discipline.

I do not know where all the conditions required for such training are to be found. A day training college is handicapped by its limited time for discussion and for the opportunities of informal talks and long periods of reading. Missionary colleges of the residential type are apt to be weak on the educational side. It was constantly said to me by missionary teachers in Africa that in the light of their African experience their preparation had been very largely irrelevant. The best of them had been trained by their hobbies, they knew what they liked and they studied along those lines. They had a general power of adaptability so that when the need came for some special piece of work they knew how to fit themselves for it.

This is not to say that training is unnecessary. It is indeed most helpful, provided it is humanized, and that it trains in the things that are really necessary. These things are mental qualities which have to be related to certain subjects. The situation that makes training necessary must condition that training. And that situation is a human problem, it is the education of primitive men and women to live in a world in which there are other men and women of a different type, and to enable them to find their feet in these new circumstances.

8.

If in the course of our investigations the idea of Christian citizenship has stood out more and more clearly as the aim of native education in Africa, we have to remember that it is an aim which cannot be realized by Africans alone. Nor can it be imposed on African education from without. There are in it elements that are "given" as well as elements that are achieved. Christian experience depends on what we do with certain factors which come to us at the outset, which life itself interprets and which in turn give to human life form and standards. However "native" the Christian Church may become in Africa it will always be a debtor not only to the Greeks but also to the Europeans.

Citizenship is of a similar nature. If it means anything at all it means individual participation of the African in responsibility for government. It depends on the presence on the same soil of two different races whose destinies are by this time inextricably interwoven.

Many there be who look upon this as a consummation devoutly to be shunned. They therefore try to counter the forces of progress by a determination that this thing shall not be. White is white and black is black, and never shall the twain meet on any terms of equality. Yet it is a hopeless position. All history is against it.

Two separate nations have never yet been able to inhabit permanently the same territory. There has come about either fusion or catastrophe. The attempt was carried on for long years in France. From the days of Étienne Marcel to those of Louis XVI. there were two distinct nations in France, a privileged class who paid no taxes and a peasantry as unfree as the beasts they tended. The cleavage between them was felt to be no shallower than that between the native African and the European.[1] But this situation came to red ruin in the French Revolution. The normal course of evolution cannot be held up indefinitely.

This has been true in our own country also. The labouring poor a century ago were neither in status nor in common opinion part of the nation at all. Those who favoured their education did so out of patronage, and those who opposed it did so out of fear.[1] Disraeli was shrewd enough to see that two nations had thus grown up side by side on the same soil. Since his day we have suffered many of the shocks and jolts that indicate the progress of fusion. Class prejudice is not dead yet, but at least it is not so respectable as it was, and in theory it is not respectable at all.

It is not likely to be different in Africa. The presence on the soil of Africa of white as well as black has permanently affected the development of each. The African can no longer be regarded as a primitive inhabitant of a primitive world capable of going his own way as if the European's arrival were no more than an incident. The European in Africa cannot work out his destiny as if he were living in another Europe beyond the seas. This fact is the rock foundation on which the education (not only of Africans but also of domiciled Europeans) must rest. Each race needs the other not only for the satisfaction of immediate wants, but in order to develop in its own best way.

Education depends on social structure. If there are two

[1] See Appendix I.

THE FUTURE OF AFRICAN EDUCATION

classes in a community one privileged and another not, a child's education will depend on the class to which he belongs. His status and his education go together, each is conditioned by the other. Similarly the status of the Native in Africa is bound up with the nature of his education. The education given to him usually corresponds with his status, in case any better education would make him wish to raise it. It is a serious limitation of the value of the Phelps-Stokes Commission Reports that their views of Native education are orientated not around the Native's political position but around American educational theory. They have dealt with education in the light of a hypothetical rural village very much as the older economists thought of human well-being in the light of a hypothetical " economic man." But the thing that in the long run determines Native education is the position that the educated Native is expected to hold in society, five, ten, or a hundred years hence. The establishment of happy self-sufficient villages, where each man lives quietly under his own vine and fig-tree, is a pleasing picture, but it is neither big enough as an aim of education nor is it relevant to the forces that hold Native life in their grip.

The education of the African thus necessarily concerns both races equally. For no unprivileged class can work out its own salvation. It needs help from its more fortunate contemporaries. The working men of England owe their advancement both to the Chartists who were men like themselves, and to the middle class Radicals who were different. The emancipation of women was the work of women and men. The growth of joint councils of Europeans and Natives in South Africa points the same lesson. But it is no less true that the privileged class requires for its own well-being the advancement of the unprivileged. It is sometimes considered that in the development of Native education it is the Whites who give and the Blacks who receive. Nothing could be further from the truth. Both of them give and both of them receive. The Whites receive security and they receive a moral basis for their own race integrity. The health of a civilization depends on the integration into it of all the elements that are present within it. Anything that is not absorbed is a potential centre of infection and decay. It was so in Greece, in Rome, in France, and it will be so again in Africa.

Of course, co-operation between the two groups will not necessarily go on to the same extent everywhere. Life in Africa as elsewhere is conditioned by climate and soil, and by other factors which we have considered as the "background" of African education. In the equatorial region it is possible that the French view of the future of the colonies is the right one, and that progress will consist in retaining the European machine of government and in associating the Native with its administration. Where one community is domiciled and another is not, there cannot be that interchange of thought and ideas which in time will produce a new and distinct civilization. This is possibry true of the Congo, but on the West Coast other influences have already been at work to neutralize the effects of geography. The closer connection with Europe and the longer experience of Europeanization have created communities who seek control of their own affairs as an electorate, and not simply as a recruiting ground for the civil service.

In those parts of Africa where both black and white can live together the problem is altogether different. The future there is inevitably in favour of integration of both black and white into one civilization. To seek to prevent it by legislative or social discrimination is to seek to sweep back the Atlantic with a broom.[1] Two races cannot possibly be kept forever separate in the same territory. Sooner or later there must come political equality, and the aim of Native education should be to bring this about by natural evolutionary methods. The only alternative to evolution is not repression but revolution.

---

[1] The objection that it will lead to intermarriage seems to me to be a complete irrelevancy. Marriage is a matter of personal preference. There is equality before the law in South Africa for the Dutch and the British, and yet not only has this not led to indiscriminate intermarriage, but it may actually have told against it. But in any case no woman would feel obliged to marry any casual person who proposed to her, simply because he was her equal before the law.

THE FUTURE OF AFRICAN EDUCATION

'The improvement of the character of the people, and keeping them at the same time in a state of dependency on foreign rulers, are matters quite incompatible with each other.'[1]

The native African is gradually losing his natural group, the tribe, and he has as yet no alternative group to which he can belong, except that if he is a Christian he has the Christian Church. But the Christian Church is not a territorial group, and although it is concerned with the highest values of life, the spiritual, it cannot take the place of a community which represents all his interests—food, clothing, shelter, marketing, police, transport. The tribe as a religious unit is reborn in the Christian Church; as a political unit it can only be reborn in the State.

But what is the " State " in Africa ? It is a pure makeshift. Its boundaries are quite arbitrarily drawn, so that an area such as Katanga which geographically and industrially and in every other way marches with Northern Rhodesia belongs to one European country and Northern Rhodesia to another. Pencil lines have been drawn upon the map of Africa and the territorial divisions have followed the map, rather than vice versa. Consequently the single greatest problem in every territory in Africa is the problem of patriotism. There is no State: the State has to be created, and it will be created not by might nor by power but by the spirit of the people. The terms " Kenya " or " Rhodesia " may convey to the Britisher the idea of an outpost of empire, still linked in feeling and thought with the mother country. But to the overwhelming majority of the people who live in those places they are home, the only home that they have ever known. And if through European pressure, the tribe, whatever may be its social influence, has been deprived of all political power, the territorial authority which has taken its place will need to invest itself with all those claims to patriotism which the tribe asserted and received.

It is this fact which makes the term " self-government " a misnomer as applied to the present States of South Africa and of Southern Rhodesia. The majority of the inhabitants

[1] Sir Thomas Munro, 1761-1827, the famous Governor of Madras, quoted in a memorandum by the Rev. A. G. Fraser, Principal of Achimota.

do not count as part of the " self-governing " nation. And yet if there is to be a nation at all it must integrate all those elements that are at present outside. Loyalty is a virtue only of citizens, as it implies a bi-lateral relationship, the governed to the governors, and the governors to the governed. Awareness to these facts has influenced the majority report of the Hilton-Young Commission to take the line that self-government in Kenya, on the exclusive terms on which it is desired by the white settlers, is for ever impossible.

I have said many things in disparagement of the usual American point of view on African education. Yet on this fundamental connection between education and status, I know no wiser words than those written by the distinguished Southerner whom I have already quoted in other contexts. I will here give two quotations from his chapter called " Our Race Security," the one dealing with the need for and nature of equality, and the second with the nature of freedom.

' Two races in ceaseless contact upon the same soil cannot be kept asunder, upon any rational and permanent basis for their differentiation, if we seek the foundations for such a basis in the self-respect of but one of the groups involved. Such a conception of our cleavage may for a brief period find its security in the passions of war, or in the immediate traditions of a poignant social readjustment; but an emotional revulsion is not a policy. Like the moods produced by artificial stimulation, the preservation of the intensity of a racial antagonism demands an increasing measure of excitation—a demand which is as futile in its permanent accomplishment as it is damaging in its social reactions. It is worse than profitless. In the slow processes of time, the powers of class animosity have always proven inadequate for the protection of the integrity of one group against the intrusion of another, unless the instincts of self-respect and of self-protection are profoundly entrenched upon both sides.'[1]

' Liberty is forever being talked about as though it were a pure abstraction. As a matter of fact it has no meaning except under its institutional expressions. Its symbol is not that of a man in a vast waste of silence sitting naked beneath a solitary tree. Its outer symbol is a perfected society itself; it is a social achievement—not a bauble strung upon a string of beads, or a state of individual isolation. Men create it together or not at all. They cannot get it by going upon a journey; nor can they give it away.

[1] E. G. Murphy, *The Basis of Ascendancy* (New York, 1909), p. 55.

THE FUTURE OF AFRICAN EDUCATION

They can bestow its institutions . . . but they can, in a fundamental sense, give freedom to no other race.

'They can, however, strike down the formal inhibitions which they themselves have imposed upon an included group; they can erase the limitations or the discriminations which they have sought to fix in the terms of their institutions. They may do so in the interest of the weaker race; they may do so as a measure of rectification toward their own social organization and as a freer and fuller expression of their genius,—an act of self-conquest and self-development. That much the stronger race may do,— and, in the interest of the fulness and the significance of its own horizons, *must* do, to the last and smallest letter of its meaning. But the more intimate processes of emancipation we cannot bestow. These, under the very necessities of the case and in the interest of the negro's own security, must be self-chosen and self-accomplished.

'His failures will at first be manifest. How soon and how largely he can overcome them no man can say. One who appeals for the wisdom and validity of fundamental policies is not therefore bound to defend the crude anticipations of an easy optimism. But it may be well to remember, as to all our social policies, that a programme is not necessarily sound in proportion to its cynicism. . . . We cannot choose for them, but we can offer them something better than despair to choose; we cannot build their righteousness, but we can do much to increase its inspirations; we cannot achieve for them the self-restraints, the peace, the wholesome securities of a racial or personal self-respect, but we can refrain from making it impossible; indeed, we may look abroad to find it, may watch with an affectionate solicitude for its delayed appearing, may do all that others can to give it solidity and truth, may rejoice in the slow rise of its dim proportions above the ooze and drift of long and unstable savagery, knowing that the rough stone of this foundation—waiting within the shadow of our common humiliations—is the other half of the double basis of our own integrity of race, the missing support of the uncompleted arch.'[1]

9.

And if it be asked, Who is sufficient for these things? the reply is that the human spirit has not changed its nature because of the colour of a man's skin.

'I have listened to thousands of old Native men of many different tribes in my time, I have heard them speak their inmost thoughts,

[1] Pp. 62-68.

not through interpreters—who ever learned anything through an interpreter ?—I have studied these people in and out of court, officially and privately, in their kraals and in the veld during many years, and I can say that I can find nothing whatever throughout the whole gamut of the Native's conscious life and soul to differentiate him from other human beings in other parts of the world,[1]

This was my own experience in Africa, even though I had to approach Native life very much at second-hand. There was nothing I saw or heard or was told by missionaries or officials or educated Natives which could not be paralleled either from contemporary English life or from history. Primitive life in Old Testament times was not dissimilar to that of the Bantu. The Middle Ages and even Victorian England exhibited a society as deeply scored by social cleavage as that of South Africa to-day. The unsophisticated mind has characteristics everywhere the same. The British servant girl who reads her weekly novelette and believes in luck and sings sentimental hymns on Sundays and is reduced to tears by the more emotional type of cinema, is part of our civilization, bone of our bone, flesh of our flesh, speaking the same language, an inheritor of the same culture. But all that Lévy-Bruhl postulates of the " prélogique " mind of the primitive he might equally well postulate of her. The differences between " higher " and " lower " are not differences of race, they are differences of integration. One life is more securely integrated than another. And E. G. Murphy speaks with truth of the " integrating force of opportunity," without which the English rustic is as much at sea as any African in the surging currents of the modern world.

This is one point to be kept in mind. Citizenship in the modern state is a responsibility which is just as likely to be as honourably carried by the educated African as it is assumed to be carried by the uneducated English man or woman. The other, and the more important, point is that the " integrating force of opportunity " is chiefly in the hands of Christian missions. The highest standard of education is not the possession of knowledge but the integration of life

[1] Peter Nielsen, *The Black Man's Place in South Africa* (1922), p. 81. Mr. Nielsen was a Native Commissioner in Rhodesia.

within a worthy purpose. It has again and again been the case in history that the Gospel of Christ has made the humble believer not only a good Christian but also a fundamentally well-educated man and the best type of citizen. Christ is the link not only between God and man, but also between man and man. If He interprets God to us, He also interprets us to one another. In His light we see light, not only for ourselves but for society as well.

It was this belief which, in spite of crudities and false emphasis and verbal inspiration, made the position of the old type of missionary essentially right. He believed that the love of God in Christ was a great regenerative force and that it could re-create men according to the Ideal of the ages. And in so far as Christ is still, in the twentieth century as in the first, not only that ideal but also the power that makes that ideal realizable, all the centuries meet in Him. In Him the distinction between prehistoric Africa and modern Britain fall away, and the spirit of man is born anew, ready for all the work that may be his vocation. The slavish imitation of European externals is always to be condemned, and there have been many mistakes made in Africa because of such a habit. Imitation of the animistic village may also be carried so far as to become a similar mistake. In these things neither circumcision nor uncircumcision availeth anything, but a new creature.

APPENDIX I.

TWO COMPARISONS.

[NOTE.—Nothing more is intended in this Appendix than to indicate lines of comparison between the status of the African and those of the mediæval peasant, the British labourer, and women in nineteenth-century England—enough perhaps to warrant the suggestion that the feeling which we call "race" prejudice is at bottom simply one form of class prejudice. These extracts do not "prove" this; they simply testify to the existence of a body of evidence which must be taken into account by anyone who wishes to prove the opposite. The burden of proof (if there *can* be proof) of the wisdom of racial discrimination as a policy rests, I think, on its advocates rather than on its opponents.]

I. THE MEDIÆVAL PEASANT.

I.

BANTU Society in its tribal form presents many similarities to that of Europe in the Middle Ages.

The empire of Charlemagne was an agricultural empire, it was composed of self-sufficient and self-conscious local groups, it was held together by local loyalties ; economically it was a closed circle and money was scarcely needed at all.[1]

From this situation Europe developed but slowly, and even where the social structure had changed the social attitude was more persistent. Society had no documentary basis, and common knowledge and immemorial custom were the recognized titles. In England the lord of the manor held the land of the manor, and his villeins held from him. In the earlier centuries rent was paid not in money but in service. This service had two aspects : if the tenant had to render service to his lord, no less was the lord bound to render service to the tenant. The tenants had occupation rights, but no ownership, and after the Conquest there were no ownership rights at all save in the King. Moreover, in theory, although not in practice, even the King himself had no absolute title. He was recognized as the embodiment of the will of the community, and only in so far as he expressed this general will was his title valid.[2]

With certain obvious differences Bantu chieftainship recognizes the same corporate life of the group, its basis on the land, its lack of absolute titles, its customary nature, and its bond of mutual service. The position of the " squatter " in a European area has also a similarity to that of

[1] H. Pirenne, *Mediæval Cities* (1925), pp. 42-7.
[2] This, at any rate, was the theory of the civil lawyers, following Ulpian. See R. W. and A. J. Carlyle, *A History of Mediæval Political Theory in the West*, Vol. I. (1903), p. 64.

a feudal villein. A squatter is "a native who lived on a European farm, used his own cattle to cultivate the whole or part of it, and received as his reward a share of the ultimate proceeds."[1]

The communal sense of responsibility is something which stands in the way of individual responsibility, but in matters of police it is an effective way of bringing offenders to justice. Edward I. in the Statute of Winchester (1285, "A monument of the persistence of primitive institutions") revived the old system whereby the hundred was held responsible for the robberies committed within it.[2] This is a well-known principle of Native custom in Africa and found expression in the Penal Code of South Africa in 1898, in the well-known "spoor law."

'The head of any kraal shall be responsible for the value and damages of any stolen animals the spoor of which is traced to such kraals.'[3]

In primitive communities of this kind based on the land, society is built up on status rather than on property. The idea of law, therefore, is one which applies to the people rather than to the place. It is a personal thing attaching to an individual as a member of a particular group rather than as a resident in a certain area.

This was a common mediæval phenomenon. Agobard of Lyons, writing in the ninth century, said that it happened constantly that of five people meeting in one room, each followed a law of his own.[4] In later mediæval times the confusion was so great at fairs and markets that special courts—the so-called courts of *pie powder*—were set up to try cases on the spot, according to the custom of the country from which the litigants came.[5]

[1] *General Hertzog's Solution of the Native Question: Memorandum No. 1*, p. 19.
[2] Stubbs, *Select Charters* (8th edit., 1905), pp. 469-74.
[3] E. H. Brookes, *A History of Native Policy in South Africa* (1927), p. 191. The law was recognized by Lord Charles Somerset in 1817. See the very interesting account of it in W. M. Macmillan, *Bantu, Boer, and Briton* (1929), pp. 55-9, where it is compared with Edgar's *Ordinance of the Hundred* (A.D. 959-75).
[4] P. Vinogradoff, *Roman Law in Mediæval Europe* (1909), p. 16.
[5] J. J. Jusserand, *English Wayfaring Life in the Middle Ages* (1909), p. 247.

I. THE MEDIÆVAL PEASANT

In the Transkei where cases are dealt with by Native law, the law is determined by the tribe to which the individual belongs. This is nowadays a principle that is recognized more or less all over Africa. It is this personal view of law which so often tries the patience of the European with the Native in his tribal state. Law is the custom of the people and in their eyes requires no further sanction. Appeals, therefore, to rules of morality obvious to the European often leave the Native cold, and it is assumed that he is a lawless and untrustworthy person. In fact, however, the sanction of custom in Bantu society (or indeed in British society !) is a far more compelling thing than the force of positive law.

The organization of crafts in Native society presents certain parallels with that of the later mediæval craft guilds. Crafts are usually hereditary. In Southern Nigeria, for instance, the craft of the blacksmith is handed on from father to son, and it is not possible to carry on the trade without this qualification by birth. This is a common feature of primitive society, and is one factor in the caste system of India. The mediæval guild lost the hereditary principle, but retained the aspect of a close corporation.

2.

The " two nations " which Disraeli saw present even in Victorian England and which are present in Africa, were there in Europe in the Middle Ages. Where human society divides along lines of status it is even more rigid than where it is divided along lines of property. It was only very slowly that villeinage and serfdom began to give way, and it was above all in the towns where the peasants *as a class* began to rise into something approaching freedom. But the man above the peasant class looked on those beneath him as of quite different clay from himself. (A " superior " white man in Africa may quite well be descended from mediæval ancestors who themselves were treated as outcasts by their own superiors !)

Meanwhile the same habits of mind show themselves wherever the *theory* of two nations is accepted. There are fear, despite, and oppression on the side of the superior class, and there is either servility or discontent or both, in the lower class.

'When the inhabitants of three villages in the south maintained, quite justly, that they would not pay for substitutes but come in person at the royal call for a levy of defence against the Spaniards, the viguier of Beziers settled the dispute with one level volley: "March to the bridge of Vidorle, or don't march, just as you please; I intend to have £12 10s. . . . You bloody peasants! Whether you will or whether you won't, you shall pay all the same!" . . . Not infrequently the most humble supplications were met with coarse language or threats, e.g. "Say no more, or I will have you thrown into the cesspool."'[1]

This is in France in 1247.

One has perhaps to go off the beaten track in Africa to see this sort of thing, but every traveller comes across it sooner or later. A visit to an acquaintance in Northern Nigeria was quite spoiled by the ungovernable rage of my host at his Native servant about the merest trifles. I have seen the same unreasonable attitude shown day after day on a boat on Lake Nyasa.

From people who were felt to be so immeasurably beneath the superior class that no reprisals need be feared, compulsory services were commonly enforced. This habit has not departed where the opportunity and the desire both exist. In the Middle Ages, for instance,

'blackmail was regularly paid to divert the royal "purveyors" from one village to another. . . . The officials imposed illegal forced labour even on Sundays and feast days. . . . The higher officials were not as a rule either tyrants or rascals, but the lower officers were coarse, dissolute, and formidable to the poor.'[2]

And in Kenya to-day the same irregularities go on. For example :—

'In September and October, 1927, men of the Seme area, Central Kavirondo, were forced out to work on bush clearing on the lake shore. . . . About eighty were turned out, and contrary to the Ordinance, were forced to work for periods up to two months

[1] G. G. Coulton, *The Medieval Village* (1925), pp. 342-3, quoting cases from C. V. Langlois.
[2] *Ibid.*, pp. 343-4.

I. THE MEDIÆVAL PEASANT 375

without pay under the orders of a fuel cutter. . . . He took the product of their labours, gave them no pay, but did give them rations of maize meal, and had several of them flogged . . . when their tally of logs did not come up to his standard.'[1]

It is not surprising to find contemporary mediæval testimony describing the bondman as one who "suffereth many wrongs, and is beaten with rods."

'Even in England, a master was amenable to no law court for beating his serf, apart from loss of life or limb, and a great man might easily kill one with impunity in fact, though not in law. It is among the special distinctions of a most courteous and saintly prior at Tournai that he had never struck a servant.'[2]

The South African Outlook is continually reporting similar miscarriages of justice towards Natives.

'Two brothers Roos pursued a Native boy some miles and then thrashed him. Subsequently the boy died, and the Rooses stuck the body into an ant-bear hole. They came before the circuit court on a charge of murder.'

The charge was reduced to one of common assault, and the defendants were let off with a fine.[3]

Another paragraph in the *South African Outlook* for the same month has an interesting quotation from the *Rhodesian Herald* of March 30th, 1928. In the case of the trial of a Gwelo butcher,

'it appears that a herd of cattle belonging to the British South Africa Company had become heavily infected with tuberculosis, and eighty of these infected cattle had been sold to the accused "on the condition"—according to the evidence of a Government Veterinary Surgeon, who acted as a go-between in the transaction—"that they were killed for Native consumption."'

This is quite in accordance, not only with mediæval principles, but also with that street cry of old London, "stinkin' butter for sarvants!"

[1] Archdeacon W. E. Owen, in the *Manchester Guardian*, Dec. 6th, 1928.
[2] G. G. Coulton, *op. cit.*, p. 52.
[3] *South African Outlook*, July, 1928, pp. 123. The recent Nafte case is still more interesting. In this case the defendant was guilty of a particularly revolting fatal act of cruelty, and was sentenced to seven years' hard labour and *twenty lashes*. Vehement protests were made against this sentence, but the Government was firm enough to let it stand.

This of course is only one side, and one which is much rarer to-day in Africa than it used to be in the Middle Ages in Europe, when there was no public opinion to keep it in check. A hard-bitten old settler in Southern Rhodesia was commended to me because (like the above-mentioned prior of Tournai) it was his special distinction that he had never struck a Native. The Farmers' Association of Graaff Reinet in June, 1927, passed a strong resolution opposing the Native poll-tax,

'as it was considered that the Natives contributed sufficiently to the revenue of the country through the customs. One farmer said that the way Natives and the poor Whites were taxed through the customs, chiefly on cheap blankets, was an everlasting disgrace to our civilization.'[1]

Women of the peasant class, of course, had no status at all in the Middle Ages. The offspring of serfs were called not "children" but "brood" (*sequelae*), and the lord treated them as such. Where a serf on one manor married a woman of another manor, the lords frequently shared the children.[2] The *ius primae noctis* was a recognized right of the lord in the case of a peasant marriage, although in fact it was almost always commuted for a fine.[3] A bondwoman was the lord's chattel.

This attitude, although not this system, persists in places in Africa. There are not many officials in the Belgian Congo who do not have a native *ménagère*, a word which means more than a "housekeeper." In the French possessions an official who wants to have a black woman living with him must contract a temporary marriage and make provision for the woman and their children when he goes on leave. The problem of half-caste children was serious enough in Northern Rhodesia in 1927 to engage the attention of the Missionary Conference. It is also a problem in Natal. One of the most notable insincerities connected with the Native problem in South Africa is that the utmost horror is expressed at the union of a black man with a white woman, while the intercourse of a white man and a black woman is

[1] *South African Outlook*, July, 1927, p. 124. There is an 80 per cent. *ad valorem* duty on cheap cotton blankets in the Union.
[2] G. G. Coulton, *op. cit.*, p. 80.   [3] *Ibid.*, pp. 464-9.

an offence that is almost venial. Even men guilty of the second will be unmeasured in their condemnation of the first.

A young student with whom I talked in a South African train assured me that " the Native is a bad lot," and against this position he was obviously amazed that there could be any argument. It is taken for granted by so many people. It was equally taken for granted in mediæval Europe that the peasant was a bad lot.

' No creatures are to be found more abominable, deadly, cunning, unreasonable, prevaricating, execrable, impudent and audacious than peasants and country folk.' [1]

This is from Hemmerlin, canon of Zurich, writing about 1450. By this time the lot of the peasant had considerably improved, and perhaps the worthy canon was afraid of the disappearance of his type of civilization at the hands of unruly peasants. He cannot find words strong enough for them. " They are intemperate in their manners, coarse and blubbery, gluttonous, rough-skinned, dirty." [2] He speaks, too, of their faction-fights, their hearty and coarse amusements, their envy.

At the same time the peasant was a great joke. There are time-honoured jests against Native Africans based upon their alleged simplicity, and usually with a suggestion of stupidity also. But this has nothing to do with colour. It has to do with class. It was the same in the Middle Ages. There is an old chestnut which goes back at least to 1450, and which in its mediæval form was told against a peasant :—

' A friar was expatiating in his sermon on the unrivalled excellences of Saint Francis . . . and seeing that with all his . . . rhetoric he could find no seat for him in heaven or earth . . . said, " Where then shall we set him ? " A certain peasant suddenly cried aloud, " Sir ! there is an empty seat here by me," and the whole congregation laughed.' [3]

3.

So far we have been considering the view that the superior takes of the inferior. Let us now turn to a few illustrations from the other side.

[1] G. G. Coulton, *op. cit.*, p. 523. [2] *Ibid.*, p. 519. [3] *Ibid.*, p. 266.

It is commonly said among a certain type of European that kindness to a Native is always taken by him as an evidence of weakness. Yet those who habitually treat him with kindness do not seem to be at all adherents of this doctrine. They are usually people who have found in the Native a fund of loyal devotion which the other people cannot command by force. It is the commonest experience of missionaries on trek to find their boys sleeping round their tent at night to protect them from all danger. A wonderful man whom I met in the Nyasaland bush, an administrator, who had lost an arm in the War, had so much got the affection of his boys that they liked nothing better than to go out with him and face a charging lion while he rested his gun on the boy's shoulder to take aim ! The defects of the Native are the defects of the child, and his loyalty is like a child's also, free, unquestioning, and generous.

A discussion I once had with some Native schoolmasters in Nyasaland was vividly reminiscent of some chapters of English history. They had been to South Africa, and were full of the disabilities from which the black man suffered. These they put down to the English servants of King George, and they were sure that if only the king himself knew of them they would be remedied. They wanted to know why the king allowed such people to be about him.

There was here the same distinction drawn between the king and his counsellors as the peasants in the revolt of 1381 (one of the few occasions in which their own point of view appears in history) made between Richard II and those who served him.

'When the king heard the news he sent his messengers to them on the Tuesday after Trinity Sunday, to ask why they were behaving in this manner, and for what object they were making insurrection in the land. And they replied by the said messengers that they had risen to save him and to destroy the traitors to him and to the realm.'[1]

The trust of the villeins in the king, although misplaced on this occasion, would appear to have been justified, for in 1391 Richard rejected the petition of the Commons that

[1] *An Anominal Chronicle of Saint Mary's Abbey, York*, English Historical Review, July, 1898, pp. 509-22, edited by G. M. Trevelyan.

villeins might not be allowed to acquire land or to send their children to school to better themselves.[1]

The king was a person to be treated with reverence, and incapable of doing wrong, save that he was so advised by evil counsel. The pathetic letter of Lobengula to Queen Victoria about the invasion of 1893 shows the same attitude.

'Your Majesty, what I want to know from you is why do your people kill me ? Do you kill me for following my stolen cattle which are seen in the possession of the Mashonas living in Mashonaland ? I have called all white men living at or near Bulawayo to hear my words, showing clearly that I am not hiding anything from them when writing to your Majesty.' [2]

4.

"Christianity in the fourteenth century was still an oral religion."[3] There were few books. The pictures on the walls of the parish church were the poor man's Bible. People were dependent for everything on the priest, and "family religion" had very little place. If they were interested in religion they listened to a wandering friar, whose graphic illustrations, drawn from that wonderful storehouse, the *Gesta Romanorum*, brought home to them the tenets of the Faith in fable and analogy.

The situation is not dissimilar in Africa. There is scarcely any literature in the vulgar tongue, and if a man had to depend on his own resources for progress in his religion he would not get very far. The Native evangelist is an interesting person. I had a conversation with one at Mbereshi and he told me how he approached people who had never before heard the Gospel. It was extraordinarily like the method used by the friars, and he had a fund of proverbs and homely

---

[1] W. Stubbs, *The Constitutional History of England*, Vol. II., pp. 485, 509. Fifteen years later in the reign of Henry IV. the right to education was recognized. "Every man or woman of what state or condition that he be shall be free to set their son or daughter to take learning at any school that pleaseth them within the realm."—Stubbs, *op. cit.*, Vol. III., p. 627.

[2] J. H. Harris, *The Chartered Millions* (1911), p. 111.

[3] B. L. Manning, *The People's Faith in the Time of Wyclif* (1919), p. 1.

illustrations which would appeal to the people. Men think in pictures rather than in ideas.

At the same time there is often a dualism in the minds of baptized Christians. This, however, is a feature of the untrained mind everywhere. Many good sober Christians of our own country carry charms and mascots, and a belief in " luck " is as universal as a belief in God. Both the mediæval peasant and the African Native show an effective belief in evil spirits, and minds that are so much obsessed with beliefs of this kind are apt, when they come under the influence of another religion, to make a syncretism of the old and the new. This commonly happened in the Middle Ages.

' The villager, at need, had his own ceremonies far more ancient than those of the priest. . . . He was well able, when occasion served to do without a priest to marry him : any old rustic could ask the couple solemnly, thrice each, whether he or she put the other to spouse ; and, after the six solemn affirmatives, they were thenceforth true husband and wife not only by village law but by church law, which here followed the ruling of pre-christian Rome. Moreover, even for the last solemn sacrament the poor man had his own substitute ; a little earth was put into the dying man's mouth instead of the holy wafer, and he went into eternity houseled as his ancestors would have houseled him before the Christian era.' [1]

The villagers believed that they could call up storms by magic, and, conversely, that they could charm away hail and thunder. Their midsummer and Christmas festivals were pagan rites with Christian names, and the Puritans of the Middle Ages are continually complaining of the use of Christian ceremonies as occasions for licence.

In these days much the same thing happens in places in Africa where Christianity has not found much depth of earth. It is one of the commonest characteristics of " Ethiopianism." In Natal I visited the village of the " prophet " Shembe, one of the most interesting places in South Africa. He has a following of several thousands of people, and he has built up a religion based chiefly on more spiritual parts of the Old Testament, keeping polygamy and dances, and with a ministry of healing. There were a number of patients in rondavels,

[1] G. G. Coulton, *The Medieval Village* (1925), pp. 270-1, based on Wernher's Poem, *Meier Helmbrecht* (1234-1250 A.D.).

I. THE MEDIÆVAL PEASANT 381

and he was building a hospital with his own hands. The children performed a dance to the accompaniment of a drum. It was a slow and measured proceeding and very impressive. The village was a model of cleanliness and order, and a Native Affairs' official who was with me said that Shembe himself had the most spiritual face he had ever seen on a Native.

Syncretism is not confined to the Native. Some theories of mission work include it as a method of approach, as indeed it was used on definite occasions in the past. The Levitical code shows an attempt to take over and sublimate in the Jewish religion some of the pagan practices of the earlier Canaanites. The early church came to a compromise with its heathen environment with regard to Christmas Day, and the process may have gone even further.

In the same way a crucifix used at Thysville on the Lower Congo had a black figure of Christ. Many of the Roman Catholic missions in Central Africa have given up the attempt to abolish the Native beer-drinking ceremonies and have come to terms about them. A paper was read at the Northern Rhodesia Missionary Conference in 1927 advocating the retention and sublimation of Native initiation ceremonies and the less obviously harmful dances. Charms and symbols are common in animistic Africa, and they are utilized in Roman Catholic and other missions. The use made of them by Natives is often quite magical and unconnected with morality. The great majority of the prisoners I observed who came on board at various landing places on the Congo to load and unload the steamer were wearing talismans with the image of a Saint. A boy I saw from the train near Sakania picked up a cigarette-end and solemnly crossed himself before lighting it !

The spirit of man, however, will not be denied. There is no permanent resting-place in externals, and from time to time some inward urge seems to burst into expression. Sometimes these movements of the spirit have individuals to lead them, sometimes individual persons are only the occasion of their outward manifestation. Movements of this kind originating among illiterate and inarticulate people often assume strange forms.

Such phenomena were constantly occurring in the Middle Ages. The year 1000 produced several of them. To a large extent the Crusades were movements of this character. We may be certain that the great number of humble people who threw away lives and fortunes in these adventures would have been hard put to it to explain what it was that impelled them. The children's Crusades were still more incoherent outbursts. So was the rise of the Brethren of the Free Spirit. The thirteenth century in Italy witnessed many movements of fanaticism. Matthew Paris has a good account, albeit hostile, of the " Shepherds " who travelled through Flanders and France and whom he came across in the year 1251. With the " Lamb and Flag " as their ensign their leader said he would win the Holy Land by humility and simplicity, for " God was not pleased with the military pride of the Franks ! " Their ranks were filled from the lowest classes of society, they were hostile to the worldly and indolent clergy and to the Universities. The movement was one of those mysterious symptoms of religious unrest, dissatisfied with the world as it is and strangely over-estimating its power to put things right.[1]

The story of Africa since the coming of the European is marked by similar movements. They are the measure both of powerlessness and of strength : strength, because they testify to the permanence of the spiritual element in man, however distorted or unenlightened ; and powerlessness, because in the particular circumstances that spirit has no proper outlet.

The famous story of that awful day in 1856, when the Amaxosa nation were overwhelmed by disaster, is perhaps the best known of all. The people had been warned by a prophetess that if only they would have faith the spirit of their ancestors would reward them by appearing in bodily form and driving out the white man from before them. The test of their faith was to be their willingness to destroy their cattle, the sole source of their wealth. The folk with implicit trust did so, and waited. It did not happen. The Xosa never recovered from this terrible blow.

[1] Matthew Paris, *Chronica Majora* (Rolls Series), Vol. V., sub. ann. 1251, pp. 246-54.

I. THE MEDIÆVAL PEASANT 383

There are, however, other cases, although not so dramatic. There is for instance the case of Dr. Wellington which I have already mentioned in the text. These things are only absurd in their local setting, like the case of our own countrymen who went to Weymouth in March, 1928, to await the end of the world, or that of the pious Americans who went to Jerusalem fifty years ago for the same purpose, and whose descendants now run the " American Colony." They are symptomatic of the dissatisfaction of the human spirit with the world as it knows it.

Sometimes, in the hands of more sophisticated people, these incoherent movements take on shape and substance.

Joachim of Flora, born in Calabria in 1132, was a product of the mysticism of South Italy. He expounded a transformed Christianity which he expressed in the " Eternal Gospel," in which there was a strange eschatological element. The great reign of the Lord was to begin in the year 1200 and continue till 1260. World history is divided into three ages, with various characteristics. The first is the age of the Father and lasted from Adam to Christ, the second is the age of the Son and began with Hosea and continued to St. Benedict, the third will be the age of the Holy Spirit. The first is the age of the patriarchs and kings, the second that of priests, and the third that of monks. The first is the age of slavery, the second of sonship, the third of liberty.[1]

The same attitude appears among Native Africans when they have begun to be interested in Christianity but are left to themselves. The " prophet " Harris on the West Coast of Africa was a Native leader who worked out a system of Christianity and made thousands of converts. There are 156 " Separatist " churches in South Africa, many of them with curious unhistorical theologies. Sometimes, as at Bullhoek in 1921, they lead to difficulties with the administration. The " Watch-Tower " movement in Southern Rhodesia is an independent native Christian movement with a theology—imported from America—not unlike that of Joachim of Flora. There are three ages or " dispensations " in history, of which that of the Holy Ghost is the last. This

[1] E. Gebhart, *L'Italie Mystique* (1890), pp. 72-77.

last age is to be the age of liberty, and for the black man it means the disappearance of white domination and the rule of the Blacks in their own country.

We may ask ourselves what are the causes of these independent native Christian movements which are called, generically, "Ethiopianism." Maurice Evans attributes them to a wooden policy on the part of European Church authorities, who insist on keeping the Natives in leading strings.[1] Professor Edgar Brookes gives various reasons—unworthy ambition, lack of intelligence, the abuse of the "open Bible," and undue subordination to Europeans.[2] All these no doubt enter in. But however they arise, a view of Church history plainly indicates that they have their origin, not in some superfluity of naughtiness in the African, but in the working of the human spirit everywhere.

In the light of these parallels can we say whether the difference between the present-day African Native and the mediæval European is greater or less than the difference between the mediæval European and his descendants to-day? Nothing would have been more unlikely to the mind of the mediæval baron or abbot than the evolution of the boorish peasant into the modern English citizen. I have attempted to show how deep was the cleavage between classes—quite as deep as that between races to-day. And yet the evolution has taken place, bridges have been thrown across the gulf.

No one would recognize in members of the British peerage or of the learned professions, men who, as their family names show, are descended from the comical, stupid, uneducable clodhoppers of the mediæval manor! What man has done man can do, and we may be certain that the road of progress open to the villein cannot be closed to the African Native. The disappearance of communal tenure has had something to do with the change. So also have the development of contract, and the growth of towns, those schools of political liberty. In England, Protestantism had much to do with it, for it developed a man's individual moral responsibility and applied that morality as a test to the affairs of the nation.

[1] *Black and White in South-East Africa* (2nd edit., 1916), pp. 88-90.
[2] *Op. cit.*, pp. 437-8.

But in whatever way the status of the mediæval peasant was altered, there was from the beginning that incalculable force with which his opponents had to reckon and which ultimately defeated them—the spirit of man himself. And in Africa the most relevant fact in the situation is not that the black man is black, but that he is a man.

II. THE BRITISH WORKING MAN.

1.

Bernard Mandeville's satirical essay on Charity Schools in England, published in 1723, shows a very apt parallel to a stock argument against Native education in Africa :—

'The welfare and felicity of every state and kingdom, require that the knowledge of the working poor should be confined within the verge of their occupations and never extended (as to things visible) beyond what relates to their calling. The more a shepherd, a plowman, or any other peasant knows of the world and the things that are foreign to his labour or employment, the less fit he will be to go through the fatigues and hardships of it with cheerfulness and content.

'Those who spent a great part of their youth in learning to read, write and cypher, expect, and not unjustly, to be employed where those qualifications may be of use to them ; the generality of them will look upon downright labour with the utmost contempt.'[1]

Education above their station will also make the poor incapable of showing the " proper respect " due from servants to masters :—

'When obsequiousness and mean services are required we shall always observe that they are never so cheerfully nor so heartily performed as from inferiors to superiors I mean inferiors not only in riches and quality, but likewise in knowledge and understanding.

'A servant can have no unfeigned respect for his master, as soon as he has sense enough to find out that he serves a fool.'[2]

This talk about education is sentimental nonsense, and is fundamentally unjust. It shows

---

[1] *The Fable of the Bees*, etc., edition dated 1772, Vol. I., pp. 216-17.
[2] *Ibid.*, I., p. 217.

'a petty reverence for the poor . . . and arises from a mixture of pity, folly, and superstition. It is from a lively sense of this compound that men cannot endure to hear or see anything said or acted against the poor, without considering how just the one or insolent the other. So a beggar must not be beat, though he strikes you first . . . and murmuring weavers must be relieved and have fifty silly things done to humour them, though in the midst of their poverty they insult their betters, and on all occasions appear to be more prone to make holy-days and riots, than they are to working or sobriety.'[1]

This sentimentalism, moreover, stands in the way of the economic interests of the country :—

'To make the society happy and people easy under the meanest circumstances, it is requisite that great numbers of them should be ignorant as well as poor.'[2]

In much the same strain the wife of a Durban shopkeeper complained to me that if this Native education were allowed to go on, how would people like herself get servants?

2.

The poor, who were also the ignorant, were to be found in both town and country. In the country they were suffering very much from the enclosures that went on in the eighteenth century, through which it became impossible for the land to support the smallholder with any degree of comfort. The small yeoman disappeared, and his successor was an agricultural labourer living in poverty at the will of the squire who had engrossed the common land. The parallel with African conditions has been pointed out in the text.[3]

Hannah More, although certainly no opponent of the education of the poor, has the same general attitude as Mandeville. In her case, however, it is based on theological rather than on political grounds. It is not unlike the Dutch attitude to the Native as contrasted with the British South African. Wilberforce, who was of the same school of thought

---

[1] Mandeville, *op. cit.*, p. 236.
[2] *Ibid.*, I., p. 216.   [3] Pp. 43 f.

II. THE BRITISH WORKING MAN

as Hannah More, in a chapter of a book which he described to Pitt as the " basis of all politics," reminds the poor that

' their more lowly path has been allotted to them by the hand of God ; that it is their part faithfully to discharge its duties, and contentedly to bear its inconveniences.' [1]

In other words the submission of the large number of the labouring classes to their inferior condition was a cardinal factor in the stability of the country. There is no hint that these " poor " were of the same race and language as those who oppressed them.

' The working classes were to have just so much instruction as would make them more useful workpeople ; to be trained, in Hannah More's phrase, " in habits of industry and piety." ' [2]

Hannah More lived in thought at a very considerable distance from the poor whom she patronized. William Cobbett, Wilberforce's bitter opponent, and the champion of the rural labourer, was nevertheless strongly opposed to grants for education, on what are often called, curiously enough, " common-sense " grounds. To what did education tend, he asked :—

' Nothing but to increase the number of schoolmasters and schoolmistresses—that new race of idlers.' [3]

' Take two men, one that can plough and make hurdles, and be a good shepherd, and one that can plough and read,' and the former ' was the best man.' [4]

3.

If the rural areas at the end of the eighteenth century were poverty-stricken the poor of the towns were still worse off. There was an underworld of overcrowding, poverty, cruelty, and violence, whose characteristics stand out luridly

---

[1] *A Practical View of the Prevailing System of Professed Christians* (1797), Chapter 4. R. Coupland, *Wilberforce : A Narrative* (1923), pp. 240, 244.
[2] J. L. and B. Hammond, *The Town Labourer, 1760-1832* (1917), p. 59.
[3] J. E. G. de Montmorency, *State Intervention in English Education* (1902), p. 239.
[4] H. Holman, *English National Education* (1898), p. 59.

in the prints of Hogarth. Unwanted infants were exposed in the streets, or trained up as professional thieves. The system of apprenticeship still held in industry, and apprentices were notoriously badly treated and were consequently idle and vicious. They were taken on by their masters as a source of profit, and the manners of the times almost excluded pity.[1]

The population of London was swollen by constant immigration from the rural districts and particularly from Ireland. Arthur Young describes the hovels in which the Irish live at home, in which the family slept on straw on the ground along with the cows and the pigs.[2] The stress of poverty drove them into the towns, where their undisciplined habits found new scope. The situation was not unlike that to-day in the back streets of Johannesburg.

These Irish frequently undercut the ordinary workman in wages, and there were constant complaints. Faction fights were common, and the watchmen were only too glad not to interfere, but to allow them to kill each other off and save trouble to the authorities.[3]

There are people in South Africa to-day who regret that "natural causes" are not allowed to operate in order to thin down the number of the Natives :—

'A member of the Southern Rhodesian Legislative Assembly in the session of 1925 took the line that the Native was being given an unfair advantage by being prohibited from obtaining European liquor !'[4]

The great occasion of expense among the very poor in London then as now was in funerals. A police magistrate gave evidence before a Committee in 1815 about a certain friendly society :—

'There is one general principle that runs through the society which I highly disapprove, and that is the ambition of the most miserable of them to have what they call a Decent Funeral.'[5]

[1] M. D. George, *London Life in the Eighteenth Century* (1925), pp. 17, 43, 228-36.
[2] *Ibid.*, p. 121. The date is 1776. [3] *Ibid.*, pp. 116-17.
[4] A. S. Cripps, *An Africa for Africans* (1927), p. 76.
[5] George, *op. cit.*, p. 303.

II. THE BRITISH WORKING MAN

Mary Kingsley used to say that one cause which attracted the West Coast Native to the Wesleyans was the fact that they were the only religious body that could provide a hearse for a funeral! A recent letter from a missionary in Accra contains this paragraph:—

'In our local press the other day I read the account of the funeral of a man who died in a town not his own, nor of his tribe. His fellow-tribesmen resident in that same town did not go to his funeral as he was not a member of their tribal club. The newspaper pointed out, however, that many local people and others attended, and then ended up as follows : " With this attendance, what might have been a poor show proved a huge success in the end, as far as mourning goes."'

The conditions among the poor in London earned the self-righteous disgust of the rich, and yet at the same time the rich equally disliked the idea of the poor rising out of their humble station. So long as the poor remained the objects of either despite or patronage their existence flattered the pride of the upper classes, but as soon as a workman showed aspirations for something higher he was viewed with suspicion and dislike. This again is a common attitude to the African Native, but it would seem to have a class rather than a racial basis.

Francis Place was one of the leaders of the reform movement which led to the great Act of 1832. He was also in earlier days a tailor at Charing Cross.

'He complains that on several occasions he lost good customers owing to their learning of his habits of study. . . . "Had these persons been told that I had never read a book, that I was ignorant of everything but my business, that I sotted in a public-house, they would not have made the least objection to me. I should have been a 'fellow' beneath them, and they would have patronized me. . . . The nearer a common tradesman approximates in information and manners to a footman, the more certainly will he please his well-bred customers ; the less he knows beyond his business, the more certain, in general, will be his success."'[1]

---

[1] Graham Wallas, *Life of Francis Place* (1925), pp. 37-8.

4.

The rise of the manufacturing districts at the end of the eighteenth century created a new problem. They were in the beginning often no better than mining camps, whose life was very rough, with the minimum of police interference. These factory towns grew prodigiously quickly, and they became a byword for lawlessness.

At the same time the lot of the factory workers was most unenviable. They were all bound apprentices, although it could hardly be said that they were apprenticed to a trade, and the conditions of their life can be shown by the provisions of an Act to ameliorate those conditions.

' Mill rooms to be ventilated . . . the rooms to be whitewashed twice a year . . . that an apprentice should not work more than twelve hours a day exclusive of mealtimes : that no work by apprentices should be done between nine at night and six in the morning : that male and female apprentices should sleep in separate rooms, and that not more than two apprentices should sleep in any case in the same bed : that the master should call in medical attendance for his resident apprentices in case of infectious disease.'[1]

This measure was opposed by the manufacturers as " injurious, harsh, oppressive, and impracticable," and they petitioned Parliament against it ! The poor apprentices were obviously not thought to have any feelings. Somewhat the same spirit underlay the remark of a well-to-do Johannesburg lady to a friend of mine, that her son, who was a medical student, was fortunate in doing his hospital practice in a *Native* infirmary. He was of a nervous disposition, she said, and was very apt to make mistakes !

The earlier domestic system of industry in which the unit of labour was the household, broke down under the new conditions. It was the custom for employers of labour to import labourers in hundreds for their factories. Robert Owen's mill at New Lanark was started with five hundred children imported in this way from Edinburgh.[2] The new

[1] *Health and Morals of Apprentices Act*, 1802. De Montmorency, *op. cit.*, p. 213.
[2] F. Podmore, *Robert Owen, a Biography* (1923), p. 72.

centres in Lancashire were created by shifting thousands of workers from other parts of the country. Their old associations were broken, and every one of them was employed on an individual contract in which his family had no share. The unit was no longer the household but the man. The same process is symbolized by the trains that can be seen coming into the Transvaal from Portuguese East Africa, and containing hundreds of indentured Natives who have left home for the first time.

5.

The objection to State interference in English education was based partly on the assumption that the family system was still effective, and partly on a belief in the baneful effect of education on an inferior class. It was well put in the debate on Mr. Whitbread's Bill in 1807, by Dr. Davies Giddy, afterwards President of the Royal Society :—

' However specious in theory the project might be, of giving education to the labouring classes of the poor, it would, in effect, be found to be prejudicial to their morals and happiness ; it would teach them to despise their lot in life, instead of making them good servants in agriculture, and other laborious employments to which their rank in society had destined them ; instead of teaching them subordination, it would render them factious and refractory, as was evident in the manufacturing counties ; it would enable them to read seditious pamphlets, vicious books, and publications against Christianity ; it would render them insolent to their superiors ; and, in a few years, the result would be, that the legislature would find it necessary to direct the strong arm of power towards them, and to furnish the executive magistrate with much more vigorous laws than were now in force.'[1]

The same point of view was expressed by writers in *Blackwood's Magazine*,

' in which it is said that mechanics' institutes would be used to form the labouring classes into a disaffected and ungovernable faction : that the only education fit for poor people was a religious one, which " renders them patient, humble, and moral." '[2]

[1] De Montmorency, *op. cit*, pp. 222-3.   [2] Holman, *op. cit.*, p. 53.

On the other hand, the more intelligent working classes themselves were somewhat suspicious of State-aided education—a suspicion confined neither to England nor to that period. The working men of Burnley in 1847 were against such education. They feared it would

'train the youthful minds to believe in that doctrine so useful to those who fatten on the industry of others—the doctrine of passive obedience and non-resistance.'[1]

This, however, was a fear of the State rather than a dislike of education. The working men themselves were passionately in favour of education. Whatever might have been the fears of reactionaries, they could not stem the tide. Brougham's Select Committee on the Education of the Lower Orders reported under the year 1816 :—

'There is the most unquestionable evidence that the anxiety of the poor for education continues not only unabated, but daily increasing; that it extends to every part of the country, and is to be found equally prevalent in those smaller towns and country districts, where no means of gratifying it are provided by the charitable efforts of the richer classes.'[2]

William Lovett, a cabinet-maker, and one of the founders of Chartism, produced a scheme of national education in 1837 more enlightened than any that the country had hitherto known. In an address to his fellow-working men he asks:

'Is it consistent with justice that the knowledge requisite to make a man acquainted with his rights and duties should be purposely withheld from him, and then that he should be upbraided and deprived of his rights *on the plea of his ignorance* ? And is it not equally cruel and unjust to suffer human beings to be matured in ignorance and crime *and then to blame and punish them* ?'[3]

He claims education " not as a charity, BUT AS A RIGHT, a right derivable from society itself."

6.

The difficulty in the way of a comprehensive system of education for the working classes was fundamentally a

---
[1] Holman, *op. cit.*, p. 79. [2] De Montmorency, *op. cit.*, p. 224.
[3] *Life and Struggles of William Lovett* (Bohn's edition, 1920), I., p. 141.

II. THE BRITISH WORKING MAN

theological one. Mankind was held to be divided by Providence into classes, and these divisions were as rigid as the order of nature. This was of course the belief of Wilberforce and Hannah More, and it was strengthened by events across the Channel. The French Revolution, at any rate in its later stages, was viewed not so much as a revolt against tyranny as a violent upheaval of the natural order of society. The upper classes had the duty of being kind and patronizing to the lower classes, but any attempt of the lower classes to better their own conditions would lead to the same kind of anarchy as had been witnessed in France.

As education became more and more a recognized need, and the upper classes became interested in it, it was, therefore, a matter of somewhat nice adjustment to give that type of education which was suitable to a person's status without giving him any desire to rise into a superior class!

Even the founder of English elementary education himself, Sir James Kay-Shuttleworth, was not exempt from this feeling. His Training College at Battersea was so organized to prevent any undue pride rising up in the breasts of its students. They did a great deal of housework both indoors and out-of-doors.

' This healthy labour was to safeguard them from the danger of forming " a false estimate of their position in relation to the class to which they belonged." ' [1]

This feeling runs through the *Report of the Commissioners appointed to inquire into the State of Popular Education in England*, laid before Parliament in 1861, and usually referred to as the " Newcastle Commission Report." It speaks of the working classes and even of the teachers as if they were almost a different species of being from the rest of society. For example, it rejects the complaint of the teachers that they cannot become inspectors, by laying down that

' it is absolutely necessary that the inspectors should be fitted by previous training and social position to communicate and associate upon terms of equality with the managers of schools and the clergy of different denominations.' [2]

[1] F. Smith, *The Life and Work of Sir James Kay-Shuttleworth* (1923), p. 107.
[2] Vol. I., p. 160.

The Commissioners complain that the teaching profession sometimes attracts persons of an ambitious temper of mind

' by the prospects which its earlier stages appear to afford of rising in the world socially as well as intellectually.'[1]

The opening of Government clerkships and other minor State appointments to people on educational grounds alone is also unfortunate, as

' their tendency is to teach the people to value education as a means of rising to a higher station in life. This is of course a reasonable object in many cases : but the main object of promoters of education must be to teach the people to value it as a source of morality, enjoyment, and comfort in the station in which the great mass of them are necessarily destined to remain.'[2]

The Dean of Bristol, in his evidence, was inclined to deprecate school education altogether.

' It is only to attempt the task of Mrs. Partington over again, to set ourselves to stem back the demands of the labour market.'[3]

Just about this time a Commission on Native Affairs was sitting in Natal. A previous Commission in 1846-47 had been condemned by the Colonists as containing only officials and missionaries. This second Commission, 1852-53, was composed chiefly of landowning colonists, practical men who " knew how to handle Kaffirs," and the educational clauses of their report are interesting :—

' All that they were concerned with, as landowners, was, to re-quote their own words, " an abundant and continuous supply of Kaffir labour for wages." With this object in view they recommended agricultural education of an elementary type for the Natives, and economic pressure, by means of hut or other taxation . . . which might constrain the Native to come out and work as an agricultural labourer on a European Farm. The Kaffirs should be taught to respect the white man . . . and realise their own immense inferiority.'[4]

Mr. Roebuck in a speech in Parliament in 1833 on the occasion of the first Government grant for education gave a conclusive answer to such narrow views as expressed in

[1] P. 163.   [2] P. 224.   [3] P. 190.
[4] E. H. Brookes, *op. cit.*, p. 55.

England. His admirable defence of a liberal education for working men's children was based on the text :—

'Education means not merely conferring the necessary means or instruments for the acquiring of knowledge, but it means also the so training or fashioning the intellectual and moral qualities of the individual, that he may be able and willing to acquire knowledge, and to turn it to its right use. It means so framing the mind of the individual that he may become a useful and virtuous member of society in the various relations of life.'[1]

The South African answer is contained in the Report of the Inter-Colonial Commission of 1903-5 :—

'No policy can be complete or sound which is limited to political or economic considerations only, and which takes no account of the irrepressible forces within each individual.'[2]

7.

The rigid division of English society into groups was as strongly marked within the ranks of the upper classes themselves as it was in society as a whole between upper and lower. Here the division was between men and women. It has already been mentioned in the text that the attitude of men to women was one of repressionism, as bitter and unyielding as that between lord and labourer, or between white and black. The case of women is almost a closer parallel to the " Native question " than that of social rank, because while money might wipe out the difference between a formerly poor man and a rich man, the physical difference between men and women was as permanent as that between white and black. And on this physical difference was based an intellectual and legal differentiation which was purely artificial.

' So late as 1868 we find an enlightened and philanthropic man of business, Mr. W. R. Greg, laying down the axiom that " the essentials of a woman's being are fulfilled by domestic servants, namely, *they are supported by, and they minister to, men*." This

---

[1] De Montmorency, *op. cit.*, p. 327.
[2] Brookes, *op. cit.*, p. 456.

was the text of a whole tribe of books. . . . These admonishers of women unite in preaching inferiority, self-repression, patience and resignation. . . . Even "a highly gifted woman" must not "exhibit the least disposition to presume upon such gifts, for fear of raising her husband's jealousy of her importance." She will gain his confidence by " a respectful deportment, and a complying disposition." . . . The "will of God," the "laws of Nature," were constantly and complacently quoted as the foundation on which the submission of women . . . was based.'[1]

A school curriculum was a "chaos of laborious trifling," and "miscellaneous learning by heart, with fancy work and' playing the piano, formed the staple of a girl's education."[4] The deliberate aim was to keep women ignorant of everything that was worth knowing, in order that their ignorance and folly might be a foil to the self-importance of men who, but for this repression, might have had no claim on their regard at all. The pioneers of women's education had an uphill fight not only against opposition, but against the brutal spirit of their opponents. Brave women such as Sophia Jex-Blake and Elizabeth Garrett Anderson were considered to have unsexed themselves and to have forfeited any rights to " gentlemanly " treatment.

8.

The British working man and the British woman, like the mediæval peasant, have broken their thraldom. In the case of the inferior classes of the nineteenth century it has been done partly by economic causes, and partly by undermining the theological and social basis of the inferiority. Thus William Lovett and Elizabeth Garrett Anderson, Joseph Sturge and Frederick Denison Maurice, the crusading spirit of Huxley, the fear of skilled German competition in the eighties, and the need for women's services in the Great War, have all played their part in this emancipation.

It is likely to be the same in the progress of African education. Tenga Jabavu and Dr. Aggrey will need to be

[1] B. Stephen, *Emily Davis and Girton College* (1927), pp. 7-10.
[2] *Ibid.*, p. 12.

followed by other Native pioneers. The work of Europeans like Edwin Smith, Father Callaway, and Dr. Loram will all be required. Economic causes are, as we have seen, already at work in both rural and urban areas. The progress of theological thought and the development of opportunities for social contact and joint service will assuredly sap the theoretical basis of conservatism.

The last great refuge of conservatism is the belief that the situation as between black and white is something quite unique, so that in the absence of precedents the " practical " man on the spot must be trusted to know what is best. On such a complacent heresy a dispassionate study of history ought to have a solvent effect, and it is with this hope that I have suggested these historical comparisons.

APPENDIX II.

THE PROBLEM OF "INDIRECT RULE."

I. A COMMENT ON CHAPTER XII, by the Right Hon. Lord Lugard, G.C.M.G., formerly Governor-General of Nigeria, Author of *The Dual Mandate in British Tropical Africa*.

II. EDUCATION UNDER INDIRECT RULE, by A. Victor Murray, reprinted, with abridgements, from the *Journal of the Royal African Society*, July 1935.

I. COMMENT BY LORD LUGARD ON CHAPTER XII.

"I feel bound to predicate that in my view Professor Murray has in some particulars mistaken the underlying principles of "Indirect Rule" in spite of the cordial appreciation which he accords to the system. Its keynote, as has often been said, is *Adaptation* of African institutions understood by the people to the changed conditions brought about by contact with Europe. It does not therefore look upon them "as a matter of static organisation" (p. 278). It is in fact the antithesis of static inertia. Or again, it is true that in their origin the Fulani were an alien race, but in a century of rule they had for the most part lost their language and by continual inter-mixture with the indigenous races most of the ruling Emirs had become completely identified with them and commanded their loyalty. The limitations on the powers of the Fulani rulers, and the repeated injunctions to D.O.'s to tour the villages and hear grievances, negative the assertion that "indirect rule of the British has established the direct rule of the Fula Emirs."

He has, I think, been misinformed also in regard to the question of education in Nigeria. The Missions have always been at liberty to establish schools with the consent of the Emir. That there was a very real suspicion at first in Sokoto and Kano lest it was the intention of the Government to undermine their religion by establishing schools cannot be denied. The official Memo. of instructions to Administrative Officers [1] emphasized the establishment of rural schools, which has always in my personal view been the most important sphere of education. It is indeed entirely inaccurate to assert that the only form of education tolerated under Indirect Rule was "that which is supposed to fit the sons of the ruling class to be rulers, and the sons of the people to be ruled" (p. 279). The first tentative school

[1] Political Memos. No. IV.

established in face of much opposition at Kano by Mr. Vischer, now Joint Secretary of the C.O. Advisory Committee on Education, was for children and adults of all classes taught by craftsmen from the city. The slow extension of education was due to the hostility of the Moslems to teachers from the South and the necessity of waiting till Moslem pupils were qualified to teach.

The Government was deeply aware of the religious attributes of Chieftainship, and Pagans have always selected their own Chiefs (p. 283).

Professor Murray considers the Transkei system " an admirable expression of the peoples' will and has their confidence " (p. 289). Though no doubt the best in South Africa, his view is not shared by Dr. Mair, or by Dr. Huggins, Premier of Southern Rhodesia, or Mr. Rogers of the Native Affairs Department, South Africa, or Professor Ifor Evans, at least prior to the Act of 1932.[1]

Where I have failed (in my book *The Dual Mandate*) to make clear the fundamental principles of the system, others, notably Sir D. Cameron,[2] and Miss Perham [3] have surely established them beyond misunderstanding.

While bound to make this caveat, I heartily welcome the new edition of *The School in the Bush*, and its powerful advocacy of principles which in the main I have also endeavoured to promote."

II. EDUCATION UNDER INDIRECT RULE.

1.

" Indirect rule " has reference in Africa to a situation which includes black and white with the white on top, but where the institutions of the black are not abolished but " progressively adapted " to modern conditions.

Even that mild statement may be disputed by some who will not like the idea that " white is on top." Yet that is not only the fact but it is the all-important fact. However

---

[1] Mair, *Native Policies in Africa*, pp. 46-8; Huggins, Southern Rhodesia, *Assembly Debates*, October 1937; I. L. Evans, *Native Policy in Southern Africa*, pp. 52-9; H. Rogers, *Native Administration in the Union of South Africa*, p. 55.
[2] Memo. on Principles of Native Administration.
[3] *Native Administration in Nigeria*, and articles in *Africa*, etc.

II. EDUCATION UNDER INDIRECT RULE   403

much we Britishers may divest ourselves of authority and allow the Native to develop along his own lines it is we nevertheless who are *allowing* him. In the last resort the suzerain's word is law, and the Native knows it. A good deal of the sentimental nonsense that is talked about indirect rule would be avoided if we frankly admitted the fact that we are the rulers.

Now, by all the laws of logic and psychology, "indirect rule" is obviously the only way to govern a backward people if we are concerned for their development and not just for their exploitation. You must argue from the known to the unknown : you must build on foundations that are already there. This is the only possible method of teaching, whether of arithmetic to children or of political ideas to nations (although the French seem to do it differently). Everything, however, depends on the people who work it, particularly the people who work it *locally*. Seen from the verandah of Government House it may and often does look quite different from its appearance to the Christian Native teacher in the small village or to the simple old pagan farmer who has to bribe one does not know how many people before his case can be heard in the local court of the Native Administration.

The preservation of Native institutions by people not themselves Natives is a kindly and desirable thing to do, and it has been well done in Nigeria. But it is necessary, as Lord Lugard has pointed out, that this preservation should not be a static thing but should permit of the transformation (and, may be, even the extinction from within) of those institutions as people become adapted to modern conditions. Progress has this irritating characteristic, that you are never done with it. The "adaptation" of to-day, if it is any good, will have antiquated itself in ten years' time, and the willingness to accept this process, over which they have only a very limited control, argues a considerable measure of faith on the part of the ruling classes. It requires, moreover, a well-thought-out educational policy which has regard to all the facts of the situation.

There are three main influences which have greatly affected the situation in Nigeria and similar countries of recent years. First of all, these countries are no longer isolated as they used to be. They are part of the world order and it is quite impossible for any European nation to put a ring-fence round any region of Africa and feel that its policy within that enclosure is its own concern. The South African Government has to its annoyance discovered that to be the case even with regard to its own Natives. It is not less the case in "backward" areas. Economic conditions—to speak of them alone—do not permit it.

Secondly, we are now seeing the fruit in these countries of a seed that was planted long ago by the missionaries. We are concerned not only with chiefs and elders on the one hand and people on the other. A third class has now arisen, and that is the class of people who have had a relatively advanced education on European lines.[1] These educated people are almost all Christian, and even though the best of them will have a real sympathy with their pagan fellows they are thankful for their own spiritual deliverance from paganism. The dislike of many "indirect rule" administrators for this class of men often passes all bounds, but they cannot be ignored. They have to be fitted in somehow.

Thirdly, a country in transition from a primitive to a more civilized state needs a great deal of personal care and attention. Yet, just at this very moment, owing to mechanical invention and improved transport, the contact of the white administrator with the black man is becoming more and more formal and perfunctory. Shorter tours make for disintegration of a man's interest. The use of motor cars has still more seriously affected the situation. Twenty years ago an officer would give a whole day to a village and stay there the night, talking with the people in their own language and getting at "the back of the black man's mind" in a way that was possible only in leisured intercourse. Nowadays a man can set out from his house and visit three or four villages in the course of the day and be back home again for dinner in the evening. Inevitably there is a greater lack of understanding between the two parties, and a more scientific knowledge of anthropology

[1] I do not like to use the word "intelligentsia" because that is a term borrowed from Continental politics which does not fit the situation in Africa.

II. EDUCATION UNDER INDIRECT RULE 405

does not make up for a less intimate contact with the people. These are days of substitutes, and we need to be constantly reminded that there are certain things which only a *person* can do and they cannot be done for him by a " method," or a subject of study, or a machine.

These factors—and there are others—seem to me to have altered the *incidence* of " indirect rule " in these days, and we need to consider how to educate the people in the present circumstances, taking all these factors into account.

2.

It is clear at once that we must take for granted a wide extension of simple education on the lines of the village school. The " three R's," hygiene, agriculture, and—shall we say ?—Scripture (seeing that elementary education is in the hands of the missions) will for many years be enough and more than enough for the great part of the population. When we realize that in the Ohafia district of Calabar, where the Scottish mission is doing excellent concentrated educational work, not as many as five per cent. of the children who could go to school are to be found in school, and even in Natal not more than twenty per cent. of the Native children attend school, we can see that there is still scope for another century of educational endeavour on these lines.

Yet even at this elementary stage progress is often prevented by a doctrinaire attitude on the part of the educational officer. We all speak nowadays of the " biological approach,"—a very sound thing, if only we know what it means,—and a great deal is said about basing Native education on agriculture. All this is highly desirable, no doubt, but it does just occasionally blind the enthusiast to the real factors in the situation. A native African is not a lump of clay or stone to be " moulded " or " fashioned " according to this or that theory of the educationist. He has his own views about these things and they are often worked out with a far shrewder idea of how many beans make five than is shown by the British official. These " imported " elements in education—reading, writing, and so on—are not only what the Native wants but they are absolutely necessary to the situation in which he lives. He has personal links with the towns and with the mines and he wants to write to his people who have gone there and they want to write back to him. He is under a European employer and he wants to be able to count his money and make calculations. And he wants the language of the European. Once, at a very remote place in Western Nigeria, with only four European inhabitants, two of them being missionaries, I came across the well-shaven greens and well-tended bunkers of a golf course, and all over the place were notice-boards informing the countryside in English, " This golf course is Private." It seemed to me that even here there was a direct incentive to the unlettered African to learn a foreign language as quickly as possible, for ignorance of the law is no more an excuse in Africa than in England.

The need for elementary education, however, is the same under " indirect rule " as under any other kind of rule. The problem we are here considering is not primarily that of the school in the bush, although we can see how a slavish adherence to the theory of " preserving Native institutions " may militate against a type of simple education which is necessary though not tribal. Our problem here is really with *political* education, for if "indirect rule " is to be a reality it cannot but involve politics.

Sir Donald Cameron admitted this in his well-known *Memorandum on the principles of Native administration* :—

'. . . the guardianship is not a permanent one and is to be exercised only until the people can " stand by themselves." That being so, it is clearly the duty of the mandatory to train the people so that they may stand by themselves at least as part of the whole community in the Territory . . . and to make its dispositions in such a manner that, when the time comes, a full place in the political structure shall be found for the Native population.'

Sir Donald's practice has been, very properly, to apply this principle not only in particular to a mandated territory like Tanganyika but also as a general aim of Native administration everywhere, wherever " indirect rule " is in vogue.

Now in " political " education a great deal more depends on the attitude of the educator than on the subjects of the

II. EDUCATION UNDER INDIRECT RULE 407

curriculum. I have spoken already of the tendency in these days to use substitutes, and in this matter of political education substitutes are all too common. History, " civics," " principles of administration," could all be made part of a high school course and yet all might be nugatory because the teacher believes in the subjects but does not believe in the pupils. There is nothing more pathetic than to see a matriculation class of Native boys in a South African school studying " civics," and becoming acquainted with all the apparatus by which the white population exercise their votes. Our belief in the Native and his future is a far more important fact in his education than what we teach him. To this extent " indirect rule " is not really a system of government at all, it is a type of motive. Men who do not believe in the African will continue to be direct rulers even under a system which professes to be " indirect." There is no way of making a machine work itself, not even a good machine. It has to be worked by somebody. The real " indirect ruler " is not an administrator of a system called " indirect rule " : he is a believer in the development of the African. This consideration should make us wary of the belief that all that is needed to carry out our ideals is a " scheme " of organisation. A scheme can be made of none effect by people who disbelieve in it, as well as by people who work it unintelligently. The weakness of even so admirable a *Memorandum* as that of Sir Donald Cameron from which I have just quoted, is that in places it is too legalistic, and in trying to achieve an ideal it occasionally gives a loop-hole to the person who does not share the ideal. For example, on page 15 he says :

' It is, of course, the duty of an Administrative Officer to advise a Native Authority to make any order which may be lawful under the Native Authority Ordinance, if he considers that it is in the interests of the people that the order should be made ; and if his advice is neglected he may then, under the Ordinance, order the Native Authority to make the required order.'

This bears out my contention that the important fact to remember in " indirect " as in any other kind of rule is that the white man is on top, and the Native only does what he is allowed or ordered to do.

3.

One of the urgent questions of the moment in the Union of South Africa is whether Native Education shall come under the Native Affairs Department or under a Department of Education *sans phrase*.[1] The urgency of the question is due to the existence of a well-educated class of Native people. It is clear that the first method is not particularly concerned with the Native as a potential citizen but rather with him as forever a member of a distinct class, while the second looks forward to a white and black citizenship of the Union.

It is sometimes held that the " purely black " areas of the tropics constitute an entirely different problem from those regions like South Africa and Southern Rhodesia where the whites also are in permanent settlement. To a large extent no doubt the problem is different, but in so far as white men are on top in both cases there are elements in the problems which are similar. If the Native is to be considered as always an inferior being, always to be governed by an alien race, his status and his education for that status will be different from what they would be if he is looked on as capable of an independent political future in the modern world. Yet it is strange that some advocates of " indirect rule," who should presumably be most keen on the education of the Native as a potential citizen, often favour an educational policy which would fit in better with a desire to leave the backward people in their own backwardness. It favours educating the chiefs and leaving the rest of the people to the simple arts and crafts of the tribe.

The number of men and women, however, who have had rather more than the mere elements of education, is getting larger every year. No amount of " biological approach " on the part of the European authorities can prevent the increase of the number of men who will insist on having a different type of education. If their own country cannot provide it they will go elsewhere. Mistaken as these Africans may be about the nature of education, and irritating as their existence undoubtedly is to the type

[1] See above, pp. 37, 123.

II. EDUCATION UNDER INDIRECT RULE 409

of official who dislikes to be criticized, they have to be reckoned with. In the wise words of the Commissioners of Inquiry into the Aba riots in Nigeria in 1929 :

' In the swiftly changing conditions to-day this sympathy and understanding must be extended both to the older and more conservative generation who retain their ancient faith and customs, and to the younger elements of the community who have become converted to Christianity and seek an outlet for their ambitions through education. And herein lies one of the most difficult problems facing the administration to-day, that of helping and guiding this increasing class, upon whom so much of the future of the country depends, to find and take its right place in the community.' [1]

At present the main careers open to educated Africans are those of teachers, inspectors of schools, native court clerks, the lower reaches of the Civil Service, traders, lawyers, journalists, and, for the very few, the medical profession and the ministry. Opportunities vary from territory to territory, and on the West Coast careers are open to Native talent in a way which causes complete bewilderment to the white South African who hears about it.

Yet for the most part these careers are those of servants—subordinates who act on some one else's initiative. I may be wrong, but I think that the present booming of " indirect rule " and the doctrine of " educating the Native on his own lines " have had a depressing effect on the opportunities before the educated Native African in Nigeria. It is doubtful whether it would nowadays be possible for an African to rise as high in the administration as Dr. Henry Carr a few years ago. The " indirect ruler " is apt to find a much keener interest in the picturesque Native chief than in the man whose education may have been quite as good as that of the European himself. Part of the trouble in Bechuanaland in September, 1933, had its roots in the antipathy of certain European officials to the educated Native, particularly when such a man added to his education the status of a chief.

Is there, then, any possibility of the African taking posts in which initiation of policy is expected and required?

[1] Report, p. 108, § 358.

There have been an African judge and a Solicitor-General on the Gold Coast, and there has been an African Director of Education in Lagos. But is the African ever to become a political officer ? They are, of course, common in the French possessions and in the Congo. These men, however, are cut off from their own people and are simply black Europeans. As Mary Kingsley used to point out, a black man administering a European system is a different thing from a black man administering an African system. " Indirect rule " can undoubtedly be more educative for the community at large, for it keeps the people together, but is it *in fact* being more educative ? It is a commonplace that " ultimately " the Africans will be able to " stand by themselves " and govern their own affairs. But what kind of African administration do we expect to find when that one far-off divine event has arrived ? And are there no steps that can be taken now to prepare the African for it, and even to hasten its arrival ?

The problem created by this intermediate class of educated men everywhere is that its existence makes a new type of stratification in the community. The mere adjustment of chiefs to people and people to chiefs is not enough nowadays. The common complaint that the old authority of chiefs has become impaired, which is the burden of so much argument on the side of " indirect rule," forgets the fact that this is the inevitable result of changing conditions.

' Subordination is sadly broken down in this age. No man, now, has the same authority which his father had—except a gaoler.' [1]

We remedy this state of things not by strengthening one factor at the expense of others but in helping to make a new adjustment wherein all factors will be duly considered. The educated Africans demand British democratic institutions and a career open to talent, and they are baulked because the whites have the top positions on the European side, and their own chiefs are confirmed in the top positions on the African side. Hence there is a good deal of yellow journalism and a passion for litigation. Yet what else can

[1] Johnson to Boswell, April, 1778.

II. EDUCATION UNDER INDIRECT RULE 411

they do? To recommend a "back to the land" policy is to give up the problem altogether. To say that they are not yet able to take positions of responsibility is to say what is no doubt true but it involves the formulation of a policy that will make them fit for such positions. A place like Achimota should be expected to provide an education not only for "civil servants" of the lower ranks but for men who will become administrative officers, comparable in these days to the remarkable group of men turned out in the 'seventies and 'eighties of last century by Fourah Bay College. There will no doubt be failures, but there are failures among the British administrators now, and certainly the system will not be perfectly adjusted again until there is an educated people as well as an educated leadership. But because we cannot take the second step there is no need why we should not take the first. And the first step is an education in "politics" in the widest sense of the term for those Africans who can profit by it, and the opening up of careers to them. Nothing educates a man for a job so well as being in the job itself.

4.

In societies under indirect rule the familiar problem of the education of chiefs and the sons of chiefs raises the preliminary question of the future of African chieftainship.

Under the old pre-European system the chief derived his authority from the tribe. He was not their officer so much as their representative person, and like all representative persons he had to endure the limitations of that position. The African chief was not at all like a Moslem emir, a ruler over "his" people; the relationship between "ruler" and "ruled" was much more intimate than that. He was a semi-sacred person, because he represented not only the tribesmen that were alive but also those that were buried in the tribal land. Nor were the limitations from which he suffered simply checks on his power imposed by his people, as the Parliament of William III limited the power of the King. They were inherent in the very position itself. He could not,do certain things because those things were "not done." The phrase "constitutional monarchy" as applied to primitive kingship savours much too much of a study of Bagehot or Anson to fit the real facts of the case. Nor was kingship strictly hereditary, according to our ideas of a "hereditary" kingship. The custom varied of course from tribe to tribe, but common to nearly all of them was the recognition of descent· within the royal house, though not necessarily from father to son. The "representative" character of the chieftainship had to be maintained and a strictly hereditary succession might not have maintained it.

Chieftainship in these days has been severely shaken by three main influences.

First of all, with the coming of the European the chief derives his status in the mixed society from the European suzerain and from nowhere else. The man whom the British Government has recognized as a chief has an entirely different position with his tribesmen from what he had before. It may look the same but it is not the same. When a man has already got the subtle kind of prestige that is involved in African kingship any addition to it by a European authority, such as an official title or official recognition, is in fact not an addition but a subtraction. This is one reason why it is often so difficult to discover the real chief of a tribe. Men are presented as chiefs and the Government may recognize them as such, only to discover long afterwards that the man who had the real prestige is some unknown person in the bush of whom no official had ever heard. This, I believe, was a frequent experience in Tanganyika. Prestige is a very curious thing. It cannot be claimed and it cannot be conferred; although the holder of it may quite well lose it. It is a very subtle relationship between a group and a person, and while it looks as if it was characterized by the person dominating the group it is in fact a case where the group recognizes it as existing in a person.[1] To "claim" it is to lose the chance of ever

---

[1] It is interesting to notice in this regard the *quality* of the hold that King George V had over the people of England. The Jubilee showed a very subtle, non-official, personal, representative quality about "loyalty" which was much more like the relationship of the African chief and the tribe than that of a monarch and his "subjects."

II. EDUCATION UNDER INDIRECT RULE

obtaining it. If the people do not give it the person cannot take it. Hence all well-meant attempts to " show " prestige or "maintain " prestige (like the firing off of howitzers over the heads of the bewildered Bamangwato people when Admiral Evans held his " inquiry " into the Tshekedi affair in 1933) appear even to a primitive people as rather silly and pointless. For good or ill, therefore, the mingling of European administration with Native life has inevitably affected chieftainship.

Secondly, the mystical relationship between a chief and his people has not been able to survive the shock of contact with Europeans. Men go away from their tribal land and from the authority of their chief and they see more of life than he knew was there. They come back—from the mines, from the towns, from school, where they have been accustomed to be treated as individual persons, and have learned to earn and use money—(" Gold and silver destroy feudal subordination," said Johnson to Boswell)—and they are no longer the same people. Of course, these experiences do not effect everybody in the same way. Many, no doubt, come back and fall easily into the old life, but the set of the new influences is in the direction of undermining the old authority. And the effect of these influences is cumulative. It is not only that the black man goes away : the white man also comes in, and he is the stranger in the midst to whom the chief's position is a very little thing.

Thirdly, there is, as I have already indicated, the presence of the educated Native, often more educated than the chief and familiar with a different thought world. Where the chief is the educated person this disturbing factor is not so evident, although the relationship between chief and people where they are at different stages of sophistication is bound to be different from the old relationship in which they moved within the same " continuum " of thought.

Now what is going to happen if the sons of chiefs are taken away by the Europeans and given a separate education ? It at once assumes a ruling class. It assumes that the kind of chieftainship of the Fulani emirs or sultans is the normal kind, and moreover that it is to be permanent.

It has at its root the same set of ideas that has dominated the English public school, namely, that its job is to train the governors while the elementary schools train the governed.

The system, however, breaks down because it creates a dissociation within " authority." Authority has two factors —both equally important. If A is trained to rule, B must be trained to obey. Where " authority " is integral, as it is in the primitive tribe in which everything depends on prestige, there is not this sharp distinction between A and B, but where there is a " ruler " and a " ruled " this distinction must be a basis of difference in education. The chief in old times did not need to be " trained to govern." He got obedience because he was what he was. The tribesmen in obeying him were obeying themselves through their own representative. But where the chief has to be trained to govern his own people this old system has broken down and a new system cannot be evolved by educating only one of the two elements in it.

Now where the people are not disposed to obey, what is to happen ? We have seen how the sahib system is going to pieces in India, because the old kind of prestige of the English having disappeared the Indians of the new generation are not disposed to take orders from an Englishman simply because he is an Englishman, while the education of many Englishmen who are in India has made it difficult for them to adapt themselves to the position of equals and not of superiors. In the same way the British working-man, having now got representatives of his class in the Cabinet and in the House of Lords, will no longer accept Oxford and Cambridge and the public schools as having an indefeasible right to train " leaders." Leaders can only lead if people are disposed to follow.

What then is the aim of the education of chiefs ? Education in agriculture such as is given at Domboshawa [1] raises no problem. But so often it is stated that the aim is to " strengthen the authority of the chief." This appears again and again as a *desideratum* in almost every discussion there is nowadays on African problems. But

[1] See above, pp. 111 f.

II. EDUCATION UNDER INDIRECT RULE 415

we might very pertinently ask against whom is the chief's authority to be strengthened ? And the answer can only be, " against his own people." I use the word " against " deliberately, because that is what it is. It cannot be authority " with " his own people, because that is something that cannot be conferred or strengthened by the intervention of a third party. It depends on the people more than on the chief. It can, therefore, only be authority " against." I have seen this happen occasionally in Southern Nigeria. Young educated men have been told by the District Officer that they must obey their chiefs, willy-nilly, sometimes when the chief has been a heathen and they as Christians have refused to perform pagan rites. But this kind of compulsion ruins authority altogether. For A to force B to obey C completely takes away the authority of C over B.

There might be a case for "strengthening the chief's authority" against the white man, for here there never was any " authority " in the proper sense of the term. Tshekedi in 1933 sent out appeal after appeal to the British Authorities to strengthen his hand against the degenerate whites who were debauching his women, but the magistrates took no action whatever until later, and that was against Tshekedi himself. Yet this was a case, if ever there was a case, for the chief's authority to be upheld. It certainly is a curious situation that we should seek to make a chief a despot over his own people and take away his power over strangers. Often the only white man against whom the chief is allowed to exercise his authority is the missionary. Some day, perhaps, there may be a kind of mixed hierarchy, with the chief below the Resident but above the District Officer and having authority not only over black but also to some extent over white as well.

The question of the Moslem Emirates is somewhat different from the ordinary African chieftainships. The relationship between the emir and his people is much more that of a master and his servants than is the relationship between a Bantu chief and the tribe. It is obvious, however, that this relationship of master and servant cannot have much stability in the modern world. People are not for ever going to be content with permanent subordination to a chief. Complications, of course, are present in Northern Nigeria, where the emirs are of one race and the people of another, although I admit that the cleavage is not so pronounced as I felt it to be when I was in Northern Nigeria in 1927. The attitude of the British Government, however, at that date certainly did add a complication, for it assumed not only a possibility but also a desirability of keeping the emirs out of touch with the modern world. Added to that was the distinct preference for Islam which made administrators of Sir Richmond Palmer's school of thought critical of those modern influences represented by Christian missions.

Sir Donald Cameron considerably modified that policy and gave the daily picture-papers in this country the joy of recording the doings of Nigerian emirs and sultans visiting England. These visits are bound to affect the outlook of these picturesque personages, but in what direction? The difficulty, of course, about visits of this kind is that the people are nearly always shown only one type of thing—battleships, army manœuvres, and other alleged symbols of the greatness of Britain, instead of the new L.C.C. schools, children's courts, youth hostels, and hospitals. The result of bringing these Nigerian chiefs out of their isolation ought to be to increase their sympathy with and their desire for a more English type of education for themselves and for their people.

The Emir of Katsina seems to have appreciated this point when in London, for he expressed a wish to send his grandsons to be educated in England. One hopes that if they come they may attend a really good elementary school and a central school afterwards! It would be interesting to see how a typical " indirect ruler," educated in this way, would affect the working of the principle of " indirect rule."

Educating the chiefs or the sons of chiefs alone, however, is only one side of the task. If we were living in the eighteenth century, or still more in the sixteenth, it would be possible to draw up a treatise on government like Bolingbroke's *Patriot King* or Machiavelli's *Prince* which might be

II. EDUCATION UNDER INDIRECT RULE

helpful to the young rulers of an African community. In these cases the people themselves did not come into the picture except as material for the ruler to work upon. But, as I have tried to show, not only is the fundamental relationship of an African chief to his tribe an organic thing but even in cases where it is not, such as in Northern Nigeria, modern conditions are all against an extension of despotism however benevolent. In whatever manner the chiefs are to be educated it must be part of the education of the community as a whole. In other words, the modern African society cannot achieve stability by educating chiefs alone.

It is important to reiterate that the authority of an African chief is nowadays a *devolved* authority. That is what " indirect rule " to-day in effect means. Part of the work of the suzerain power is devolved upon a lower authority. All sovereignty, however, rests in the suzerain. A good deal of the argument for the special education of sons of chiefs is based upon a tacit recognition of this fact. The chief is recognized as a British official and is to be trained for his job just like any other British official. But in so doing he becomes a very different kind of person from the chief in an independent tribal condition.

It is indeed very doubtful whether to-day there can be any such thing as " indirect rule " at all. The most apposite definition of " indirect rule " seems to me to have been made by two Native chiefs and it is not at all in correspondence with what we nowadays call " indirect rule." At Sir Charles Warren's meeting with Khama on May 13th, 1885, Khama declared :

' I accept the friendship and protection of the Government of England. . . . Further, I give to the Queen to make laws and to change them in the country of the Bamangwato, with reference to both black and white. Nevertheless I am not baffled in the government of my own town, or in deciding cases among my own people according to custom ; but again I do not refuse help in these offices. Although this is so, I have to say that there are certain laws of my country which the Queen of England finds in operation and which are advantageous for my people and I wish that these laws should be established.' [1]

[1] Cd. 4588 of 1885. No. 34.

On the day before he had declared :

'What we want is to go forward and improve, and I think we can do so if we are wisely connected with the English, for after what we have seen of your ways we shall take up some of them.'[1]

These are the words of an independent chief who feels free to take the initiative in a discussion and to make suggestions and not simply to wait for the other party to declare his will and accept it. Moshesh, the chief of the Basutos, took the same line. He said to Sir Philip Wodehouse in 1862 :

'If the Government send magistrates the Basuto will not understand. It will be like a stone that is too heavy for them to carry. . . . If I obtain an agent I will be under the Queen as her subject, and my people will be her subjects also, but under me. . . . I wish to govern my own people by Native law, by our own laws, but if the Queen wish after this to introduce other laws into my country I should be willing, but I should wish such laws to be submitted to the Council of the Basutos and when they are accepted by my Council I will send to the Queen and inform her that they have become law.'[2]

These two Native chiefs stated excellently the principles of " indirect rule." It is true that England was the stronger power but neither of them accepted or assumed the position of a conquered chief, and they were devolving their authority upon Britain rather than having the British take away their power and restore some of it—which is what has happened in other territories. Miss Perham has insisted[3] that a Protectorate is a very different thing from " indirect rule," and yet the conditions which gave rise to the Protectorates of Bechuanaland and Basutoland contained more possibilities of adequate " indirect rule " than did the conditions in those territories where " indirect rule " has become the vogue. And the primary factor was this—that the conditions of change were in the hands of the Native people and not merely of the suzerain. If the people wished for English education and Christianity and wished to give up their ritual dances and beer drinks they could do so, and there would be no local Resident or Assistant District Officer in the name of a mistaken belief in anthropology to say them nay. Unfortunately, through lack of firm and wise leadership on the part of the

---

[1] Cd. 4588 of 1885. No. 34.   [2] Lagden : *The Basutos*, pp. 314-5.
[3] In *Africa*, July, 1934.

II. EDUCATION UNDER INDIRECT RULE

British (firm in Basutoland and wise in Bechuanaland), the Protectorates made no advance at all and Miss Perham's opinion is quite justified. Here is a case where in the absence of chiefs like Khama and Moshesh a system such as that in Nigeria might have arrested the decline.[1]

Under " indirect rule " is it possible for the people to change their rulers, or have we so stereotyped the situation that no change of any kind is possible save on our own initiative ? Is any effective criticism of the ruler possible on the part of the people ? We reserve to ourselves the right to criticize their system and to introduce considerable changes in it in the interests of what is called " natural justice," but what possibilities are there for the African to make changes in *our* system ? According to Sir Donald Cameron, the Report of the Aba riots, Lord Lugard, Sir Theophilus Shepstone and all other administrators and writers on these subjects, Native institutions are only to be preserved in so far as they are " not repugnant to natural justice." The phraseology is that of the eighteenth century and implies a *consensus communis* regarding the " rights of man," but while this is, no doubt, admirable and proper, it is, nevertheless, partisan. It means, in effect, so long as they are not repugnant to the *European's* views of what is " natural justice." That is no doubt quite justifiable, but in some places it makes of tribal government a totally different thing. Everything in the tribe hangs together, and it is not for the outsider to pick and choose and then to imagine that what he has left has been left as it was. Human sacrifices at Aro Chuku were an abomination unto us and were properly abolished, but the religious and social system of the Aros is quite a different thing without them. If then we ourselves assume the initiative in these matters it seems a little hard not to allow the African to assume the initiative regarding what he will take and what he will reject of what we bring to him from our side. This was

[1] The danger of the Protectorates from the Union seems to have stirred the Dominions Office into life, and Sir Alan Pim's reports on the Protectorates (Swaziland, 1932; Bechuanaland, 1933; Basutoland, 1935) have begun to be implemented. Swaziland is a special case, where " indirect rule " has been moderately successful, but complicated by extraordinary conditions of land tenure.

obviously the intention of Khama and of Moshesh, and ought to be inherent in any adequate system of "indirect rule."

5.

The position accorded to women is a good test of the nature of any society. However much we may differ in our estimate of Victorian society in England, there is no doubt that tried by this test we have immensely improved on our forefathers. There is no need to labour the point.

The position of women in African society has often been misunderstood. It has often been assumed that a woman was merely a chattel with no rights and no authority of her own, and that *lobola* was, in the well-known words of that flamboyant hero, Sir Harry Smith, " the sin of buying wives." The matter is not quite so simple as that, and the effective status of some women in certain tribes and of all women at certain times in all tribes has been considerable. *Lobola*, moreover, while it may depress the position of women as against men, has undoubtedly enhanced their position as against other women. Nevertheless, it is generally true that what we should consider a menial status has been the lot of women in the African tribe.

Now the position of women has been undergoing radical changes in the last fifty years. New agricultural methods have displaced a good deal of field labour for women and have had a marked effect on polygamy. So also has the habit of the Government of putting increased taxes on the possession of extra wives. But there has also been growing up a greater self-respect among women themselves, and among the educated ones the age of marriage has risen considerably. In Lagos it is almost as late as that of European women, and the widening gap between the time when the girls leave school and the time when they marry constitutes a very serious social problem. The question of careers for these town dwellers is a very urgent one, and in Lagos we are beginning to see African women as shop assistants in the big " factories," as well as women teachers, nurses, and

II. EDUCATION UNDER INDIRECT RULE

typists. Lagos is, as we know, a unique place, but it simply illustrates to-day what will be more and more the situation in all African towns a generation hence.

Now the changing position of women in African society is not confined to those territories that are governed under the system of "indirect rule," but is general throughout Africa. As, however, I am concerned here only with education under "indirect rule" it will be well to ask if there are any problems peculiar to such territories.

I have suggested that the real problem of education under "indirect rule" is that of the political education of the people and the place that the people so educated can find in the administration and government of the country. This "political education," in order to be thorough, will have to be carried a good deal further than the school education of men. It will have to include that of women and, still more important, it will have to include the education of men into sympathy with women's education. In the winter of 1931-2 I travelled throughout Nigeria as educational adviser to the Christian Council. I had a score of conferences with African teachers in different parts of the country at which no other European was present, and some of the discussions went on —as they would, of course, in Africa—for many hours. One of the things which impressed me most was the fairly general prejudice of these educated men against educated women. Of course it was not unanimous by any means, but the considerable balance of opinion was against the educated women. All teachers were willing to allow that the girls might be educated up to, say, Standard II (in Nigeria about equivalent to Standard II in an English elementary school), but the majority felt that anything much beyond that was undesirable. They felt that education prevented girls being good housewives and made them "intractable."

The *Saturday Review* used to take precisely the same point of view seventy or eighty years ago with regard to girls' education in England. The aggressive male is not a peculiarly African phenomenon !

Nevertheless, this problem will have to be faced if the peoples of these African territories are to be trained to "stand by themselves" in the modern world. Illiterate wives may flatter the self-importance of those educated African men who like this sort of thing, but they will be a handicap in the education of the children and they will really be a handicap in the devlopment of the men themselves. In the tribal society girls had their initiation ceremonies as well as boys, and as far as the life of the tribe was concerned there was equality of education for both sexes. In the transitional African society that we see to-day one sex has suffered from educational segregation. (I am not, of course, here or anywhere else speaking of the simple bush school.) The leeway is being made up, but it is not sufficient to have girls' high schools and colleges parallel with boys' high schools and colleges. What is needed is a proper attitude of the educated man to the position of women. This cannot be inculated by Europeans who themselves are often quite uneducated on the subject of their own women. It can only be done by sympathetic and cultured Europeans, by a more humanistic higher education for Africans, and by the efforts of educated African women themselves. The Aba riots showed what an enormous influence the tribal women could wield when organized : the influence of educated women could be just as great. A good deal of the energy of educated African men goes in seeking for themselves an adequate place in the life of the community, and it is natural and proper that it should. But there are many other things they could do as well, and not the least important is to seek to raise their own women to the level at which they will be worthy wives and mothers of a potentially free and independent people. This is the sphere in which the Bantu and other non-Moslem communities have the possibility of far outstripping the more picturesque and superficially more powerful emirates of the North.

6.

The place of missions in the African territories under " indirect rule " is bound to be a difficult one, and it constitutes a problem which can be solved more easily along lines of personnel than on a system of paper safeguards and restrictions. The problem presses in many ways. In some

II. EDUCATION UNDER INDIRECT RULE

territories there are schools run by the Native Administrations and occasionally such schools are in opposition not only to mission schools but even to schools run by the Government Education Department. Is this competition a good thing? Is a Native Administration, administering Native law, the best body to deal with a school which teaches subjects which are *not* Native, and which, by their very existence, are a symbol of the imported civilization? If not, is the mission the best agency to continue to do it? Then, again, on the other side, if the African is to develop his own community, and to be free to take what he thinks fit from the European civilization, and if the Government has taken up the responsibility of educating its potential citizens, what place is there in the higher branches of the educational service for such a *tertium quid* as the missionary? Behind all this problem of contrasted and competing persons and agencies there is the greater problem of Christianity as a possible basis for the new African society. There are able officers who believe that Islam is the best religion for the African. In territories where white men take this point of view life is apt to be difficult for other men of the same race who take a quite different point of view. Then, again, even if we admit the value of Christianity, how can we separate it from all these apparently warring sects—Anglicans, Methodists, Roman Catholics, Seventh Day Adventists and all the rest of them? All this constitutes a problem difficult at the moment but likely to be still more difficult later on in territories where the avowed aim of the Government is to preserve Native institutions and develop them to stand up to modern conditions without losing their essential characteristics.

These questions are complicated by the peculiar nature of Christianity. A political officer in Northern Nigeria can study Moslem law and preside over its administration without feeling at all committed to Mohammedanism as a way of life for himself. In the same way an administrator may make an intensive study of animism and thoroughly appreciate its value without being an animist. But it is not so with Christianity. It makes a personal challenge every time. If a man is willing to accept that personal challenge he will give a fair hearing to Christianity as a way of life for the African. But if he is hostile to it, or indifferent to it, he will never be able to understand his fellow countryman, the missionary, and, still less, the *African* Christian.

In the government of African territories personnel is nine-tenths of the problem. The ordinary villager cares little whether he is living under " direct " or " indirect rule," and on the boundary of Katanga men go and come without any consideration as to whether they are on Belgian or on British soil. But the local officer counts very much indeed. According to the personal attitude and sympathies of this official the African under him feels happy or uneasy. The Bechuana chiefs in September, 1895, on a visit to England, implored Chamberlain to give them as a Resident

' a good man who knows our speech and customs, and is not bad-tempered and impatient, and who loves us.' [1]

This is an African point of view all over !

This matter of the relations between missions and government is also largely a matter of personnel. The mere official and the mere propagandist will never really see eye to eye. This is obvious all the time when discussing with officials the sins of missionaries and with missionaries the sins of officials. Behind a vigorous official advocacy of Native Administration schools in certain areas in Nigeria I once found a dislike of certain missions, while an equally violent opposition to these schools was due to the missionaries' dislike of certain officials. I do not see how this personal equation can be eliminated. A rigid demarcation of rights and duties would be an unfortunate thing in a situation like the government of backward peoples where a right use of *discretion* is a necessary instrument.

The question of the suitability or otherwise of Native Administrations being made the authorities for education cannot, however, be settled on purely personal grounds. Where they are used as a stick with which to beat the missions, and where they are opposed merely as a competitive element, the right use will not be made of them. They need

[1] Cd. 7962 of 1896. No. 22.

II. EDUCATION UNDER INDIRECT RULE   425

to be considered as part of the general policy of the country. A Native Administration which is purely artificial, created by the fiat of the European official, is likely as much to do harm to an indigenous Native authority as to help it. The line of advance seems to be to consider not a ruling class at all, at any rate not the " vested interest " of a ruling class, but an entire community, chiefs and people being equally part of it, and to consider a new form of administration which will prevent Native customs being changed at a speed greater than the people can understand, yet will allow for them to be changed. It will need to provide opportunity for the educated Christian men and women to play a part in the life of the community adequate to their ability, while still carrying their own people with them. (Experience in French and Belgian Africa shows that the educated African can be just as much an exploiter of " Natives " as any foreigner.) And it will need steadily to advance the level of general education so as to lessen that gap between educated and uneducated which is necessarily a first result of all education everywhere. Under " indirect rule " a European system of government is certainly not suitable, but in the changing conditions of to-day neither is a purely " Native " system of administration suitable. " Indirect rule " should mean not the preservation of Native tribal life nor its destruction, but a careful regulation of the rate of change. It may be concerned to preserve, but it is also surely concerned just as much to alter. It is the assumption that " indirect rule " means only " preserving " and " safeguarding " that has done so much damage.

Now it is certainly true that where the business of " indirect rule " *has* been assumed to be only to " preserve " it has found in Christianity a very hostile influence. Christianity and a non-Christian tribal system cannot exist together. The attempt to make them do so is due to a misunderstanding of both. General Smuts, in a most unfortunate speech at the educational conference in Johannesburg in July, 1934, suggested that a blend of Christianity and paganism was the best thing for the Native. Dr. Lucas, the Bishop of Masasi, a well-known missionary leader whose sympathetic attitude to African life commands our respect, in an interview with the *Manchester Guardian* made the strangely contradictory statement that

'it is difficult, if not impossible, to interfere with any part of the elaborate structure of an old society without causing damage to the whole structure, and the educators of a Native race must *therefore* respect ancient customs and make use of all that is valuable in them, while taking out everything that was opposed to Christian morals and putting something good in its place.'[1]

The new African society, however, will never be a mosaic carefully put together by either the European statesman or the European bishop according to his own personal predilections. To think that it will is to rule out altogether the personal initiative of the African—the very element that the new society requires for its stability. What the African thinks and what we think that he thinks are not necessarily the same thing.

Such artificial syncretism is not helpful. But at the same time Christianity as concerned with a spirit of life and not with this or that custom undoubtedly has its part to play in the new Africa. This is tacitly recognized even by opponents of missions. I have referred to the continual recurrence of the phrase "repugnant to natural justice" in the literature dealing with "indirect rule." Customs "repugnant to natural justice" must be ruled out. But what is this sense of "natural justice" in the European races if it is not the deposit of Christianity? We cannot divest ourselves of our heritage even when we quarrel with it. The theory that moral ideas somehow exist in the air and are independent of history is a complete fallacy. The language in which we think, the categories we use, and the standards by which we judge are not born with us; they have come to us from the society in which we live, and even the non-Christian humanist has his debt to pay to Judaea.

How far, then, is animism compatible with modern conditions? In other words, how much longer can the animistic village continue in a world of motor cars, railways, newspapers, wireless and economic solidarity? The answer

---

[1] *Manchester Guardian*, February 25th, 1935. I have italicized "therefore."

II. EDUCATION UNDER INDIRECT RULE 427

is that it can do so indefinitely. The animistic outlook is part of the make-up of every civilized being, and it can coexist quite easily with a civilization which denies it. There is an animistic streak in every religion and in every ritual, in hard-headed, non-churchgoing men who put on aprons and pinafores in freemasons' lodges, in giddy young women who collect mascots and charms, and indeed in all of us. And the African who works electrical machinery in a mine and comes home to kill a cock and sprinkle its blood before his ju-ju is only exhibiting in a more glaring way a contradiction of a type in which we all indulge in a less spectacular fashion. Animism of a kind is certainly compatible with modern conditions.

But as a moral discipline it is quite incompatible. This is what differentiates the tribe as it really is from this rather strange invention of the Bishop of Masasi. The acts and customs and rituals of the tribe are not ends in themselves —they are expressions of an inner spirit, of a life which has a very real and in many ways very admirable and sane hold upon its followers. Tribal religion has a *sanction*. The difficulty about the tribe in these days is not that these customs are disappearing but that the tribe as a moral force is in decay. The new mixed society in which people live has not got this tribal religion at the back of it to keep it morally stable, nor can it have. A thoughtful African who is at all educated beyond the elementary stage cannot remain in animism as an educated Indian can remain in Hinduism. That is why these attempts to salve this or that piece of tribal custom are not really salvage at all. Tribal life is not an assortment of pieces—pieces of ritual, pieces of custom, pieces of proverbs and so on. It is a whole thing, with an informing principle. Customs and such like are matters of convenience or adaptation—they are not the root thing with which we are really dealing. The choice, therefore, before the African, at any rate outside the Moslem areas (and one wonders sometimes if this exclusion is absolute), is between Christianity and scepticism. It certainly is not animism. There are shallower minds who can view without shrinking the second of these alternatives, but even the Colonial Office feels that religion must come in. Yet there is a school of thought known as the scientific humanists who feel that the sweetness and light fostered by modern science is somehow available for the African instead of Christianity. I wonder how far that is likely. I feel myself that science in these days when it sets up as an alternative to Christianity is developed over against those forms of Christianity which are least intelligent and most superstitious, and yet that the advocates of science have quite as superstitious a regard for their own subject as the people they condemn have for the church. Superstition in these days is not confined, nor even *chiefly* confined, to members of religious bodies. And the assumption that science can give the African what he needs in the modern world is to credit him with being less of an all-round person than he really is. The African's need is for religion, and no greater disservice can be done to the principle of " indirect rule " than to take the line that it means the discouragement of Christianity and an amateur experimentation with " Native " cults.

At the same time we may agree with all this and yet not agree with the manifestations of Christianity which meet the bewildered education officer who takes over a district for the first time. All kind of names that he had never heard before, theories of life and conduct often as strange as those of the Native folk themselves, prejudices and ignorances that he had thought to have died out at the time of the Renaissance in Europe confront him at every turn. And still worse than that, there appears to be no standardization within the groups themselves. Among Anglicans there are some who believe in the Mass, some who hate it like the devil, there are verbal inspirationists and modernists ; people of every degree of " breadth " and of " height." The label " Methodist " tells you nothing whatever about a missionary except the name of the body that employs him. In the same way with all other religious bodies. Even among the Roman Catholics there are White Fathers, Jesuits, and dozens more, agreeing certainly on their main propositions but different in outlook and even in policy. What is the education inspector to do ? He does what is natural under the circumstances and pays attention to the man and ignores

II. EDUCATION UNDER INDIRECT RULE 429

his label as much as he can.[1] Sooner or later something will have to be done about this fissiparous element in African education. Men emerge from their tribes only to fall into a new classification of European sects. At the very time when African society most needs to hold together it has these wedges driven into it. Fortunately the African has often a greater sense of humour than we have, and these things do not bother him so much as we think they do.

Yet the need for religion remains. Too much has perhaps been said in some quarters to emphasize this point, as if it is the African alone whose education must be "based" on religion while the Europeans have outgrown this stage. From the other side this need for religion is often used to justify the existence and the continuance of any and every mission as if interference with a particular mission indicated opposition to "religion." But the "sanction" in the tribal life of the African is religion, and while the tribe as an institution is inevitably decaying, the need for a sanction is the more urgent. Where is it to be found ? The apparatus of European justice with its law courts and its prisons and its often disproportionate fines is no sanction at all, as anyone familar with African prisons will tell you. Public opinion is in much too chaotic a state in these days of transition to be any guide. It is often thought that European "prestige" would act as a sanction to the African in contact with the whites, but too many contradictory things have happened and are happening to prevent the African continuing to take the white man at his own estimation. Sometimes "patriotism" is preached to the African as something which he will appreciate, and he is expected to be loyal to his "country" and to be a better person in consequence. But what is "Northern Rhodesia," for example, to an African ?—it is a mere geographical expression. "Nigeria," perhaps, is less so, because it is a more coherent unit. But much too much is expected of the African in this regard, and we too easily assume that a mere official

---

[1] At the same time I have often felt it to be a pity that the Government official does not spend a little more time trying to understand these divisions. The *Church Times*, the *Universe* and the *British Weekly* are "documents" quite as relevant for the study of religion as a ju-ju or a totem.

incantation in the name of the King will solve this spiritual problem for us. None of these external things touch the real problem, for the real problem is the existence or creation of that inward informing principle which gave coherence to the tribe. I believe that Christianity can do that, although I do not believe that every mission can do it or that every Government servant can foster it. The thing which cannot do it is animism resuscitated under European auspices. The desired thing, I think, is being done at Achimota, which is a semi-Government college, and at a number of excellent missionary institutions I could name. In order to be done it requires on the part of the European an acceptance of the Christian Gospel as a sanction for his own life as well as for those of the Africans. This is where the man of real Christian conviction, whether an official or a non-official and whether he expresses it by a dogmatic adhesion to a creed or not, has the pull over the man without it. He is not insisting on the African having something which he himself does not wish to share. A European urging Mohammedanism or animism on Africans is, when we think of it, a person in rather an odd position, but so, too, is the European official or missionary who urges Christianity upon the African as a kind of stock requirement but without the spirit of Chaucer's parson, who

> Christes lore and His apostles twelve
> He taught, and first he folwed it himselve.

Where words and theories about God and destiny are made the staple of " Christian " education the work is not being done. And when mere proselytism is the aim the work is being definitely hindered. But that is not a reason for not trying to get it done properly.

Having said all that, I shall probably be accused of trying to steer a course " between partiality on the one hand and impartiality on the other " if I say something on behalf of the denominational missions. Denominational missions, unfortunately, are inevitable. The thing that matters is not their origin but their attitude. They are supported by voluntary contributions from home, often at very great sacrifice, whereas, of course, the Government raises its money

II. EDUCATION UNDER INDIRECT RULE 431

compulsorily by tax. In order to raise money in the voluntary way there must be a clientèle to which you can appeal. A *general* appeal for money for the missionary societies would interest nobody. And when all is said and done it is a very remarkable thing that thousands of folk at home, many of them in poor circumstances, are sufficiently interested in the welfare of people beyond the seas as to save up money for them. That, of course, does not justify proselytism? But *is* it proselytism? Missions on the field have before now competed with each other for the attention of the Africans and some of them are competing still. The jibe that missions bribe Africans with education has its justification in certain places even yet. But the whole trend of missionary thought is against such competition, not only as a competition of rival groups but even as competition of rival theologies. More and more every missionary society is seeking to pursue as its aim the purpose of the London Missionary Society which so much attracted Livingstone :

' to preach the Gospel of the blessed God.'

Where a mission does *not* do so, the puzzled and annoyed administrator might ask himself before he condemns " missions " whether this particular mission really represents the policy of, say, the Conference of British Missionary Societies.

Then, again, on the " field " local groups are inevitable. There are tribes and there will inevitably be denominations. A vague, generalized, unorganized " Christianity " appeals to nobody, least of all to the African. He must have the local group with a well-defined objective and community life, and there is no harm whatever in his doing so. But, as I have said, everything depends on the attitude. If these groups are concerned with their own self-perpetuation and aggrandizement then the means has been mistaken for the end. It therefore comes down once again to personnel, and I have a great deal of sympathy with the official who concerns himself with the missionary as a man and not with the label he carries.

There is one further point about education. If the missions are giving a " secular " as well as a religious education, and if, still more, it is accepted that a religious "basis" is important for African education, the missions are doing something that is necessary to the State, and which the Government would do if it could. It was, however, a continual source of complaint to me when I was in Nigeria that teachers in mission schools were relatively very badly placed compared with teachers in Government schools as regards both salary and pension. This complaint was just, but in order to meet it a comprehensive survey of education is needed in every territory. Education in Africa is very much where English education was immediately after the Education Act of 1870, and the history of the working of that Act, and particularly the Report of the Cross Commission eighteen years later, are very suggestive as to the probable trend of education in Africa. There must some day be a State service of education, although that does not rule out mission schools in Africa any more than it has ruled out Church schools in this country. The teachers are the most vocal class and on the whole the ablest class, and many people have to go into teaching who could quite well be those Native administrators who will be needed if their country has to "stand by itself." At present, teaching is the best thing for them. It is obviously fair that teaching should be considered a "service" as it is in this country, and whether it is done in a mission or in a Government school should make no difference.

What then is the conclusion of the whole matter? "Indirect rule" has to advance to a further stage, a stage which can be prepared for by education. The work of general education must of course go on. There are still ninety per cent. of the children to be taught reading, writing, gardening, hygiene, and a few more things. That is not particularly a problem of education under "indirect rule." Our problem is with higher education and what is to come of it. There must be careers opened up for people educated to follow them, there must be opportunity, and above all things there must be *initiative*. No people can ever get very far along the road of progress if they are only allowed to carry out other people's orders. Among the educated classes

II. EDUCATION UNDER INDIRECT RULE 433

must be included chiefs, and the great need for the sons of chiefs is for a general education and not education in the " art of government." The art of government is an equation between the governor and the governed, and a mere segregation of the governors may even unfit them for the special task. And any education of the sons of chiefs which assumes that chieftainship in its tribal form is bound to continue is an education in the face of the evidence. What African society will become we do not know, because the African himself has not yet been in a position to speak. After all, it is he who will have to make it.

APPENDIX III.

Scheme of work at the Girls' Community Centre, Ituk Mban, Uyo, Port Harcourt, Nigeria, April 1938.

TYPICAL WEEKLY TIME-TABLE, GIRLS' COMMUNITY CENTRE, ITUK MBAN, UYO, NIGERIA.

	7.0	8.30	8.45–9.15	9.20–9.40	9.40–10.30	10.30–11.15	11.20–12.0	3.0–5.0
Mon.	Students' own housework	Prayers	Students' own laundry		Physical exercises and games	*Talks* on Laundry methods and soap- and starch-making	1. Reading 2. Reading 3. Preparation for soap-making	Mending and ironing
Tues.			Scripture	1. Preparation for soap-making 2. Reading 3.		*Talks* on Housewifery and 'Compound' sanitation	1. Writing 2. Writing 3. Writing notes	Mending, ironing and marking
Wed.			Scripture	1. Figures or spelling 2. Soap-making 3.		1. Simple dictation 2. 3. Write up notes	*Talks* on midwifery, mothercraft and child-training	Sewing
Thur.			Scripture lesson in 'story' form			*Talk* on Food values and cooking methods followed by Practical work		Knitting, pattern making
Fri.			Hymn singing and scales	Catechism class and/or silent reading		1. Reading or writing 2. Written work, recipes, etc. 3.	*Talk* Home Nursing and simple First Aid	Fancy stitches for garments
Sat.			Cleaning their own house and all the contents		Bible Class	Sweeping compound and other such work Arrange class room for Sunday		Holiday occasionally, games in evening
Sun.						To village church for service		Afternoon service, Sing-song in evening

1. Fees are 2s. for the course. Centre provides beds, blankets, books, etc. Girls provide food and cooking utensils.
2. Class 3 consists of those who have come for domestic training only. They are usually Standard IV and V girls.
3. Soap-making is done in small groups, in order that each person may learn. Oil is plentiful.
4. The more advanced girls learn to cut and make their own patterns and garments, and do individual cooking. The course begins with "invalid" cookery, possible in their own homes, and goes on to considerations of balanced diet.
5. Girls buy in the local market material required for cooking lessons, and are given the money for it.
6. A large, 14 lb. sugar tin is the much-coveted prize for the best mending and laundry work for the session.

INDEX.

ABA, riots at, 409, 419, 422.
Abercrombie, Lascelles, *The End of the World*, 324.
Abyssinia, viii, 20.
Accidia, 69.
Achimota, vii, 94, 98, 101, 132, 215, 260, 308, 330, 350, 411, 430; conference at 350; constitution of, 348 f.; cost of, 101; refresher course at, 93, 312.
Achterberg, N. D., *South African Introductory Arithmetic for Native Schools*, 161.
Adaptation in education, *see under* Slogans.
Adult School Movement, 353.
Africa: area, 3; geography, *chap. i*; history, *chap. ii*; mystery of, 5, 20; population, 3; scenery of, 18, 188 f., 220; exploitation of, 44, 271 f.; administration of, 270 ff.
— East: economic effects of climate, 10; Indians in, 13; Portuguese in, 24; land-holding in, 41 f. *See under* Kenya.
— North, 13; Islam in, 21 f., 317 f.
— South: economic effects of climate, 10; regional survey of, 15 f.; Dutch in, 25 ff., 34; languages in, 141.
— South, Union of: history, 34 ff.; politics in, 34 f.; native policy, 35 ff., 52 ff., 408; native poverty in, 53, 56 f.; tribalism in, 305.
— West: imitation of Europe, 8; climate of, 8 f.; regional survey of, 13 f.; education in, 14, 99, 101, 222; Portuguese in, 23; Dutch in, 25 f.; land-holding in, 41; different from the rest of Africa, 333.
African (*see also under* Bantu): status, 20, 132, 341, 361; culture, 19 f., 313 ff., 321 ff., 335 f.; characteristics, 20, 88 ff., 371 f.; adaptability, 25; Europeanization, 8, 74 f., 317, 323 ff.; inarticulate, 86; comparison with British Tommy, 86, 88; comparison with Irish, 89; games, 90, 96; family, 93, 192, 353; language, 146, 152; methods of counting, 160 f.; memory, 161; comparison with Old Testament society, 174 f., 366; social sense, 181 f.; appreciation of nature, 18, 189, 219 f.; cleanliness, 190; sleeping habits, 190; interest in sex, 190 ff., 219 f.; lack of time-sense, 203; art, 213 ff.; religious nature, 234; formalism, 243 f.; spiritual heritage, 323, 327 ff., 336; compared with unsophisticated Europeans, 366; loyalty, 378.
African Lakes Corporation ("Mandala"), 12.
Aggrey, Dr. J. E. K., 201, 260, 396.
Agobard of Lyons, 372.
Agriculture: primitive, 43 f.; engrossing of, 50 f.; co-operation in, 57 ff., 61; and taboo, 85; and intelligence, 163 f., 231; in school, 168, 183, 185 ff.; and religion, 186.
Akan, 141.
Albert, King of the Belgians, and Protestant missionaries, 33.
Algeria, 22; 272.
Al Hajji 'Omaru, 23.
Alice, Cape Province, 81, 114.
Allier, Professor Raoul, 315 *n*.
Alsace, 143.
America, United States of: and the Peace Conference, 259; Negroes of, 292 ff.; development of, 293; race problem in, 364 f.; Southern, compared with Africa, 154, 304 f., 307 f.
Americans, 145; in Africa, *chap. xiii*; funds for African education, 259 f., 291.
Anderson, Elizabeth Garrett, 396.
Anglo-Catholics, 252 f.; and Government co-operation, 255.
Angola, 23, 24.
Angoni, 141.
Animals, care of, 193 f.

439

Animism, compared with Hinduism and Islam, 338 ; and modern life, 426, f.
Anthropology : not an adequate clue to Africa of to-day, 2, 313 ff. ; and missions, 262, 328, 422 ff. ; and use of the term " culture," 19, 313 f.
Appreciation : of Nature, 18, 188 f., 219 ; of art, 217 ff., 242 ; of science, 223 ff.
Apprentices, 100 ; in eighteenth-century London, 388 ; after the Industrial Revolution, 390.
Arabic, 21, 279.
Arabs, 20 ff., 317 f.
Aristotle, 304.
Arithmetic : numbers in, 135 f. ; compared with reading and writing, 157 ; nature of, 158 ff. ; meaning of " practical," 161 ; " adaptations " of, 301.
Army and Religion, The, 88, 172.
Arnold, Matthew, ix, 172, 261, 319, 324.
— Dr. Thomas, 72, 229, 232.
Aro Chuku, 110, 419.
Art : and culture, 147 ; values in, 210, 215 ; in school, 212 ff. ; and the Y.M.C.A., 221 ; and working women's college, 221.
Arts and crafts, native, 51 f., 221 f., 273, 373.
Ashanti, 2, 282, 341.
Asiatics at the Cape, 27.
Assimilation, rule by, 271, 286 f.
Atmosphere : a blessed word, 237 ; conditions of religious, 237 f., 242 f.
Atta, Nana Sir Ofori, 5 *n*.
Attendance, school, 81 ff.
Augustine, St., x, 211.
Authority : of the teacher, 244 ; of the Church, 247 ; of the Bible, 248 ; nature of tribal, 412 ff. ; devolution of, 402 f., 417.

BABOO English, 153.
Backgammon, 96.
Bacon, Rev. G. N., 136.
Bagdad, 22 *n*., 318.
Ba-Ila, the, 64, 96 *n*.
Ball, W. W. Rouse, *String Figures*, 90 *n*.
Bamangwato, 289, 413, 417.
Bamu'ta, Y. S., 143.
Band's Gazette, The, 167 f.
Bantu, the (*see also under* African) : adaptability, 25 ; staple food, 25 ; at the Cape, 28 ; factors making for survival, 39 ; capacity for leadership, 50 ; tribal organization, 84, 282 f. ; continence, 84 ; capacity for progress, 166, 289 ; lack of history, 319 ; and "white" civilization, 326 ff.
Barrie, Sir J. M., 145.
Barry, F. V., *A Century of Children's Books*, 177.
Basutoland, 83, 286, 418, 419.
Battersea Training College, 393.
Beaverbrook, Lord, *Success*, 179.
Bechuanaland, 286, 289, 409, 418, 419, 424.
Bedford College, 331.
Behaviourism, 296.
Beira, 12.
Belgians, the, 21 ; absence of self-criticism among, 33. *See also* Congo, Belgian.
Belief, the place of, 73 f., 340.
" Belle Sauvage," Doctrine of the, 248, 336.
Bengali literature, 153.
Benin, Bight of, 4.
Bentley, W. Holman, 120 *n*.
Berlin Conference, 31, 271 f.
Beyrout, 273.
Bible, the : in Africa, 152, 174 ff. ; and the reading lesson, 168 ; educational value of, 170 f. ; in English schools, 172 f. ; alleged " devotional " use of, 174 ; historical view of, 174 f. ; and European civilization, 248.
— Authorized Version of the, 149 ff. 173.
Bible for Youth, The, 176.
Biography, 201 f.
Biology, educational value of, 188.
Birmingham, King Edward's School, 349.
Black and White : relationship, 7 f., 61 ; and the Great Trek, 29 f. ; in America, 292 f., 306 ff. ; inevitably linked, 328 f., 359 ff. ; equality of, discussed, 330 ff.
Blackwood's Magazine, 391.
Blankets, tax on, 376 *n*.
Blantyre (Nyasaland), 331 ; Cathedral at, 76, 242.
Bloemfontein, students of, 37.
Board of Study for the Preparation of Missionaries, 258.
Boksburg, 194.
Bolingbroke, *Patriot King*, 416.
Bornu, 22 *n*., 279.
Botha, General, 36, 101.
Bowen, Edward, 207 *n*., 246.
Brethren of the Free Spirit, 382.

INDEX 441

Brévié, M., 287.
Briey, Comte de, *Le Sphinx Noir*, 120.
British, the : 15 f., 21 ; at the Cape, 28 f. ; in India, 271, 280 ; in Africa, 271 f. ; temperament of, 272 ff., 280 ff. ; in Palestine, 272 ; and Moslems, 280 f. ; and Roman Catholics, 281 f.
British and Foreign Schools Society, the, 234.
British South Africa Company, 31 f., 272 ; relation to natives, 20 ; and Portuguese, 24 ; and native lands, 42 ; and native education, 111.
British Weekly, The, 144.
Brookes, Professor Edgar, *A History of Native Policy in South Africa*, 29, 372, 384, 394, 395 ; *Native Education in South Africa*, 37 *n*.
Brookings Graduate School, 294.
Brougham, Lord, Select Committee of, 82 *n*., 392.
Bryce Commission (1896), 355.
Buildings : value of good, 238 ff. ; examples of, 240 ff. ; Domboshawa, 111, 241 ; Mkhoma, 241.
Bullhoek, 383.
Bunyan, John, 71, 81.
Burke, Edmund, 150, 279, 297, 300.
Burnet, Professor John, *Ignorance*, 201 *n*.
Burnley, working men of, 392.
Bushman paintings, 213, 217.

CABBAGE, 82.
Calabar, 46, 405.
Callaway, the Rev. Geoffrey, 88, 397.
Calvinism, 21, 27 f., 254.
Cam, Diego, 23.
Cambridgeshire Syllabus of Religious Education, 172 f., 176.
Cameron, Sir Donald, 402, 416 ; *Memo. on Principles of Native Administration*, 406 f., 419.
Cameroons, 13 *n*., 22 f., 287.
Cape Coloured, The, 27, 35.
Cape Native Teachers' Association, 95.
Cape Town, 16, 46 ; locations of, 47 f.
Carlyle, R. W. and A. J., *A History of Mediæval Political Theory in the West*, 371 *n*.
Carnegie Corporation of New York, 261.
Carpentry, examples of, 207 ff.
Carr, Dr. Henry, xii, 409.
Casement, Sir Roger, 120 *n*., 340 *n*.

Cat's Cradles, *see* Games, African.
Cattle, 11, 15.
Causation primitive view of, 85 ; in education, 167, 231.
Celebrations, school, 244 *n*.
Celibacy, in mission work, 72 f.
Chamberlain, Rt. Hon. J., 424.
Character-building : conditions of, at Mbereshi, 110 ; historical element in, 117 ; and Scripture, 170 f. ; and manual training, 206 f., 210 ff. ; and boarding-schools, 232 ff.
Charlemagne, 23, 371.
Chartists, the, 361, 392.
Chaucer, 146, 151, 153, 430.
Chemistry, educational value of, 188.
Chesterfield, Lord, 331.
Chief : tribal position of, 38 f., 41, 178, 282, 371 f., 411 ff. ; in Belgian Congo, 41, 283 ; in Transkei, 41 ; in the Gold Coast, 278 ; as European magistrate, 283 ; in Tanganyika, 283, 412 ; in Uganda, 283.
Chikaranga, 113.
Chiliasm, 250.
Chimanica, 113.
Chinyanja, 136, 141.
Chirombo, 136.
Chisolo, 96.
Chizezuru, 113, 149.
Christianity : and native life, 51, 323 f. ; and tribalism, 62 f. ; and Scripture, 170 ; an historical religion, 172 ; nature of, 236 ; and education, 237 f. ; world-wide mission of, 257 ; prejudice against in Nigeria, 283 f. ; method of advance, 327 f. ; in the Middle Ages, 379 ff.
Church, the Christian : replaces the tribe, 64, 363 ; position in England and in Africa, 247 f., 359 ; Anglo-Catholic view of, 252 f. ; social view of, 343.
Ciskei, 57.
Citizenship, education for, 341 f., 346 f., 359 ff.
Civics, 203, 407.
Clapham Sect, The, 29.
Class divisions, 343, 393.
Clifford, Sir Hugh, 41.
Climate, effects of, 8 ff.
Clinton, D. K., *The South African Melting Pot*, 29 *n*.
Coal, 12, 15.
Cobbett, William, 387.
Cocoa, 9, 290.
Coleridge-Taylor, 189.

Colonial Office, British : on the place of the vernacular, 139 ff. ; and union languages, 142 f. ; Advisory Committee on Native Education in Tropical Africa, 260, 261.
" Colour Bar " Act, 35.
Commission : East Africa (1925), 226 f. ; West Africa (1926), 227 ; Phelps-Stokes, *q.v.* ; Hilton-Young (1928), *q.v.* ; on Popular Education in England (1856-61), 393 f. ; on Native Affairs in Natal (1852), 394 f. ; Cross (1888), 432 ; Devonshire (1870), 197.
Commonwealth Trust, 261.
Community centres, 353 f.
Compounds, native, 47 ; at Springs, 47.
Conferences : Missionary, 125 ff. ; Nyasaland (1927), 125, 127, 136, 196 ; Le Zoute (1927), ix, 119, 261; Tanganyika (1925), 124 f., 127, 191 *n.* ; Northern Rhodesia (1927), 126, 193 *n.*, 253, 262, 376, 381 ; Achimota (1927), 350 ; Congo (1928), 126 ; Transkei (1927), 126 ; Southern Rhodesia, 127 ; Edinburgh (1910), 257 f. ; British Missionary Societies, 258, 431 ; International Missionary, 258.
Conflict of civilizations, 1 f., 40 ff.
Congo : climate of, 9 ; exploitation of rubber, 11, 32 ; mineral wealth, 12, 16 ; survey, 14 f. ; General Missionary Conference, 126 ; the river, 188 ; native sailors, 190 ; craftsmanship, 242 ; British in, 272 ; Arab villages, 317.
— Belgian : history of, 31 ff., 286 ; and public opinion, 33, 119 ; land-holding, 41 ; labour, 45, 81, 332 ; education, ix, 118 f. ; language, 142 ; missions, 253 f.; native women, 376.
Congo et les livres, Le, 120.
Congo Free State, 31.
Congo, Mission News, The, 126.
Conolly, James, *Labour in Ireland*, 319.
Continuity in culture, 320 ff.
Contract : and causation, 85 ; and formalism, 89 f.
Conversion, magical view of, 73.
Co-operative Movement, 333, 353 ; in Ireland, 58.
C.O.P.E.C. (" Conference on Christian Politics, Economics and Citizenship "), 251.
Copper, 12.

Coquilhatville, 33.
Cordova, 318.
Cotton : in Belgian Congo, 33 ; in Uganda, 290.
Coulton, G. G., *The Medieval Village*, 374, 376, 377, 380.
Council of Europeans and Natives, Joint, in Johannesburg, 36 *n.*, 37, 361.
Coupland, R., *Wilberforce : A Narrative*, 387.
" Cowper-Temple " Clause, the, 133, 172.
Craftsmanship : native, 51 f. ; and agriculture, 186 f. ; nature of, 187 ; an education of the emotions, 209 ; in missions, 212.
Cripps, Arthur Shirley, 149, 237 ; *An Africa for Africans*, 388 *n.*
Crown Colony Government, 286.
Crusades, the, 382.
Cullen, Archbishop, 280.
Cultivation, methods of, 11 f., 44.
Culture : African, 19 f., 313, 316 ff., 320 ff., 330 ff., 336 ; two senses of, 19, 313 ; village, 43 f. ; and poverty, 60 ; and the vernacular, 134, 139 ff. ; English, 147, 319 ; Matthew Arnold's use of the term, 319 ; meaning of, 316 f., 320 ff. ; European, 326 f., 329 ; stages in, 330 ff.
Curriculum, content of the, *chap. vi, chap. ix.*
Curtis, L., 35.

DA GAMA, Vasco, 24.
Daily Herald, The, 144.
Danish language, the, 141.
Dante, 146.
Darwin, Charles, *Origin of Species*, 249.
Davies, Miss (of Nashville), 293, 354.
Dead, the, and the tribe, 39, 83.
Denominationalism : in English education, 172, 234 ff. ; at Domboshawa, 111, 133 ; at Fort Hare, 133 ; at Achimota, 133 ; and missions, 266, 428 f., 430.
Detribalization, 12 ; causes of, 42, 45, 50 f., 61, 282 ff., 323 ff. ; effects of, 48 f., 61, 307, 324 ; and Christianity, 163 f. ; and morality, 178; and indirect rule, 278, 283.
Deuteronomic Code, the, 64 *n.*
Development, doctrine of, 249 f.
" Devonshire " Commission (1870), 197.
de Wall, D. C., on the Matabele, 5, 20.

INDEX

Diamonds discovered, 16, 31.
Differentiation : policy of, 36 ; Dr. Edgar Brookes' views, 36 ; and the Phelps-Stokes reports, 309 ; follows equality, 330 ff.
Direct rule, 271, 287.
Director of Native Education, work and qualifications of, 122, 128 f., 345 f.
Discipline, 229 f., 233 ff., 244 f.
Disease, ravages of, 46.
Disraeli, Benjamin, 360, 373.
Domboshawa (Rhodesia), viii, 111 ff., 414.
Donnelly, Sir J., 322.
Dramatic Method at Mbereshi, 110.
Drawing, 216 ff.
Drinkwater, John, *Abraham Lincoln*, 326.
Driver, Professor S. R., *Deuteronomy*, 64 n.; *Genesis*, 176.
Dualism, 335, 380 ff.
Dube, the Rev. Dr. John, 99.
Duff, Alexander, 114.
Duffy, T. Gavan, *Let's Go*, 340 n.
Dunster, 109.
D'Urban, Sir Benjamin, 29.
Dutch, the, 15 f., 21 ; history in Africa, 25 ff.
Dutch East India Company, 26 f.
Dutch Reformed Church, 27 f., 252, 254.

EALA, 33.
Economics : relation to geography, 17 f. ; basis of, in Africa, 53 f., 58 ; versus politics in Africa, 284 ff.
Eddington, Professor A. S., 295.
Edgeworth, Maria, 177.
Edinburgh Conference (1910), 257 f., 276.
" Edinburgh House," 258, 265 f.
Education : meaning of the word, 201 ; nature of, 231 f. ; Christian, 264 ; self-deception regarding, 306 ; and social structure, 306, 309, 346 f., 360 f., 390 ; purpose of, 325 f. ; requires faith, 335 f. ; factors in, 338 ff. ; and citizenship, 340 f., 346 f., 406 f. ; and labour, 393 f.
— African : moral aim of, 2, 17 f., 76 f. ; economic aim of, 10 ; in Natal, 10 f., 129 ff., 344 f. ; in Nyasaland, 12 ; agencies in, 66, 338 ff. ; " fourth dimensional " nature of, 83 ; indigenous system of, 83 ff. ; and theory of causation, 85 ; compared with early European, 98 ; types of, *chap. vi ;* grading of, 99 f. ; administration of, *chap. vii ;* too literary, 226 f. ; relation to African society, 231 f., 306 f. ; and the Americans, 259 ff. ; in Northern Nigeria, 273 ff., 278 ff. ; and indirect rule, 288 f., Appendix ii ; and anthropology, 314 f. ; rationale of, 329, 333 ; compared with women's education in England, 330 ff. ; results of, 335 f. ; direction of 339 ff. ; future with the Government, 344 ff. ; neglected factors in, 351 ff. ; arguments against compared, *see* Appendix i.
Education, American, 293 f.
— English, 234 f., 330 f., 339 ; and working men, 333, 385 ff. ;. and the State, 391 f.
Education Gazette (Cape), 95.
Education : liberal, 188 ; through carpentry, 207 f.
— Principles of, as a subject, 357.
Educational administration : principles of, 106, 124 ff., 130 ff., 344 ff. ; Gold Coast, 93, 96, 124 ; Natal, 94 f., 129 ff., 344 f. ; Cape Province, 95, 116 ; Northern Rhodesia, 99, 199 ; Southern Rhodesia, 99, 120 ff., 208, 353 f. ; Southern Nigeria, 105 ff., 123 ; Belgian Congo, ix, 118 f., 252 ; Nyasaland, 124, 161 n., 199 ; West Coast compared with East and Central, 125 ; French territory, ix, 119 ; Portuguese territory, 119.
' Educationist ' distinct from teacher, 311.
Edwards, Sir Owen, 246.
Efik, 13 n., 160, 354.
Egypt, 3, 19.
Electorate, a native, 347, 355.
Elisabethville, 6, 12, 15, 16, 17, 48, 59.
Elizabethan literature, 189.
Elmina, 23.
Enclosures of common land, 17, 43 f., 386.
Engineering, 210, 233 f.
English : place of, in school, 137, 141 ff., 148 f., 153 f. ; and the vernacular, 139, 151 ff. ; in Nigerian Moslem schools, 279 f.
Equatorial region : crops of, 9, 11 ; survey of, 14 f.

Erastianism, 21.
Erosion of soil, 11.
Ethics, contemporary, 262 f.
Ethiopianism, 291, 380, 384.
European civilization, 44 f., 46, 325, 326 ff.
Evangelical Revival, The, 28, 249 f.
Evans, Admiral, 403.
— Maurice S., 71; *Black and White in South-East Africa*, 164, 384.
Evolution, doctrine of, 247, 249.
Exhibitions, native school, 95.
Expert, position of the, 277.
Ezekiel, 64.

FACTORY system, in England, 17.
Fallacies, educational, 73 f., 92, 164, 209, 356.
Family, importance of the, 93, 192, 352 ff.
Fernando Po, 25.
Feudal System, 371 f.
Fichte, 143.
Finance of missions, 264 ff.
Flexner, Professor, *Do Americans Really Value Education?*, 294.
Folk Tales, 202, 204.
Form: European life versus African, 243 f.; value of, 238 ff., 244.
Fort Hare, South African Native College, 37, 56, 101, 117, 166, 289.
Fosdick, Harry Emerson, 173.
Fourah Bay College, 101, 411.
Fowler, H. W., *Dictionary of Modern English Usage*, 201.
" Fraktur," 143.
Franchise, the Cape, 35 f., 43 n., 116, 330.
Franck, Louis, 10 n.; *Études de colonisation comparée*, 118, 286.
Fraser, the Rev. A. G., 274, 363 n.
Frazer, Sir J. G., *The Golden Bough*, 1.
Freeman, Arnold, *see* Hayward, F. H.
Freetown, 14.
French: the, 21; and Moslems, 22 f.; aims in Africa, 23, 272; at the Cape, 26; and African education, 119; method of rule, 271, 286 f., 288, 362; monument at Beyrout, 272 f.; system of intermarriage, 376.
— Revolution, the, 28, 249, 360, 393.
Frissell, Dr., Principal of Hampton, 303.
Froebel, 218.

Fula, the, 23, 278, 401, 413.
Fundamentalists, 251, 253 f.; and Government co-operation, 255.
Funerals, 9, 388 f.

GA, 141.
Gaboon, 22.
Galsworthy, John, *Loyalties*, 178.
Games, African, 90, 96.
Garnett, J. C. Maxwell, 303.
Garratt, G. T., *Hundred Acre Farm*, 305 n.
Garvey, Marcus, 291 f.
Gebhart, Emile, *L'Italie Mystique*, 383 n.
Geography: alternative to agriculture, 185, 194; human, 196, 204; connection with history, 204; as school subject, 205 f.
George V., King, 378; Jubilee, 412 n.
George, M. D., *London Life in the Eighteenth Century*, 388 n.
Germans, the, 21, 272.
Gesta Romanorum, 103, 379.
Giddy, Dr. Davies, 391.
Gilchrist, Mr., M.L.A., Southern Rhodesia, 342 n.
Girl Guides, *see* Wayfarers.
Girls, *see* Women.
Girton College, 331.
Gladstone, The Rt. Hon. W. E., 272.
Glasgow, slums in, 190.
Glastonbury, 314.
Glenelg, Lord, 29.
Gold, 12; effect of its discovery in South Africa, 16; in Manicaland, 24; in Rhodesia, 31.
Gold Coast, economic effects of climate, 8 f., 51, 290.
Golf in West Africa, 406.
Government and Missions, relations of: British territory compared with others, 101, 118 ff.; well balanced in Southern Nigeria, 106 f.; difficulties of, in the Cape, 106; need for a policy, 119 f., 285; in Nyasaland, 124 f.; Conferences, 127; nature of co-operation, 99, 127, 129, 132, 260 ff., 309, 340 f., 347 f.; in Natal, 129 ff., 344 f.; at Hope Fountain, Southern Rhodesia, 132, 353 f.; on the Gold Coast, 132, 261; in education, 365 f., *chap. xii*; *Appendix ii*; in Northern Nigeria, 273 ff., 279, 280 ff.; in politics, 344 ff., 347 f., 355, 422 ff.
Government House, view from, 403.

INDEX 445

Graaf Reinet, Farmers' Association of, 376.
Grace, doctrine of, 268 f.
Grammar : place of, 198 f. ; study of, 199 f., 217.
Grants, 101 ; in Southern Nigeria, 105 ; in Southern Rhodesia, 121 f.; principles of, 118, 122 ff. ; effect of, 265 f.
Green, T. H., 332.
Grenfell, George, 120 *n*.
Grondwet, the Transvaal, 30 *n*.

HADDON, K., *Cat's Cradles from Many Lands*, 90 *n*.
Hadfield, J. L., 122 *n*.
Half-caste children, 346, 376.
Hall, R. J., *Civics : An Introduction to South African Social Problems*, 203 *n*.
Hammond, J. L. and B., *The Town Labourer*, 387 *n*.
Hampton Institute, 260, 303, 304.
Hankey, Donald, 86.
Happy Homes and How to Make Them, 220.
Harlem (New York), 305.
Harris, J. H., *The Chartered Millions*, 379 *n*.
— the " Prophet," 383.
Hausa : traders, 13 *n*. ; in Northern Nigeria, 278.
Hawkins, Sir John, 4.
Hayward, F. H., *A First Book of School Celebrations*, 244 *n*. ; and Freeman, A., *The Spiritual Foundations of Reconstitution*, 244 *n*.
Hazelwood School, 207 *n*.
Health : in the tropics, 10 *n*. ; as a school subject, 300.
Hebrews : growth of individualism among the, 63 f. ; taboos, 84 f. ; theory of causation, 85.
Hegel, 143.
Hellenism, Byzantine, 318.
Hemmerlin, 377.
Herbartianism, 303.
Hertzog, General J. B., 35, 36, 57, 292, 330, 372 *n*.
Hiawatha, 189.
Hill, Matthew Davenport and Rowland, 207 *n*.
Hilton-Young Commission, 288, 342, 364.
Hinduism, 338, 427.
History : meaning of, 175, 202 ff., 315 f., 320 f. ; nature of African, 19, 203 f., 316, 323 ; and biography, 201 f. ; as a school subject, 202 f. ; and geography, 204 ; and language, 318 f.
Hobbies, value of, 70, 359.
Hofmeyr, J. H., 36.
Hogarth, 388.
Holman, H., *English National Education*, 238 *n*., 387 *n*., 391 *n*.
Home and Colonial Training College, 355.
Hospitality, 88.
Hottentots, 27.
How to be Happy Though Married, 220.
Huguenots, the, 26, 27.
Huileries du Congo Belge (Lever Brothers), 41, 59, 81, 119, 290.
Humanism, 195 f.
Humanization of factors in African education, 342 ff.
Huxley, Professor T. H., 172, 295, 322, 396.
Hygiene, as nature study, 189 ff.

IBADAN (S. Nigeria), 105.
Ibo, 142.
" I.C.U.," *see* Industrial and Commercial Workers' Union.
Ila, *see* Ba-Ila.
Imagination, use of, 89 f.
Imperfection, the cult of, 76 ff., 239.
Imperial East Africa Company, 31, 272 ; relation to natives, 20 ; and native lands, 41 f.
Inanda (Natal), 48.
India : missionary education in, 114, 274 ; motherhood in, 191 f. ; Montagu-Chelmsford reforms in, 263 ; British rule in, 271, 280 f., 286 f. ; comparison with Africa, 338, 373 ; sahib system in, 414.
Indians : traders, 13 ; attitude to Africans, 13.
Indirect method of approach, 89.
— rule, x, 272 ff., 288 ; and British temperament, 272 ; in Northern Nigeria, 273-86 ; weakness of, 278 f., 282 f. ; and tribalism, 282 f., 288 f. ; and education, 290, Appendix ii.
Individualism : growth of, 46 ; need for, 61 ; in the Hebrew prophets, 63 f.
Industrial and Commercial Workers' Union, 49 f. ; legal position of, 49 ; excommunicated by Roman Catholic missions, 50, 253.
Industrial Revolution, the, 16, 28, 284 f., 319, 337, 390 f.

446 THE SCHOOL IN THE BUSH

Industrialism : at Mombasa, 1 ; in South Africa, 16 ; in Rhodesia, 16 f. ; in Katanga, 16 ; in Transvaal, 31, 34 ; European, in Africa, 44 ff., 62, 284 f.
Initiation ceremonies : sublimation of, 77, 87, 262, 381 ; in education ; 84 ; effect of, 87.
Inspection of schools, 123 f. ; in Natal, 129 ff.
Insurance Act, the, 343.
Intelligence, development of, 164 f. ; connection with skill, 196 f., 208 f.
Inter-marriage, 276, 362 n., 376 f.
International Institute of African Languages and Cultures, 262.
International Review of Missions, 258.
Iraq, 274.
Ireland, agricultural co-operation in, 58 ; in the eighteenth century, 388.
Irredentism, 143.
Irvine, Helen D., *The Making of Rural Europe*, 43, 44.
— J. T., xii, 119 n.
Isidukaduk, 137 f.
Islam and Moslems : on West Coast, 14 ; and Arab invaders, 21, 22, 317 ; in North Africa, 21 f. ; native policy of, 21 f. ; unprogressive, 21, 317 f. ; in British territory, 22 ; and the French, 22 f. ; Emirates in Nigeria, 271, 273 ; in Zaria, 273 f. ; attitude to Christian missions, 276 ; and Government, 284, 416, 423.
Italians, the, 21.
Ituk Mban, 354, Appendix iii.

JABAVU, Professor, D. D. T., 58.
— Tenga, 396.
Jameson, Dr. (Sir), L. S., 5.
Japan, 337.
Jeanes, Anna C., fund, 261, 354 ; teachers, vii, 113, 261.
Jerusalem, American Colony at, 383.
Jerusalem Missionary Conference, ix.
Jewish civilization, analogy to, in Africa, 327 f.
Jews in South Africa, 34.
Jex-Blake, Sophia, 396.
Joachim of Flora, 383.
Johannesburg, 16, 31, 388 ; labourers in, 45 ; Bantu Social Centre, xii, 166, 312.
John of Salisbury, *Polycraticus*, 98 n.
Johnson, Dr., 410, 413.

Johnson, Sir Harry H., *A History of the Colonization of Africa by Alien Races*, 24, 27 n., 32.
Jokes, against peasant and native, 377.
Jonah, 175.
Jones, J. D. Rheinallt, xii, 223.
Jones, Dr. Thomas Jesse, 259 f., 304, 307, 308 ; *The Four Essentials of Education* 300 ff.
Journal of the African Society, 156.
Junod, Henri A., *The Life of a South African Tribe*, 96, 160, 161.
jus primæ noctis, 376.
Jusserand, J. J., *English Wayfaring Life in the Middle Ages*, 372 n.
Jutland, battle of, 147.

KADALIE, Clements, 49.
Kambole Industries, 222.
Kambove, 16, 46.
Kano (Nigeria), 52, 274, 280, 285, 318, 401, 402.
Kanuri, 22 n.
Karoo, the, 11.
Katanga, 12, 16, 32, 272, 363, 424.
Katsina, 280, 319 n. ; Emir of, 416.
Kay-Shuttleworth, Sir James, 122, 393.
Keith, Sir Arthur, 247.
Kenya : climate of, 10 ; public opinion, 33, 287 f. ; land, 41 f., 290 ; taxation, 44 ; native reserves, 53 ; Ki-Swahili, 143 ; Jeanes school, 94, 261 ; policy, 288, 290, 342, 363 ; compulsory labour, 374 f.
Kepler, 219.
Kgotla, 289.
Khama, 180 f., 289, 417 ff.
Kidd, Dudley, 88.
Kilindini, 1.
Kilpatrick, Professor, *Source Book in the Philosophy of Education*, 298.
Kimberley, 16.
" Kimberley brick," 111, 241.
King William's Town, 29, 95, 117 ; location in, 48.
Kingdom of God, doctrine of the, 250, 340.
Kingsley, Mary, 389, 410.
Kinshasa, 15, 126.
Kirk, Sir John, 31.
Ki-Swahili, 141 ; as a *lingua franca*, 142 f.
Kitchen-Kaffir, 153.
Kongo, King, 23.

INDEX 447

LABOUR: effect of, on European health, 10 n.; in Congo, 15, 45, 59, 81; in Portuguese East Africa, 45; Europeanized conditions of, 48.
— compulsory, 23 f., 81, 374 f.
Lagos, 153, 243; marriage in, 420.
Land: in South Africa, 15, 34 ff., 42 f.; tenure of, in primitive societies, 38 ff.; tenure of, in Scottish Highlands, 40; and tribalism in Africa, 38 f., 50 f.; in Kenya, 41 f.; in Rhodesia, 41 f.; insecurity of tenure, 58 f.; tenure of, in the Transkei, 57; and education, 307 f.
Landseer, Sir Edwin, R.A., 147 n.
Language (*see also* Vernacular): " direct method," 137; technical sense of, 144 f.; African, flexibility of, 145 f., 152; function of, 165 ff.; uneducated use of, 198; connection with grammar, 198 ff.; values in, 200; " authorities " on, 145, 200.
Laws, the Very Rev. Dr. R., 196 n., 340 n.
Leaders, training of, *see under* Slogans.
Le Grand, Father, S.J., 33.
Leisure, sense of: necessity for, 69 f.; at Mbereshi, 110; problem of, 219 f.; in school work, 245.
Leopold II., King of the Belgians, 31 f., 120 n., 272, 286.
Leopoldville, 126. *See also under* Kinshasa.
Lever Brothers, *see* Huileries du Congo Belge.
Leverhulme, Lord, 41.
Levitical Code, 381.
Lévy-Bruhl, Professor Lucien, 89 n., 315, 366.
Lewis, Wyndham, 213.
Leys, Dr. Norman, *Kenya*, 308.
Le Zoute: conference at, ix, 261 f.; and the Portuguese, 119.
Liberia, 14, 293 n., 354.
Life, corporate, nature of, 66 ff.
Lingua franca, question of, 142 f.
Literalism, 89 f., 92.
Literary studies, 195 ff.
Literature: for teachers, 94 f.; and culture, 146 f., 148; conditions of a great, 150 ff.; vernacular, need for, 151, 154, 169.
Livingstone, David, 21, 24, 30, 431; *Missionary Travels and Researches in South Africa*, 248 n.

Livingstone, W. P., *Laws of Livingstonia*, 340 n.
Livingstonia: organization of, 66, 99; a village school of, 79 f.; apprentices, 100.
Lobengula, 42, 112, 379.
Lobola, see Ukulobola.
Locations, native: 47 f.; Cape Town, 47; King William's Town, 48; Elisabethville, 48; Port Harcourt, 48; Christian missions in, 63; Boksburg, 194.
Locke, John, 166, 177, 219.
Lodge, Sir Oliver, 81.
Lokele, the (Congo), 81, 90, 224.
London in the eighteenth century, 388.
London Mercury, The, 144.
Loram, Dr. C. T., xii, 260, 397; *The Education of the South African Native*, 136 n.
Lovedale, 37, 98, 100, 114 ff., 289, 308, 309, 349; bookshop, 177, 213 n., 220; Phelps-Stokes report on, 309.
Lovett, William, 392, 396.
Loyalty: tribal, 181 f.; education of, 181 f., 233, 333 f., 363.
Lubumbashi, 48.
Lucas, E. V., 168.
Lugard, Lord: and the dual mandate in Africa, 44, 271; on African education, 227 ff., 279 f.; and Nigeria, xi, 273 ff., 403, Appendix ii.

MABIE, Dr. Catherine, 97.
Machiavelli, 416.
Macmillan, Professor W. M., xiii; *The Cape Colour Question*, 29 n., 30 n.; *Bantu, Boer and Briton*, 372 n.
Madagascar, 287.
Madan, A. C., *Living Speech in Central and South Africa*, 200.
Madari, 112.
Maitland, F. W., 246.
Mambo Leo, 94.
Manchester Guardian, 143 n., 294 n., 375 n.
Manda (Tanganyika), 6, 13.
Mandates, 22, 258 f., 263, 270 f., 286 f., 288.
Mandeville, Bernard, *Essay on Charity Schools*, 385 f.
Manica, 24.
Manning, B. L., *The People's Faith in the time of Wyclif*, 379 n.
— Cardinal, 251.

Manual work: and intelligence, 196 f.; in school, 206 ff.
Mariannhill (Natal), German Roman Catholic (Trappist) mission: excommunicates " I.C.U.," 50; farmers' association, 58.
Masasi, Bishop Lucas of, 425 ff.
Mashona, the, and Mashonaland, 23, 34, 39, 111, 112, 113, 121, 319, 379.
Mashonaland Quarterly, The, 169.
Masters and Servants Acts, 49.
Matabele, the, and Matabeleland, 5, 20, 34, 42, 111, 121, 141.
Matadi, 14.
Maternity: Letters from Working Women, 191 *n*.
Mauretania, the, 224.
Maurice, F. D., 332, 396.
Mbereshi (Northern Rhodesia): 137; description of girls' school, 108 ff.; mothercraft at, 190 ff.; carpentry at, 207 f., 210; water-course at, 239.
McDougall, Professor William, *An Outline of Psychology*, 296.
Meanings and equivalents, 135 ff.; and relationships, 186.
Mechanics' Institutes, 353, 391.
Medical training at Yakusu, 103.
Memory, nature of, 166 f.
Ménagère, 376.
Mende, 160.
Mensuration, 158.
Methodist Ecumenical Conference (1921), 307.
Middle Ages: labour conditions compared with S. Africa, 15; society compared with African, 244, 366, 371 ff.
Migrations: of labourers, 12, 17, 45 f.; of students, 98.
Miller, Dr., of Zaria, 273.
Millin, Sara Gertrude, *The South Africans*, 293 *n*.
Minerals, effect of discovery of, 12.
Mission, the Christian: interior life of, chap. v; relation to education, 65; aim of, 73 f., 256 f.; and citizenship, 366 f.; and indirect rule, 422 ff. See also Government and Missions.
Missionary Societies: establishment of, 248 f.; Denominationalism and, 266, 428 f.; Roman Catholic, 72, 251 f., 254 f.; Society of S. John the Evangelist (Cowley Fathers), 72; Community of the Resurrection, Mirfield, 72, 77; Universities' Mission to Central Africa, 72, 77; Baptist Missionary Society, 104, 253; Dutch Reformed Church of South Africa, 169; Protestant, 256 ff.; Fundamentalist, 253 f.; Anglo-Catholic, 252 f.; American Baptists, 253; American Presbyterians, 253; Disciples of Christ, 253; Plymouth Brethren, 256; Church Missionary Society, 273; London Missionary Society, 353, 431.
Missionary training: aim of, 110; content of, 256 f., 356 ff.
Mohammed, 337.
Mohammedism, *see* Islam.
Mombasa, 1, 31, 101; Arab school in, 196, 281.
Montagu-Chelmsford reforms, 263.
Montmorency, J. E. G. de, *State Intervention in English Education*, 387 *n*., 390 *n*., 391 *n*., 392 *n*., 395 *n*.
Moral instruction, 176 ff., 202.
— tale, the: history of, 177; in folk stories, 202.
Morale, as basis of government, 263 f., 341.
Morality: nature of, 178 ff.; and religion, 74; and primitive custom 178, 373; African and British, 180 f.; and school life, 233 f.; in human relationships, 289 f.; and science, 295; Christian, 334.
Moravians, the, 27.
More, Hannah, 386 f., 393.
Morel, E. D., 120 *n*.
Morris, William, 147 *n*., 222; *Message of the March Wind*, 322.
Morrow, George, 168.
Moshesh, 418 ff.
Mothercraft as nature study, 190 ff.
Motive, the missionary, 248 ff., 266 f., 366 f.
Motor-car, lesson of, 224, 325 f.; influence of, 404.
Moulton, R. G., *Shakespeare as a Dramatic Artist*, 238 *n*.
Mozambique, 24.
Mthenga, 94, 169.
Muller, E. H. W., *The Administration of the Transkeian Territories*, 56 *n*.
Mumford, W. B., and Orde-Brown, G. St. J., *Africans learn to be French*, 119, 287.
Munro, Sir Thomas, 363, *n*.
Murphy, E. G., *The Basis of Ascendancy*, 292, 307 *n*., 364 f., 366.
Murray, Rev. Dr. W. H., 136.

INDEX

Music: in school, 218; appreciation of, 221.
Mussolini, x, 20, 313.
Mweru, Lake, 31, 108, 336.
My Duties, 176 f., 178 ff., 202.

NAFTE, case of, 375 *n.*
Names: nature of, 165 f.; primitive respect for, 166.
Napoleon's Book of Fate, 220.
Nash, Paul, 213.
Natal: climate, 10 f.; population 11 *n.*; labour in, 10 f.; aim of education, 11; children in school, 83, 405; *Native Teachers' Journal*, 94 f., 129, 130, 131; opinion on the vernacular, 139 f., 145 f.; Scripture syllabus, 176, 344 f.; scenery of, 188; educational system of, 129 ff.; Native Affairs Commissions, 294.
National Society, the, 234.
Nationalism: in Latin countries, 120; and culture, 313; and social view of the state, 343 f.
Native Administrations, 403, 423 ff.
Native Affairs Department Annual (Southern Rhodesia), 149 n.
Native Farmers' Association (Cape), 58; (Southern Rhodesia), 111.
Native Teachers' Journal (Natal), 94 f., 129, 130, 131.
Nature: study of, 183 ff.; appreciation of, 188 f., 220; study of, for town children, 194.
Needham, W., 322.
Nesfield, J. C., *English Grammar*, 145, 199, 200.
Newcastle Commission Report, 393 f.
Newman, J. H., Cardinal, 173 *n.*, 280.
News of the World, The, 144.
Nibelungs, Lay of the, 146.
Nielsen, Peter, *The Black Man's Place in South Africa*, 366 n.
Nigeria: land holding in, 41; indirect rule in, 271, 415 f., 419, 423; (*see also* Nigeria, Northern); and Islam, 22 *n.*, 317 f., 423 f.
— Northern: educational system, 2, 274 f.; indirect rule in, 273 ff., 416; effect of railway, 6 *n.*, 284; history of, 317 f.
— Southern: mines of, 12; languages of, 142; crafts in, 373. *See* Schools, *and* Government and Missions.
Nietsche, 344.

Non-European Conference, 13.
Northumbrian villages, 89.
Norwegian, 141.
Nsaka, 109.
Numa, the religion of, 51.
Numbers, vernacular, 135 f.
Nunn, T. P., *Education: its Data and First Principles*, 229 *n.*
Nyasaland: soil of, 12; aim of education in, 12; transport in, 12; migration of labourers, 12, 46; conditions of schooling in, 81; educational administration in, 125, 281; education conference in (1927), 125, 127, 136, 196; tentative code for village schools (1927), 161 *n.*, 199; Roman Catholics in, 281; talk with school-masters in, 378.

OGAN, Dick, xi, 106.
Ohafia, 405.
Ohlange (Natal), 99.
Old Testament: development in, 63 f.; in Dutch religion, 27 f.; and African life, 174 f., 366.
Oldham, J. H., xi, 258, 261.
Opus operatum, doctrine of, 74, 170, 185 f., 212, 299, 301, 318.
Orange Free State, 30.
"Organized Science Schools," 197, 227.
Ormsby-Gore, The Rt. Hon. W. G. C. 227.
Owen, Archdeacon, W. E., 375 *n.*
— Robert, 390.
Oxendale, Messrs., 1.
Oxford Movement, the, 249, 253.
Oyo (Nigeria), 52.

PAGE, Gertrude, 44.
— Walter, H., 293.
Palestine: society of, 174 f.; British in, 272.
Palmer, Sir Richmond, 318 *n.*, 416.
Panda, mines at, 16.
Papini, Giovanni, *Life of Christ*, 176.
Parable of the straw and the lamp, 304.
Paris, Matthew, 382.
Parrot, alleged adequate symbol of African education, 227.
Pass Laws, breach of, 49.
Pathfinders, 222 f.
Patriotism, problem of, 363, 429 f.
Patterson, J. R., *Kanuri Songs*, 22 *n.*
Paul, St., 182, 329, 334; *Epistle to the Romans*, 327.

450 THE SCHOOL IN THE BUSH

Paulinus, 23.
Peace Conference, the, 258 f., 270.
Peake, A. S., *Commentary on the Bible*, 176.
Peasant : Slavonic, 43 ; mediæval, 373 ff.
Peasants' Revolt (1381), 378.
Perfection, the cult of, 74 ff., 239.
Perham, Margery, ix, 402, 418 f. ; and Curtis, L., *The Protectorates of South Africa*, 35 *n*.
Perrault, Charles, 177.
Phelps-Stokes Commissions, 127, 140, 173, 236, 259 f., 280, 303, 304, 306, 308 ff. ; belief in " adaptation," 162 *n*.
— — Fund, 259, 304.
" Phenomenalism," 262.
Philip, Dr. John, 29.
Pie-powder, courts of, 372.
Pim, Sir Alan, 419 *n*.
Pirenne, Henri, *Mediæval Cities*, 371 *n*.
Pisé-de-terre, 93, 112, 241.
Pitt, William, 387.
Place, Francis, 389.
Plunkett, Sir Horace, 58.
" Plus-fours " in Africa, 1, 45.
Podmore, F., *Robert Owen : A Biography*, 390 *n*.
Police, mediæval European, and African, 372 f.
Politics, contemporary philosophy of, 262 ff.
Ponthierville, 7, 15.
Poor whites, 54, 327.
Port Harcourt, 48, 104.
Portuguese : unprogressive, 12 ; history in Africa, 20 f., 23 ff. ; and compulsory labour, 23 f. ; aims in Africa, 24 ; and Dutch, 25 ; and native education, 119.
Prester, John, 5.
Prestige, nature of, 412, 413, 429.
Principe, 23.
Printing presses, use of, 169.
Privacy, value of, 67, 75.
Progress, nature of, 166, 321,. 426 f.
" Project method," the, 184.
Propaganda, opposed to education, 173.
Prophecy, Old Testament, 175.
Protestants, 21 ; missionary aim of, 251, 256 f. ; and the scientific temper, 257 ; and progress, 384.
Psychology : influence of, 250 ; scientific method applied to, 295 ff. 357 f.
Punch, 147.

QUEEN ADELAIDE, Province of, 29.
Quelimane, 24.
Questionnaire, method of the, 297 f., 303.
Quiller-Couch, Professor Sir Arthur, 150, 173 ; *On the Art of Reading*, 150 *n*.
Quixotism, British, 280 f.

RAILWAYS, 6 ; in West Africa, 14 ; in Rhodesia and Congo, 16.
Rand, the, 12, 16, 47, 290.
Rationalists, unscientific, 249.
Rattray, R. S., 2, 282.
Reading : value of, to missionary, 71 ; popularity in school, 83, 168 ; relation to experience, 148 f. ; compared with arithmetic, 157 f. ; nature of, 164 ; dependent upon literature, 169 ; for leisure, 220.
' Reconstruction,' 293, 308.
Reform Act (1832), 284.
" Refresher " courses, 93 f.
Religion : as basis of education, 132, 170, 234 ff. ; and agriculture, 185 f. ; and sex, 191 ; comparative study of, 249 f.
Religious instruction : and writing, 125, 163 ; different from religion, 170.
Reserves, native, 17, 42 f., 52 ff.
Retief, Piet, 29.
Reverence, teaching of, 245 f.
Rhodes, Cecil J., 5, 57, 340 *n*.
Rhodesia : exports of, 12 ; migration of labourers, 12 ; public opinion in, 33 ; land-holding in, 41 f. ; native policy in, 53.
— Northern : mines of, 12 ; education code, 99, 199 ; Missionary Conference (1927), 126, 193 *n*. ; indirect rule in, 278.
— Southern : economic effects of climate, 10 ; export of cattle, 12 ; railway, 16 ; migration of labourers from, 46 ; constitution of, 57 ; debate on native education, 341 ; education code of, 120 ff.
Rhodesian Herald, The, 375.
Rhodes Scholars, American, 293.
Richard II., 378.
Risorgimento, the, 143.
Ritual : primitive, 85, 243 f. ; meaning of, 243.
Roads, 6.
Robert, M., *Le Katanga Physique*, 16 *n*.

INDEX 451

Rodin, Auguste, 215 *n*.
Roebuck, J. A., 394.
Roman Catholics and Roman Catholicism, 21, 340; in Belgian Congo, 33, 118 f.; and Lever Brothers, 119; present position of, 251 ff.; and Government co-operation, 254 f.; and missionary training, 256 f.; in British territory, 281 f.; and native policy, 346; and pagan practices, 381.
Romance of the Rose, The, 146.
Roman Empire, 271, 284.
Romanticism in English Literature, 189.
Rotherham Advertiser, The, 204 *n.,* 235.
Rousseau, J. J., 107, 177.
Royal Niger Company, 272.
Rugby, 229.
Rural civilization, 43 ff., 50 ff., 61; in the Transkei, 55 ff.; reconstruction of, 57 ff.; study of, 183; problem of, 219 f.; " adaptation " to, 301; idealization of, 305, 324 f., 361; in America and in Africa, 305 ff.
Rusk, R. R., *Experimental Education,* 297.
Ruskin, John, 147 *n.*; *Unto This Last,* 297 *n.*
Russell, the Hon. Bertrand, 296.

SACRED TRUST, idea of the, 258 f., 270, 342.
Sadler, Sir Michael E., 207 *n.*
Sakania, 16, 381.
Salaries of teachers, 432.
Salisbury (Rhodesia), 94, 111.
Salutations by the way, 88 f.
Samori, 23.
Sanderson of Oundle, 224.
San Paulo de Loanda, 23.
— Salvador, 23.
— Thome, 23.
Sarraut, Albert, *Études de colonisation comparée,* 119, 286 f., 288.
Scenery, African, 18, 188 f., 220.
Sceva, 213 ff.
Schauffler, Dr. H. P., *Adventures in Habit Craft,* 182 *n.*
School, the village: *chap vi;* case for inefficient schools, 82 f.; relation to society, 231; compared with boarding-schools, 185, 332 f., 348.
Schools, Boarding-: arguments for and against in England and Africa, 230 ff.; social life of, 244; necessity for freedom, 348 ff.

Schools, English public, 228 f., 279.
Schools, Government:
Achimota (Gold Coast), *q.v.*
Dar-es-Salaam, 348 *n.*
Domboshawa (Southern Rhodesia), *q.v.*
Fort Hare (Cape), *q.v.*
Hope Fountain (S. Rhodesia), 132, 353 f. *See also* Schools, Mission.
Ibadan (Nigeria), 105.
Kabete (Kenya), 94, 132, 261.
Makerere (Uganda), 101.
Mazabuka (Northern Rhodesia), 132.
Nyasaland, 132.
Salisbury (Southern Rhodesia), 120.
Tanganyika, 156, 163.
Tjolotjo (Southern Rhodesia), 111, 112, 120.
Tsolo (Cape), 113 f., 197, 232.
Schools, Mission:
Amanzimtoti (Natal), 112, 241.
Aro Chuku (Nigeria), 110.
Blythwood (Cape), 106.
Chikuni (Northern Rhodesia), 251.
Hope Fountain (Southern Rhodesia), 108, 132, 310, 353 f.
Imbizana (Natal), 82.
Inanda (Natal), 48.
Ituk Mban (Nigeria), 354, Appendix iii.
Kafue (Northern Rhodesia), 204, 235 f.
Kambole (Northern Rhodesia), 222.
Kilnerton (Transvaal), 230.
Kimpese (Congo), 93, 97, 108, 126, 167, 190, 326.
Kisantu (Congo), 101.
Kota-Kota (Nyasaland), 76.
Likoma (Nyasaland), 77, 217.
Livingstonia (Nyasaland), 66, 75, 79, 99, 100, 169, 240.
Lovedale (Cape), *q.v.*
Madzi Moyo (Northern Rhodesia), 112.
Mariannhill (Natal), 50, 58.
Mbelele (Northern Rhodesia), 81.
Mbereshi (Northern Rhodesia), *q.v.*
Melsetter, Mount Selinda (Southern Rhodesia), 112.
Mkhoma (Nyasaland), 93, 94, 169, 213, 241.
Morgenster (Southern Rhodesia), 169, 207.
Nengubo (Southern Rhodesia), 106, 242.
Penhalonga (Southern Rhodesia), 112, 232, 245.

Schools, Mission (*cont.*):
St. Cuthbert's (Cape), 78, 221, 241.
St. Matthew's (Cape), 106.
Tigerkloof (Cape), 98, 106, 112, 325.
Umzumbe (Natal), 80.
Uzuakoli (Nigeria), 104 ff., 326.
Yakusu (Congo), *q.v.*
Zomba (Nyasaland), 240 f.
Schools, Native African : on West Coast, 99 ; Ohlange (Natal), 99.
Schreiner, W. P., 36.
Scientific point of view, 153, 257, 328 ; criticism of, 295 ff.
Scotland, United Free Church of, 321.
Scott, David Clement, *Cyclopædic Dictionary of the Mang'anja Language*, 136, 200 ; builder of Blantyre Cathedral, 76.
— Captain R. F., 179.
Scouts, *see* Pathfinders.
" Scramble for Africa," 49, 271.
Scrimgeour, Professor, *Arithmetic in the Primary School*, 160 *n*.
Scripture : in Natal schools, 131, 344 f. ; and religion, 170 ; teaching of, 170 ff. ; in English education, 172 f. ; county syllabuses, 173.
Sechuana, 141, 289.
Segregation, 42 f., 52 ff., 364 f. ; in the Transkei, 55 f. ; African views on, 312.
Self-government, meaning of, 363 f.
Seminarism, 173 *n*., 230, 280.
Senegal, 22, 271.
Serbia, rural conditions in, 43.
Serowe, 289.
Sesuto, 141.
Sex : and tribal custom, 84 ; in African life, 191 ff., 219 f.
Shakespeare, 151, 238, 323, 326.
Shaw, G. Bernard, *Saint Joan*, 326.
— Mabel, 193 *n*.
Sheffield, munition workers in, 60.
Shembe, 380.
Shepherds, The (" Pastoureaux "), 382.
Shepstone, Sir Theophilus, 419.
Shiré river, 6.
Shropshire Lad, A, 149.
Sidgwick, Henry, 332.
Simplicity, an achievement, 324 f.
Sindebele, 141.
Sisal, 12.
Slavery and the slave-trade, 5, 14, 23, 24, 27, 28.
Slogans : examination of, 299 f. ; " education must be based on religion," 132, 170, 234 ff., 260, 299 ; " the vernacular enshrines the soul of a people," 140 ff., 149 ; " adaptation," 130, 162, 299, 301, 307 ; " indirect rule," 274 ff. ; " the educated man must go back to his own people," 181 f., 312, 333 ff. ; " training of leaders," 197, 334 f. ; " education by doing," 196 f., 299 ; " manual training develops character," 207, 210 ff., 212, 299 ; " back to the land," 220, 305 ; " African education has been too literary," 226 ff., 299 ; " educate the native along his own lines," x, 276, 283 f., 299, 306, 312, 316 f., 319, 324, 328 f., 332, 335 ; " keep the native in his place," 204, 235, 306 ; " white civilization in danger," 327 f.
Smiles, Samuel, *Self Help*, 176, 179, 181.
Smith, Edwin W., xiii, 397 ; *Way of the White Fields in Rhodesia*, 10 *n*. ; *Christian Mission in Africa*, 10 *n*., 119 *n*., 262 *n* ; *The Golden Stool*, 282 *n*. ; and Dale, A. M. ; *The Ila-speaking Peoples of Northern Rhodesia*, 64 *n*., 96 *n*.
— Frank, *Life and Work of Sir James Kay-Shuttleworth*, 393 *n*.
— Sir George Adam, *Isaiah*, 176.
— Sir Harry, 420.
Smuts, General J. C., 34, 425.
Société pour la Protection des Indigènes, 33.
Sofala, 24.
Sokoto, 279, 401.
Somaliland, 22 f.
Somerset, lake villages of, 41, 314.
Somervell, D. C., *Short History of our Religion*, 176.
Somerville College, 331.
" Soul of a nation," the, 140, 143 ff., 145 ff.
South African Institute of Race Relations, 50 *n*.
South African Outlook, 375, 376 *n*.
Spaniards, the, 20, 25.
Specialists, effect of, in mission work, x, 75 f., 256 f., 269.
Spencer, Herbert, *Education : Intellectual, Moral and Physical*, 188, 299, 303.
Spoor Law, 372.
Squatting, 43, 371 f.
Stanley, Sir H. M., 30, 31, 272.
Stanleyville, 3, 15, 102, 103, 104.
Star of the Congo mine, 16.

INDEX

State : social theory of the, 342 ff. ; nature of the African, 363 f.
Steenkamp, Anna, 22.
Stellenbosch, 37.
Stephen, Barbara, *Emily Davis and Girton College*, 396 n.
Stevenson, Robert Louis, 135.
Stewart, James, 115.
Stool, the Golden, 2, 282, 341.
Stubbs, W., *Select Charters*, 372 n. ; *Constitutional History*, 379 n.
Sturge, Joseph, 396.
Sudan, 14, 21, 317.
Suggestions for the Consideration of Teachers (Cape), 95.
Superstition : not necessarily cured by teaching agriculture, 185 f. ; mediæval, 380.
Swahili, *see* Ki-Swahili.
Swaziland, 419 n.
Swedish, 141.
Switzerland, " soul " of, 145.
Symbolism : value of, 70 ; varieties of, 238 f.
Syncretism, 380 f., 426.
Syria, 274.

TABOO : system of, 84 f., 192 ; and morality, 178 ; and children, 351 f.
Tanganyika : Lake, 31 ; school in, 156 ; education conference (1925), 124, 127, 191 ; Medical Services' schedule on maternity, 191 ; indirect rule in, 278, 283, 287, 288, 342, 412.
Tarsus, 271.
Tatler, The, 144.
Taxation, nature of, in Africa, 44 f.
Taylor, Jeremy, 356.
Teacher, the native : connection with the mission, 65, 80 f. ; vocation of, 91 f. ; training of, 92 f., 354 ; at Yakusu, 103 ; at Uzuakoli, 105 ; in Southern Rhodesia, 121, 353 f. ; organization of, 95 ; professional feeling of, 96 f. ; and nature study, 194 f.
Temple, C. L., *Native Races and their Rulers*, 275 ff., 283 ff.
Temple of Vision, 224 f.
Templecrone (Ireland), Co-operative society of, 58.
Text-books : Physiology, 97, 167 ; Arithmetic, 161 ; Geography, 205 ; Civics, 203 n ; History, 102, 202.
Theology : and missionary work, 247 f. ; and development, 249 ff. ; contemporary, 262 f.
Thomson, Professor J. Arthur, 229, 295 n.

Thonga : numerals of, 160 ; memory for arithmetic, 161.
Thorndike, Professor, 357 ; *Educational Psychology*, 297.
Thought and expression, 165 ff.
Thysville, 46, 381.
Timbuktu, 5.
Time sense in history teaching, 203.
Tobacco, Rhodesian, 12.
Towns : growth of, 45, 59 ; effects of, 61 f. ; in Europe, 384.
Traders, Africans as, 13, 59, 317.
Trade Union Congress, 333, 353.
— Unionism, Native, 48 ff.
Training of teachers, *see under* Teacher, the Native, *and* Missionary Training.
Transkei, the, ix, 36, 55 ff., 166, 289, 291, 373, 402.
Translation, nature of, 135, 149 ff.
Transvaal, 30, 34 ; Wayfarers' Council of, 222 f. ; syllabus of drawing, 216 f.
Trek, the Great, 29.
Trevelyan, Professor G. M., 378 n.
Tribe : nature of, 39 f., 61, 181, 419, 427 ; break up of, 42, 50 f., 61 ; and religion, 51, 282 f. ; and Christianity, 63 f. ; the Hebrew, 63 f. ; and education, 84 ff. ; and morality, 178 ff. ; development of, 288 f. ; significance of, 305, 307 f. ; loyalty to, 363 ; and the mediæval system, 371 ff.
Tshekedi Khama, 413, 415.
Tshuba, 96.
Tsolo (Transkei, Cape Province), 113 f.
Turner, J. M. W., 147 n.
Tuskegee, 303, 304, 305.
" Two-nation theory," 360 ff. ; compared with Middle Ages, 373 ff.
Tylor, E., *Primitive Culture*, 313.
Tyrol, Southern, 143.

UBUNTU, 39, 88, 223, 316.
Uganda, 3, 31, 39, 51, 173, 191, 272, 289, 290, 354 ; Ki-Swahili in, 143.
Uitlanders, the, in the Transvaal, 34.
Ukulobola, 11, 262, 316, 420.
Umcebisi Womlimi Nomfuyi, 56.
Umtata, 55, 291.
United Council for Missionary Education, 258.
Universities, growth of, in Europe, 98.
Utility in school studies, 187 f., 227 f.
Uzuakoli (Nigeria), viii, 104 ff., 326

VAN DER STEL, 26.
Van Riebeeck, 26 f.
Verbal inspiration, 173, 249, 253 f., 367.
Vernacular, the: chap. viii; in Mashonaland, 113; psychological argument for, 134 ff.; cultural argument for, 139 ff.; static study of, 149.
Versailles, Peace Conference at, 258, 270.
Victoria Falls, 188; bridge over, 210, 224.
— Nyanza, 31.
Victoria, Queen, 248, 379, 417, 418.
Vinogradoff, Professor Sir Paul, *Roman Law in Mediæval Europe*, 372 n.
Vischer, Major Hanns, xii, 260, 402.
Vocation, special: " living Native," 78.
Vocational training, 206 ff.
Voortrekkers, 29, 34.

WALKER, Professor E., *History of South Africa*, 27 n., 30 n.
Wallas, Graham, *Life of Francis Place*, 389 n.
Wankie, 12, 16.
War: Franco-Prussian, 30, 143; Napoleonic, 28, 143, 248; Great, 259, 270, 274; American Civil, 292 f.
Ward, James, *Psychology Applied to Education*, 297.
Warren, Sir Charles, 417.
Washington, 294.
Washington, Booker, T., 305 f.
Watch-Tower Movement, 151, 292; *The Divine Plan of the Ages*, 321, 383.
Wayfarers, 222 f.
Webb, C. C. J., *Group Theories of Religion and the Individual*, 315 n.
" Wellington, Dr.," 291, 383.
West, A. S., *English Grammar*, 200.
Westermann, Professor, on the vernacular, 140 ff., 150, 154.
Westminster, Statute of, 35.
Weymouth, end of world at, 383.
Whitbread, S., 391.
White Man's Wonders, The, 102, 224.

Whitman, Walt, *To the Man-of-War-Bird*, 336 n.
Wilberforce, William, 29, 386 f.
William the Conqueror, 175.
Willoughby, Professor W. C., *Race Problems in the New Africa*, 282 n.
Winchester, Statute of, 372.
Witchcraft, 87 f., 262; and agriculture, 185 f.
Witney, 109.
Wodehouse, Sir Philip, 418.
Women: in European domestic service, 48; European, in celibate missions, 72 f.; education of native, 93, 102, 107 f., 191 ff., 351 ff., 420 ff.; school at Mbereshi, 108 ff.; attitude to marriage, 108, 420 ff.; history of education in England, 330 ff., 395 f.; in the Middle Ages, 376; attitude towards, in Africa, 376; emancipation of English, 331, 396.
Women's Co-operative Guild, 353.
— Institutes, 353.
" Wonder," " the Renascence of," 18, 188 f., 193, 245.
Wordsworth, 189, 302.
Workers' Educational Association, 353.
Writing: compared with arithmetic, 158; in education, 167 f.
Wycliffe, 151, 153.

XENOPHON, 113.
Xosa, 29, 141; disaster to, 382.

YAKUSU (Congo): native market at, 60; village schools of, 80; conference with native teachers, 97, 312; description of, 102 ff., 107; printing press, 104, 169, 201, 224.
Y.M.C.A., 221.
Yorubas, 3, 39, 317.
Young, Arthur, 388.

ZANZIBAR, 21, 31, 338.
Zaria, C.M.S., mission at, 273 f., 280.
Zimbabwe, Great, 169; problem of, 319.
Zomba (Nyasaland), 13, 240 f.
Zulus, 23; language, 131, 136, 139 f. 141, 146, 148, 152.

For Product Safety Concerns and Information please contact our EU
representative GPSR@taylorandfrancis.com
Taylor & Francis Verlag GmbH, Kaufingerstraße 24, 80331 München, Germany

www.ingramcontent.com/pod-product-compliance
Lightning Source LLC
Chambersburg PA
CBHW071135300426
44113CB00009B/982